The African-American Atlas

Black History and Culture–An Illustrated Reference

Macmillan USA
An Imprint of Simon & Schuster Macmillan
New York

Prentice Hall International
London Mexico City New Delhi Singapore Sydney Toronto

The African-American Atlas

Black History and Culture–An Illustrated Reference

Molefi K. Asante and Mark T. Mattson

Macmillan USA
An Imprint of Simon & Schuster Macmillan
1633 Broadway
New York, New York 10019

Library of Congress Catalog Number: 98–25556

Printed in the United States of America

Printing Number
  1 2 3 4 5 6 7 8 9 10

Library of Congress Cataloging-in-Publication Data
Asante, Molefi K., 1942–
        The African-American atlas : Black history and culture--an
    illustrated reference / Molefi K. Asante and Mark T. Mattson.
            p.   cm.
        Rev. ed. of: The historical and cultural atlas of African
    Americans. c1991.
    Includes bibliographical references and index.
        ISBN 0–02–864984–2 (hc. : alk. paper). —ISBN 0-02-864985-0 (pbk. : alk. paper)
    1. Afro-Americans. 2. Afro-Americans--History.   3. Afro-Americans—History—Maps.
    I. Mattson, Mark T. II. Asante, Molefi K., 1942– Historical and cultural atlas of
    African Americans.
    III. Title.
    E185.A79 1998
    973' .0496073—dc21   98-25556
                                                                                                   CIP

This paper meets the requirements of ANSI/NISO Z.39.48-1992 (Permanence of Paper).

Contents

Figures and Tables

CHAPTER 13

Preface

African American culture is sewn into the very fabric of American society. Indeed, to speak accurately of American culture and history or world history and culture one has to consider the enormous contributions of African people in the United States. The impact is particularly significant in the contemporary American context because African American culture is a major component of what constitutes being American. In this regard, Africa in America has meant that America is more than a European nation on Native American soil; it is a combination of many cultural influences that provide the special character of the American nation.

African American culture is also African at its most elemental and fundamental level. From the sentence construction in Ebonics to musical appreciation, the legacy and heritage of thousands of years of human responses to the African environment have had an impact on the nearly four hundred years of the African American sojourn in North America.

The atlas has proved to be a major reference work with interest for libraries, scholars, government workers, businesspeople, tourists, and individuals with an interest in presenting a portrait of the African American community. The original atlas was directed toward an American as well as a world audience. In revising the atlas we have endeavored to enliven the spatial representation of some of the most important events, personalities, and facts about African Americans with new maps, charts, and photographs.

An atlas, however, is not an encyclopedia. One will not find every item of importance to African American history included here.

We have selected information, events, and personalities that represent a great expanse of the cultural spectrum. Thus, we have been motivated by the desire to include the contributions of those individuals and groups that have had influence on the national and world character of the African American people. Yet we are the first to admit our limitations and our selectivity which could be questioned by any other historians and authors. Nevertheless, it is our sincere wish that the readers of this revised atlas will find that it not only contains the same warmth and information of the first edition but that it has an expanded set of interpretations, explanations, and a fresh statistical update of the conditions of the African American community.

A basic purpose of the atlas is to provide detailed maps of information and events. As a reference work, this volume should be useful for those interested in a technical and historical guide to knowledge about how African Americans have organized their lives culturally, socially, and economically. In addition, we sought to give the reader a sense of the historical and cultural origin of African Americans. We have tried, in this edition, as in the first, to demonstrate that African Americans, though domiciled in the Americas, are not absolutely detached from the long history and cultural traditions of the continent of Africa itself.

Therefore, we have carefully created maps and charts to give the reader a holistic view of the African American people. In doing this, we have avoided a strict chronological order, preferring to interweave themes into certain broad time lines. Furthermore, we have painstakingly integrated the maps,

statistical information, and cultural data into narrative segments that should be easy to follow. Of course, we have tried not to repeat information found in the maps and charts in a word-for-word fashion. This type of redundancy serves no purpose for this atlas and we have avoided it as much as possible.

The atlas makes a head-on confrontation with several issues that have plagued African and African American historiography. In the first place, we have used the term African Americans to refer to American citizens whose racial, cultural, or ethnic backgrounds are historically rooted in the indigenous people of the African continent. Although nearly 75 percent of this population have racially or culturally plural backgrounds and more than 99 percent have ethnically plural backgrounds, we have followed the general practice in the United States of defining the African American population by its general African rather than its European or Native American elements. Furthermore, we have not tried to separate the Yoruba from the Ibo, or the Asante from the Ga, or the Congo from the Angola, inasmuch as we have recognized that these groups have been thoroughly amalgamated in the African American population.

Historically, leading African Americans, regardless of color or degree of non-African genes, have defined themselves in this manner since the seventeenth century. Had they defined themselves any other way it would not have mattered in a legal sense anyway. Thus, in the United States the African population, with all of its mixture, has avoided the legal classifications of people by color as was recently done in South Africa and Brazil.

Using the new Afrocentric paradigm as a guide, we have attempted to view Africa holistically, that is, as one giant interrelated sector rather than as sub-Saharan and north-of-the-Sahara parts of the same continent. It is no longer fashionable to think of Africa as a continent of separate, discrete regions where people of one region never interact with people of another.

The European slave trade, a principal part of the past 500 years of the African experience, contributed to the view of Africa as segmented and disjointed. Separate ethnic and linguistic experiences exist and are accounted for in the new paradigm by also recognizing similarities in African myths, symbolism, and cosmologies.

Nothing is so central to the African American experience as the spirituals, which we have chosen as the organizing principle, the structuring device for this atlas of African Americans because the spirituals have ennobled the experiences of the people in ways that no other social or artistic form has done. No image is more significant or more appropriate in connection with African American culture than these epic songs. They tell the story of Africans in America more poignantly than any prose. Consequently we have used them as keepers of the traditions.

The first chapter is "I Got My Religion from Out of the Sun," and serves as the introductory statement. It examines some of the ancient origins of the people who are now African Americans. Four hundred years ago where were no African Americans; only Africans with various ethnic names and identities existed. This chapter looks at African origins of the human race as well as critical ancient historical sites. Chapter 2, "I Don't Care Where You Bury My Body," is about adventure. Africans have migrated all over the earth, often by force but also because of curiosity and a spirit of adventure that often govern human movements. The third chapter, "Dark Clouds A'risin," discusses the beginnings of the slave trade that was to transport millions of Africans from the continent of Africa to the Americas.

The fourth chapter, "De Udder Worl Is Not Like Dis," examines the effect of the Great Enslavement on the African population. The fifth chapter, "And Before I'd Be a Slave," is a celebration of the resistance movement. The aim is to demonstrate the resistance in several areas of African American life. Chapter 6, "All My Troubles Will Soon Be Over With," shows the African American culture of resistance, the abolition movement, and the attack on the pro-slavery elements. Chapter 7, "My Lord Gwinter to Rain Down Fire," discusses the approach and waging of the Civil War. Chapter 8, "Swing Low, Sweet Chariot," is dedicated to the emancipation and Reconstruction, and the struggle of African Americans against white prejudice.

Chapter 9, " Now Ain't Them Hard Trials," is concerned with the wanton murder of many African Americans during the late nineteenth century and early twentieth century. Lynching became a national disgrace as Ida B. Wells Barnett became a leading voice against the murder of black men. Chapter 10 is called "And Still We Rise" as a testament to the achievements of African Americans in many fields of endeavor. Chapter 11, "Great Day, Great Day, the Righteous Marching" discusses the Civil Rights Era when Martin Luther King Jr. rose to prominence and led the most consistent and persistent battles against the injustice in the American social and legal systems. This chapter also discusses the attendant political and organizational situations that textured the nature of the struggle. Chapter 12, "Before This Time Another Year," is a portrait of the cultural and historical elements that have gone into the creation of a resilient culture. Chapter 13, "Didn't My Lord Deliver Daniel," presents data on employment, literacy, poverty, identity, and mortality.

Other features of this atlas that should aid readers in understanding the persistence of certain themes are the similarity of adventures and the preponderance of particular responses to society that are the biographical and thematic snapshots strategically placed to highlight given events and personalities. In general the chapters are presented in chronological order; however, biographical, photographic, and thematic shapshots that cross time lines occur as an African American improvisation. The aim of this feature is to provide an instant opportunity for comparison, reflection, and information. We have deliberately not included snapshots in every section but have done so in those cases where we think it would make good sense.

Finally, we are pleased to be issuing this new edition during a time that we can truly say that the computer has lived up to its previous billing about accessing information. We are able to use the most up-to-date information for our book, to tap into the greatest source of data ever organized in the world, and to have fun re-presenting the African American Atlas.

Acknowledgments

This book seeks to express the vitality and energy within the African-American community. We recognized very early that it would be impossible to capture the spirit of the historic African-American people without the contributions of many others. Chief among the scholars and writers who have informed our work in one way or another are Maulana Karenga, California State University-Northridge; Vincent Harding, Ilief Theological Seminary; St. Calir Drake, Professor Emeritus, Stanford University; Lerone Bennett, *Ebony* magazine; Ivan van Sertima, Rutgers University; John Hope Franklin, Professor Emeritus, Duke University; Sterling Stuckey, Northwestern University; Mary Berry, University of Pennsylvania; and John Henrik Clarke, Professor Emeritus, Hunter College. What we have received most from them is a sense of the magnitude of the African-American culture. Beyond the inspiration of the works of these contemporaries have brought to our *African-American Atlas* is the tremendous intelligence with which they have worked in this field. They were preceded by Benjamin Quarles, Benjamin Brawley, William Wells Brown, Langston Hughes, Merle Epps, Carter G. Woodson, and W. E. B. Du Bois. They, too, sang the complex songs and danced to the intricate rhythms of African-American culture. To both our contemporaries and our forerunners, we are grateful and forever indebted for understanding the vastness of this cultural and historical experience.

An undertaking such as this atlas is impossible without the assistance of many persons and institutions. Among the major resources that were made available to us and that we consulted were the Paley Library at Temple University, particularly its archival department; the Charles Blockson Afro-American Collection at Temple University; Lincoln University's Langston Hughes Library; Special Collections, the Schomburg Center for Research in Black Culture; the Institute for Afro American Culture in Los Angeles; and the newly formed Institute of the Black Peoples in Ouadougou, Barkina Faso. Catherine Hooker at the Schomburg in New York and Lillian Anthony of the Afro-American Heritage Project in Louisville, Kentucky, came through with some excellent ideas and suggestions at key moments. During the initial period of gathering maps, statistics, and photographs, we spent considerable time in archives, on the telephone, and using facsimile machines—tracking down information. There were times when we had reached our mind's end regarding where to look for certain information for the atlas. We were fortunate enough to have Pam Austin of the Temple University Archives as a ready source of knowledge during these moments of impasse. She inevitably came through with bits of information and ideas that assisted in moving the project along.

The presence at Temple University of the nation's first doctoral program in African American Studies provided us the opportunity to work with many competent research assistants who made valuable contributions to the atlas. We owe special thanks to five students, Karyn Lacey, Cecil Gray, Daniel Black, Rodney Patterson, and Eddie Glaude, who arrived on campus from Oberlin, Virginia, Clark-Atlanta, South Carolina, and More-house for the Temple experience and became part of our research team. Karyn Lacey particularly helped to keep track of material and data during the early days of the project. Also, we would like to thank Angelic Justin, whose many trips to our library resulted in much useful information.

During production of this second edition, we are particularly indebted to William Kampf, who researched statistical, historical, and biographical information throughout the entire volume. Bill also contributed through the production of most tables and many illustrations. We wish him success as he enters law school in the fall of 1998.

We have also benefited from the intellectual ideas and encouragement advanced by H. Patrick Swygert, President, State University of New York at Albany, formerly the Executive Vice President of Temple University, and Peter Liacouras, President, Temple University; they represent the best tradition of administrators who are also scholars. We would like to acknowledge the support of the Department of African American Studies and the Department of Geography and Urban Studies.

Though it should be known, we should say explicitly that none of the people whom we have mentioned bears responsibility for anything appearing in this volume.

We thank Catherine Carter, our editor, and Jane Andrassi, our production supervisor. We thank them for their insights and support.

Finally, we acknowledge each other for the wonderful joy of working together on a worthy project. We also say thanks to our families, with special attention given to our wives, Kariamu and Cathy, for their enduring understanding and love.

"I Got My Religion from Out of the Sun"

1

AFRICAN ORIGINS

African Americans originated on a continent that is nearly four times the size of the continental United States or three times the size of the United States including Alaska (figure 1.1). Even Texas, at 267,339 square miles and legendary for its size, appears small when compared to the Sudan (997,499 sq. miles), Congo (904,991), South Africa (472,359), or Tanzania (363,707).

Distances can be very great on the continent. This makes travel and communication very difficult. The distance from Cairo to Capetown is approximately 5,000 miles; Dakar, Senegal, to Mogadishu, Somalia, is nearly 5,000 miles. It is possible for a person to travel 1,000 miles in Nigeria in order to reach the largest city, Lagos. One can be 800 miles from Dar es Salaam, the capital of Tanzania, and still be within the country. Similar distances occur in Congo, Algeria, and Sudan. One of the most important challenges facing Africa is transportation.

The continent has virtually no major barriers to human movement. Relatively few internal barriers exist since most of the land consists of flat savanna or rolling plains. One might compare Africa to the American Midwest between the Rocky Mountains and the Alleghenies (see figure 1.2, page 3).

The huge Sahara is the most pronounced feature on the continent, roughly the size of the United States. But the desert is no barrier; every day thousands of Africans regularly traverse it. Camels from Libya, Algeria, Morocco, and Egypt went back and forth from Timbuktu, Katsina, and Ouagadougou. Salt, gold, ivory, gum arabic, spices, glassware, iron tools, and blankets were traded between these places. The Sahara trade was the source of much wealth for many African kings. They used the taxes from the permissions to travel to aid in the development of their state systems.

The second largest obstacle on the continent is the Congo Rain Forest. It is the most extensive area of swamps, forests, and dense vegetation on the continent. The Zaire River drains the largest area of any river except the Amazon.

Africa, the world's second-largest continent, is geographically diverse. It contains almost every type of topography found on the earth. There are deserts, the largest being the Sahara, but both the Kalahari and the Namibia are formidable features of the continent's landscape. Rain forests—in which a day without rain is a phenomenal and momentous event—contain more tropical plants, flowers, and herbs than does any other tropical area of the world except the Amazon Basin.

Rivers crisscross the vast surface of this continent. The great Nile, mother of African civilization, has carried, along with its currents, ideas, concepts, and people from near the Mountains of the Moon in Uganda–Zaire to the Mediterranean, the longest distance of any river, since time immemorial. The fabled Congo River, more massive than any river except the Amazon, is ten miles across in some places. Crossing the equa-

Figure 1.1. Comparison of the United States and Africa in terms of size.

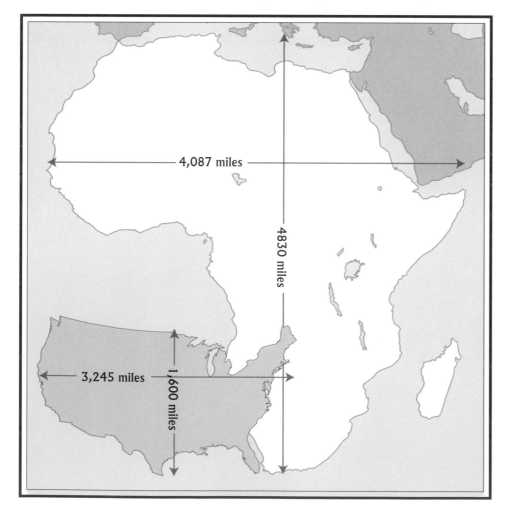

4,087 miles

4830 miles

3,245 miles

1,600 miles

tor twice, which occurs with no other equatorial river, the Congo maintains a steady volume of water that is unaffected by the seasons: when the dry season transpires in one part of the river, the rainy season is occurring in the other and vice versa. The storied Niger, witness to caravans of faith and gold merchants and site of ancient cities such as Timbuktu, Gao, and Jenne, traverses the colorful and artistic West African region while laying claim to its place as one of the most majestic rivers of the world.

The fast-moving Zambezi, cutting through stones and forest, is famous for being the source of Musi wa Tunya ("The Smoke That Thunders")—Victoria Falls. A plaque at the falls says that David Livingstone, on seeing the Zambezi pound over the mile-wide cliff, once said, "No more beautiful sight has ever been seen on earth."

There are lakes in profusion. Most are natural, a few human-made for generating enormous supplies of electricity. The largest of these are the results of giant dams such as Akosombo in Ghana, Aswan in Egypt, Kariba in Zimbabwe-Zambia, and Cabora-Bassa in Mozambique.

Some lakes have produced strange chemical reactions, emitting gasses in the air, sometimes with deadly results as in the Cameroon. Lake Bosumtwi in Ghana is a sacred lake dedicated to the deities. Its shape is almost a perfect circle.

Mountains are prominent. Snowcapped peaks occur in Kenya and Tanzania.

Grasslands, called savannas, dominate in the west between the coast and the rain forest. Tall grasses have been used for centuries to make beautiful baskets and sleeping mats.

Africa's geographical diversity produces a variety of human responses to the environment. We see this diversity reflected in art, food, and the fabrics, such as kente, bokolanfini, asoke, adinkra, and faso dan fani, all harmonizing with the people, cultures, and environments of their origin.

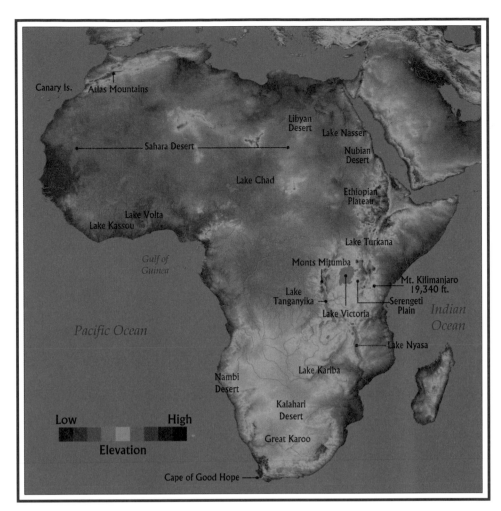

ARCHAEOLOGICAL EVIDENCE

Archaeological and biological evidence points to East Africa as the place where the modern human and the earliest human society had their origins (see figure 1.3, page 4). Louis Leakey and other anthropologists have established that the the human remains they have found there are the oldest known. Indeed, Leakey's work in the Olduvai Gorge in northern Tanzania, near Lake Rudolf in Kenya, and near the Omo River in Ethiopia has shown that hominids were using tools in this area more than two million years ago. These early humans were the first to use the handaxe, although the name most often associated with the implements, "Acheulian," refers to similar tools found in western Europe. Anthropologists now know that the African sites in the Olduvai Gorge region contain the oldest tools known to humans.

Donald Johanson, an American pale-

Figure 1.2. Physiography of the African continent. There are few mountain ranges on the African continent. Mountains appear dark orange in this figure. Green colors and light oranges indicate the predominance of lowland savannas, deserts, rain forests, and rolling plains.

oanthropologist, contends that the skeleton known as Lucy, which he discovered in 1974 at Hadar, Ethiopia, and other fossilized bones found in both Ethiopia and Tanzania belonged to a single hominid species called *australopithecus afarensis.* According to Johanson, afarensis was the common ancestor of *australopithecines* and humans. The date for these fossils was put at 3.5 million years ago, about 1.2 million years after the divergence of humans and apes. Hominid activity in the East African region predates any such activity elsewhere in the world. With the appearance of the Omo humans and their toolmaking ability, a new phase in evolution had been reached.

Climatic changes occurred over the period of human evolution in Africa. Glaciers did not cover the continent of Africa during the Ice Ages, as occurred in Europe, but there was an appreciable effect on the African climate because of the vast icecaps at both the North and South Poles. The Wurm Glaciation, which covered Europe between 70,000 and 10,000 B.C.E., produced a cooler and wetter eastern Africa and a cooler and drier western Africa. This condition altered the balance between the forest and savanna regions, making what are now forest regions more open and habitable by large groups of humans.

In the open African savannas, early humans found adequate supplies of game animals and permanent sources of water. The chill of the nights in the highlands of Africa probably encouraged the development of the next major technological achievement: the making and control of fire. About 60,000 years ago, African humans were using fire, an instrument for cooking and warmth. Thus, the adequacy of the food supply and the ability to make meat tender gave the early Africans a method for expanding the size of communities.

Accordingly, the Sangoan culture (named after the typesite at Sango Bay on Lake Victoria in Uganda), with its distinctive stone tools, represents the most prevalent type of early human culture in Africa. Following the Sangoan culture was the Mousterian culture, which evolved as a Stone Age culture between 35,000 and 8000 B.C.E.

The Isonghee abacus, found in what is now the Republic of Congo, is the earliest example of humans using bone to create instruments for calculation. According to experts, it is nearly 28,000 years old.

Evidence of human societies is rich in the central and eastern parts of the African continent. Indeed, the ancient Egyptians claimed to have come from the Mountains of the Moon. The countries of Kenya, Congo, Egypt, Sudan, Ethiopia, and Uganda are keys to ancient African history. In these regions of Africa are found the origins of philosophy, mathematics, religion, architecture, art and the maing of cyclopean stone tombs, among other achievements.

Figure 1.3. Origin of humans in east Africa.

ANCIENT HISTORICAL SITES

Fabled cities of the fertile valleys of central and southern Africa as well as long-vanished towns and villages in the Sahara Desert demonstrate the richness of Africa's human record (see figure 1.5, page 6).

Africa possesses the longest record of biological and cultural relics of early humans. Indeed, the Olduvai Gorge in Tanzania affords us a record of human biological and social evolution that is not only a standard reference for the continent but has become, by virtue of the fullness of the record, a world standard.

Ancient toolmaking sites have been found throughout Africa, many older than 1.5 million years. Stone Age and Lower Paleolithic sites between 700,000 and 100,000 years old are numerous. The later emergence of other sites, particularly in western and central Africa, represented increased in-migration from other African regions. Thus, sites established by 10,000 B.C.E. (such as Tiemassas in Senegal; Yengema Cave in Sierra Leone; Adwuku in Ghana; Rim in Burkina Faso; and Iwo Eleru, Jos, Ukpa, and Mejiro, near Old Oyo in Nigeria) provide evidence of organized human activity and early technology in these regions. Human activity and early social technology had occurred before, but the record indicates a greater concentration of people and a wider variety of activities about this time.

African rock paintings are older and more numerous than such paintings elsewhere. Most of the paintings and engravings occur in areas where there are protective rock shelters, ledges, caves, or massive rock overhangs, so the naturalistic and schematic representations of the works have endured until today.

The African continent is rich in historical and cultural sites both preceding and following the pyramids, the oldest monumental constructions on the earth. Erected around 2500 B.C.E., the pyramids remain the most perfect example of African architectural antiquity (figure 1.4). With the spread of human populations to western and central Africa as a result of numerous internal political and agricultural imperatives, large empires were welded together by outstanding military and political leaders (see figure 1.6, page 7). Many of these empires lasted into the twentieth century as fragmentary states within the more modern state structures established as a result of the colonial policies of the European nations. units. Even today, the Asante, Yoruba, Mossi, Lozi, Congo, and Fante nations exist as functional within modern states (see figure 1.7, page 8).

WEST AFRICAN EMPIRES

The migration of people from East African to the savannas of West Africa occurred over thousands of years; the pace of migration was especially high from the third century B.C.E. to the tenth century A.D. Dynamic civilizations arose as a direct result of the interaction among numerous empires and kingdoms. Among the names of civilizations that must be considered in connection with the rise of organized states in Central and West Africa are Nok, Ghana, Mali, Songhay, Mossi, and Kanem. Nok, which predates the Christian era, is known primarily for its developed art. Mossi, Kanem, and other empires of the Sudanic belt, running east to west along the grass-

Figure 1.4. An Egyptian pyramid of the type seen here is a funerary monument from the Old Kingdom (c. 2686–2181 BCE). Pyramids are also associated with Pre-Columbian cultures in Central America giving credence to the notion that ancient Africans crossed the Atlantic Ocean. Credit: Michael Maslan Historic Photographs/Corbis.

Figure 1.5. Ancient historical sites.

lands, just north of the rain forest, have contributed to the richly textured history of the civilization of West Africa. The Peul, Yoruba, Akan, and Wolof people brought to the west of art, warfare, and religion, which had been developed in the eastern part of the continent. Africa traditions. However, Ghana, Mali, and Songhay are the best-documented civilizations of the region (see figure 1.7, page 8).

Ghana

The empire of Ghana developed prior to the Islamic penetration of West Africa around 300 B.C.E. and shows highly developed artistic and governmental modes (see figure 1.7, page 8). While not all areas in this region came under the direct control of the Ghana Empire, its influence was felt throughout the region through the control of both the gold trade, upon which its economy was based, and the salt trade. Numerous adventurers, writers, and scholars from the eleventh to the fifteenth centuries attested to the presence of a complex government in the region that stretched from the Atlantic Ocean on the west to the Niger River valleys on the east and from the southern Sahara on the north to the Atlantic Ocean on the south. Indeed, Ibn al-Bakri said that kingship in Ghana was derived from the matrilineal pattern, meaning that the king was the son of his predecessor's sister rather than the son of his predecessor. The king ruled as an autocrat who communicated to his subjects through a mediator, much like the present okyeame in contemporary Ghana. The king was also the central figure in the religion of the people. Upon his death, his retainers were buried with him. According to al-Bakri, the king had an army of 200,000 men, of which 40,000 were archers.

By the time al-Bakri wrote, the empire, which arose in 300 B.C.E., was in decline. After the Almoravids, an army of blacks from Morocco, conquered Ghana in 1076, there was no longer a strong central government. Disorganized by constant internal battles and unable to find its former glory, the country fell prey to

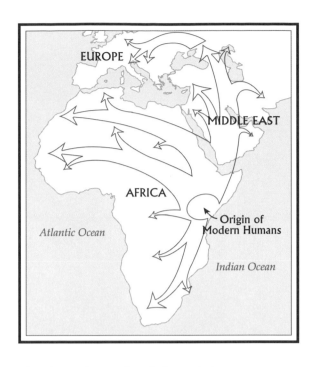

Figure 1.6. Dispersion of ancient peoples from their eastern African origins.

the Soninkes, who defeated the Almoravids in 1087 and divided the land into several smaller states. By 1203, it was possible for Sumanguru, king of Sosso, to annex the now smaller Ghana territory. However, in 1240, Sundiata, the legendary king of the Mande kingdom of Kankaba, vanquished the remnants of the Ghana Empire at the battle of Kirina and created the empire of Mali.

Mali

The kingdom of Mali existed from the first century (see figure 1.7, page 8). Indeed, the Mali Empire's history is the history of the famous Keita family of West Africa. This family ruled the empire for nearly thirteen centuries—one of the longest dynasties in world history. However, it was not until the Sundiata, who was born with one leg shorter than the other, as military leader led Mali onto the world scene as a mighty nation. In 1230, Sundiata ascended the throne left by his father, Nare Maghan I. He achieved quick, decisive victories over the enemies of Mali, organized the state to administer civil authority, and gave women powerful positions as governors.

Military generals were given responsibility for the regions they conquered. In the great thirteenth-century epic of Sundiata, as retold by D. T. Niane, we

Figure 1.7. African cultures from various periods in history.

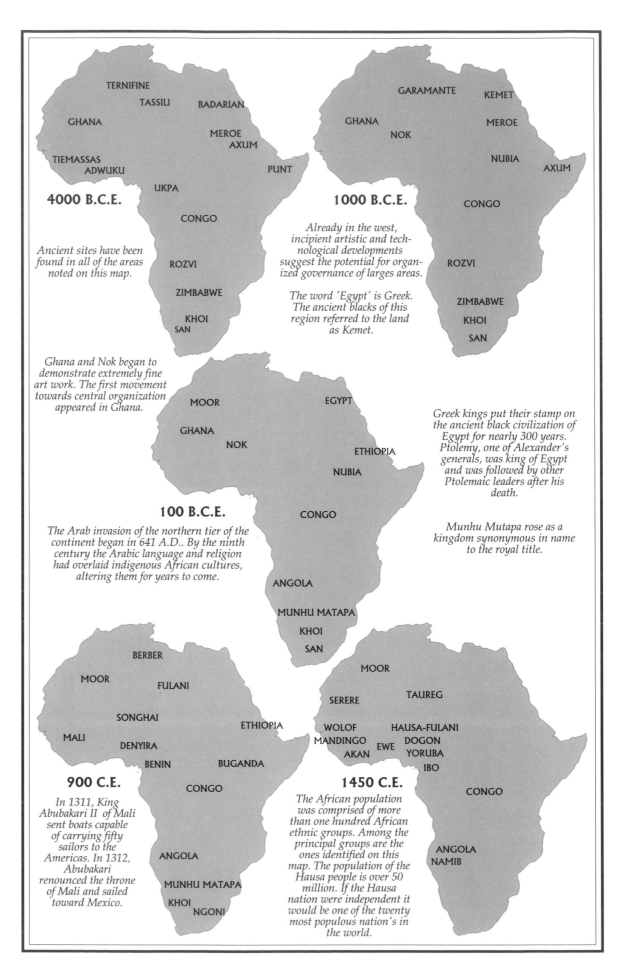

4000 B.C.E.

Ancient sites have been found in all of the areas noted on this map.

Ghana and Nok began to demonstrate extremely fine art work. The first movement towards central organization appeared in Ghana.

1000 B.C.E.

Already in the west, incipient artistic and technological developments suggest the potential for organized governance of larges areas.

The word 'Egypt' is Greek. The ancient blacks of this region referred to the land as Kemet.

100 B.C.E.

The Arab invasion of the northern tier of the continent began in 641 A.D.. By the ninth century the Arabic language and religion had overlaid indigenous African cultures, altering them for years to come.

Greek kings put their stamp on the ancient black civilization of Egypt for nearly 300 years. Ptolemy, one of Alexander's generals, was king of Egypt and was followed by other Ptolemaic leaders after his death.

Munhu Mutapa rose as a kingdom synonymous in name to the royal title.

900 C.E.

In 1311, King Abubakari II of Mali sent boats capable of carrying fifty sailors to the Americas. In 1312, Abubakari renounced the throne of Mali and sailed toward Mexico.

1450 C.E.

The African population was comprised of more than one hundred African ethnic groups. Among the principal groups are the ones identified on this map. The population of the Hausa people is over 50 million. If the Hausa nation were independent it would be one of the twenty most populous nation's in the world.

learn that laws and codes of conduct for the military leaders were put into force to provide proper guidance and protocol for the conduct of society. Everywhere in the empire, Sundiata and his story were repeated by griots who used the legend of the military genius who became king as an instrument of instruction. By the time he died in 1255, Sundiata had placed Mali in the annals of world history. It was an empire and a civilization equal to any in the world at that time. Sundiata was succeeded by kings with lesser political genius, some of whom distinguished themselves in other ways. Responsible for sending longboats to the Americas, Abuba-kari I himself sailed to Mexico in 1312. In 1324, Emperor Mansa Musa went to Mecca in a pilgrimage that impressed the world with his wealth. Mansa (King) Musa's entourage spent so much gold in Cairo that they left a legacy of inflation in the Egyptian capital.

Songhay

Songhay, emerging from the vassal state of Gao, succeeded the Mali Empire due to the consistent and intelligent military prowess and discipline of the army of Sunni Ali Ber, the last descendant of the dynasty established by Dia Assibia (see figure 1.7, page 8). In 1464, when he became sovereign of the Songhay state, Sunni Ali Ber defeated the Tuaregs at Timbuktu, captured the city, and established himself as the most important West African leader. Sunni Ali Ber, known as "the Great," extended his empire by controlling the Niger River with a navy of large boats that patrolled both shores of the river. Refusing to accept Islam, Sunni Ali Ber advanced the traditional religions and cultures of the Sudanese people.

His death in 1492 created a vacuum in the political life of the country. His son, Bakori Da'as, was unable to hold the empire together and was soon deposed by Mamadu Toure, who ascended to the throne under the name Askia Muhammad and ruled from 1493 to 1529. During his reign, the University of Sankore reached its greatest heights as

Askia Muhammad restored the tradition of Islamic learning that had been discouraged under Sunni Ali Ber. The outstanding intellectual Akmed Baba, the last chancellor of the university at Timbuktu, was credited with writing more than forty books on subjects as far ranging as logic, theology, ethics, mathematics, and rhetoric. He is considered one of the great intellectuals of the sixteenth century.

The major contribution of the reign of Askia Muhammad was the promotion of education and the advancement of science at the University of Sankore. He permitted scholars from Asia and Europe to come to Songhay to learn and teach at the principal centers of education: Gao, Jenne, and Timbuktu. Students studied law, rhetoric, grammar, literature, and medicine. Indeed, by the turn of the sixteenth century, the region was developing a literature fully its own and based upon the traditional myths, beliefs, patterns of behavior, and philosophies of the people of West Africa.

Muhammad had made all of this possible through expert institutionalization of banking systems and laws regulating the business of the empire. So successful did Songhay become under Askia Muhammad that other people envied the nation.

After his son pushed Askia Muhammad from the throne, the decline of Songhay set in. This was followed by a period of instability that was only halted when Songhay began to expand its boundaries in an effort to prevent dissension in the center. This, however, was to no avail as the nations on the boundaries continued to attack the outposts of the empire. Soon Songhay's decline was set on a permanent path. Various smaller states long accustomed to paying tribute to the Songhay Empire reneged on their obligations due to the weakness of the empire. The struggles with its vassal states gave an opening for stronger nations to attack the mighty Songhay.

In 1591, the Moroccans brought cannons across the desert in order to fight the army of the Songhay Empire. While most of the Moroccans died in the battle, their cannons overpowered Songhay's army, which was still fighting with swords and spears. The technology of warfare in West Africa had now changed. This war was a prelude to the coming defeat of the African nations and empires by Europeans armed with the most modern weapons of warfare. The Mighty Golden Age of West Africa was over. It would be nearly 400 years before Africa would regain some of its past glory. The intervening years meant the destruction of the centers of learning and power and threw Africa into political and social chaos. The eminent Senegalese scholar Cheikh Anta Diop was among the first scientists to explore the relationship of the ancient Kemetic civilization in what is now called Egypt to the West African empires and states. Diop found that the languages of more than twelve West African states could be traced directly to ancient Egypt. Thus, he had opened an entirely new field, linking all of Africa to its classical cultures in the Nile Valley. His dictum, often repeated during his lifetime, was, "Egypt is to the rest of Africa as Greece is to the rest of Europe" (Diop 1974, xiv).

Cities long claimed by the marching sands of the Sahara Desert connected West African cities and villages to those farther east. Movements and migrations of people due to natural disasters (e.g., droughts, pestilence, and floods) or human catastrophes (e.g., war and internal conflicts) caused Africa to be a continent of powerful human interactions along the natural waterways such as the Niger, Nile, Congo, and Zambezi rivers. The cities, especially along the Niger, created and kept in their trust the ancient memories of the societies of secrets. Along this river grew the towns—Timbuktu, Gao, Jenne—that were to become famous in all of Africa. Caravans crossed the desert from the banks of this river as they still do today. African Americans carry within them the heritage of these cities and caravans of the savanna.

WESTERN AFRICA

The story of human societies in the western part of the African continent has not been fully documented in writing, and yet the people convey as orature (i.e., proverbs, rituals, dramas, divinations, incantations, adages, myths, legends, and epics) the entire kaleidoscope of a creative and productive heritage inherited from the East and enriched in their Western experiences. Aboubacar Moussa Lam of the Cheikh Anta Diop University in Dakar, Senegal, has discovered place names stretching from the Nile Valley to the Atlantic Ocean that show the migration patterns of the Peul people from the east to the west of the continent. in the past millennia the great Lake Chad functioned as a location of early shipbuilding and even today reveals the secrets of sail. This is documented in his work *l'origine Egyptien des Paul*.

Here the Niger River, one of the four majestic rivers of Africa, roams through richly textured lands—the Sahel savannas, green hills, and rain forests—as witness to the color and vibrancy of the region.

Here the names of history are studded like diamonds in our memories and remind us once more of the heritage of African Americans: Nok, Queen Amina of Zaria, Asantehene Osei Tutu, Ghana, Sundiata, Queen Nzingha, King Njoya, King Akwa, Okomfo Anokye, Yaa Asantewaa, King Odudua, Queen Idia, Dokua, Okru Banin, Abubakari, Mansa Musa, Timbuktu, Sankore, Nsibidi, Benin, Uthman dan Fodio, Gao, Jenne, Ouagadougou, Segu, Dogon, King Ansa, Touba, Keita, Mali, Shango, Oshun, Ogun, Kumasi, Agades, and thousands of other names of people, places, and ideas interconnected in the western region of Africa (see figure 1.7, page 8).

The empires of Ghana, Mali, and Songhay and the kingdoms of Benin, Asante, Oyo, Congo, and Angola left their political and cultural stamps as markers to political and material greatness. From these political jurisdictions and their remnant political and military organizations came many of the Africans who were brought to the Americas. The ethnic names with which the Africans came included Mandingo, Fante, Ibo, Efik, Yoruba, Hausa, Serere, Wolof, Tuareg, Dan, Vai, Angola, Baule, Touculeur, Sherbro, Baga, Asante, Ga, Ewe, Fulani, Douala, and over 100 other names. In some cases, the entire ethnic group was wiped out in Africa by the European slave trade.

This vast region—containing more square miles than the continental United States—was poised, by virtue of indigenous village industries and widespread trade networks, to make rapid advances in technical development. The appearance of Portuguese ships along the Moroccan, Mauretanian, and Senegambian coasts was to alter fundamentally the manner and rate of West Africa's technological advancement.

The Mourning Time

W. E. B. Du Bois estimated that over 100 million Africans were uprooted from the continent in the European slave trade. Others have suggested figures between 15 million and 50 million transported across the Atlantic Ocean to the Americas and the Caribbean. Millions were dislocated on the African continent itself, leaving broken bodies, spirits, and industries. There was nothing regular about what the scholar Marimba Ani has called in Yoruba the *maafa*, the Great Disaster, in which Africa was literally robbed of its human and material wealth. When the trade ended it was as if a massive hand had indiscriminately plucked people from villages, towns, and cities. Hereditary kings and queens, princes and princesses, courtiers, okyeames, and queen mothers were faced with the indignity of having their titles stripped in the presence of their nations. Throughout the huge continent, millions of Africans were in political, social, economic, and spiritual turmoil during the period of the Great Disaster. Wars were fought and captives taken on the basis of an entirely new ethic of warfare never before seen on the continent. The level of violence inflicted on historical enemies had rarely

approached the level of slaughter that was brought in with the new European weapons. This was the mourning time for Africa.

When the European slave trade began, the West African traditional nations and kingdoms were undergoing wide-scale turbulence caused by inroads of Islam in the west. Already established in the arid regions of Mali, Senegal, and Mauretania, Islam pushed into the heart of the tropical forest region by converting many people of present Guinea. The struggle against Islam weakened most nations and made those without Islamic allies easy prey for the superior weapons of the Europeans.

The millions of transported Africans, seariders who became landless in a strange land, re-created and re-formed Africa in thousands of farms, villages, and towns in the Americas and Caribbean. Langston Hughes, often called the "Poet of the African American People," summed up the pathos in the soul of African Americans in many of his poems. He was fond of using the river metaphor. In one of his early poems he wrote, "I have known rivers, ancient dusky rivers and my soul has grown deep like the rivers." This metaphor is a mighty current running through the works of many African American authors as different as Mari Evans, Vincent Harding, and Houston Baker. It speaks to the enormity of the experience of being dislocated; it speaks to movement; it speaks to the variety of circumstances that engages the African soul in the rhythmic movements of history. Whether it is the Mississippi, Ohio, Congo, Nile, Niger, Zambezi, or Red River of Arkansas, the African knows rivers. They have carried the hearts and souls of the people from place to place.

Artists have enshrined the river in the African American culture. One sees it in the dance of Kariamu Welsh Asante or Alvin Ailey or Pearl Primus. It is the mother metaphor in the lyricism of Wynton Marsalis's horn or Michael Jackson's movements. John Coltrane and James Brown are connected by it; Aretha

Franklin and Ruby Dee are sisters because of the river. In the end, it must be viewed as it was, a mighty turbulent ocean.

AFRICAN HISTORY AND CULTURE

It is certainly true to say that there are many cultures in Africa, but it is equally true to say that there is an African culture, just as one might speak of an Asian or a European culture. Variations in cultural and political styles and in religious and social institutions are found throughout the African continent. Yet the commonalities of the continent are plentiful. From music to dance, from foods to celebrations, from theological concepts to rituals, one finds great similarity. The enslaved ancestors of present-day African Americans brought with them all of the abundantly complex rituals, symbols, and ideas of their large and diverse continent. West Africa represents the immediate ancestral home of the vast majority of African Americans. While it is true that Africans were enslaved in the Americas from East and Southern Africa as well as Madagascar, the principal areas of the European slave trade were the regions adjoining the concavity of the African coast created by the Atlantic Ocean. The political institutions developed in the Senegal-Gambia region, the Niger River Valley, and the Zaire River basin were built on the foundations of cosmological and epistemological principles derived from the social and political environment. They included systems of governance where the village constituted the key unit in the effective administration of law and rules. Numerous villages held together in confederation might constitute a large kingdom. Several kingdoms would become an empire. In every case, the organization was created out of the belief systems of the people.

Most African empires had a hierarchical form of governance. The king stood at the top of the power structure. In all cases, however, the king was subject to the ancestral traditions. This meant that the king paid homage to those who had gone before him. He was the representative among the people of the distant power of the deities and the ancestors. In some instances, the king could not rule alone. In those cases, he had advisers and councillors appointed by the kingmakers who made the rules and laws governing the society. West African rulers typically related their prowess, courage, virility, wisdom, health, rhythm, and longevity to some primordial site of the nation.

In the myths of West African peoples one finds the names of Bosumpra, Yengema, Zenebi, Mbanza Ngungu—ancient African sites as animating forces in the philosophical and religious systems of the various states. All across the continent the integration of the historical sites with the special, primordial ancestors is recognizable. In West Africa, this spirit is present everywhere.

Nevertheless, there was to be no appreciation of the ancestral sites and particular spirits of the African landscape during the 300 years of the slave trade beginning in the fifteenth century. Indeed, the same disregard of Africa's historic place and the African sense of history was to occur in the nineteenth century. At the Berlin Conference of 1884–1885, Africa was balkanized in totally irrational ways as far as the interest of Africa was concerned. But for Europe the conference had worked out compromises to prevent European wars.

During the periods of the slave trade and colonization, the lack of roads aided the African kingdoms in maintaining isolation from the coastal regions. However, the rudimentary system of highways built by the European powers in every nation made it easier to transport raw materials from the interior to the coast and for the white administrators to penetrate the interior with laws and ordinances.

AFRICAN AMERICAN IDENTITY

These factors and many others make the discussion of African American identity one of great complexity. Of course, it is simple to speak of the African Americans as those blacks who live in the United States or who were born in the

Americas, North, Central, or South. But at a more profound level the question Who are African Americans? raises deeper reflections and requires much more complex answers.

Most Americans do not know the names of the African ethnic groups that make up the African American population. Numerous African ethnic groups with long histories and traditions were victimized by the slave trade. Who, then, are African Americans?

In part, the answer to the question must be historical—that is, it must deal with origin and history on the African continent. One must consider the cultures and civilizations that constitute the African heritage: Egypt, Meroe, Ethiopia, Tichitt, Nok, Ghana, Kanem-Bornu, Carthage, Nubia, Katanga, Tekrur, Mali, Songhay, Hausa, Birgirmi, Wadai, Mossi, Fulani, Yoruba, Denkyira, Akwamu, Asante, Benin, Kongo, Luba, Kuba, Lunda, Angola, Munhu Matapa, Lozi, Bemba, Xhosa, Zulu, Basotho, Swahili, Buganda, Bunyoro, Galla, and Somali. Many additional and smaller cultures and civilizations exist, and these made considerable contributions to human harmonization with the environment. Furthermore, because of the disruption of enslavement, members of the African American population normally are unable to identify their African nation of origin. The entire continent becomes the ancestral home to the African American population when each individual chooses a particular cultural group or region because of the resonance one feels with it.

All European ethnic groups have a heritage that extends prior to their arrival in America. But no other ethnic or racial group in the United States has been under such intense pressure to forget origin and to abandon its cultural past as the African American community. At times, African Americans have obliged. When the Colored Convention met in Philadelphia in 1817 to decide how to respond to the issue of sending Africans back to Africa, the speakers (the leading citizens of the major urban centers) agreed that African Americans should

refer to themselves, not as Africans, but as colored Americans. The pressure for Africans living in the North to abandon any relationship with Africa was due in large part to the African leadership's concern with how white Americans would view the idea of Africans, a separate community, agitating for freeing Africans in the South. Thus, they assumed the posture that they were not Africans, at least for the purpose of agitation, but colored Americans.

This action predictably put a damper on anyone wanting to hold to traditions or to seek out African ancestry. But when the leading citizens of the major urban centers called for a new policy, they usually carried the day. This is precisely what happened when the convention debated the merits of the terms "African" and "Colored." But a strong minority held to the name "African," and in fact it never disappeared from institutions from the time that Richard Allen named his church the African Methodist Episcopal Church, in 1793.

Other institutions carried the word "African" in their titles as well—the Free African Society, for instance, founded in 1761 in New York. In the eighteenth century, during the age of the African Methodist Episcopal Church, the African Free Society, the African Free School, and the African Benevolent Society, outstanding men and women understood that they were of African heritage although they lived in the United States.

Yet the relocation of African Americans in a psychological space that allows for agency and responsibility has already been successful in contemporary times with a solid political awareness developing in the urban areas.

Afrocentric scholars have begun to uncover much information about the African past. Indeed, the entire continent has become one vast worksite for historians, anthropologists, political scientists, and geographers interested in precolonial Africa. Cheikh Anta Diop, Chinweizu, Theophile Obenga, and Ayi Kwei Armah in Africa and Miriam Maat Monges, Abu Abarry, Maulana Karenga, and Kwame

Ayeke on both sides of the ocean have examined the political, social, and cultural organizations of Africa societies from the standpoint of African agency as opposed to marginality. This atlas will link the African American more firmly to historical roots than most previous works have done because the aim of a considerable body of scholarship has been to dislocate and dissociate continental Africans from Africans in the Americas and Caribbean.

The relocation of the African American in a world context has already begun in several places. One finds this attitude permeating the meeting of the Organization of African Unity, where observer status is regularly accorded African American delegations. In addition, several agencies of the United Nations have begun to bring African Americans more fully into the discussion of the African world. Thus, the UNESCO project "The Route of the Slaves," a multiyear, transnational, and transcontinental project for documenting the slave trade, has involved the talents of outstanding African American scientists, even though African nations first promoted the idea. Documentaries for radio and television have situated African Americans in larger African as well as American context.

To a great degree the presence of prominent continental African and Caribbean authors and artists in key academic positions in the United States has made a difference in linking African Americans to the rest of the African world. International figures such as Wole Soyinka, Ngugi wa Thiong'o, Ali Mazrui, Ama Aidoo, Isidore Okpewho, Chinua Achebe, and Maryse Conde are accepted within the African American community as a part of the same African world.

Not since the abandonment of the name "African" in the nineteenth century by the most prominent blacks of the period has there been such a drastic return to Africa. The term "African" had always been correct. Now the literature reflects the attitudes of the people—that is, the literary people have begun to listen to their inner voices.

Sterling Stuckey, among others, has written perceptively about the culture of Africans during the enslavement, noting the continuity of ideas and ideals in the thinking of the early African Americans. The ancient kingdoms serve contemporary society by pointing to the sources of many ideas, customs, behaviors, and styles that live fully in the African American.

CLASSICAL AFRICA

The earliest civilizations of Africa arose along the Nile River in the northeastern part of the continent. These civilizations, Egypt, called Kemet, Nubia, Meroe, Kush, and Axum are among the first in the world to construct the basis of writing, architecture, law, medicine, political organization, literature, philosophy, and geometry. We are still astonished at the immensity of these civilizations' achievements and their bequests not only to Africa but to the world.

From the First Dynasty of Egypt around 3100 B.C.E. to the rise of Axum in the third century C.E. our attention is captivated by the accomplishments of the African people of the region. They are engaged not simply in city building and architecture but also in philosophy and religion. The legacy of these civilizations would prove to be as great in the area of human morality and ethics as in the material development of their nations.

Egypt itself stands at the head of all ancient nations in terms of the prodigious nature of its artists, scholars, and rulers. No nation at a comparable time in history has come close to the productivity of the Egyptian civilization. In Egypt we see the evidence of cultural production long before the presence of the First Dynasty. By the time Menes (Narmer) united Upper Egypt with Lower Egypt the land had seen many centuries of human development. But when Menes came down from the South—that is, Upper Egypt— and conquered Lower Egypt, the delta area in the North, he set in motion the most marvelous period in African history. The stability, strength, energy, and science of Egypt were without peer.

Of course, even in the days of the ancient civilization of Egypt, there was speculation about the impact of Nubia on Egypt. So ancient is Nubia that they are the first people identified in the writings of the Egyptians. But they are even older than their appearance in the consciousness of Egypt. Nubia may very well be the mother of Egypt, as has been argued by scholars such as Yosef Ben-Jochannan and more recently by Miriam Maat Ka Re Monges in her book *Kush: The Jewel of Nubia* (Trenton, NJ: Africa Word Press, 1997). We know that ancient Nubia was adjacent to Egypt and that there was considerable intermingling among the people of the two countries. The names of Mentuhotep, Rameses, Piankhy, Shabaka, Tarharka, and Nefertari are just a few of those associated with both Egypt and Nubia. There were times when the two nations were ruled as a united country by Egyptian and Nubian kings.

Other ancient nations such as Axum, Punt, and Kanem-Bornu brought their own gifts to classical Africa and in time the spread of African people from the East to the South and West meant that many of the concepts, ideas, and institutions of the East were transplanted to the West and South. Since all humans originated in East Africa and the earliest civilizations come from this region, it is most understandable that migration to other parts of Africa would occur. Thus, periodic migrations from East to South and West occurred over the millennia, and these migrations peopled the various regions of Africa. But when people migrate they not only take themselves to their new homes but their ideas and customs. Scholars have speculated on the reasons for the various migrations to the South and to the West. Some migrated to find better sources of food, others migrated for religious and spiritual reasons, and still others migrated after war and violence on their communities.

Munhu Matapa

One of the most significant civilizations of southern Africa was called Munhu Matapa. The Munhu Matapa Empire began in the first century C.E. and lasted for 1500 years in the area that is now the nation of Zimbabwe. Kings of the region were called Munhu Matapa, and the empire took its name after them.

Shona and Lozi people, descendants of the ancient Munhu Matapa, are credited with the more than 400 sites of stone ruins that were once flourishing villages found in South Central Africa. Stretching over Zimbabwe, Zambia, South Africa, and Mozambique, these ancient sites hold histories yet untold.

The largest of the sites is the Great Zimbabwe, literally "stone house," located in Southern Zimbabwe. There are two parts to the sites. One part is located on the top of a hill and the other larger area is located in the plains below. Both are extremely impressive and show excellent skill and artistry.

Made of the local granite, the huge stones that make up the structures were expertly chiseled to fit without the use of any cementing element. The site atop the hill and the valley or plains site both display a dignity and strength that suggest nobility. In *Lost Cities of Africa* (Boston: Little, Brown, 1970) Basil Davidson wrote that "everywhere these structures are marked with an originality which seems to owe nothing to the rest of the world" (p. 247).

The ruler or Munhu Matapa was legendary in South Central Africa. Whenever a new Munhu Matapa rose to power he attempted to outbuild the previous lord of the land. Indeed, at the height of its glory the ancient Zimbabwean kingdom traded with India, China, and the Arabs. There is no record of a European merchant or missionary reaching this empire. The deities, beliefs, and methods of civilization remained within the confines of the society itself. This was sufficient to make the empire respected by those who visited to trade.

Europeans who finally reached the site in the nineteenth century could not believe that Africans had erected it. They sought all kinds of excuses for the high quality of the work, the apparent organizational ability of the people, and the extent of their trade with the outside world. How could a people dominated by Europeans, a people despised by them, have created so a splendid civilization? This was to plague the white colonists' minds in Africa.

Jebel Uri

Toward the west of the Nile Valley, the civilization of Kanem emerged. Under the emperor Dunama Dibbalemi, who ruled Kanem from 1210 to 1224, the Kanemic Empire stretched from the western banks of the Nile to an area just northeast of the Niger River. The successor kingdom to Kanem was the mighty Bornu, the remnants of which can be found in the present Nigerian sultanate of Bornu. Caravans from the Niger to the Nile—and perhaps, as some authors claim, from the Niger to Somali—passed through the territory of the Kanem Bornu Empire.

During the sixth century C.E., Nubian Christians were buffers between the kingdoms to the west and the Islamic invasions coming from the northeast. It was not until the thirteenth century that the Nubians were finally conquered by Islamic culture. Evidences of their last stands are found in the ruins of churches that dot areas of Egypt, Chad, and Sudan.

The incredible ruins of Jebel Uri appear in this region. This ancient city with its nine-stepped auditorium to the cemetery of the long-vanished Daju people is one of the largest ancient cities of Africa. The city was constructed of stone within a strong circular wall. From the size of this ancient community it is believed that a large population lived here for four or five centuries. Much like the architects of Great Zimbabwe, the builders of this city used no mortar. A mighty causeway of huge blocks of stone ascends to the top of the site. The earliest dates for the site suggest the time of Harkhuf, the traveler, around 2400 B.C.E.

WEST AFRICAN ANTIQUITY

Wahb ibn Munnabeh wrote of the migrations of African peoples from the east to the west and into the interior in 738 C.E. He spoke of the people of the Sudan as the Goran, the Zaghawa, the Habesha, the Copts, and the Berbers. In 947 C.E., the greatest geographer of the period, El Mas'udi, wrote in his book *Meadows of Gold and Mines of Gems* (Beirnt: Maktabat Khayyat, 1965, p. 22) that "the sons of Kush . . . traveled toward the west and crossed the Nile. There they separated. Some of them, the Nubians and the Beja and the Zanj, turned to the rightward, between the east and west; but the others, very numerous, marched toward the setting sun."

According to H. Lhote and other scholars, the Sahara has long been occupied by black people. In fact, Lhote reported that a painting in the Tassili area is similar to one of the same style found in Cote'd' Ivoire. The desiccation of the Sahara forced Africans to move farther west and south from the eastern area. We now know that human beings have probably lived in the West African region longer than 30,000 years.

The records of antiquity in West Africa have become more numerous as scholars begin to investigate cultures that have occupied the savannas. Art historian Bernard Fagg reported that tiny fragments of charcoal from the Kanjeran pluvial produced an age of 39,000 years. Lhote has suggested that Africans invented portraiture art, painting men and women with sensitivity and realism as early as 3000 B.C.E.

THE EUROPEAN SCRAMBLE

The transformation of the world's power arrangements over the last 500 years brought about major changes in international relationships. Africa became the favorite region for forced laborers and cheap raw materials. Seeking to expand its own power base, Europe found Africa a ready-made continent of economic opportunity.

Colonial interests of the European nations followed the early merchant and missionary inroads into the continent. The scramble, as it was called, for Africa was fed by the national desires of European states to reap the most benefit from a continent rendered too weak to defend itself by the tremendous upheavals from within and the avarice of nations from without. Like birds of prey, the colonial powers pounced upon any African state or kingdom that seemed to limp along in political disarray, economic disorganization, or worldly indifference to the European encroachments in the continent (see figure 1.8, page 18). European nations with fleets quickly outfitted them and headed for the coasts of Africa. The initial entry into Africa was for gold. Only when the Americas were being exploited did the need for laborers supersede the desire for gold. Not oil, but Africans were the original black gold.

MODERN DIVISIONS

Modern African states are the creations of boundaries established in the interest and for the benefit of colonial European powers (see figure 1.9, page 19). The borders of most states in Africa have no rational basis, except that they were set up in the various charters of the European nations. When the Berlin Conference of 1884–1885 was over, the African continent had been politically organized in the interest of Europe in ways that were to confirm the historical division of the continent created by the rise of the European slave trade itself.

Sensing the inherent weakness in an arbitrarily divided Africa, the most eminent African scholar of the twentieth century, Cheikh Anta Diop, called for the redrawing of the boundaries of the continent to take advantage of natural and historical interests (*Cultural Unity of Black Africa*, Chicago: Third World Books, 1986). In a similar vein, Molefi Kete Asante delivered a speech to an international African conference in London in January 1987, later published as "Six State Continent" in the African Concord, in which he provided guidelines for redrawing the continental boundaries. Kwame Nkrumah, the leading spirit for the development of the Organization for African Unity, initiated the call for a united Africa in the 1960s.

African Americans are largely descended from the western region of the continent. This area was much more accessible to Europeans seeking to transport Africans to the Americas. East coast and southern coast Africans had been taken by Arab and Portuguese slave traders to Asia and the Arabian peninsula. The Arabs under Tippu Tib continued their trade until the 1800s.

The anomalies produced by arbitrary division of the continent have resulted in tensions, disputed territories, political unrest, ethnic distrust, and frequent challenges to central governments. Thus, one finds Yoruba people in Nigeria and Benin; Mandingo people in Guinea, Senegal, Sierra Leone, and Mali; Akan people in Cote D'Ivoire and Ghana; and Ewe in Ghana and Togo. Consequently, the borders of national states are often violated by individuals who are seeking to make contact with relatives and friends of the same ethnic groups. Divisions such as these did not exist during the European slave trade. Europeans invaded or traded with unitary African states. For example, an agreement might be made between the Dutch and Fante nation or the English and Benin. The modern African nation-state is now laid over the traditional nations, often over several of them.

Figure 1.8. Lagos, Nigeria. While largely rural, Africa is dotted with many large cities. Like most third-world urban areas, Lagos is crowded, noisy, and polluted by Western standards. Credit: Daniel Lainé/Corbis.

MOROCCO
TUNISIA
SPANISH SAHARA
ALGERIA
LIBYA
EGYPT
MAURITANIA
MALI
NIGER
CHAD
FRENCH SOMALIA
SENEGAL
GAMBIA
PORTUGUESE GUINEA
GUINEA
UPPER VOLTA
DAHOMEY
NIGERIA
ANGLO-EGYPTION SUDAN
SIERRA LEONE
IVORY COAST
GOLD COAST
SOMALIA
LIBERIA
ETHIOPIA
TOGO
UBANGUI-SHARI
CAMEROON
ITALIAN SOMALIA
SPANISH GUINEA
BUGANDA
KENYA
GABON
BELGIAN CONGO
RWANDA URUNDI
FRENCH CONGO
TANGANYIKA

COLONIAL AFRICA ANNEXATION

- English
- French
- Spanish
- Portuguese
- Italian
- Belgian
- Independent

ANGOLA
NORTHERN RHODESIA
MOZAMBIQUE
NYASSALAND
SOUTH WEST AFRICA
SOUTHERN RHODESIA
MADAGASCAR
BECHUANALAND
SWAZILAND
SOUTH AFRICA
BASUTOLAND

Figure 1.9. Colonial Africa.

COUNTRIES GAINING
INDEPENDENCE

Before 1945

Between 1950 and 1960

In 1960

After 1960

Countries Fighting for
National Liberation

Figure 1.10. Present-day Africa.

"I Don't Care Where You Bury My Body"

2

THE TRANSATLANTIC JOURNEY

The migration of Africans from the Nile River Valley to the Niger River area in West Africa was but the beginning of movement on the continent of Africa. The eastern cradle of Africa gave birth to numerous migrations.

When historian Ibn Amir Hajib asked Emperor Kankan Musa of Mali about navigation on the Atlantic Ocean, the king replied:

> The monarch who preceded me would not believe that it was impossible to discover the limits of the neighboring sea. He wished to know. He persisted in his plan. He caused the equipping of two hundred ships and filled them with men, and of another such number that were filled with gold, water and food for two years. He said to the commanders: do not return until you have reached the end of the ocean, or when you have exhausted your food and water.
>
> They went away and their absence was long: none came back, and their absence continued. Then a single ship returned. We asked the captain of their adventures and their news. He replied: Sultan, we sailed for a long while until we met with what seemed to be a river with a strong current

flowing in the open sea. My ship was last. The others sailed on, but as each of them came to that place they did not come back nor did they reappear; and I do not know what became of them. As for me, I turned where I was and did not enter the current.

In 1311 and 1312, according to scholar Fadl Ailah al-Omari, the Malian prince Abubakari II, brother of Emperor Mansa Musa, sent shipping vessels across the west African sea (Atlantic Ocean). The historian and anthropologist Ivan Van Sertima, in his book *They Came before Columbus: Africa and the Discovery of America* (Philadelphia: Innes, 1920), tells us that Abubakari's fishing vessels landed in Mexico, where the African settlers affected the local culture's language, rituals, myths, religions, and agriculture. Sertima's work, like that of Michael Bradley, was based on earlier work by Leo Wiener, who had argued in the early part of the twentieth century that Africans had discovered America.

Other scholars have argued that Africans came to central America long before the fourteenth century. Indeed, evidence in the Mayan and Mexican forests—pyramids and large African sculptures (the Olmec heads)—suggests an early African presence (figure 2.1).

The Olmec civilization of Mexico, the first complex culture of the Americas, is thought to have been influenced by the classical African civilizations of Ethiopia, Kemet, and Meroe (see figure 2.2, page 23). The Olmec civilization flourished between 1200 and 400 B.C.E., when it fell into regional conflicts and finally became one of a series of smaller cultures of Mesoamerica.

The Olmec culture was centered on the Gulf Coast of Mexico, but its economic, political, and social influence extended into the central Mexican highlands and southeast to the Pacific up to El Salvador and into other regions of Central America. Many later American civilizations trace their history to the Olmecs.

By 1200 B.C.E., Olmec civilization was fully developed at San Lorenzo, the earliest major ceremonial center. Later,

Figure 2.1. Olmec head.

around 900 B.C.E., the power center of the civilization shifted to La Venta, where huge African heads of basalt have been found. Weighing several tons and resembling the faces and hairstyles of Africans of the same period of time, these heads lend support to the claims by Van Sertima and Bradley that the Olmec civilization was the first civilization established by Africans outside of the continent of Africa.

The inspiration for the massive public works projects—clay building platforms and stone drainage systems—seems to be ancient Egyptian. Actually, the large human heads and fine jade carvings suggest African, perhaps Nubian, influences at an early period. A further relationship to the classical African civilizations has been suggested through the similarity of the hieroglyphic systems of writing. The Nile Valley in Africa and the Mesoamerica region share several similarities, including the later development in the Americas of pyramids. Since there are no direct written records of the African origin of Olmec civilization, the arguments for African influences, substantial as they are, have been based upon the carved images of Africans, the similarity of cultural expressions, and, as in the case of the Mali sailors, the presence of African customs, myths, and ceremonies in certain parts of Mexico.

Enough evidence exists to show that ancient Africans not only sailed to the Americas but were able to make boats that would take them across the oceans. However, it was as sailors and soldiers in European expeditions that Africans became known in more recent times.

The first African to enter what is now the United States of America was Estevanico. He entered the southwest as one of the principal explorers in a Spanish expedition. Estevanico's route covered a considerable part of the American southwest. After Estevanico's journey, it seemed fashionable for Spanish, Italian, and Portuguese explorers especially to have African assistants along because of their prowess, courage, linguistic ability, and ingenuity.

Figure 2.2. Early African presence in North America: Olmec sites in Mexico.

The skill and courage of the African sailor was such that when European explorers sought to sail to unfamiliar lands they often relied upon Africans as navigators and ship hands. For example:

- Pedro Alonso Nino accompanied Columbus to the Americas.
- Alvarado, who is usually given credit in textbooks for his exploration of equatorial South America, was assisted by nearly 200 African sailors, many veterans of several voyages to sea.
- In 1513, when Balboa reached the Pacific Ocean, thirty Africans looked upon the same scene as the Spaniard.
- The first wheat crop sowed in the "New World" was planted by an African with Hernando Cortés's expedition.

Unfortunately, many African explorers remain nameless for three principal reasons: (1) they traveled under the flags of nations other than their own; (2) histories were written from the viewpoint of the expedition's principal leader; and (3)

Table 2.1. African Explorers of the Americas.

Time Period	Explorer	Accomplishment
1450–800 B.C.E.	Olmec (Nubian-Kemetic) Africans arrive in Central America (Mexico)	Trading, teaching, learning
1305–1312 C.E.	Abu Bakari II, the King of Mali, sends one fleet of ships and later leads another across what is now the Atlantic Ocean	Exploration
1310–1491	Mandingo merchant explorers	Make over fifty trips to various Caribbean and Central and South American points including what are now called Panama, Honduras, and Haiti.
1492	Pedro Alonzo Nino	Pilot and navigator for Columbus.
1513	Nuflo de Olano	With Vasco Nunez de Balboa when Balboa claims the "South Sea" for Spain. Olano and twenty-nine other Africans are with Balboa in the crossing of Panama.
1514	Group of Africans	With Pedrarias de Avila when he takes the title of royal governor of a Spanish colony on the Isthmus of Panama.
1523	Group of Africans	With Pedro de Alvarado when Alvarado's expeditionary force enters Guatemala.
1527	Estavanico (Estebanico/Esteban; called "Little Steven")	Leads Panfilo de Navaes's unsuccessful expedition from Spain to the southwest of North America. Leads three surviving Europeans on eight-year transcontinental journey from Florida through Texas and northern Mexico to the Gulf of California and Mexico City.
1532	Twelve Africans	With Francisco de Montejo's first campaign to the Yucatan Peninsula.
1539	Estavanico	With Desoto when he journeys to the Mississippi River.
1540	Group of Africans	Lead expedition (which includes Friar Marcos de Niza) giving Europeans their first contact with Arizona and the land of the Zuni people (now New Mexico).
1565	Group of Africans	With explorers who found St. Augustine, Florida.
1745	Jean Baptiste Pointe Du Sable, the father of the city of Chicago	Born in St. Marc, St. Dominique (Haiti). Builds the first permanent home on the northern bank of the Chicago River in 1779. Later establishes a thriving trading post that grows into the city of Chicago.
1781	Twenty-six Africans	Help found Los Angeles, California, with eighteen others.
1798–1866	James Pierson Beckwourth	Born in Fredericksburg, VA. Explores western United States long before John Fremont. Assists William Ashley of the Rocky Mountain Fur Co. until 1825. Serves as chief scout for Fremont starting in 1848. Well liked by the Blackfoot and Crow nations, the Crow make him a chief (Bull's Robe). Discovers pass through Sierra Nevada mountains in 1850 later used by wagon trains, pioneers, gold seekers, and the Western Pacific Railway. The pass, a valley in Nevada, and a Methodist church in Denver, Colorado bear his name.
1810	Five Africans	With Lewis and Clarke expedition. One of the five, Rourk, is the group's scout, trapper, and trader.
1820	George Bonga	Opens a trading post on the northern Great Lakes. Marries a Chippewa. A town in Cass County, Minnesota, bears his name.
1843	Jacob Dotson, Mifflin Gibbs, Andrew Jackson, and don Jesus Picos	With John Fremont. Dotson is a marksman and an expert with the lasso. Fights beside Fremont in the Mexican War and against Kit Carson in the Bear Flag Party during the Civil War.
1848–1849	Mammy Pleasant	Helps build San Francisco and aids Africans escaping slavery.
1909	Matthew Alexander Henson	Arrives at the North Pole; returns to carry Robert E. Peary physically to the North Pole.

Africans were conscripted as soldiers and servants to support the expeditions. The African explorers whose names we know usually rose far beyond the station assigned to them (see figure 2.3, page 24).

Estevan de Dorantes (Estevanico, "Little Steven" in English) was born in Africa and became one of the greatest explorers of his day. Sold as a servant to the conquistador Andres Dorantes de Carranca, Estevan later joined him in 1527 on an expedition to the Americas under an experienced explorer named Panfilo de Narvaez.

In 1528, when the expedition of 600 men entered Florida, Panfilo divided them into two groups. One group he led into the jungles of Florida, another group he directed to march toward the southwest to Mexico. The expedition was wiped out by sickness, Native Americans defending their lands, and internal squabbles. The four who survived—Estevan, Andres Dorantes, Castillode Moldonado, and Alvar Nuniz (also known as Cabeza de Vaca)—were captured by the Native Americans and made to work for them for six years. Estevanico escaped and, attracted by the story of the seven cities of gold in the southwest, became a scout for an expedition led by one Father Marco. Traveling alone over vast reaches of the west, the African explorer sent messages to the main party by friendly Indians. The last message received from Estevanico was a huge cross—symbol of a great discovery. This message led the expedition to the Zuni Pueblo, which Estevanico had thought was one of the legendary seven golden cities. When the main body of the expedition reached Zuni Pueblo, the Indians had already killed the explorer who had opened what are now Arizona and New Mexico to Africa and Europe.

THE MARINE TRADITION

When the West Africans crossed the Atlantic Ocean (West African sea), they brought with them patterns and customs that had been found in East Africa as well. Bradley has shown in his book *The Black Discovery of America* (1981) that the West African culture is the protocivilization for many of the cultures of the Americas. Whether one examines the bronze objects, portraiture in ceramics, weaving, dyeing, or mud-brick houses, one sees the relationship to the cultures of Mexico and the Andes. Since Nubians built large boats with sails as far back as 3100 B.C.E., it is logical that Africans who lived near the sea, either in the eastern or the western part of the continent, had that capability.

When Bartholomew Diaz and Vasco da Gama entered the Indian Ocean they found that Africans carried on an energetic trade from the Zambezi River eastward across the sea to China. When Columbus reached Cape Verde islands in the Atlantic Ocean he had been preceded by Mailian adventurers more than a century before. The records of these early mariners are found in the archaeological evidence in the Americas, the books by Moorish scholars, and the African plants, such as cotton and the pan-gourd, now found in the Americas.

AFRICAN ADVENTURERS, COWBOYS, AND PIONEERS IN THE AMERICAN WEST

There is a long line of adventurers, cowboys, and trailblazers who added to the exploration of the American West. Some of the more colorful characters included Nat Love, the famous cowboy, and Isom Dart, who was considered one of the most feared men of his time (see figure 2.4, page 27 and figure 2.6, page 28). Both Love and Dart were known for their ability to hunt and track wild animals as well as for their skill with guns. Bill Pickett was an Oklahoma cowboy who became famous for inventing and popularizing steer wrestling as a performer with the 101 Wild West Show. Pickett was elected to the Cowboy Hall of Fame for his innovations.

Perhaps one of the most exciting stories of an African adventurer in the West is that of Gobo Fango, a South African who went to Utah in 1861 with a white family named Talbot. According to the book *Our Pioneer Heritage* published in 1965 by the Daughters of Utah Pioneers,

Figure 2.3. African-American builders of the New World.

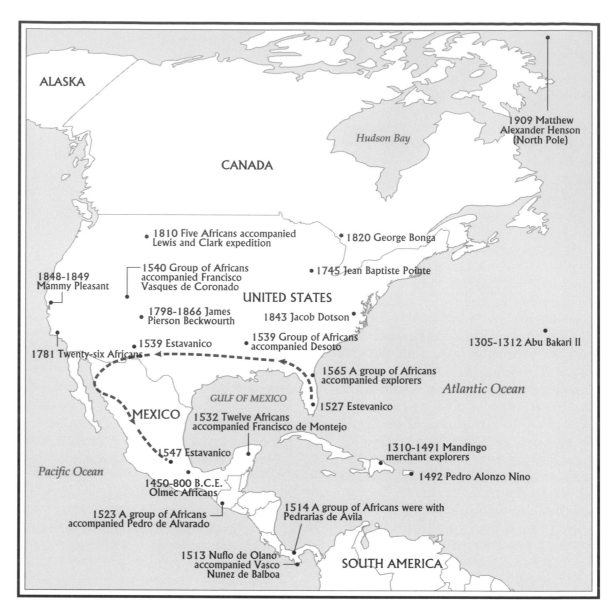

Gobo Fango was hidden under the skirt of one of the white women traveling in the party when a group of Confederate troops stopped them, looking for Africans who had escaped from slavery. When the danger had passed, the young Gobo was taken to Grantsville, Utah. From there he was taken by Mary Anne Whitesides to Kaysville, Utah, to assist in herding sheep. As a young boy, Gobo was given the responsibility of herding sheep on the plains. He learned the intricacies of tracking and rounding up sheep and became well known for his ability to survive in the outdoors. Often he went from ranch to ranch assisting in sheepherding duties. He was able to make a living hiring himself out for extra money. Gobo was used for many chores by the family of Mary

Ann Whitesides. Her husband, Edward Hunter, paid the previous "owner" of Gobo about thirty dollars a month until the end of the Civil War. Although Utah was not governed by the laws of the Confederacy, many sympathizers lived in the state. When the war was over, Edward Hunter began to pay Gobo the thirty dollars. This caused the previous "owner" to sue Hunter to no avail.

With his freedom, Gobo became famous as a sheepherder in the Oakley region of Utah. In 1880, he took Edward Hunter's sheep to the market in Oakley to run them on shares. A cattle war broke out and Gobo was shot by a man named Bedky, who had pretended to be his friend. Gobo was badly injured but managed to crawl to the home of Walt

Matthews. He was to live for only a few more days, but before his death he wrote a will leaving money for Mary Ann Whitesides and $500 to the Grantsville Relief Agency.

Throughout the towns, mountains, rivers, and passes of the American West, people celebrate the fact that Africans were early settlers and pioneers (see figure 2.5, page 26). The African American army private George Washington was responsible for persuading Billy the Kid to meet with Lew Wallace. Edward Booth was a pioneer in the gold fields of Alaska. Clara Brown lived in Central City, Colorado, from 1859 to 1877. She had been born into slavery in Missouri. Clara Brown owned a laundry and gave much money to charity in Central City. When she died the town dedicated the Opera House to her honor.

The Conestoga wagon is well known for having transported many travelers across the West. Independence, Missouri was one of the leading centers for the construction of the wagons. The city had become known for its Conestoga wagons because of the work of Hiram Young, builder of the famous wagons upon which thousands of people depended.

Young employed more than fifty men who operated the twenty-five forges in his smithy. His reputation was without peer as a builder of Conestogas. Many of the early settlers in the West would insist on using a Hiram Young carriage for transport. So important to the westward movement were Young's vehicles that cities and towns in Missouri got the recognition for being the places where the West truly began. This could certainly be said of Independence, Missouri, because of the work Young's smithy did in building the finest Conestogas around.

The tradition of adventurers, cowhands, and philanthropists came together in the finest examples of African American openness to difference and challenge in the American West. This tradition did not end with the closing of the nineteenth century. A spirit of exploration and adventure led to Matthew Henson's trek with Admiral Robert E. Peary to the

Figure 2.4. Nat Love (1854–1921). Born a slave but freed at the end of the Civil War, he obtained a job at a cattle ranch and soon headed west, becoming a cowboy in frontier lands.

North Pole on April 6, 1909 (see figure 2.7, page 26). Henson was the first man to walk on the North Pole. Peary could hardly walk because of frostbite and illness and Henson returned to carry him to the North Pole. The record of the exploits of the two men, one black and one white, in the Arctic Region is one of inspiration and victory. When Matthew Henson planted the flag of the United States of America at the North Pole, he was following in the path of many African explorers and adventurers before him, most of whom have remained anonymous to history because their stories were never written.

The ascendancy of free spirits among African Americans was based upon the same kind of aspiration that captured the imagination of whites who set out to explore regions new to them. Thus, the early pioneers, cowboys, trailblazers, scouts, and adventurers were curious about the world and wanted to increase their knowledge of it. Some among them were hunters and trappers, seeking to make a profit from their expertise. Others were seekers after gold in the mountains and valleys, but all were devoted to the free expression of their curiosity.

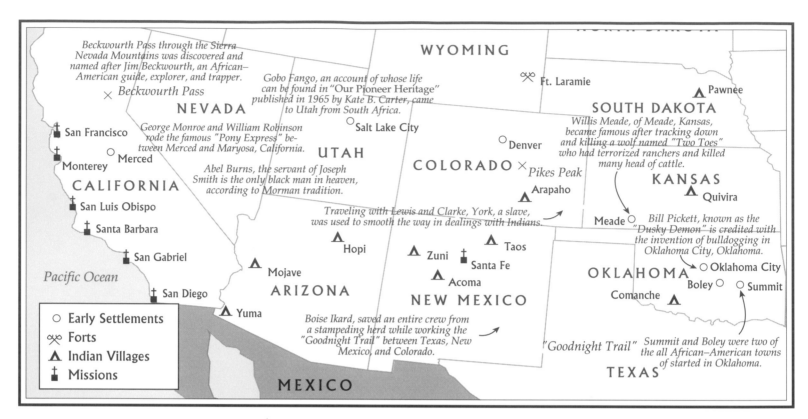

Beckwourth Pass through the Sierra Nevada Mountains was discovered and named after Jim Beckwourth, an African–American guide, explorer, and trapper.

× Beckwourth Pass

Gobo Fango, an account of whose life can be found in "Our Pioneer Heritage" published in 1965 by Kate B. Carter, came to Utah from South Africa.

George Monroe and William Robinson rode the famous "Pony Express" between Merced and Maryosa, California.

Abel Burns, the servant of Joseph Smith is the only black man in heaven, according to Morman tradition.

Willis Meade, of Meade, Kansas, became famous after tracking down and killing a wolf named "Two Toes" who had terrorized ranchers and killed many head of cattle.

Traveling with Lewis and Clarke, York, a slave, was used to smooth the way in dealings with Indians.

Bill Pickett, known as the "Dusky Demon" is credited with the invention of bulldogging in Oklahoma City, Oklahoma.

Boise Ikard, saved an entire crew from a stampeding herd while working the "Goodnight Trail" between Texas, New Mexico, and Colorado.

Summit and Boley were two of the all African–American towns of started in Oklahoma.

WYOMING
NEVADA
✕ Ft. Laramie
▲ Pawnee
SOUTH DAKOTA
✝ San Francisco
○ Salt Lake City
UTAH
○ Denver
KANSAS
✝ Monterey ○ Merced
COLORADO ✕ Pikes Peak
▲ Quivira
CALIFORNIA
▲ Arapaho
Meade ○
✝ San Luis Obispo
✝ Santa Barbara
▲ Hopi
▲ Zuni ▲ Taos
■ Santa Fe
OKLAHOMA
○ Oklahoma City
✝ San Gabriel
Pacific Ocean
▲ Acoma
NEW MEXICO
Boley ○ ○ Summit
✝ San Diego
▲ Mojave
ARIZONA
Comanche
▲
○ Early Settlements
✕ Forts
▲ Indian Villages
✝ Missions
▲ Yuma
"Goodnight Trail"
TEXAS
MEXICO

Figure 2.5 (above). African Americans in the Wild West.

Figure 2.6. Isom Dart (1849–1900). Freed when the Civil War ended, Dart led an exciting life as a horse thief in Mexico, then as a miner, and eventually as a cowboy.

Figure 2.7 (above). Matthew A. Henson (1866–1955). Accompanied Robert Peary to the North Pole and was the first person to reach that point on April 6, 1909, but did not receive credit for his accomplishment until much later because of his race.

Figure 2.8. Typical African cowboy of the 19th century.

Figure 2.10 (above). An African American marshall.

Figure 2.9. African American pioneers pose for a rare photograph near their sod house on the American plains.

"Dark Clouds A'risin'"

3

African Resistance to Enslavement

African resistance to foreign invasion was pervasive and aggressive across the continent during the entire period of the slave trade. Every region was engaged in warfare against either Arab or European intruders who sought to exploit the human and natural resources of the African continent.

The African people were not amused when they saw European nations competing to send missionaries, traders, and ambassadors to royal courts in an effort to obtain advantages over each other. The list of wars protecting the African homeland is long; the heroes and heroines who fought as patriots are now ancestral figures in various panoplies of recent deities throughout the continent. The wars for the control of the National Golden Stool between the Asante and the British, the wars between the Zulu and the British and between the Zulu and the Boers (to prevent expansion), the Yoruba wars, the Angolan resistance, the Baule resistance, the Shona Chimurenga wars, and the Benin wars were all fought for African honor. Nowhere in Africa did the Europeans enter uncontested once the people were aware of the potential disruptions. Unfortunately, in most cases African awakening was too late.

Meeting in Berlin during the winter of 1884–1885, several European nations conferred on an agreement that divided the African continent among themselves. The major players were Britain, France, Portugal, and Belgium, although Spain and Germany were given power over significant African territories. Consultation with African people was nil.

Imposing political and military will on the African people through force of arms, the European nations succeeded in dominating most of Africa by 1900. Wars of resistance caused widespread destruction of life and property in every region. The Germans killed thousands of people in Namibia; the British shot on sight every African they encountered in the territory of Zimbabwe; the Portuguese murdered the royal families of Angola; and the French punished the resisters in Guinea and Mali.

Two principal factors most often led to the defeat of Africans: (1) cultural differences and (2) military inequality. According to the late Senegalese scholar Cheikh Anta Diop in his book *The Cultural Unity of Black Africa,* Africans have usually been xenophilic while Europeans have been xenophobic. The result is European aggression on people perceived to be weak. European adventurers often wrote in their diaries that Africans were childlike or perceived Europeans as lost deities. Upon closer scrutiny what we see is a cultural misinterpretation. Numerous travelers into African territories were received with hospitality by kings and queens of the continent. Given passage through the various countries, Arab and European visitors often viewed Africans as naive. Their openness to strangers created the false impression that Africans did not care about the protection of their countries or their people.

Africa's lack of vigilance as well as its lack of military technology to counter the intruders often allowed access to the resources and people of the continent. Thus, the cultural factor coupled with the military and technological inventions of warfare made Africa's struggle to protect itself unwinable within the context of the times.

Asiento

So profitable was the European slave trade that the Roman Catholic Church entered the business as a grantor of commercial privilege to prevent Christian nations from engaging in fratricidal wars of access to the African coast. Usually the pope and a slaving nation signed an agreement that ensured that nation's right to a specific region of Africa (see page 33). A fee was paid to the church for this asiento (or license). When there were competing claims to territory, the church could stay in and determine which nation had its consent by virtue of the correct asiento. Since no European nation exercised complete hegemony over others, the church became—and remained for several hundred years—the primary moral sanction for the brutal institution of slave trading.

The asiento of 1713 between England and Spain granted England a monopoly of the Spanish colonial slave trade for thirty years. With the contract signed by the pope, the kings of England and Spain were each to receive one-fourth of the profits of the trade. England advanced Spain 200,000 crowns for each African imported. The contract was ended in October 1750.

Bartolome de Las Casas, who lived between 1474 and 1566, is considered the first proponent of using Africans instead of Native Americans as forced laborers in the Spanish colonies of America. He was one of the first missionaries to the Americas, arriving in Hispaniola in 1502, but was not formally ordained until 1512. His campaign to prevent the harsh treatment of the Native Americans culminated in his persuading the Spanish crown and the Catholic church to permit the importation of Africans to the region.

Monopolies of the trade changed hands between the leading slave powers: Portuguese, Dutch, French, and English. The European slave trade was the largest single employer in Holland and Portugal between 1500 and 1750. Thousands of individuals were employed in some aspect of the trade or a related industry. Millions of dollars in capital were placed at the disposal of the pioneering and adventuring slave captains.

Due to the intense competition in the business of trading in humans, the Portuguese, who had been the first Europeans in the trade, did not become one of the key nations in the later stages. Its power had run its own natural course. By the middle of the sixteenth century the three biggest trading powers were England, Holland, and France. Spanish merchants had been effectively held out of the trade by the papal arbitration of 1493, which allowed other nations to import Africans to Spanish territories in the Americas. In Europe, Portugal was first in the slave trade. The small Iberian nation was the leading seafaring country of the fifteenth century when Prince

The Asiento
1713, March 26

The Asiento, or contract for allowing to the Subjects of Great Britain the Liberty of importing Negroes into the Spanish America. Signed by the Catholick King at Madrid, the 26th Day of March, 1713.

Art. I.
"First then to procure, by this means, a mutual and recprocal advantage to the soveriegns and subjects of both crown, her British majesty does offer and undertake for the persons, whom she shall name and appoint, That they shall oblige and charge themselves with the bringing into the West-Indies of America, belonging to his catholick majesty, in the space of the said 30 years, to commence on the 1st day of May, 1713, and determine on the like day, which will be in the year 1743, viz. 144000 negroes, Piezas de India, of both sexes, and of all ages, at the rate of 4800 negroes, Piezas de India, in each of the said 30 years, with this condition, That the persons who shall go to the West-Indies to take care of the concerns of the asiento, shall avoid giving any offence, for in such case they shall be prosecuted and punished in the same manner, as they would have been in Spain, if the like misdemeansors had been committed there."

Art. II.
Asientists to pay a duty of 33 pieces of eight (Escudos) for each Negro, which should include all duties.

Art. III.
Asientists to advance to his his Catholic Majesty 200,000 pieces of eight, whcih should be returned at the end of the first twenty years,...

[John Almon, Treaties of Peace, Alliance, and Commerce between Great-Britain and other Powers (London, 1772), I. 83–107]

Henry, called the "Navigator," took an interest in the coast of Africa. Arabs had occupied a portion of Africa since the seventh century and had participated in their own slave trade, transporting millions of Africans to various parts of the Arab world. However, under the leadership of Portugal and Spain, after the defeat of the Africanized Muslims, Europe struck its own chord for slavery. Every major European nation of the time became involved in the lucrative trade. Portugal had not been permitted to license a company until 1692, when the Portuguese Company of Cacheo was allowed to compete in the slave business.

Until then the Portuguese had been content on leaving the slave trade in the hands of merchants who proved ineffective against other nations. By the time the Portuguese Company of Cacheo entered as a regular slave trading company, it could only gain the profits left over from the big three.

Portugal was the first nation to acquire the asiento to import four thousand Africans annually into the Spanish colonies in the Americas. The asiento was granted by King Charles V, who succeeded King Raymond and Queen Isabella.

The Dutch had initiated their company, the Dutch West India Company, in 1621 with the purpose of gaining control of the sea routes to the Americas. By the middle of the century, Dutch ships appeared in every port in the Americas.

The French transformed Rouen and some other Norman towns into centers for slave trading. In 1634, a group of Norman merchants had secured a patent from the government to begin the slave trade. However, other companies followed, including the French Company of the West Indies. France was having great difficulty competing with Holland and England until the establishment of the Royal Company of Senegal in 1673. This company gave France a foothold on the coast of Africa and made it a formidable trading nation. During the Seven Years' War with England and the American War of Independence, the African colonies of the two nations changed hands quite frequently. In the end, the French efforts at slave trading proved more profitable in areas where they did not have to compete with the English. Angola and Congo became regions of lively activity among French slavers.

England came to dominate the trade by aggressive attacks on other slave powers and intense competition for new regions. So successful were the English that long after the passing of Sir John Hawkins, the originator of the English slave trade in 1562, the English barons and imperial merchants had written the most daring story in the history of European slave trading. As John Hope Franklin wrote in his book *From Slavery to Freedom,* the system for prosecuting the slave traffic was the product of English ingenuity.

The process of slave trading was not merely sailing to the African coast, securing a load of Africans, and sailing off again to the Americas. The ships spent considerable time on the African coast, capturing or negotiating for Africans to be sold into slavery. Wars of resistance at certain ports seemed constant. The crews of slave ships were often soldiers who fought against African kingdoms in order to stabilize the trade. Gaining enough Africans to make the negotiations profitable meant that some of the ships had to stop at several ports and engage in various kinds of force, pressure, and coercion for Africans.

EUROPEAN SLAVE TRADE

The European slave trade overlapped and superseded the Arab slave trade on the African continent. From the fifteenth century until the last quarter of the twentieth century, Africa was in the vise of European colonial exploitation and domination; it has yet to overcome the powerful cultural and psychological impact of Europe. Evidence of the damage to the African image in the world as well as Africa's own image of itself has been seen in the way African history has been written. The negation of African achievements and accomplishments has largely been a product of the past 500 years.

The achievements of Africa and Africans had been known to the Greeks, the Persians, and the Arabs. Historians and travelers from the Arab states had written of the riches of the various African kingdoms and empires in a matter-of-fact manner. For hundreds of years, caravans in the Sahara linked the savannas in the south with those in the north and joined cities such as Gao, Jenne, Ouagadougou, Agades, and Tedmekka. Visitors to this region, such as al Fazari, al Yakubi, al-Bakri, al Omari, and Ibn Battuta, recorded the wealth of the West African empires from the eighth to the fourteenth centuries. Al Fazari wrote in the eighth century that the ancient kingdom of Ghana in the western part of the continent was a significant political and commercial entity. Nearly a century later, as reported by al Yakubi, the evidence was still coming in that Ghana was a force to be considered in world civilization and that it had amassed its wealth from the gold mines in its territory. By 1067, al Bakri could provide the fullest picture of the Ghana empire ever given. In his record he described how the kingdom's capital was divided into two sections. The king and inhabitants occupied the central part of the town while the foreign merchants were given their own portion of the city. According to al Bakri, the king was surrounded by governors and viziers and flanked by guards who held gold-handled swords. Gold seemed to have been everywhere in the kingdom of Ghana.

Al Omari saw the great wealth and power of Africa displayed in the reign of the Malian king, Mansa Musa, who journeyed to Mecca in 1324 with so much gold that he distributed it freely to officers of the local governments and various other officials in Mecca and Cairo. Thus, whether buying, selling, or gift giving, Mansa Musa made his presence indelible on the imagination of the people of Cairo as he passed through the city on his way to and from Mecca. Al Omari wrote that "the Sultan of this kingdom presides in his palace on a great balcony . . . flanked by elephant tusks . . . his arms stand near him, being all of gold. . . . Behind him there stand about a score of Turkish or other pages which are bought for him in Cairo. . . . One of them . . . holds a silk umbrella surmounted by a dome and a bird of gold" (Omari 1927).

Ibn Battuta, the greatest traveler of the Middle Ages, visited several African kingdoms. An African of the Islamic faith, born in Tangiers, Ibn Battuta was a lawyer and scholar who traveled to places as distant as Samarkand, China, Sumatra, Crimea, and India during the fourteenth century. But his most important travels were in the kingdoms of West Africa. In the African country of Mali he observed a people who lived in complete security because injustice was rare. According to Ibn Battuta, "the Blacks are of all peoples those who most abhor injustice" (Battuta 1971, p. 43).

Neither the scholars and travelers nor the African emperors of the empires of Mali and Songhay could predict the fate that lay in store for the people of Western Africa a little less than 100 years later when the Portuguese began their cruises down the coast of Africa. People from every major ethnic group of the western and southern coasts were brutally uprooted and taken to the Americas and enslaved. Records show that when slavers came with their armies to invade the coast they encountered strong resistance from the Africans. In some cases, women and children took up swords and spears against the invaders; thus, the names of Nzingha and Yaa Asantewaa are forever in the annals of African resistance to enslavement and colonization.

The initiation of the European slave trade began the largest forced migration in the history of the world. No more tragic episode has ever been recorded in human history given its continuing impact on contemporary societies. In addition to the Africans taken from the continent, others were brutalized through warfare with the Europeans and subsequent warfare among Africans over the control of access to European goods. Long, forced marches from the interior to the coast, detention camp diseases, and the horrible Middle Passage across the ocean to bondage often killed one-third of the people captured by the enslavers. This brutish business depended upon force of arms, and Europeans ventured into Africa with their arms ready to snatch Africans from their villages. In addition to this practice, they turned to purchasing prisoners from African kings who were often lured by greed and intimidation into the transactions. However, the overwhelming majority of Africans taken from the continent had to be taken by force and were often held in fortresses until slave ships came. Almost every European nation had agents (called "factors") who "stocked" these fortresses (or "factories") with human beings. While such dehumanizing practices brought untold pain and suffering to Africans, the practices also meant that Europeans became numb to the brutality they caused. The guilt and distrust created over five centuries of enslavement and resistance to enslavement have persisted to the present era. As we shall see later, the infamous trade cast its shadow on every part of the modern world.

The European slave trade fueled the Western economies for four centuries and turned Africa into a continent of spent energies and lost people. Entire nations were disrupted and more than 100 small ethnic groups disappeared from the face of the earth in the great maafa of slave trading. Broken economies and shattered political orders littered the continent with dangerous tenants of once proud kingdoms and empires.

Prince Henry of Portugal sent Captain Gonzales to the coast of West Africa in 1441, where he captured three Africans who quickly offered ten other Africans as ransom. Gonzales accepted the trade and Africans were brought to Portugal as curiosities and presents for royalty. In 1444 Portugal began trading with the Guinea Coast. By 1482, Portugal had begun building El Mina in Ghana and King Ansa of the Fanti had granted the Portuguese the right to occupy the coast for gold trade. This soon became a major fortress for the European trade in human beings.

Spain joined Portugal in the European enterprise in 1517; England began in 1530 under William Hawkins and later his son, John, who began the trade in earnest when he went to Africa in 1562 with the good ship *Jesus*. In 1624, France joined the trade, followed by Holland and Denmark.

The fact that the English were late in getting into the trade did not mean that they would be less determined to make their money in the market. It took two wars for the British to succeed in taking control of the trade from the Dutch. Although Britain had granted rights to a special trading company in 1618, by 1662 other companies had received their charters. By 1698, the government had opened the trade to all British merchants who were capable of paying 10 percent duty on the English goods taken to Africa. So integral was the European slave trade to Britain that when it accepted the Peace of Utrecht in 1713, it also demanded to have a thirty-three-year exclusive right to transport Africans to the Spanish colonies in America.

The British trade with the coasts of West Africa principally involved the people of what is now Ghana, Nigeria, Benin, and the Cameroons, but it was by no means limited to these areas. Yoruba, Asante, Fante, Fon, Ijaw, Ibibio, Ibo, and Douala were a few of the nations decimated by the British slave trade. As the major slaving power, Britain controlled access to the coasts for more than 100 years. Other European nations took up any slack left by the British and consequently devastated entire ethnic groups.

THE TRADE TRIANGLE

The routes of the European slave trade formed more of a rectangle, not the classic triangle depicted in American history books. This is particularly so in relationship to the Africans who eventually landed in the United States of America. The slave ships left Europe, traveled to Africa where they took on Africans, and sailed to the West Indies where Africans were "broken" and trained for enslavement. Then the Africans were transported to the North and South American mainlands. Sometimes the "orientation" process took months and sometimes it took years. Of course, many Africans escaped and became Maroons; others were brought to the United States, where they were given to "breakers" who tried to break their spirits. Some succeeded, others failed.

The trade in Africans disrupted the normal pattern of industrial and social development of the African continent, particularly the West African empires and nations. Actually, the period of the most intense trade in slave activity occurred

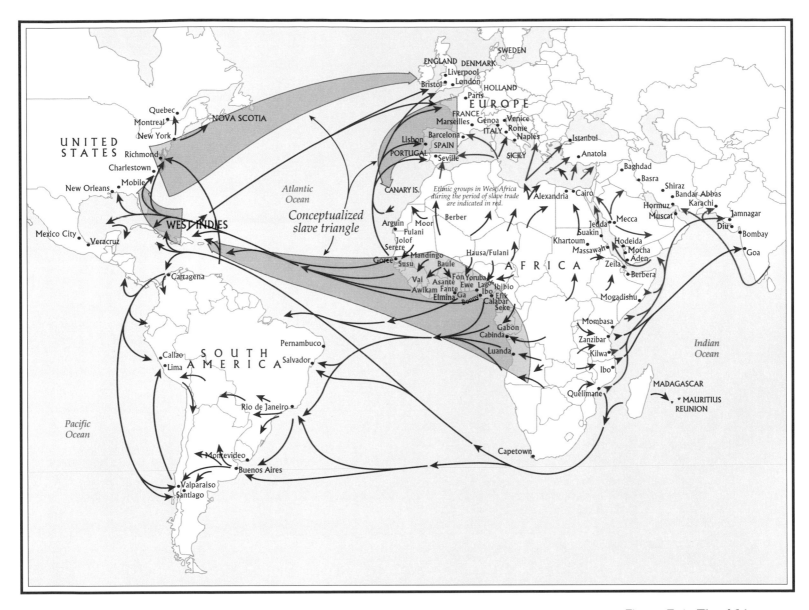

just as the Songhay Kingdom was breaking up in the West African region. From about the third century B.C.E. to 1492, there was a solid period of growth, commerce, education, art, and science developing in the kingdoms of Ghana, Mali, and Songhay. With the breakup of these savanna kingdoms due to internal struggles, Arab Islamic missionaries, and European traders, Africans were increasingly used in the slave economies of South and Central America and eventually North America.

Most of the leading European nations of the sixteenth century were involved in the trade in slaves (see figure 3.2, page 38). Entire European villages found their economic livelihood on the ravishing of African villages. Shipbuilders, sailors,

moneylenders, outfitters, mercenaries, and missionaries from Europe headed to Africa in order to partake of the huge profits that were to be derived from supplying Africans to European settlers in the Americas.

Captain Antonio Gonsalves of Portugal landed his ship near Cape Bojador in what is today the country of Senegal. Gonsalves's troops captured ten African villagers along with the cargo he had been ordered to obtain. The Africans were presented to Prince Henry as gifts. In turn, he presented a few of the Africans to the pope of the Catholic church, for which gift Prince Henry received from the pope, without the African kings' knowledge, the "full possession" of Africa's coastal regions. By

Figure 3.1. The African dispersion and the conceptualized slave triangle. After research by and permission from Joseph E. Harris.

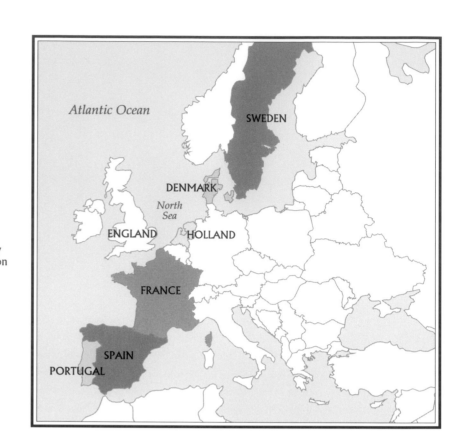

Slavery in the
American Colonies

Colony	Statutory Recognition
Massachusetts	1641
Connecticut	1650
Virginia	1661
Maryland	1663
New York	1665
South Carolina	1682
Pennsylvania	1700
New Jersey	1702
Rhode Island	1703
New Hampshire	1714
North Carolina	1715
Delaware	1721
Georgia	1755

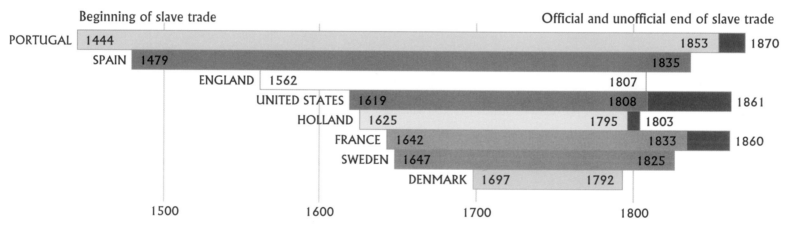

Figure 3.2. Countries involved in the European slave trade.

1481, with nothing more than the papal bull giving them what did not belong to them, the Portuguese had established the first European settlement in Africa at El Mina (the Mine) in what is now Ghana. With the advantage of heaven on their side the Portuguese dominated the gold, spice, and slave trade for nearly a century before European nations such as England and Holland were greatly involved. But the Portuguese importation of Africans was not only for the Americas; 1,000 Africans were brought each year into Portugal itself for domestic use. In fact, the Portuguese population, it is claimed, gradually took on African characteristics

as more and more Africans were absorbed (*Ebony Pictorial History of Black America*, 1971, p. 43).

Like Portugal, Spain also had a great influx of Africans. Many Africans of the Iberian peninsula were on voyages with explorers such as Columbus, De Soto, Cortés, Mendez, Pizarro, and Balboa. The Iberian monopoly was directly challenged by the Dutch, British, French, Swedes, Danes, and Prussians (Germans) by the beginning of the sixteenth century. While the church may have given the Portuguese and the Spaniards a head start, technology and efficiency were to ensure that the British would be leaders in the trade for the next few centuries. After a long struggle to acquire the coveted asiento, the British government finally succeeded in 1713 and quickly moved into the trade. Liverpool became the center of Britain's quest for black gold and numerous local industries grew up to support the trade. Already a shipbuilding center, Liverpool flourished as a city where the young British men could easily lease a ship, hire a crew, or hire themselves out to a ship, and go off to Africa in search of adventure and wealth through the trade. The British slave trade worked overtime to compete with the Portuguese, Spaniards, and Dutch, achieving between 1713 and 1793 the buying and selling of 308,000 individuals from Liverpool alone.

The European nations became very skillful in acquiring Africans for the slave trade. They would often dock their ships and make excursions into the interior of the continent from a "safe" fortress such as Cape Coast Castle or El Mina in search of unprotected Africans; they would purchase Africans who had been captured in war with another ethnic group; they would raid other European nations' holding centers for Africans; and they would attack unsuspecting African villages and towns with guns and cannons and take away men, women, and children (figure 3.3). Marched in chains, often for great distances, the Africans were held in small cells until enough had been gathered to fill a cargo ship. Then they were placed on board and shipped to various parts of the world.

The staging areas were particularly horrifying. Hundreds of Africans together in chains—wailing—constantly discussing the fate of one's brother, children, husband, wife—trepidation and apprehension—drunken European sailors prone to violence and sexual assaults against men and women—and then the coming of the ships: despair.

Figure 3.3. West African ports of embarkation.

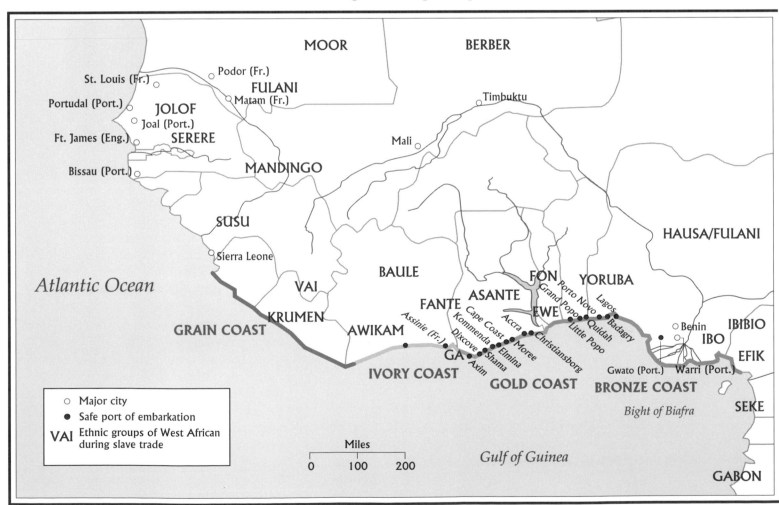

The awesome "Middle Passage" would be talked about for generations. Africans who crossed without dying often wished they had died like nearly one-half of those who boarded the ships in the coastal forts of Africa. The trip could take from five to eight weeks depending upon the winds. Although many people died while trying to escape, perhaps more died from suffocating in the foul air of the ships' holds, in which human beings were packed body to body, often with less than eighteen inches between ceiling and floor, of which there were layers upon layers, to get as many people in the ship as possible. Defining

Figure 3.4. Slave ship and instruments of captivity.

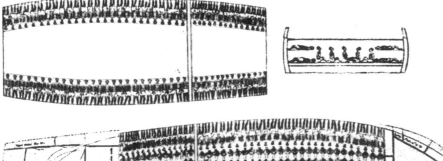

the limits of the possible, the most efficient management of space, the most profitable arrangement of bodies became the constant talk of shipbuilders and slavers (figure 3.4).

Captives were shackled two-by-two on a ship and forced to crouch, with their knees up to their chins, in areas that were no more than four feet high. Only one entry led to the hold. Few clothes were allotted to the captives and consisted mainly of cloths around their waists, whether men or women. To quench their thirsts the captives received a pint of water a day. In order to prevent serious circulation problems the slave captains made the Africans come on the deck and dance by the lash (see figure 3.5, page 41). Needless to say, the Africans found this the greatest outrage and insult since dancing in African society was more than exercise. It was always a way to be in concert with ancestral spirits and national traditions.

Because Africans were often taken from several different ethnic communities and placed on the same ship, physical assaults were commonplace. In these cases the slavers would also have to take care that fights to settle ancient animosities did not occur. On the other hand, they were always afraid that Africans would organize insurrections on board the vessel. Caught between a desire to keep a full cargo for "sale" in the Indies or Americas and safety on the ships, white captains often killed weak Africans to place fear in the minds of others. But even so, Africans who survived the crossing carried with them the memory of the suffering as well as the victory of their fellows. The journey was a voyage of terror. They became witnesses to the long night of brutality visited upon their brothers and sisters and yet kept in their hearts the dream of freedom, which never died.

The major European nations involved in the slave trade experienced internal economic growth as a direct result of the profits from the trade in Africans. The shipping industry, the munitions industry, the suppliers of rope and iron, and the food suppliers became wealthier because of the competition to outfit the ships in the Atlantic trade.

AFRICA'S UNDERDEVELOPMENT

Walter Rodney has written in his major work, *How Europe Underdeveloped Africa*, that the European slave trade is responsible for stifling Africa's natural pattern of development. Evidence (see John Hope Franklin, *From Slavery to Freedom*, New York: Vintage, 1966, pp. 48–66) is shown in terms of the amount of natural and human resources taken out of the continent during the time of the slave trade and colonialism. Key contributors to the industrialization of Europe, even after the end of the slave trade, were often colonial officials serving in some capacity for the governments of Europe. For example, John Cadbury of Britain became wealthy and influential in the chocolate business as a direct result of his control over the cocoa board of West Africa. Instead of Africans controlling their own resources, whether diamonds, iron ore, gold, or ivory, other people had unlimited access to these resources. It would not be until the twentieth century that African nations would gain virtual independence and seek to control their own resources. This movement would usher in a new day of assessment in which the toll of the slave trade and the colonial experience would be determined.

Europe's eagerness to exploit the new economic opportunities was seen in the speed with which Pope Alexander VI made his international decree soon after Columbus's first voyage. The pope, of Spanish heritage, declared that the world outside of Europe would be divided into two zones, one each on either side of a line running south to north 640 kilometers west of the Azores. The papal decree gave Spain all lands "discovered" in the western zone and Portugal all lands "discovered" in the eastern zone. An intense battle between the Spaniards and Portuguese was set up over this line. The Portuguese insisted that the line be moved 2,400 kilometers west of the Azores before they would sign it. The Spaniards finally agreed and the Treaty of Tordesillas of 1494 made it law between the two governments. Soon thereafter the Portuguese claimed all of Brazil, which was now east of the line. When Pedro Alvares Cabral led his expedition to the Brazilian coast in 1500, he had acquired for Portugal the largest territory of the period.

Few nations outside of Spain and Portugal accepted the Treaty of Tordesillas as binding on them. In 1497, John Cabot had claimed Newfoundland for the English; in 1524, Giovanni de Verrazano charted the Atlantic coast from the Carolinas to Nova Scotia on behalf of the French; and ten years later Jacques Cartier, a Frenchman, made his journeys up the St. Lawrence River. For the most part, the Dutch, English, and French were content to share the commercial treasures of the Spanish finds.

Figure 3.5. Africans on deck of slave ship.

AFRICAN RESISTANCE TO ENSLAVEMENT   41

THE STRUCTURE OF DEPENDENCY

The history of the colonization of the continent of Africa shows that the colonizing powers put into place a structure of dependency. This structure remains in place in most African nations. From the beginning of the colonization scheme, Africa was placed in the role of supplier to the industrial engines of Europe. The decentered position of African states meant that Africa did not serve its own interests but the interests of the conquering powers of Europe. It is in this sense that Rodney speaks of the underdevelopment of Africa.

The structure of dependency is maintained by the colonizing powers controlling the industrial development of the colonies, forcing the colonies to accept an agricultural role, expropriating the material and human resources of the colonies for service in the colonial power sphere of influence. However, for the system to function, the colony must acquiesce in its own demise. Thus, the colonizing and conquering power cannot allow voices of resistance to the structural measures to be heard. Those voices must be stifled at all costs because once the people are aware of the manner in which they are oppressed and exploited, the possibility of revolt occurs. Such was the condition of Africa at the beginning of and during the slave trade.

Africans arriving in the Americas from the continent of Africa were placed in the system of exploitation that was to further underdevelop the continent itself. The need for more and more human and material resources to feed the capitalist engine was generated in large part by the effectiveness of the slavery system in stimulating development in the colonial power centers. Thus, the creation of the banking system, the backbone of the international trade in people and goods, was parallel to the rise of the slave trade itself. Contradictions were inherent in the nature of the system from the beginning. Inasmuch as the system of exploitation depended upon the agreement of the enslaved and colonized people, it would only be a matter of time when people would no longer accede to their humiliation and exploitation. When that time arrived, it would be the end of the system of exploitation by which human beings were dehumanized in order to serve the categories of existence created by force.

Dehumanization of the victims of slavery was necessary to maintain the structure of dependency. The structure depended on the colonizer as much as the colonized—that is, the colonizer had to believe in the process. If the colonizer developed a weakness for moral or ethical principles, or viewed the Africans as human beings entitled to the same rights and privileges as himself or herself, then the system of dependency could not go on existing. As the structure was designed, it meant that there could not be an appreciation for the African as a human being.

To view the African as human meant that the white man would have to redefine the structural relationship. That is particularly why the indoctrination normally given to sailors prior to sailing to the coast of Africa had a lot to do with the "savage" nature of the inhabitants of the coast of Africa. Furthermore, many people had been prepared by the writers, preachers, and political leaders of Europe to accept the dehumanization of Africans.

It is no wonder that the brutality meted out to Africans was so callous. When the leading intellectuals of Europe, including George Hegel, succeeded in creating an anti-African attitude, even the common Europeans came to despise and hate Africans without having met any.

In general, the population of the colonizing country did not care very much about the creation of this anti-African hysteria. They believed the stories they heard—many of the more fanciful stories were passed around from city to city and from country to country.

Obviously, semiliterate and illiterate whites visiting a strange land would see different customs and ceremonies with which they had no experience and make fantastic accounts of these events. Such would probably be true about visitors from Africa or Asia to Europe. But in the case of the European powers, these fanciful stories served the purpose of exploiting the culture and resources of the African people.

It was necessary for the European colonizing powers to retain control of this image of Africa because it assisted in the underdevelopment of Africa. It allowed the colonizers to have faith in the mission of enslaving the African in a strange land. Without such faith, the tension in the system would be broken and the Europeans on the frontlines of the struggle to support the structure would cease to work for its maintenance.

The most extreme manifestation of the attack on the African was the physical abuse, even death inflicted upon those who resisted. There was nothing discreet about the process of dehumanization because the European involved in the process did not see it as necessary to be subtle—after all, the African had been defined as subhuman. Thus, whatever the colonizer wanted to do was possible within the moral framework in which he operated throughout his life.

One should not underestimate the psychological impact of this process on both the European and the African. The African was reduced to a thing, objectified in the worst possible manner, as brute strength, sex, emotion.

This arrangement was so successful that Africans began to use the same arguments for themselves as the Europeans had used. This was the ultimate victory in support of the structure of dependency. Africans had succumbed to the bombardment of ideas and concepts about themselves, brought by outsiders, that reduced them to objects within the social and cultural system of Europeans. When Africans no longer controlled the ability to define themselves, the victory of the structure of dependency was won by the colonizers.

Every African idea, object, ceremony, ritual, or invention had to be explained in the context of the savagery that had been constructed in the mind of Europeans. African art, taken from the continent by the hundreds of thousands of pieces, was interpreted in the light of this negative view of the people. Indeed, Africans participated in this process by being so psychologically destroyed that they often presented to the Europeans some of the most historical treasures of the land. But having been told over and over again that their religion was pagan, that their deities were nothing, that they were alone in the world and could not do anything without the help of the Christianizing European, it was a small step to accepting dehumanization. So the psychological warfare on Africans, those enslaved and those colonized, was severe in the extreme.

The structure of dependency was put into place over the entire period of European contact with Africans. Waiter Rodney is correct to assert that Africa's underdevelopment was directly responsible for European development. He believes that African industry, commerce, and institutional development could have evolved more naturally without the disruptive intervention of Europe. Every index of modernity, from the making of iron to taxation to support a central government, existed in West Africa long before the coming of the European. Evidence from the major savanna empires—Ghana, Mali, Songhay, Mossi, and Bornu—suggest that West Africa would have established unified central governments over vast territories had there not been the intervention of the slave trade.

The breakdown of ritual patterns, the political interference of slave traders (European and African), the murder of traditional priests, the imprisonment of kings and queens, the internecine battle over the slave trade, and the introduction of the gun conspired against African potential. Out of the ashes of slavery, disintegration, and colonization Africa would find difficulty in molding a stable economy for the next 400 years. Dependency on Europe would become the single most powerful motivator in African economies as the European colonizers turned the interest of Africa away from Africans.

"De Udder Worl' Is Not Like Dis"

4

THE GREAT ENSLAVEMENT

Slavery was preeminently a social system because of the interlocking nature of its various parts: labor, etiquette, overseers, importation, brutality, politics, products, leisure, punishment, and profit. In the United States this draconian system played out its singular role on individual plantations throughout the South, although the North had its share of plantations as well. Nevertheless, it was on the southern plantations that African labor tied together the entire system of slavery. Africans and whites were caught in the locks of this system, bound by its grinding motion in a veritable wheel of hell.

Different colonies developed crops according to the capabilities of their soils. For example, Virginia, Maryland, and North Carolina were centers for the growing of tobacco. In South Carolina and Georgia, indigo and rice (and later, cotton) were the principal crops. The major crops of the southern plantations were tobacco (Virginia and North Caro-

lina), cotton (South Carolina, Georgia, Alabama, Mississippi, Louisiana, and Texas), indigo (Georgia), and sugarcane (Florida, Georgia, and Louisiana) (figure 4.1 and see figure 4.2, page 47). The South, with its fertile soil and abundant sunshine, was the center of agriculture in the United States during the eighteenth and nineteenth centuries. Agriculture demanded lots of land and was labor intensive. Unlike the northern industrial cities, the agrarian South depended upon Africans for every aspect of the economic life of the region.

From the beginning of the nation, the Great Enslavement of the African was a thorny political problem as well as a major moral issue. When the first Constitutional Convention met in Philadelphia in 1787, many abolitionists thought it would declare slavery ended. They had hoped that the men sitting in deliberative assembly would address the issue that had burned itself into the consciences of many people. This optimism

Figure 4.1. Principal African settlements and the slave economy of colonial America.

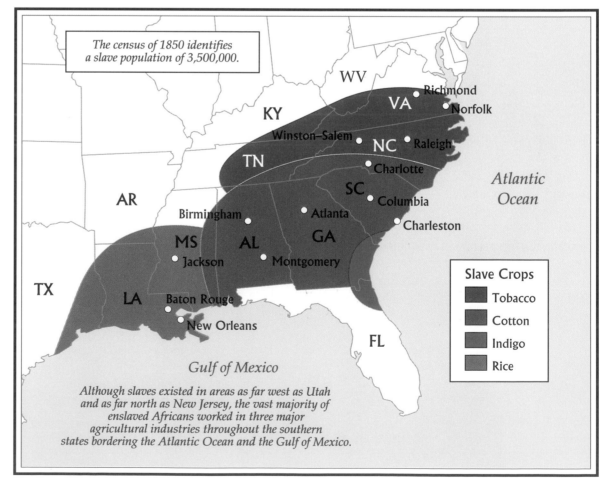

The census of 1850 identifies a slave population of 3,500,000.

WV

KY

VA · Richmond
· Norfolk

Winston–Salem · · NC · Raleigh

TN · Charlotte

AR

SC · Columbia

Birmingham · · Atlanta

MS AL GA · Charleston

· Jackson · Montgomery

TX

LA · Baton Rouge

· New Orleans

FL

Atlantic Ocean

Gulf of Mexico

Slave Crops
Tobacco
Cotton
Indigo
Rice

Although slaves existed in areas as far west as Utah and as far north as New Jersey, the vast majority of enslaved Africans worked in three major agricultural industries throughout the southern states bordering the Atlantic Ocean and the Gulf of Mexico.

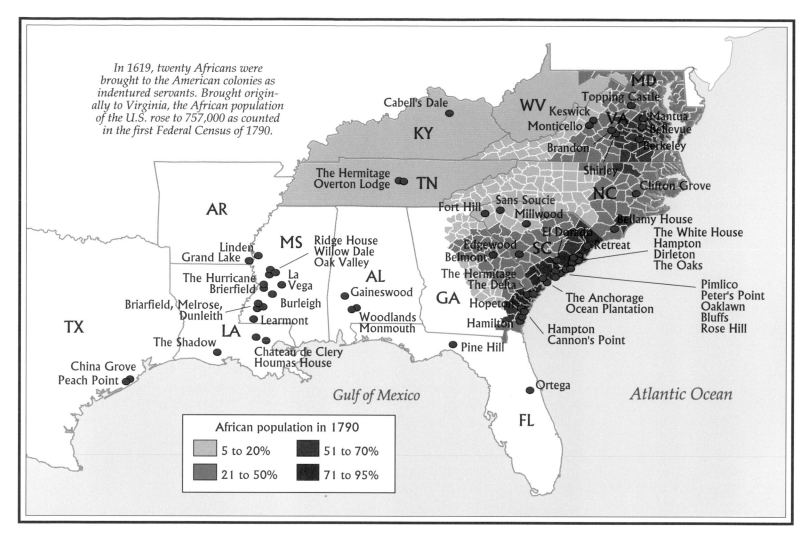

In 1619, twenty Africans were brought to the American colonies as indentured servants. Brought originally to Virginia, the African population of the U.S. rose to 757,000 as counted in the first Federal Census of 1790.

African population in 1790
- 5 to 20%
- 21 to 50%
- 51 to 70%
- 71 to 95%

Figure 4.2. Plantations of the antebellum South and concentrations of Africans.

was not rewarded. The Constitutional Convention put into law what would become the mode of operation in the country for the following decades, even beyond the Civil War. The northern lawmakers placated the southerners by granting them twenty more years to import Africans into slavery. In the future, many who understood the moral dilemma facing the nation would take the option of appeasing the elements that demanded gradualism in freedom and liberty to Africans. This pattern has been broken often enough, but the will of the nation is more frequently dictated by those who believe in the social and economic dream of a united nation.

During the Constitutional Convention, another concession was made to the southern plantation owners. Article IV, Section 2 of the Constitution states that "No person held to service or labor in one State, under the laws thereof, escap-

ing into another, shall . . . be discharged from such service or labor, but shall be delivered up on claim of the party to whom such service or labor may be due." Thus, Africans held in bondage against their wills were not safe and secure even if they were able to escape to the North. Some communities in the North, such as Gap, Pennsylvania, developed reputations as residences for noted slave-catchers. An African escaping to the North and coming through such a town or city could be captured, held in prison, and returned to the South. The danger of physical enslavement did not end with an escape; it followed the African to every city and town in the United States.

The Constitutional Convention also made the crucial compromise that ruled, in effect, that Africans were three-fifths of whites in political weight when it came to voting for political offices. This meant that each time a vote was taken for political office, the African, who could not vote in most cases, was counted as three-fifths of a white man. The conventioneers set in motion the system for the political inferiority of Africans. Even the articulate Thomas Jefferson said, "As a property, they are lawfully vested and cannot be taken away." He had not freed his hundred-odd slaves on his own plantation at Monticello and did not believe that the Constitutional Convention should allow this issue to divide the deliberative body. Later, when the scientific genius Benjamin Banneker, who was born in 1731, wrote to him contesting his attitude about the races, Jefferson opted to stand behind the principles of white supremacy, believing as he expressed that the African was inferior to the white person.

Earlier in his life Thomas Jefferson had made several philippics against slavery. Indeed, during the deliberations on the Declaration of Independence he raised the possibility of prohibiting the slave trade but felt that because it was supported by the king of England, it would be difficult for the colonists to control the high seas in order to stop the slave trade. The Americans who favored slavery were against Jefferson's views because they knew that if an attack against the slave trade prevailed in the Declaration of Independence, it would mean further attacks on the institution after independence. Thus the Declaration was written and adopted with no mention of slavery. Once the idea of African inferiority had been accepted by omission in the Declaration of Independence and by compromise in the Constitution, it would take nearly seventy-five years to eradicate this negative view.

Very early in the colonies, certain cities and towns held special places in the minds of Africans. Among the towns that attracted large numbers of Africans because of their owners' business or occupations were the growing industrial towns of Boston, New York, Philadelphia, Baltimore, Charleston, and Richmond (see figure 4.3, page 49).

Because of their high concentration of Africans it was natural that these cities would also be the leaders in agitation for African rights and the establishment of institutions for them. Several of these cities became principal centers for antislavery propaganda and supporters of the political program of Africans in the North. They gave money and protection to African antislavery organizers.

Boston had been the leading seat of protest against the British and in that capacity had attracted the attention of its African residents. Crispus Attucks had been the first person to die in the Boston Massacre in March 1770 (see figure 4.7, page 52). Subsequent Africans had fought in the American Revolution—more than 5,000 Africans fought the British. Among them, Peter Salem and Salem Poor distinguished themselves for valor and courage. Both were excellent soldiers who made other Massachusetts recruits proud. In succeeding years, Boston became a major arena of African American protest. David Walker wrote his famous Appeal to the Colored Citizens of the World in 1829 while a resident of the city.

Philadelphia was also a major antislavery community. Its Quaker background gave it a sense of fair play and justice that did not always appear in other cities. The Quakers had protested the enslavement of Africans since the 1787 rally against slavery. Africans in Philadelphia led the way in creating in institutions such as schools, churches, lodges, benevolent organizations, and literary societies.

PRINCE HALL

The presence of Africans in the cities of the North meant immediate attention to the betterment of the condition of Africans. Prince Hall, the most successful activist of his time, established the first Masonic lodge for Africans. Born in Barbados in 1748, he worked his way to Boston aboard a ship in 1765. He rose from obscurity to become a light for freedom in the colonies.

Hall led demonstrations and protests against the dismissal of African troops from the Continental Army. Under

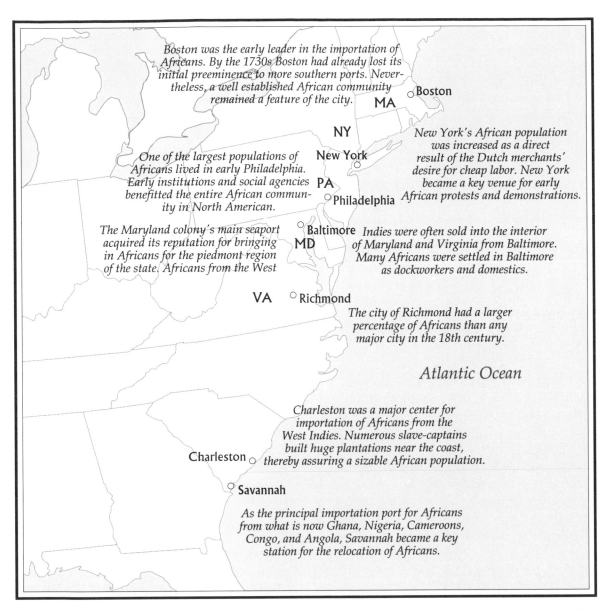

Figure 4.3. Colonial centers of commerce based on African slavery.

Boston was the early leader in the importation of Africans. By the 1730s Boston had already lost its initial preeminence to more southern ports. Nevertheless, a well established African community remained a feature of the city.

MA

○ **Boston**

NY

New York ○

New York's African population was increased as a direct result of the Dutch merchants' desire for cheap labor. New York became a key venue for early African protests and demonstrations.

One of the largest populations of Africans lived in early Philadelphia. Early institutions and social agencies benefitted the entire African community in North American.

PA

○ **Philadelphia**

○ **Baltimore**

MD

Indies were often sold into the interior of Maryland and Virginia from Baltimore. Many Africans were settled in Baltimore as dockworkers and domestics.

The Maryland colony's main seaport acquired its reputation for bringing in Africans for the piedmont region of the state. Africans from the West

VA ○ **Richmond**

The city of Richmond had a larger percentage of Africans than any major city in the 18th century.

Atlantic Ocean

Charleston was a major center for importation of Africans from the West Indies. Numerous slave-captains built huge plantations near the coast, thereby assuring a sizable African population.

Charleston ○

○ **Savannah**

As the principal importation port for Africans from what is now Ghana, Nigeria, Cameroons, Congo, and Angola, Savannah became a key station for the relocation of Africans.

General George Washington's policy of excluding blacks from the armed forces, Africans were denied the opportunity to fight until the protests by Hall and others caused a change in opinion. In one of the first petitions to a legislature (in Massachusetts) in support of African rights, Prince Hall signed his name to indicate his support. The petition made the case that the petitioners had the same rights as the Americans claimed when they charged the British with unlawful trampling of their rights.

The most impressive achievement of this African was the founding of the first African Masonic Lodge, African Lodge No. 1, in Boston. He had asked to be initiated into a white Masonic lodge but was turned down by the white Americans. He sought out a British regiment encamped near Boston and asked the Masons in the regiment to initiate him and fourteen other Africans. The British Masons initiated him into a British military lodge. After the British Army withdrew from the Boston area, Hall set up lodges in Philadelphia and Providence, Rhode Island.

Prince Hall's concern for his fellows did not stop with his establishment of the Masonic Temples. Rather, he continued his petitions on behalf of African people. Indeed, his petition to the Massachusetts legislature for the education of African children is remarkable for its clarity of purpose. The petition said in part, "We must fear for our rising offspring to see them in ignorance in a land of gospel light, when there is provision made for

THE GREAT ENSLAVEMENT   49

them as well as others and they cannot enjoy them, and no other reason can be given than that they are black." When Prince Hall died on November 4, 1807, he had become a wealthy and respected man throughout the Commonwealth of Massachusetts and other states. There are few African Americans who have accomplished as much as Prince Hall on behalf of the downtrodden. His work places him in the front ranks of those who have served the nation well.

Figure 4.4. Poster advertising the sale of slaves used for cotton and rice production.

GANG OF 25 SEA ISLAND
COTTON AND RICE NEGROES,
By LOUIS DE SAUSSURE.

On **THURSDAY** the 25th Sept., 1852, at 11 o'clock, A.M., will be sold at **RYAN'S MART**, in Chalmers Street, in the City of Charleston,

A prime gang of 25 Negroes, accustomed to the culture of Sea Island Cotton and Rice.

CONDITIONS.—One-half Cash, balance by Bond, bearing interest from day of sale, payable in one and two years, to be secured by a mortgage of the negroes and approved personal security. Purchasers to pay for papers.

Figure 4.5 (right). Phillis Wheatley (1753?–1784). Brought to the United States as a slave from Senegal, her poetry has been recognized for its importance in the historical development of African-American literature.

PHILLIS WHEATLEY

The mid-eighteenth century was the period of Phillis Wheatley (figure 4.5). Wheatley was born in Senegal around 1752 and arrived in Boston in 1761 on a slave ship. As a child of eight or nine years old she was sold to a wealthy merchant and tailor named John Wheatley.

Phillis Wheatley was able to win acclaim and acceptance during the Revolutionary period. Her book, *Poems on Various Subjects, Religious and Moral,* was the first book by an African woman to be published in America and the second book to be written by a woman in America. She could not be called an activist or a radical; she did not use her talents to attack the system of slavery. However, what she did was significant because her works proved to some doubting whites that Africans could think and write. At a very early time in American history she gave the lie to the view that Africans had no mental or intellectual gifts. The fact that she was effective in the literary world, thought at the time to be outside the capability of Africans, makes her a figure of historic proportions.

The Wheatley family of Boston raised Phillis more like a daughter than a slave. They taught her how to read and write in English. She astonished the people of Boston by her ability to speak, write, and read in fluent English while she was still in her teens. She wrote a blank verse eulogy about Harvard College as her first poem. Because she was such a novelty in the literary and intellectual world, many white American and European people of literature heard about Wheatley and wanted to read what she had written or hear her speak. Even Voltaire wrote that Phillis Wheatley wrote "very good English verse." In 1773, she had the fortune to visit England, where her volume of verse was published and she became almost immediately celebrated as an American phenomenon.

There is no militancy in Wheatley's poetry and she concentrates mostly on religious themes, praising, for example, the circumstances that brought her in contact with the Christian religion. In addition to writing about religion, she wrote about American patriots such as George Washington. When Washington was commissioned as commander-in-chief of the United States Military Forces in 1776, Phillis Wheatley wrote a poem expressing her genuine delight over the occasion in a tribute to the general. Washington wrote her a short note inviting her to visit him at his headquarters. She accepted and met the "father of the nation."

PAUL CUFFE

Paul Cuffe was an original protester against the system of exploitation of Africans. He was born in 1759 on Cutterhunker, Massachusetts, an island near Bedford, Massachusetts. While he was still a teenager, Cuffe went to sea on a ship bound for the Gulf of Mexico. The name Cuffe is an Anglicized version of the Akan name Kofi found among the Asante and Fante people of West Africa. Determined to make a difference, Paul Cuffe decided to enter the business world.

When he was twenty-one years old, Cuffe was threatened with jail by the Massachusetts authorities for not paying his personal taxes. Cuffe took a direct position on the question of Africans paying taxes. He argued, as the Americans had argued, that there should be no taxation without representation. He wanted to be exempted from taxation. The tax collector did not accept Cuffe's logic, so the young Cuffe paid the nominal sum.

Angered by the incident and believing that Africans were exploited, Cuffe sent a petition to the Massachusetts legislature, appealing his case. He wrote that blacks ought to be granted immunity from taxation since they had "no voice or influence in the election of those who tax us." Cuffe's case was argued in the legislature. When the appeal was finally decided, a law was passed granting Africans the same rights as other people in Massachusetts. The audacity of this young man caused his stature to rise in the black community. He was also recog-

nized by the white community as a leader among Africans.

When his father died, Cuffe inherited some land, which he promptly sold and bought a ship, which he captained himself. Cuffe became a prosperous ship-owner within a few years. He owned a small fleet of ships and a shipyard, where he built and repaired his ships.

Captain Cuffe was not distracted by his wealth. He remained committed to his ideals and principles, believing that Africans were discriminated against and needed the support of the government. He was the wealthiest African in America during the 1790s. He built a school and opened it to anyone who wanted to learn.

Figure 4.6. Poster advertising a raffle of a horse named "Star" and a girl named "Sarah."

Figure 4.7 (right). Crispus Attucks (1723–1770). First person to die in the Boston Massacre in March 1770.

Figure 4.8 (below). William Talbott of Lexington, Kentucky, advertises for a large lot of negroes on July 2, 1853.

$1200 TO 1250 DOLLARS!
FOR NEGROES!!

THE undersigned wishes to purchase a large lot of NEGROES for the New Orleans market. I will pay $1200 to $1250 for No. 1 young men, and $850 to $1000 for No. 1 young women. In fact I will pay more for likely

NEGROES,

Than any other trader in Kentucky. My office is adjoining the Broadway Hotel, on Broadway, Lexington, Ky., where I or my Agent can always be found.

WM. F. TALBOTT.

LEXINGTON, JULY 2, 1853.

This was to be an example of what education ought to have been for all citizens. Cuffe's point was that education is valuable to all people and that no one should be denied the opportunity to learn.

Near the end of his life, Cuffe gave much attention to the colony of Sierra Leone. He furthered the cause of Africans who wanted to emigrate. He visited the colony himself and in 1815, two years before his death, he transported thirty-eight immigrants to Sierra Leone in West Africa at his own expense. Cuffe furnished the immigrants with all necessities for their new environment.

AFRICANS IN THE ENGLISH COLONIES

The first recorded presence of Africans in the English colonies as indentured servants was 1619 in Jamestown. The Africans had been seized from a Spanish ship and brought to Virginia in a Dutch warship. This was to be the beginning of a long hard sojourn in North America for Africans. When Mathiu da Costa, an African, had arrived in Nova Scotia in 1608, it was not as an indentured servant to European settlers. However, the Spanish and Portuguese had already supplied their earliest colonies with Africans from the east and west coasts of the continent of Africa.

The pattern of interracial interaction was established very early in Virginia. Initially there had been white indentured servants prior to the coming of Africans. For a brief time, both groups had served as indentured servants. Within a few years, the status of Africans had decreased and the relationship between the Africans and Europeans had been degraded to the point where only Africans were legally enslaved.

By the middle of the seventeenth century the condition of Africans as servants for life, or slaves, was clearly a part of the generally accepted codes in Virginia. In 1640, when three servants ran away and were captured, the penalties exacted showed unequal treatment. Each of the runaways received thirty lashes with the whip. The two white servants were required to give their masters an additional year of service and three years of service to the colony. On the other hand, the African servant was sentenced to servitude for life.

Throughout the seventeenth century, a century of transition for the business of slavery in America, the African was consistently valued more than the white in terms of wealth, thus indicating the change of status. The African could be held for life and was therefore more valuable as property than the white who remained essentially an indentured servant, normally serving no more than twenty-one years. Virginia court cases during the 1650s indicate that in the buying and selling of Africans servitude for life was usually mentioned. Furthermore, the status of life servitude was inherited by the children of the enslaved person.

Africans who entered the colonies after this period lacked indentures; they were enslaved for life. Africans indentured and freed earlier participated in fighting against these laws because some, like Richard Johnson, a carpenter, and Anthony Johnson, a landowner, had acquired black and white servants of their own.

The gradual legalization of slavery resulted in a psychological and cultural dislocation of Africans to rival the economic and physical dislocation. In 1661, the first legal reference to slavery is made in an act that decreed that if a white and black servant fled together, then the white was to make up the time missed by the black. In 1662 the Virginia House of Burgesses reversed the long-standing English common law that children followed the status of their fathers. Since the colony was seeing an increasing number of children who had white fathers and black mothers, the House of Burgesses passed a new law that said children would follow the status of their mothers, bond or free. Thus, the children of a free white father and an African woman who was herself enslaved would be enslaved. The debates in the Virginia House of Burgesses expressed the moral agony that had afflicted some members of the society over the question of enslaving

Christians in perpetuity. A number of the Africans had become Christians. How was a Christian to hold another Christian in perpetual bondage?

It had been a different story for the earlier white colonists. In effect, they had enslaved Africans who had not signaled their acceptance of the Christian religion. So strong was the propaganda regarding the moral advantage to the Africans of being enslaved that the white colonists never considered the possibility of

Figure 4.9 (above). On May 13, 1835, Sarah, Dennis, Chole, Fanny, Dandridge, Nancy, Mary Ann, Fanny, Emma, and Frank are offered for sale at the New Exchange in New Orleans by an owner who is departing for Europe.

Africans becoming Christians. When the decision had to be taken, however, the Virginians came down on the side of their commercial and material interests. In 1667 they enacted a law that decreed that baptism does not alter the condition of bondage or freedom. The African was caught in the Great Enslavement, and every law, code, and custom would be rearranged if necessary to make the system function.

White servants still formed the mainstay of the farm labor force in 1671. The total population of Virginia at that time was 40,000. Of this total, there were 2,000 African slaves and 6,000 white servants. By the turn of the century African enslavement had taken precedence over white servitude.

Unlike Virginia and to some extent Maryland, slavery in Carolina was expressly called for in the Fundamental Constitutions of 1669. There was no period of uncertainty about the institution. Carolina engaged in the importation of Africans with a vengeance, opening up the great tobacco plantations to intensive farm labor. Georgia, founded in 1733, attempted to forgo slavery. The proprietors thought that slavery was unsound on mercantilist grounds. By 1750, however, Georgia settlers were pressing for their own importation of Africans. South Carolina had demonstrated the feasibility of using African laborers in intensive agriculture.

South Carolina and Georgia had heavy concentrations of Africans along the low-lying areas of the Atlantic seacoast. In fact, South Carolina had several counties that were dominated numerically by Africans during the eighteenth century (see figure 4.2, page 47).

In the southern colonies the large numbers of Africans created fear of insurrection and riot for the white population. Laws were passed with the intention of governing every aspect of the enslaved African's life. Among the more common regulations found in the plantation states were prohibition on Africans carrying firearms, prohibition against Africans owning property, and the requirement that all Africans carry passes when they left the plantations. When South Carolina discovered insurrectionary activities in 1739 and again in 1740, the legislature tightened the codes controlling the sale of liquor to Africans and prevented Africans from assembling without permission of their owners.

The late eighteenth century was a period of dramatic change in the status of Africans in America. Two unrelated events held sway over the future of the enslaved African in America. The first was the signing in 1787 in Philadelphia of the U.S. Constitution. The second was the development in 1793 of the cotton gin. Both events were to put a damper on the antislavery movement.

There had been some relaxation of the stringencies of the slave system during the American preoccupation with the Revolutionary War. Some of the key leaders of the Revolution believed that it was inconsistent for the colonists to be fighting for their own freedom while maintaining the enslavement of Africans. Some blacks had fought in the Revolutionary War. The antislavery movement had been organized in 1775 and reorganized in 1787 with Benjamin Franklin as president. In New York, the Society for Promoting the Manumission of Slaves was established in 1785 with John Jay as president. Quite a number of Revolutionary era leaders sought to end slavery during this period of egalitarian spirit. But the Constitution was a certain stop to the movement.

Opposition to the slave trade and to slavery was raised at the Constitutional Convention, but the strength of the slave states produced a compromise that was to eliminate any action that would lead to a quick end to slavery. Taking the doctrine of John Locke as their guide, the conventioneers chose to protect property rights—that is, the ownership of slaves—over the protection of human rights. The Constitution accepted and legitimized the enslavement of Africans. Three ominous clauses were entered into the Constitution with the effect of setting back the antislavery movement. An

African was to be considered three-fifths of a white man for purposes of taxation and apportioning representation in the House of Representatives; the slave trade was allowed to continue until 1808; and states were bound to return fugitive slaves to their owners.

The second development that affected the lives of Africans in America was the invention of the cotton gin. Eli Whitney is credited with inventing the cotton gin in 1793, although some believe that it was invented by an enslaved African who could not be cited for the invention as a slave. Whatever the case, the appearance of the cotton gin radically changed the fate of the African population. Cotton had been domesticated first in Africa and later in Arabia and India, but with the invention of the cotton gin and the techniques for spinning and weaving that were developed in England, it became a rather inexpensive textile. The demand for African labor was almost insatiable. No longer would cotton be second or third to tobacco, rice, and indigo in the various regions of the South—cotton would be king.

The expansion of the use of Africans on farms and the serious interest in cotton were dramatic given the context. Now that a machine could separate the seeds from the lint, laborers could be used to plant and harvest more of the white gold. New lands were staked out and placed under cotton cultivation. Within ten years of the invention of the cotton gin, the numbers of Africans involved in cotton production had tripled. Georgia and South Carolina became the prime areas for cotton growing. In 1803, more than 20,000 Africans were imported from Africa to those states. The principal function of the enslaved Africans in those states was to grow and harvest cotton.

Although indigo, tobacco, rice, and later sugarcane were the major crops in the Gulf states of Louisiana, Alabama, and Mississippi, after 1795 those regions eagerly accepted the cotton gin and became producers of cotton as well. The expansion of cotton production to more states meant a further increase in the number of Africans used in cotton production.

THE HAITIAN REVOLUTION

The French loss of Haiti to the Haitian revolutionaries was to have a major impact on slavery in the United States. When two religious leaders, Papa Boukman and a woman whose name now escapes history, met in the woods to plan the revolution against the French, they had no idea of the significance their actions would have for Africans in the United States. Activated in part by the French Revolution of 1789, the Haitian revolution was centered on freedom from the control of the French elite in Haiti.

Actually, the French refusal to extend to the Africans the rights they had won during the French Revolution was the immediate reason for the revolts in Haiti. No similar uprising had occurred after the American Revolution because the Africans who had fought in the Revolutionary War believed that the Americans would grant freedom to the black population in keeping with the grand ideas of liberty and rights. However, In Haiti the situation was different. The Africans greatly outnumbered the French in the colony, producing a fear on the part of the French that they would be dominated by the Africans if they extended the rights of the French Revolution to them. In 1791 the African Haitians rose up and killed their white masters, which prompted the French Assembly to withdraw even the limited rights of the Africans. They also felt compelled to send soldiers from France to put down the disturbances. To gain some kind of acceptance among the people, the French issued a decree stating that all who supported the French government would be granted freedom.

Toussaint L'Ouverture, the military leader of the Haitian revolution, was able to wrest control of the island nation from the French army. L'Ouverture was the dominant military presence on the island even with the French army on patrol. An able soldier and astute tactician, he was able to elude capture by the French. When Napoleon tired of the fact that L'Ouverture was the one person who could prevent a French empire in the Americas, he sent General Le Clerc with 25,000 troops to subdue the Haitians. Le Clerc's army was finally able to capture L'Ouverture, but they could not pacify the island. Defeated by the Africans of Haiti, Napoleon was forced to sell the Louisiana Territory to the United States in 1803.

The impact of the Haitian revolution on the Africans in America was awesome. When word circulated that a black army had defeated the grand army of Napoleon, the African population was stunned. Never had they dreamed that it would be done in Haiti. Furthermore, the fact that the Haitians would now be in control of their own destinies was too much to imagine. W. E. B. Du Bois (in his book *The Suppression of the African Slave Trade*) had said, in effect, that L'Ouverture created a problem for the Western Hemisphere and caused France to sell the Louisiana Territory, thus setting up the inevitable end of the slave trade by the United States in 1807. Therefore, the Haitian revolution had both psychological and practical implications for Africans. In the first place, the overwhelming victory by L'Ouverture's army meant that it was possible for Africans to be free. Second, the importation of Africans was dramatically reduced, if not stopped altogether. The white settlers did not want to import trouble.

Concern about Haiti filled the minds of most white Americans. This was particularly true of the southerners. There was terror caused from the reports coming in from Haiti, each more frightening than the previous. Blacks were in revolt; they were ruthlessly killing their white masters, taking their land, and destroying their homes. Not even the war between the French and English in 1812 could occupy minds of the Americans more than the events in Haiti.

South Carolina and Georgia, heavily dependent upon African labor, became timid in regard to importation of Africans. They wanted more enslaved persons to assist in running the farms but they were reluctant because of the situation in Haiti. No white person wanted to see the condition in Haiti become the condition in South Carolina. In 1792, the colony of South Carolina refused to allow Africans into the colony for two years. North Carolina passed a law to prevent further importation of Africans from the West Indies or Africa.

The Haitian revolution convinced some whites that they were bringing into the country Africans who could create future revolts. As early as 1790 the Meeting of Friends in New York and Pennsylvania asked Congress to legislate against the slave trade. But the activities of Toussaint L'Ouverture and his Haitian army quickened the pace of the discussions about prohibiting importation. Indeed, by 1794 a bill was passed seeking to prevent the slave trade between the United States and foreign ports and to prohibit the outfitting of foreign ships for the slave trade at U.S. ports. More than the eloquence of the newly formed anti-slavery movement, it was the fear that the Haitians might spread their revolution to the southern states that reduced support for the slave trade.

Another aspect of the enslavement business that caused considerable fear in the plantation south was the fugitive slave. Since the American Revolution, Africans had moved around from one place to another in search of safe havens. Indeed, even Caribbean Africans had escaped from the islands into the United States. With the escapees from plantations in the United States and the continued influx of Africans from the West Indies, the threat of violent uprisings grew increasingly more possible. After all, Haiti had shown that it was within the realm of Africans to ruthlessly overthrow their owners. Fugitives had to be controlled.

The U.S. Constitution had provided for the return of fugitives. This provision had not been effectively implemented. The first fugitive slave law was passed in 1793. This law empowered the slave owner to travel to any state or region and seize an African who was claimed to be a chattel of the slave owner, carry the person before a magistrate, and obtain a warrant to remove the person from the state from which he or she had fled. The law did not provide trial by jury and allowed the African to be convicted on the oral testimony of the claimant or with an affidavit from a magistrate in the state from which the African was to have fled.

Numerous antislavery groups protested the passage of the law, but the idea had already taken hold due to the fear that arose from the Haitian uprising. While the fugitive slave law of 1793 appeared on the books, it was a difficult law to enforce. Africans continued to escape and move around the country from state to state and from region to region. Elaborate schemes were created to hide them from their pursuers.

The Louisiana Purchase and New Orleans

The Louisiana Purchase was connected with the Haitian revolution in political, economic, and social ways. Many of the Africans brought into the Louisiana area had come from the Caribbean (see figure 4.11, page 59). When France sold the territory in 1803 as a direct result of the Haitian revolution, thereby thwarting the French empire in the Americas, the western farmers in the United States gained greater and freer access to the mighty rivers of the area. Sugarcane was now a fast-growing crop in the region. Both the Spanish and French had begun to grow sugarcane for commercial reasons before the territory became a part of the United States. Already by this time the number of Africans in the Louisiana territory was growing at a steady rate. Both the Spanish and French settlers had brought Africans in as slaves, and there remained a strong contingent of these early Africans, often creolized, as the Americans took over the governance of the territory. New Orleans became the centerpiece of the territory. It was a combination of all of the influences in the area. Africans, French, Spanish, English,

and Native Americans gave New Orleans a special place in American slave society. Africans, of course, were as elsewhere the laborers who fed the engine of New Orleans society.

An outbreak of slave revolts, caused in part by the lingering effects of the Haitian revolution and excited by the masses of Africans who had come into the Louisiana territory from the Atlantic seaboard, created havoc in the new territory. The biggest such revolt occurred in 1811. Four hundred Africans in New Orleans rose up against ill treatment and their enslavement. The federal government sent troops to New Orleans to quell the insurrection. Several dozen Africans were killed.

Louisiana was the southern state with the largest free African population and New Orleans was the vanguard city in Louisiana. Many had come to the city during the Haitian revolution, and they remained to become a sizable part of the population. Free Africans were more numerous than often thought, and played a major role in New Orleans life, contributing to various American communities as artisans and artists. In 1836, there were 855 free Africans in New Orleans. They owned 620 other Africans and paid taxes on property assessed at $2,462,470. Twenty-four years later, the free Africans in New Orleans had increased their property holdings to $15 million.

New Orleans also had a relatively large population of persons of mixed racial ancestry who were the offspring of white men cohabiting with black women and in rare instances black men cohabiting with white women. These persons were usually treated by the law as all other blacks. In fact, as early as 1816, New Orleans passed an ordinance requiring separation of the races in public accommodations. Definitions of who was an African were a part of the legal exercises that brought the most debate about social styles in the southern states. Most state legislatures agreed that if a person had one drop of African blood then that person had to be defined as an African.

African Religion in New Orleans

The fundamental religious practices of the Africans in New Orleans in the early period were influenced by two elements: the Congo religions and the Yoruba religions. The Congo religions came from the African groups that were brought into Louisiana and Texas. The Yoruba religions were imported from Haiti and Cuba. Both of these religious influences played a major part in the development of the African American religious outlook in New Orleans, despite a heavy concentration of Catholicism. Still, Catholicism served the interests of the various African deities in New Orleans as it had done for Africans in Cuba, Brazil, and Haiti.

Yoruba beliefs came to dominate the religion of the Africans of New Orleans perhaps more than any other region of the country. Much as in Haiti, the religion was called Voodoo in New Orleans. In other places in the South the religion took on different names. It may be called Santeria, Obeah, Hoodoo, Myal, or Roots. The idea behind the religion is the same: the power of God is manifest in many different ways to alleviate human problems. Thus, there are more than 400 orishas, or deities of Yoruba religion.

The major powers used in the religion in New Orleans during the Great Enslavement were Ogun, Shango, Ifa, Legba, Obatala, and Oshun. Ogun is the deity for ironworks and creativity; Shango is the deity for thunder and lightning and the elements; Ifa is the deity who knows the beginnings of knowledge and wisdom; Legba is the deity of uncertainty; Obatala is the deity of reproduction and fertility; and Oshun is the deity of the Oshun River. She is one of the many deities in female form.

From its inception, New Orleans held a special place in African American history. Under the southern skies of this city on the Mississippi River, Africans created song, practiced magic, rewrote religious catechisms, explored the limits of freedoms, and challenged the racial order.

This was not merely a population concerned with material possessions.

Spiritual matters were always on the minds of the Africans in New Orleans. The city was the center for numerous spiritual movements and leaders. Some of the spiritual leaders had small followings, a few had considerable influence throughout the city.

New Orleans hosted Madame Marie Laveau's religious regime in the nineteenth century. No person held such power over New Orleans as did this priestess of the African religions. She was charismatic and persuasive. Africans and whites came to her for advice. They sought Madame Laveau's wisdom on all matters of fate, fertility, love, wealth, death, impotence, enemies, and happiness. In the twentieth century, New Orleans was to become the home of jazz, but in the nineteenth century it was whatever music Madame Laveau chose to play.

Four Thieves Vinegar Spell of Madame Laveau

Madame Laveau was a Voodoo priestess in New Orleans. Four Thieves Vinegar potion was used by her in ways she claimed would drive away ones enemies.

First, smear the liquid on the doorknob of one's enemy. It was sure to be touched and its effects felt.

Second, put a small amount of the potion in a bottle together with the enemy's name written on parchment paper. Throw the sealed bottle into the fast moving water of a river or a stream. It was said to draw one's enemy with it as it floats away.

Figure 4.10. Voodoo priestess Madam Laveau developed spells for followers in New Orleans. Following instructions such as these, believers in Voodoo rid themselves of

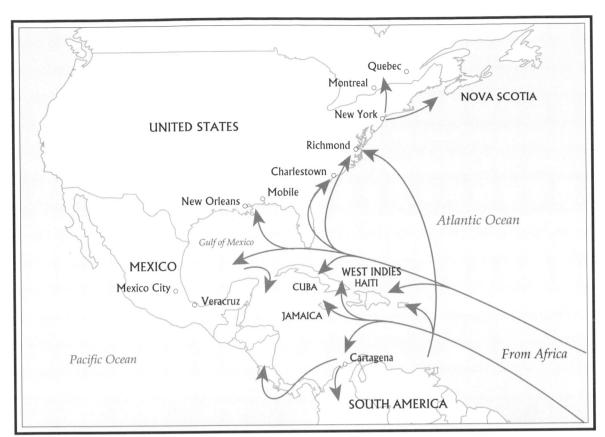

Figure 4.11. Slave connection between West Indies and the United States.

Figure 4.12. Like Madame Laveau, Voodoo priestess Yaffa practices ancient African religion. Credit: Philip Gould/Corbis.

Figure 4.13. Voodoo Museum in New Orleans features articles from African religions of the 19th century. Credit: Robert Holmes/Corbis.

THE GREAT ENSLAVEMENT   59

"And Before I'd Be a Slave"

5

REMEMBERING AND ORGANIZING

The impact of the Great Enslavement on Africans was psychological, political, social, and economic. Torn from the continent of origin, Africans developed responses to the different environment that indicated resistance and accommodation experienced by those who had been unfairly captured, abused, enslaved, and discriminated against. Both attitudes, resistance and accommodation, coexist within the African American community as a result of the psychological dislocation often felt in a Eurocentric hegemonic culture. The psychological dislocation is perhaps as important a factor in African American history as physical dislocation was at one time. Continuation of the psychological dislocation is no longer dependent upon the actual physical removal of Africans from the continent. It is now the result of more than 370 years of a condition that the philosopher Maulana Karenga calls "the cultural crisis."

The first and second generations of Africans enslaved in America remembered or were told about Africa. They knew the names of rivers, towns, and mountains. They had at their disposal the rituals, ceremonies, dances, and music of their respective ethnic communities. They knew how to worship the deities and to give praise to the elders and ancestors in their own language. The loss of this sense of connectedness and the inevitable loss of self-respect drove Africans to the development of novel responses to the Great Enslavement, responses that never had to be made in Africa itself. Even those who had been fortunate enough to have been captured and made to serve in the employ of Africans still found the circumstances in America difficult beyond imagination. In order to secure psychological space and spiritual peace, Africans found that the ability to create forms of resistance and accommodation that allowed them to reconstruct dignity within the confines of the slave situation was necessary.

These forms were expressed as music, speech, and dance. Using the Sunday morning church services that were eventually permitted, Africans combined all of the elements of resistance and accommodation, in dance, music, and speech, into one festive occasion "in the name of the Lord." Taking the one day of rest to renew their spirits and to reestablish connections to the African deities through the medium of Christianity, the enslaved Africans gave permanence to a transmuted and transfigured social and cultural reality.

This was not a slave culture. It was the expression of an elegant African culture under duress. When the African musicians were prohibited from using drums, they expressed the percussive elements with sticks, cans, bottles, and even the human body as in hand-clapping or the hambone.

Yoruba, Asante, Mandinka, and Angola were different languages, yet the Africans were able to combine elements of these languages, mainly syntax, with lexical items from English to create a pidgin and later a creolized language to communicate with each other and the whites. In language as in music, Africans demonstrated a willingness to resist the enslavement through creative uses of structure and words.

Physical resistance was not out of the question. However, after petitions and demonstrations, many Africans felt that freedom was worth the threat of death. Thus, cultural resistance was only one method of attacking the enslavement.

FREE AFRICANS IN THE NORTH

During and after the colonial period there were free Africans, some of whom had never been enslaved in North America, although their numbers were small and their power insignificant (see figure 5.1, page 63). John Hope Franklin reports that there were 59,000 free Africans in the United States in 1790. Of that total, 27,000 were in the North and 32,000 were in the South. By 1860, there were 488,000 free Africans, and 46 percent of them lived in the Atlantic South, and 44 percent lived in the industrial North. The remainder lived in the West or central states.

By 1860, the concentration of free

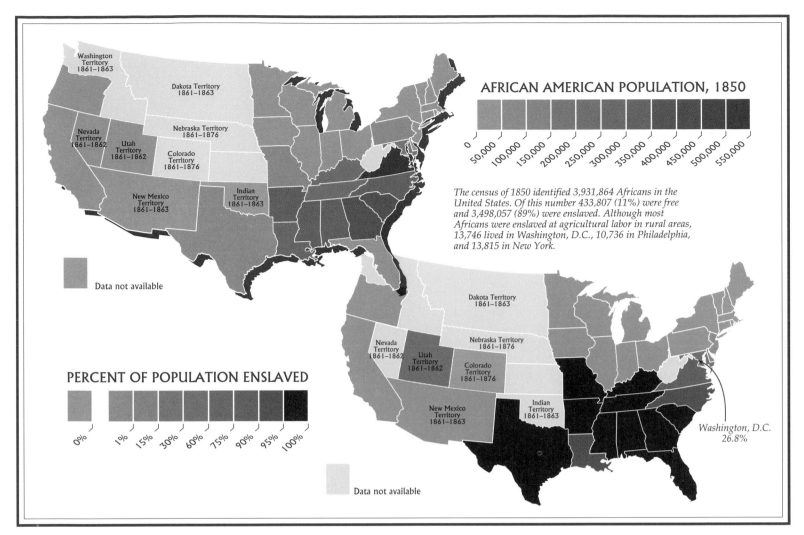

AFRICAN AMERICAN POPULATION, 1850

0 50,000 100,000 150,000 200,000 250,000 300,000 350,000 400,000 450,000 500,000 550,000

The census of 1850 identified 3,931,864 Africans in the United States. Of this number 433,807 (11%) were free and 3,498,057 (89%) were enslaved. Although most Africans were enslaved at agricultural labor in rural areas, 13,746 lived in Washington, D.C., 10,736 in Philadelphia, and 13,815 in New York.

Data not available

PERCENT OF POPULATION ENSLAVED

0% 1% 15% 30% 60% 75% 90% 95% 100%

Washington, D.C. 26.8%

Data not available

Africans was in the following cities: Baltimore, Washington, Charleston, Mobile, and New Orleans in the southern region; Boston, New York, Cincinnati, and Philadelphia in the northern region. The largest concentrations were in Baltimore, 25,600; Philadelphia, 22,000; New York, 12,500; New Orleans, 10,600; and Charleston, 3,200. Isolated pockets of free Africans were found in places like Cass County, Michigan; Hammond County, Indiana; and Wilberforce, Ohio.

Soon after their arrival in America, the Africans organized churches and other institutions for social relations as well as spiritual comfort. The major church was the African Methodist Episcopal (AME) during the later eighteenth century. Other churches had been started and had disappeared.

The church represented the one institution in America where the African could conceivably keep council with the ancestors. It was a "place of refuge in a stormy time." Evidence exists of churches being set up in Petersburg, Virginia, in 1776, in Richmond in 1780, and at Williamsburg in 1765.

In Georgia, as early as 1779, Africans set up their own churches after the Revolutionary War. George Liele, who had shown industry among the Africans in Savannah, Georgia, established a Baptist church before finally settling in Jamaica. Andrew Bryan, Liele's assistant, continued to preach at the church, urging both blacks and whites to treat others as they wished to be treated. Bryan was arrested and imprisoned after the Americans won the Revolutionary War, but his church, according to John Hope Franklin, became the nucleus of African Baptist churches, and probably influenced the religion of Africans in South Carolina (from *Slavery to Freedom*, New York: Vintage, 1966, p. 162).

Figure 5.1. Free versus enslaved African population, 1850.

However, it was in Philadelphia with the work of Richard Allen that the rise of the free churches truly began. Richard Allen was born in Philadelphia in 1760. He was the founding bishop of the African Methodist Episcopal (A.M.E.) Church, the first major black institution in the United States, with Allen the first major leader of African Americans in the country. Born of slave parents, Allen grew up in slavery in Delaware and became a zealous Methodist minister whose many converts included his master, who let him buy his freedom. Allen returned to Philadelphia around 1786, where he brought so many African Americans into St. George's Methodist Church that friction soon developed in the church between whites and blacks. Allen proposed a separate church for blacks and by 1787 had formed the Free African Society, one of the first official organizations of African Americans. It was dedicated to self-improvement and advancement. In the same year, whites segregated blacks by assigning them to the gallery at St. George's Church. Allen and Absalom Jones led an exodus of black parishioners from that church, and Jones and members of the Free African Society established St. Thomas's Free African Church within the Protestant Episcopal Church. Allen, in turn, formed the Bethel African Methodist Episcopal Church (Mother Bethel). Ordained a bishop in 1799, he gained complete control of his church in 1816.

Bethel was truly Mother Bethel. It quickly developed branches in Wilmington, Baltimore, Camden, and Norristown, Pennsylvania. By 1816, the churches under the leadership of men such as Daniel Coker, Morris Brown, and Nicholson Gilliard were able to formalize themselves into a conference. Coker was elected bishop but resigned and Allen was elected to fill the place. By 1820 there were 4,000 African Methodists in Philadelphia, and the church had spread to Pittsburgh in the west and Charleston in the south.

As in Philadelphia, Africans in New York and Boston were expressing an interest in their own churches at the turn of the century. The establishment of the African Methodist Episcopal Zion Church in New York in 1796 was led by Peter Williams, James Varick, George Collins, and Christopher Rush. They ordained themselves and by 1822 had elected their own bishop.

In Boston, the African population organized its own Baptist church under the leadership of Reverend Thomas Paul in 1809. Paul traveled to New York to assist in setting up the Abyssinian Baptist Church. Between Boston and Charleston, despite the intervening condition of the slave system, Africans set about establishing churches that reflected a desire for freedom from constraints imposed by the attitudes of whites.

The African American church did not develop as an independent organization in earnest until the eighteenth century, although Christianization had begun in the seventeenth century. Independent churches in the South did not appear in numbers until after the Civil War, when recently freed Africans began to assert their spirituality through the formal Christian church. Concurrent with the Christian church have always been the Hoodoo, Roots, and Cuba religions with elements in traditional African religions. Strong semi-independent and independent churches reflected an eagerness for self-direction and leadership. These churches, most of them Baptist and Methodist, became the leadership-training institutions for the community. Early preachers also became the interpreters of black social and political agendas, placing themselves between white society and the membership. Forced by this position to assume a leadership role, the African American preacher often became the lead-off witness against racism. By their tone and behavior, they taught their membership what and how to think on the leading social and political issues.

Richard Allen's break with the Methodist church in 1794 and Bishop George Stallings's break with the Catholic church in 1989 represent the motive force in the progressive African American church. Resistance to discrimination coupled with a humanizing mission provides the best example of the African American church. Determined to throw off the shackles of inferior treatment and secure independence from white conceptual hegemony, early Africans in America found religion a possible ally. Allen's establishment of the African Methodist Episcopal Church was a prime example of the will to freedom. His spirit is the spirit of his creativity, invention, resistance, redefinition, reconstruction, and restoration. The most honorable path in African American history has been this road to freedom—born of a commitment to the belief that Africans were as capable as any Americans despite the social, political, and economic attempts to deny this fact.

Anxious to develop leadership and education, Africans found the church and some fraternal organizations to be excellent proving grounds. In March 1775, when a British lodge of Freemasons attached to the British army under General Gage initiated fifteen Africans, including Prince Hall, they started a revolution. Many African groups were established in the larger cities to care for the social welfare of the growing populations swelled by the influx of newly arrived Africans from the West Indies as well as escaped Africans. Organizations such as the African Society (founded in Boston in 1796), the African Free School, and the African Benevolent Society are socially and historically connected to the religious themes of Bishop George Stallings in the twentieth century.

Throughout the history of African Americans there would be men and women who challenged the stereotypes held by whites. They would be in every profession, live in every region of the country, and have many different political views. Yet the common goal would be to disprove the inferiority of the African.

Preachers were the first line of offense in the struggle for decency and respect. Early African preachers took to the pulpit as a justifiable avenue of protest, admonition, and indeed, if need be, insurrection.

Many of the revolts in African American history were the work of preachers who had seen certain visions. Given permission to learn the Bible in order to preach to Africans, the preachers learned first of all the verses in the Bible that supported slave uprisings and revolts. Although the slave owners also had their verses and just as easily told the enslaved Africans that the "Lord wanted them to obey their masters," the preachers could teach the Africans that "to obey the devil is a sin against God."

Scientists also rose up to say with a collective voice, "And before I'd be a slave, I'll be dead and buried in my grave." They demonstrated by their productive and qualitative enterprises that Africans could do anything that was possible for others. Whether in nuclear fission, aeronautical engineering, biology, or agricultural chemistry, the record is the same when the African American is given an opportunity to pursue, to the fullest extent, his or her chosen field.

The achievements of scientists such as Benjamin Banneker would continue to refute the claims that Africans were less intelligent than whites. Banneker's accomplishments in the eighteenth century were to be followed by even greater technological and scientific work by other Africans in the nineteenth and twentieth centuries. The scientific world recognized the contributions of individuals such as Katherine Johnson, Percy Julian, Lewis Latimer, Charles Drew, Ernest Just, Daniel Hale Williams, and George Washington Carver. While these are the names that are most memorable, literally hundreds of men and women, under the worst technological circumstances, succeeded in establishing a remarkable record for African Americans in medicine, biology, chemistry, agriculture, and technology.

Banneker's letter to Thomas Jefferson explaining his objection to Jefferson's view about the African race was exceptional because of the absence of an abundance of examples of achievement among the enslaved Africans of his day. However, since the time of Banneker,

African American scientists have been in every field and discipline working for the advancement of the human race. By taking the initiative, these men and women have moved mountains of apathy to etch their names in the annals of history.

Preachers and scientists represent only two of the professions that have been involved in the resistance to cultural, physical, economic, and political enslavement of the African American community. Artists, particularly musicians, have done an incredible job of retaining or attempting to retain the African roots of cultural resistance. From break dancing to rap, from jazz to gospel, the cultural and psychological message is the same: resist domination. The reason that this attitude governs most of the thinking of African Americans is that the quest is always for liberation, for freedom from color and racial prejudice. There is no other American quest accepted so well by the African American people.

FREEDPERSONS

Although the overwhelming majority of Africans in the United States were enslaved, there were free Africans from the beginning of the country. The categories of free Africans included those who were neither indentured nor enslaved, those who had escaped to freedom, those who had been manumitted by previous owners, and those who had purchased their own freedom. In the first class were individuals whose ancestors had descended from Africans who had entered the Americas in the sixteenth century with Spanish explorers and were not legally bound by Anglo-American enslavement. Many of these people, like most free Africans, had to constantly defend their right to be free. The second class included those who had successfully escaped and eluded capture or whose parents had done so. These individuals constituted a category of Africans in large towns and cities, both North and South, who were technically free but who were always in danger of being captured by slave hunters. The third class was composed of Africans whose owners had freed them as a moral act, usually in their wills or on their deathbeds. Such Africans were able to live among enslaved Africans in the South or travel to the North. They usually took menial jobs, occasionally serving as overseers or domestics in the towns. The fourth class of free Africans was characterized by determined and proud individuals who had purchased their freedom. Sometimes slave owners would give Africans the opportunity to work extra time to pay their purchase cost plus interest. Many did so and lived with great pride because of their achievement.

Although they could never be sure that they would not be challenged for their liberty, the majority of free Africans found gainful employment. The chief positions were in agricultural, manufac-

Figure 5.2. Am I not a man and a brother?

turing, and domestic work. While the North did not have as much agricultural work as the South, it was not without its share of farm work and need for farm laborers. Just as in the South, the majority of the free Africans worked on farms and as domestics. However, the Africans in the North owned their own labor, while in the South the laborer was owned by the slave master. The freedperson was at liberty unknown in the South.

James Forten

James Forten was born in Philadelphia in 1766. Like many of his contemporaries in Philadelphia, Forten was a sailor. He served aboard a privateer during the American Revolutionary War. When the war ended, Forten devoted considerable time to the betterment of the African race in Philadelphia and elsewhere. He was one of the signers of a petition asking Congress to modify the Fugitive Slave Act of 1793. Active throughout the city for the good of the entire community, Forten joined Richard Allen in 1814 to organize a force of 2,500 Africans to defend Philadelphia against British forces.

Forten was committed to the idea that Africans in America who lived in the North were "colored citizens" and deserved as many rights and responsibilities as any other citizens of the United States. He was one of the leaders of a major meeting in 1817 to protest the American Colonization Society's scheme to send Africans back to Africa. This meeting, held at the Bethel African Methodist Episcopal Church in Philadelphia, was attended by delegates from as far away as upstate New York. Forten chaired the meeting and assisted in writing the resolution that declared that the free blacks of the North were opposed to any attempt by the southern planters to send Africans back to Africa so as to separate them from their enslaved brothers and sisters.

THE CHURCH AND THE PROFESSIONS

During the last half of the nineteenth century African Americans flocked to the churches as havens of peace and understanding. How else were Africans who were oppressed, brutalized, and disconnected from roots to make sense of the world around them? The end of the Civil War brought great activity on the part of several denominations that sought to exploit the newly found field of potential believers. Black church membership grew phenomenally; the Baptist church alone gained 500,000 members by 1870. But growth was also recorded by the Methodist Episcopal church, which had divided into a northern and southern church over the slavery issue. The African Methodist Episcopal Church, one of three black-controlled denominations at the time, increased its membership as well. It had gone underground in the South during the struggle to eliminate slavery. The other black denomination in the United States was the African Methodist Episcopal Zion Church. It increased its membership from 25,000 in 1860 to 200,000 in 1870. A third church, the African Baptist Church, would have its greater growth among the Africans who went with the defeated British to Halifax, Nova Scotia, at the end of the eighteenth century.

The Catholic church made its progress in the District of Columbia and the state of Louisiana. Father Patrick Healy and his natural brother James Augustine Healy were appointed to important posts in the Catholic church. In 1873, Patrick Healy became president of Georgetown University in Washington, D.C., and James Augustine Healy was appointed to the post of bishop there in 1875. He was later made an assistant to the papal office. The church, however, was not an avenue for professional growth. Those who found favor with the hierarchy of the church could excel within limits, but always for Africans there was a ceiling to their ascendancy.

A GALLERY OF HONOR

A transgenerational group of Africans has demonstrated the highest levels of achievement, as we will see throughout this atlas. The following

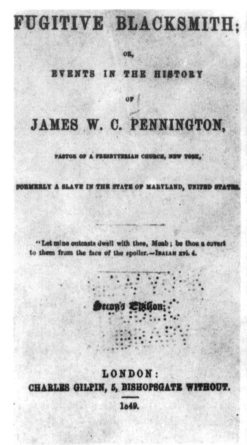

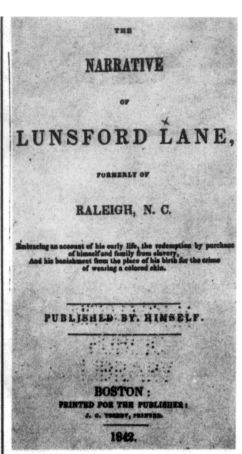

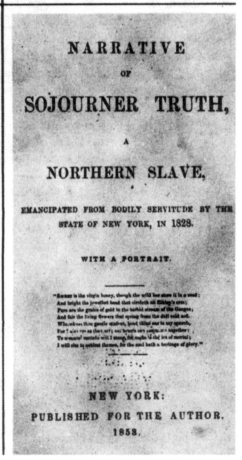

summaries of some of the outstanding achievers serve as reminders of the talents of this historic people.

Bishop Henry McNeal Turner

Bishop Henry M. Turner was born in Newberry Court House, South Carolina, on February 1, 1833. He was freeborn due to his mother's freedom. Her father of royal blood in Africa was never enslaved. He was brought to America and declared free. Therefore, Henry grew up amidst slavery but was a free child. This did not make his life any easier, as the whites that he worked for often had overseers who wanted to use him as a test case for the enslaved Africans. He was hired out to several places where he had to fight the overseers. He was determined that no white man's lash would ever scar his back. He resented every attempt to whip him. One dream stood out in his mind as a child: to impart knowledge to his people. Against all the odds for an African in the South, Turner learned to read. He was appointed in 1863 by President Lincoln as the first commissioned African chaplain in the army.

Benjamin Banneker

Benjamin Banneker (1731–1806) was one of America's earliest scientists. He made a clock out of wooden parts while he was still a young man. It was the first wholly American made clock in the country. His clock kept time accurately for twenty years.

Banneker, who was born in Ellicott, Maryland, of a free mother, attended a private school until he received the equivalent of an eighth-grade education. As a child he loved mathematics and soon published almanacs, mastered astronomy, and became a surveyor. Secretary of State Thomas Jefferson recommended Banneker to President George Washington for the post of surveyor,

Figure 5.3. Covers from several publications of Sojourner Truth.

along with Pierre L'Enfant and Andrew Allicott, for laying out the nation's new capital in the District of Columbia. L'Enfant's resignation made Banneker a key figure in the planning process. He was the first African given a presidential appointment. On August 19, 1791, Banneker wrote Thomas Jefferson, sending him a copy of his annual almanac and disputing Jefferson's claim that Africans were inferior to whites.

Henry Blair

Henry Blair was the first African to receive a patent for an invention in the United States. Blair was born in Maryland in 1804 and received a patent for a corn planting machine in 1834. Two years later he received a patent for a cotton planting machine. Blair was designated as "a colored man" in the official records. Since enslaved Africans could not receive patents, it is most likely that Henry Blair was a free African.

George R. Carruthers

George R. Carruthers was one of the two naval researchers who helped to develop the Apollo 16 lunar surface ultraviolet camera/spectrograph, which was placed on the moon in April 1972. Carruthers designed the instrument and William Conway adapted it for the Apollo mission.

Carruthers was born in Chicago in 1940 and made his own telescope at the age of ten. He is only one of dozens of creative African Americans who work for the space program of the United States. With a Ph.D. in physics from the University of Chicago, Carruthers was well qualified to receive the Exceptional Scientific Achievement medal from the National Aeronautical Space Agency, as he did in 1972.

Charles Richard Drew

Charles Drew was born in Washington, D.C., in 1904. At his death in 1950 he was celebrated for his outstanding achievements in the field of blood research. He pioneered in the development of techniques for preserving blood, making it possible to save thousands of lives of American and allied soldiers during World War II.

Drew attended Amherst College, where he established a reputation as an athlete and a scholar. He received the Messman Trophy for bringing the most distinction to his college. Drew received his medical degree from McGill University in Toronto in 1933. He perfected the techniques for separating and preserving blood at McGill. He then went to Howard University to teach pathology. Believing that he needed to explore blood research more deeply, he enrolled in the doctoral program at Columbia University. His work on "banked blood" brought him to the attention of the British government, who asked him to set up the first blood bank. He later directed the American Red Cross and became chief surgeon at Howard University.

Corporal Eugene Jacques Bullard

Eugene Jacques Bullard was born in Columbus, Georgia, in 1894 of a Martiniquan father and Muskogee mother. While he was still a teenager he ran away to France and in 1914 joined the French Foreign Legion, enlisting in the 170th. He earned his wings in 1917, becoming the first military pilot of African descent. The plane he flew in combat during World War I was the Spad VII with the Spa93, Group Brocard. During his combat missions he claimed two victories, one over a Pfatz and the other over a Fokker DR I. Both victories were won over the Verdun region. Bullard was a much-decorated pilot, winning the Legion of Honor, the Chevalier, Medaille Militaire, Croix de Guerre, Croix de Combattant 1914–1918, Medaille Commemoration Française, and the Medaille Verdun.

He settled comfortably in Paris after the war with Germany and opened a nightclub. However, within twenty years the Germans and the French were at war again and Bullard quickly joined the French resistance. In battles with the German invaders he was wounded at Orleans, and his friends arranged for him to be smuggled out to the United States as France fell to the German forces.

In 1954 the French invited Bullard to return for the ceremony of relighting the eternal flame at the Tomb of the Unknown Soldier at L'Arc de Triomphe. He was given the honor of lighting the flame and then returned to New York, where he lived his last years. He is buried in the Federation of French War Veterans Cemetery at Flushing, New York.

Katherine Johnson

Katherine Johnson was born in West Virginia in 1918. She became well known for her work as an aerospace technologist while working at the National Aeronautics and Space Administration's Langley Research Center in Hampton, Virginia. Her research involved more sophisticated ways to track manned and unmanned space vehicles. She became an expert at analyzing data from the manned and unmanned moon missions.

Percy Julian

Percy Julian was born in Montgomery, Alabama, in 1898 (figure 5.4). His major achievement was in the development of derivative drugs that aid in the treatment of arthritis. Julian attended Harvard University and the University of

Figure 5.4. Percy Julian (1898–1975). Chemist whose research led to over 100 patents as a result of discoveries related to the manufacturing of drugs, hormones, and vitamins, including a synthetic drug to treat glaucoma.

Vienna. He taught at Fisk, Howard, and West Virginia State universities before deciding to concentrate on medical research. He worked first with soybeans and specialized in the production of sterols, thus enabling arthritis sufferers to be able to afford cortisone, a sterol derivative, more inexpensively. In 1935, Julian synthesized the drug physostigmine which is used to treat glaucoma.

Samuel L. Kountz

Samuel L. Kountz was born in Lexa, Arkansas, in 1931. Kountz was a brilliant surgeon who attended the University of Arkansas Medical School—he was the first black to enroll at the school. He was the international leader in performing kidney transplants during his life. He was responsible for more than 500 kidney transplants during the time he was head of surgery and chief of general surgery at New York state's Downstate Medical Center and Kings County Hospital Center, respectively. He also worked with other surgeons to develop the prototype of a machine that can preserve a kidney for fifty hours from the time it is taken from a donor to the time it is transplanted. He contracted a strange illness while on a visit to South Africa in 1980. His illness was never diagnosed and he remained brain damaged until his death in 1981.

Though there were other scientists before Kountz, none achieved so many practical results in such a brief career.

Sengbe and the *Amistad* Mutiny

Sengbe, a Mende-speaking African, called Cinque by the Spaniards, was seized and carried off to be sold into slavery in 1839 (see figure 5.5, page 71). His father was a rice farmer from the Mende region of West Africa. The slave ship took Cinque to Cuba. In Havana, two Spaniards purchased fifty Africans, including Cinque, and placed them on a ship called the *Amistad*, which means "friendship" in Spanish, bound for Puerto Principe, Cuba. On board the ship with the Africans that had been purchased were the captain, two other enslaved Africans, and two whites serving as a crew.

When it was night, Sengbe and other Africans surprised Captain Ferrer and the cook, killing both. In command of the ship, Cinque tied the owners of the cargo to the bridge and instructed them to steer the ship toward the African coast. The Spaniards guided the ship toward the United States, steering it north and west instead of east and south. For nearly two months the ship zigzagged in the Atlantic Ocean. Ten Africans died before the *Amistad* finally reached Long Island, New York. They had been without adequate food and water for several days. In the New York waters the vessel was sighted by a United States Navy ship, which sent a group of sailors aboard to investigate.

The Americans were shocked to find only Africans in charge of the ship. They ordered the Africans below deck at pistol point and took the ship to New London, Connecticut, where all of the Africans with the exception of three small girls were charged before the United States Circuit Court with murder of the captain and mutiny. All of the Africans were imprisoned in anticipation of the trial.

None of the Africans in New Haven could understand the language that was spoken by the Africans who had captured the *Amistad*. Nevertheless, the Africans found many friends and supporters in the New Haven area. There were newspaper articles about them. The daring feat they had accomplished was spoken of in the highest terms by students and faculty at Yale University as an example of the human spirit overcoming adversity. An Amistad Committee was also formed to raise money for the defense of the Africans. Lewis Tappan was a chief supporter of the Africans. In fact, the American Missionary Association was formed out of the Amistad Committee. The aim of the American Missionary Association was to combat "the sins of caste, polygamy, and slaveholding."

Since Africa has several hundred languages and the African American population was composed of individuals whose descendants came from more than 100 different ethnic/linguistic groups, it was difficult to find someone in New Haven who understood the Mende language. The language problem presented the court with serious difficulties until a Yale professor, Josiah Willard Gibbs, discovered a method for determining the exact language spoken by the Africans. He found a way to have them say the words for different numbers and then looked for Africans who understood those numbers. With this kind of research Gibbs was able to locate James Covey, a Mende sailor, who worked on a British ship in New York City. Covey was asked to serve as an interpreter for the Africans.

Once Covey began to interpret the information from the Africans, more details of the heroic story began to unfold. When Covey explained that Cinque told him that they had been kidnapped from their homes and taken to Cuba against their wills, the public sentiment, already pro-African, changed even more in their favor. The abolitionists in Connecticut and New York rallied to their support, claiming that since the Africans had been taken from their own lands without their consent they had a right to use any means necessary to obtain their freedom, just as other free men would do.

The case attracted national and international attention. There were many legal details and fine points of law to be decided in this case. Africans had mutinied and killed a white captain in international waters in order to free themselves from bondage, and the vessel had been seized in the United States waters. The entire law class at Yale University was dismissed to attend the trial because the professors considered it to be the trial of the century.

When the trial began, Sengbe testified in his own behalf. From his carriage and countenance, everyone could see that he was a man of considerable natural intelligence and dignity. He handled his testimony with deftness and eloquence. Covey, himself a Mende speaker, translated Sengbe's words quickly, without hesi-

Figure 5.5. Sengbe aka Cinque (1814?–unknown). Led the revolt by slaves on the ship *Amistad* in 1839; testified in the Supreme Court case involving the *Amistad* and eventually won the freedom of all Africans aboard the ship. Credit: New Haven Colony Historical Society, gift of Dr. Charles B. Purvis, 1898.

tation. The court ruled in favor of the Africans. However, the decision was appealed to the Supreme Court. Former president John Quincy Adams was emotionally moved by the plight of the Africans and undertook to argue their case before the Supreme Court. President Adams was convinced that the case should be decided in favor of the Africans. On March 9, 1841, Adams argued for eight and a half hours in support of the Africans. The Africans were freed. Later, Adams would express his feeling that the practice of slavery had to be ended in the United States and that, if it took everything he had, he would do it because the practice of judging some people to be slaves and others to be free because of their color was intolerable and not within the bounds of human decency.

Before he left for Sierra Leone in 1842, Sengbe and some of the other Africans who had led the mutiny learned a great deal in the United States. They learned to speak English, studied the laws and political systems of the New England states, and were regularly taken to the Christian churches in the area. When they left for Africa, they were accompanied by several missionaries who believed that Sierra Leone was a good place to establish a mission against the slave trade.

The *Amistad* affair had aroused so much controversy and interest in the United States because of the intensifying of the antislavery struggle. Already by the 1830s a number of functioning committees had been set up in the northern communities from Boston all the way to Philadelphia. New York had one of the more active chapters of the abolition movement, and their sentiment, along with the intellectual community of Yale and other colleges, worked to create an environment favorable to a positive solution. Of course, the fact that the former president of the United States decided to argue the case for the Africans did not hurt. The entire incident and its resolution was claimed as a victory for the spirit of fairness in the courts. However, not all enslaved Africans won their cases, nor were all permitted to have their cases

fairly judged. The vast majority of Africans remained in the prison of forced labor after the *Amistad* had been forgotten. Some who escaped were captured and forced back into slavery.

The Sad Story of Anthony Burns

Anthony Burns was arrested on May 24, 1854, and placed under guard in the federal jury room in a Boston court building. He was charged with being a runaway from enslavement. Burns's former owner, Charles Suttle of Alexandria, Virginia, wanted him back. When news that Burns had been arrested spread through the streets of Boston, many citizens jumped to defend him. In fact, three outstanding lawyers came to court the next morning in his defense: Charles M. Ellis, a member of the Boston Vigilance Committee, Richard Henry Dana Jr., author of the book *Two Years before the Mast*, and Robert Morris, Boston's most prominent African American attorney.

The famous Fanueil Hall was filled to capacity the next night to protest the capture of Burns. Among those in attendance were two of the historic names in the struggle to end slavery: Wendell Phillips and Theodore Parker.

A commotion was started in the hall when a man shouted, "When we go from the cradle of liberty, let us go to the tomb of liberty—the courthouse." The audience poured out into the streets and headed for Court Square. Already leading a group to the courthouse were Reverend Thomas Wentworth Higginson and Lewis Hayden. They had begun battering down the door of the courthouse to rescue Burns. Constables were inside the building with pistols and clubs. In the melee that followed, Reverend Higginson was killed and the military reinforcements came in to rout the abolitionists. The abolitionists had been unable to free Burns by force. They despaired that they would ever free him by legal means. Consequently, it was decided to raise the $1,200 needed to purchase his freedom. The United States Attorney refused to permit the transaction. He insisted that, according to the Fugitive Slave Law, the escapee must be returned to the state from whence he had escaped.

When Burns came to trial, soldiers guarded every door. President Franklin Pierce wired the court to spare no expense in executing the law. After a week of testimony, Burns was ordered to return to slavery. More than twenty military units had been brought to Boston to see that he did not escape. More than 2,000 horsemen and marines escorted him through a crowd of 50,000 supporters crying, "Shame!"

The Heroic Nat Turner

Nat Turner (figure 5.6) is an epic figure alongside Frederick Douglass, Booker T. Washington, Martin Luther King, Harriet Tubman, Marcus Garvey, Malcolm X, and W. E. B. Du Bois. He remains larger than life in the inner core of the African American's soul. His story is a central motif in African American culture because around it revolves the

pathos, the dreams, and the resistance to oppression that have characterized the African experience in America. Turner's revolt was the culmination of a preparation that began soon after his birth on October 2, 1800. He was considered exceptionally precocious by his family. At twenty-one years of age, Turner ran away from his owner and, after staying away for a month, returned voluntarily.

After considerable preparation and meditation, Nat Turner and his guerrilla army began their campaign in 1831. Their intention, pure and simple, was to free all slaves. Galvanized by his religious belief that he was to be the avenger for the sufferings of Africans, the messianic Turner left a path of blood through rural Virginia (see figure 5.7, page 74).

When Nat Turner was finally captured, the white population of the slaveholding states was stunned. They had never felt so completely vulnerable. New laws were enacted to tighten the already

Figure 5.6. Nat Turner on the road to freedom.

Figure 5.7. Typical southern plantation house of the type raided by Nat Turner in the Fall of 1831. Credit: Dave G. Houser/Corbis.

harsh regulations that restricted African movement and discussion. Turner was hanged for his involvement in the uprising. Rather than bringing an end to African revolts, the death of Nat Turner seemed to embolden other heroic figures.

The nineteenth century experienced the most widespread outbreak of resistance to white domination since it had begun in the fifteenth century. Revolts occurred throughout the globe and included the eleven Asante wars, the Zulu wars, the revolts of Zeferina and Balaio in Brazil, and numerous other attacks on slavery and oppression. In this context, Nat Turner's rebellion was a testament to the courage and will of Africans in America to overthrow slavery.

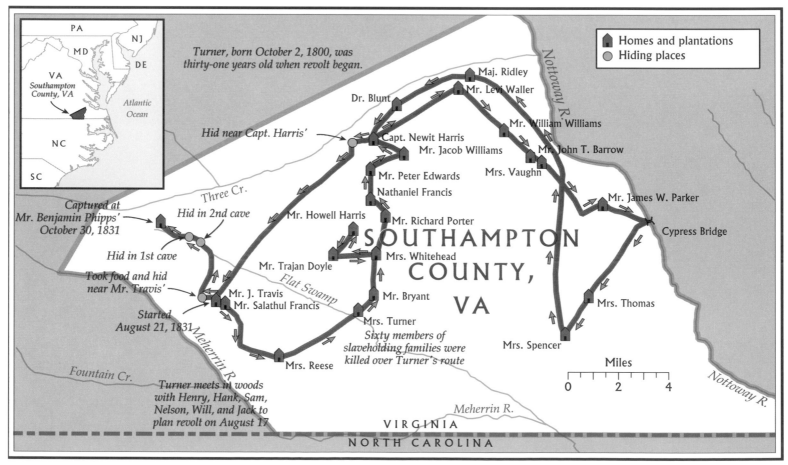

Figure 5.8. Route of Nat Turner through Southhampton County, Virginia.

Important Events in Nat Turner's Life

1822

Nat Turner sold to Thomas Moore when Samuel Turner died.

1825

Nat Turner's first religious vision. He begins to preach to those who would listen.

1825

Nat Turner baptized a white believer, Ethelred Brantley, who had declared himself a believer in Jesus Christ.

1830

Moved to the home of Joseph Travis when the widow of Thomas Moore married Travis.

August 13, 1831

A daylong atmospheric phenomenon in which the sun appeared bluish-green. Turner saw this as a sign from heaven.

August 20, 1831

Nat Turner asked two of his trusted friends, Henry and Hark, to meet him the following day to plan the revolt.

August 21, 1831

Hark, Henry, Nelson, Sam, Lack, and Will meet in the morning at Cabin Pond to cook a pig and drink brandy. At 3:00 P.M. Nat Turner joined them and began planning the revolt.

August 22, 1831

The seven left about 2:00 A.M. to go to the Travis house, where they were joined by Austin. Entering the house, they killed Travis, his wife and child, and the two younger males, Putnam Moore and Joel Westbrook. They had committed their first act of rebellion against the evil system of slavery.

August 22, 1831

(2:00 A.M. to dawn) The revolutionaries reached the house of Salathul Francis, whom they killed.

August 22, 1831 (2:00 A.M. to dawn)

The revolutionaries reached the home of Piety Reese, whom they killed, as well as her son, William. The farm overseer, James Barner, was severely wounded.

August 22, 1831 (5:00 A.M.)

The revolutionaries visited the Wiley Francis house but after a confrontation with Francis's workers withdrew without violence.

August 22, 1831 (5:30 A.M.)

The revolutionaries reached Elizabeth Turner's house, where they killed her, Mrs. Newsome, a neighbor, and the overseer, Hartwell Peebles. They were joined by eight others at the entrance to the Newsome house.

August 22, 1831 (6:00 A.M.)

The revolutionaries divided: one unit on horseback (nine men) went to Mrs. Catherine Whitehead's house where they killed her, her mother, her son, her four daughters, and a grandchild. One of the daughters, Margaret, was the only person Nat Turner admitted killing himself. The other unit (six men) went on to Henry Bryant's home, where they killed him, his wife, his son, and his wife's mother.

August 22, 1831 (6:30 A.M.)

One unit of revolutionaries went to Richard Porter's house where they found no one home. They then went to Nathaniel Francis's house where they killed the overseer, Henry Doyle, and two boys who were nephews of Francis. Mr. Francis and his mother were away at the time and Mrs. Francis was hidden in the attic by her own enslaved Africans. The other unit of revolutionaries went to the home of Howell Harris. No one was home, but the group met and killed Trajan Doyle on the road outside the house.

August 22, 1831 (7:30 A.M.)
Some of the revolutionaries met and killed Mrs. John K. Williams and her child in the lane to the Francises' house.

August 22, 1831 (8:40 A.M.)
Nat Turner led a group of men to the home of Peter Edwards, which was found empty. About this time both units rejoined at the home of Captain John T Barrow, who was killed by the first unit to reach him. There were now more than forty armed and mounted African men in the revolutionary force. Word had obviously spread among the landowners that a revolt was occurring because increasingly the whites seemed alerted.

August 22, 1831 (9:00 A.M.)
The revolutionaries arrived at Newitt Harris's home to find the family had fled.

August 22, 1831 (9:15 A.M.)
The revolutionaries came to Levi Waller's home soon thereafter and killed Waller's wife and ten children in school at his house. Waller observed the attack from hiding and later became a principal prosecution witness in several trials.

August 22, 1831 (10:15 A.M.)
The revolutionaries went to the house of William Williams, where they killed him, his wife, and his two sons.

August 22, 1831 (11:00 A.M.)
The revolutionaries reached the house of Jacob Williams, where they killed his wife, three of their children, the plantation overseer's wife, Mrs. Caswell Worrell, her two children, and a visitor, Edwin Drewry.

August 22, 1831 (noon)
The revolutionaries reached the house of Rebecca Vaughan, where they killed her, her son, and her niece. At this point the revolutionary force had grown to sixty mounted and armed men. The decision was taken to march on the village of Jerusalem. Believing it was better to die than to live a slave, Turner persuaded the force to attack the village. However, they were met by an armed group of landowners who exchanged shots with them. No one was killed on either side, but the revolutionaries knew that they would face increasing resistance.

August 22, 1831 (2:00 P.M.)
Turner discovered that the main road to Jerusalem was guarded and attempted to cross into the village via a lower bridge. It, too, was guarded. The revolutionaries decided to redraw their strategy and took shelter near the Ridley house. Some men deserted the force, reducing Turner's number to about thirty men.

August 23, 1831 (daybreak)
Turner leads his force to the house of Dr. Simon Blunt, who had given his enslaved Africans weapons. They fought a bitter battle against the revolutionaries. Men were killed on both sides and Turner's forces were reduced to about twenty-five men. Hark was wounded and captured.

August 23, 1831 (7:00 A.M.)
The revolutionaries met the armed landowners, whose force had now grown to more than 100 men in a final battle. When the battle was over, most of the revolutionaries had escaped and several were killed, including Will.

August 23, 1831 (9:25 A.M.)
the patrols and patterollers because of the support he received from people working on the farms. He changed his hiding place several times but was always in this same general area. Nat Turner was alone, his men scattered or dead.

August 23–October 30, 1831
Nat Turner went underground to avoid detection. He hid in the vicinity of the Travis farm. A number of enslaved Africans gave him food. He managed to avoid the patrols and patterollers because of the support he received from people working on farms. He changed his hiding place several times but was always in the same general area.

October 30, 1831 (noon)
Nat Turner was captured when his hiding area was discovered by a dog. He was taken to the Peter Edwards farm and held captive by Benjamin Phipps.

October 31, 1831 (noon)
Turner was surrendered to Edward Butts, the deputy sheriff of Southampton County, and put in the county jail.

November 1–3, 1831
Nat Turner is questioned by Thomas R. Gray in his cell. Gray claims that Turner dictated his "Confessions" during this time.

November 5, 1831
Nat Turner was tried in the Southampton County Court, found guilty, and sentenced to be executed.

November 11, 1831
At the age of thirty-one, Nat Turner was hanged for leading the most serious African uprising in U.S. history. The severity of regulations governing the conduct of slaves was intensified beyond any degree known in prior years, so great was the white fear of an African uprising throughout the South. Nat Turner's name was whispered among blacks and whites in the immediate vicinity. The killing of Turner was meant to suggest to the African that death would be swift for anyone who attempted to overthrow their enslavement. Many enslaved mothers named their sons Moses while actually meaning Nat.

"All My Troubles Will Soon Be Over With"

6

THE GATHERING
OF FREEDOM FIGHTERS

During the 1830s Africans outnumbered whites in several southern cities such as Charleston, Savannah, New Orleans, and Richmond. Both Mobile and Norfolk were close to having black majorities. Thirty years later, in the 1860s, Africans were not a majority in any major city. The pace of white population growth was much faster due to immigration. Furthermore, few Africans were being brought into these areas. Whites had begun to sell as many Africans as they could to rural areas in order to prevent revolts, insurrections, and riots.

City life was politicizing for Africans because many free blacks lived in the urban areas. For example, out of the 18,000 Africans who lived in Baltimore in 1830, nearly 14,000 were free. By 1860, the free population was 25,000 out of 27,000. At the beginning of the Civil War, Baltimore was the fourth largest city in America and it had more free Africans than any other city.

There were several reasons for Baltimore's position in terms of free Africans. It was an active seaport, particularly engaged in commerce with cities farther south. This was not the same for New York or Philadelphia to the extent it was in Baltimore. The city was between the North and the South both in a geographical sense as well as in a psychological sense. Africans from the Deep South could always find a ship going to Baltimore. Once an African was in Baltimore there were enough free Africans in the city to provide food, shelter, and advice. In time a strong antislavery spirit developed among the enslaved Africans in Baltimore. This was the city of Frederick Douglass and Harriet Tubman, among other famous leaders.

In the Deep South, New Orleans was the capital of free blacks. In 1830, it had 8,000 freedpersons out of 17,000 Africans, and in 1860 it was 10,600 free out of 24,000.

The first U.S. census was taken in 1790, and at that time free Africans constituted 8 percent of the African population in the nation. There were 59,000 free Africans out of 698,000 total. Seventy years later in 1860, there were 488,000 free Africans out of 3,953,000, or 12 percent.

Although the North took measures to end slavery in the 1780s, in 1790 there were more enslaved Africans than free Africans in the northern states. Indeed, more free Africans lived in the South than in the North. In 1790, 32,000 free Africans lived in the South compared to 27,000 in the North. Some 40,000 of the North's 67,000 Africans were enslaved.

In 1860, when slavery had been eliminated in the North, there were still more free Africans (250,000 to 238,000) in the South than in the North. The states with the largest numbers of free Africans in 1860 were Maryland (84,000), Virginia (58,000), and Pennsylvania (56,000). Cities with the largest free African population in 1860 were:

Baltimore	25,600
Philadelphia	22,000
New York	12,500
New Orleans	10,600
Washington	9,200
Charleston	3,200

RESTRICTIONS ON FREE AFRICANS

To be free did not mean that there were no restrictions on Africans. Severe codes were placed on free blacks to keep them in check. So called "slave codes" were drawn up to keep free Africans from socializing with enslaved Africans. Free Africans needed licenses to own guns for hunting. They could not have schools or hold meetings during the 1830s. Church services could only be held in the presence of a white adult. Movement was restricted to the county. Free Africans could vote in Maryland, Tennessee, and North Carolina, but that right was abolished in 1810, 1834, and 1835, respectively. The fear of free Africans infected every security decision made in the South.

The historian John Hope Franklin has spoken of the Africans who were not enslaved as "quasi-free," reflecting their dubious status within a racist society. They were always suspect and had to be vigilant in order to maintain freedom.

The prohibition of slavery in certain northern states and the constant influx of escaped Africans meant that the free population would increase with time. This increase in population did not bring with it much power of consequence or any significant influence in the affairs of the states. On the other hand, the free Africans in the South proved to be a thorn in the side of the slavery system since they were symbols of the possibility of freedom for Africans. Whenever free Africans were able to successfully negotiate their livelihood, establish strong families, keep their farms prosperous within the context of the system, and demonstrate concern for their enslaved brothers and sisters, they proved that Africans could control their own lives and families. Such examples, however quietly they were lived, were dramatic within the environment of the South.

The South maintained slavery until the end of the Civil War. Thus, many of the free Africans in the South existed because white slave owners often manumitted the Africans who worked for them. Some did this as an act of conscience. Religious conversion was frequently given as the reason for a change of heart. Others manumitted Africans who were their own children from slave mothers. Some slave owners, like John Randolph, who provided in 1833 for the freedom of 400 enslaved Africans on his plantation, made provisions through their wills for the release of their enslaved persons. There was no particu-

Figure 6.1. 1816 through 1892: African Methodist Episcopal Church.

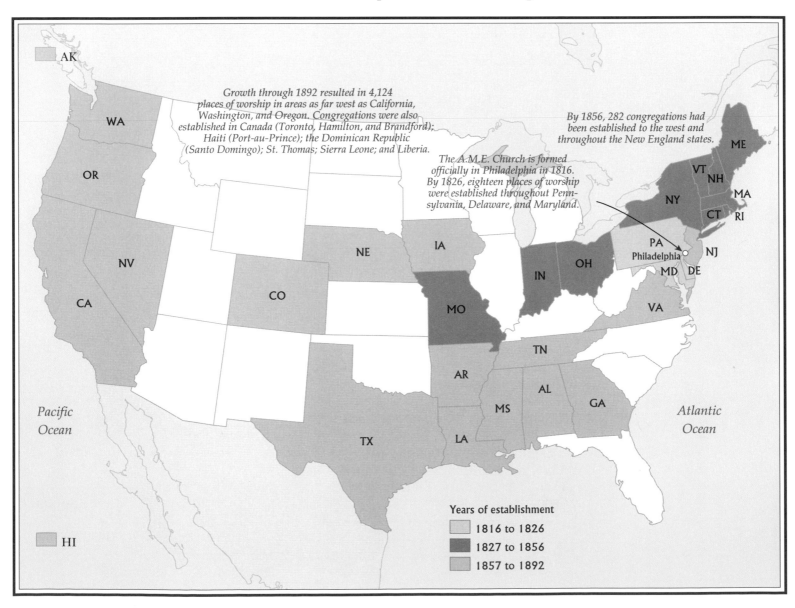

Growth through 1892 resulted in 4,124 places of worship in areas as far west as California, Washington, and Oregon. Congregations were also established in Canada (Toronto, Hamilton, and Brandford); Haiti (Port-au-Prince); the Dominican Republic (Santo Domingo); St. Thomas; Sierra Leone; and Liberia.

By 1856, 282 congregations had been established to the west and throughout the New England states.

The A.M.E. Church is formed officially in Philadelphia in 1816. By 1826, eighteen places of worship were established throughout Pennsylvania, Delaware, and Maryland.

Years of establishment
1816 to 1826
1827 to 1856
1857 to 1892

lar path to freedom in the slave South. The African who saved the Georgia state capitol from being burned to the ground was freed in 1834 by the state. Peter Chastang of Mobile was freed because of his valor and courage in the War of 1812.

JAMES PIERSON BECKWOURTH

James Pierson Beckwourth was born in Fredericksburg, Virginia, on April 6, 1798 (figure 6.2). His father, who had fought in the Revolutionary War, moved the family westward when James was about eight years old. The succeeding years of his life proved to be historic because he became one of the best-known trappers and mountain men of his day. Indeed, James Beckwourth became a leader among the Absaroka (Crow) people and one of the heroic figures of the nineteenth century.

James Beckwourth was sent to school in St. Louis. He studied for four years, which was a respectable time of study on the frontier unless one was going to become a preacher or lawyer. Apprenticed to a blacksmith, Beckwourth soon left this position and decided to travel to the lead mines for work. In a party of 100 men and 8 boats he struck out for Galena. Met by an army of Sac and Fox peoples, the party had to negoti-

ate a treaty that would allow them to work the mines. In the meantime, Beckwourth became friendly with the Native Americans. They liked him and he liked them. After working for a while in the mines he traveled down the Mississippi to New Orleans.

At the age of twenty-five he signed on with the Ashley Rocky Mountain Fur Company in the fall of 1823. This was to be Beckwourth's ride to fame in the annals of American history. Alongside the experienced mountain man Black Harris, he rode ahead to buy horses from the Pawnee. The long trip to Pawnee territory undertaken in the middle of the winter nearly exhausted the two before they were assisted by two Pawnees. When they returned to where they had left the Ashley party, the group had already gone ahead without them, thinking they were dead. Beckwourth stayed in the territory packing furs. Upon his return to St. Louis the following spring he met General Ashley, who was outfitting another group of trappers. He asked Beckwourth to join them and to carry about $1,000 in gold to one of the leaders of the group, Tom Fitzpatrick.

Soon Beckwourth became skilled in the culture of the Native Americans. The Absaroka people gave him the name White Handled Knife because of his bravery. When a fellow trapper named Greenword told a group of Absaroka people that Beckwourth had been born a Crow but was stolen in a raid by the Cheyenne when he was a boy, they believed the story because of Beckwourth's knowledge, bravery, and skill.

Captured by the Absaroka people while trapping beavers, Beckwourth was taken before Chief Black Lodge. When word got out that he was indeed an Absaroka himself, stolen from them as a baby, and as an adult had killed many Blackfeet, the enemy of the Absaroka, there was general rejoicing. Beckwourth married one of the daughters of Chief Black Lodge, Still Water. He was now given the Absaroka name Morning Star. On several occasions he demonstrated his bravery when the Absaroka engaged their

Figure 6.2. James Pierson Beckwourth (1798–1866). Famous trapper and mountain man who became a leader of the Absarok (Crow) people.

enemies. After defeating so many Absaroka enemies, the tribe gave him the name Antelope which meant respect and courage. Beckwourth later received many more names of honor from the Absaroka people.

Beckwourth took leave of the Absaroka nation to work for the American Fur Company, started by John Jacob Astor. He then became a courier in New Mexico and later joined the gold rush in California. In 1866 he was persuaded by the American government to return to the Absaroka to work out a treaty with them. When he returned the people met him with much praise and admiration. They pleaded with him to remain with them. His own son, Chief Black Panther, asked him to stay among the people. But Beckwourth told them that he could not remain with them since he had many attachments outside of the nation. After a festive meal, Beckwourth died and was buried among the Absaroka. It has been surmised that because they loved him so much he was poisoned by the people to keep him from returning to the outside world.

The spirit of adventure is found throughout African American history. The examples of this adventurous spirit are numerous.

Waller Jackson was one of ten Africans to "round the Horn" in 1849 to prospect for gold near Downieville, California. The Ninth and Tenth Cavalry, African regiments formed from black Union troops, were sent to combat against the Apache and Cheyenne. The Cheyenne gave the African regiments the name "Buffalo Soldiers" because of their complexion and hair texture. Henry O. Flipper, the first African American graduate of West Point, was the first black officer named to the Tenth Cavalry. Allensworth, California, was founded by a famous African American soldier, jockey, and adventurer who gave his name to the town.

Charlotte Forten Grimke, born of wealthy free parents in Philadelphia, was one of the first persons to volunteer to teach Africans in the South (see figure

6.4, page 84). Jean Baptiste Du Sable established a fur-trading post around 1788 in the area that was to become the city of Chicago. The site where he constructed his log house is accepted as the original settlement of Chicago.

Henry Riding, an African pioneer in Iowa, was credited with stopping a railroad crew at gunpoint from laying tracks across his land. The company finally paid him $21,000. Isaiah Thornton Montgomery founded the town of Mound Bayou in 1887 as a place where

Figure 6.3. A warning to Africans about kidnappers and slave catchers in Boston.

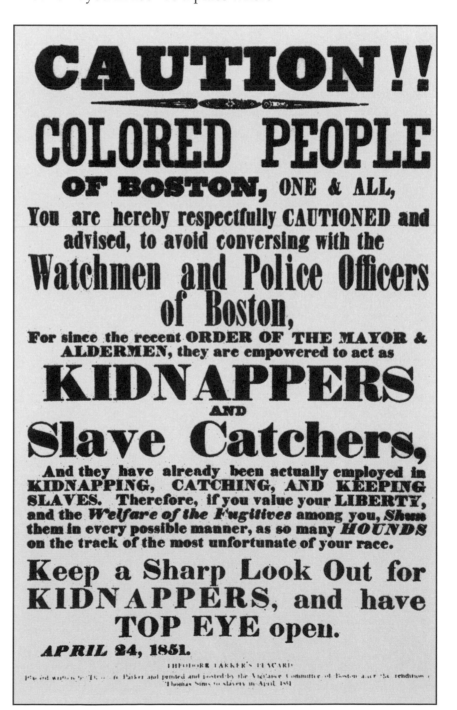

CAUTION!!

COLORED PEOPLE

OF BOSTON, ONE & ALL,

You are hereby respectfully CAUTIONED and advised, to avoid conversing with the

Watchmen and Police Officers of Boston,

For since the recent ORDER OF THE MAYOR & ALDERMEN, they are empowered to act as

KIDNAPPERS

AND

Slave Catchers,

And they have already been actually employed in KIDNAPPING, CATCHING, AND KEEPING SLAVES. Therefore, if you value your LIBERTY, and the *Welfare of the Fugitives* among you, Shun them in every possible manner, as so many HOUNDS on the track of the most unfortunate of your race.

Keep a Sharp Look Out for KIDNAPPERS, and have TOP EYE open.

APRIL 24, 1851.

THEODORE PARKER'S PLACARD.

Placed written by Theodore Parker and printed and posted by the Vigilance Committee of Boston after the rendition of Thomas Sims to slavery in April 1851.

Figure 6.4. Charlotte L. Forten Grimke (1837–1914). Born in Philadelphia to wealthy, free parents, she began to educate slaves as the Union took control of territories in the South.

African Americans could obtain social, economic, and political rights in a racist South. George Washington Carver was born and raised in Diamond, Missouri. He was kidnapped when he was only six weeks old and ransomed for a horse valued at $100. Carver made his way through Minnesota, Kansas, and Iowa before he was asked to work at Tuskegee Institute by the famous Booker T. Washington in 1896. William Robinson and George Monroe worked for the famous pony express postal service carrying mail between St. Joseph, Missouri, and Sacramento. The riders, including Buffalo Bill Cody and Wild Bill Hickok, had only ten days for the trip.

THE PROSLAVERY POSITION

The whites who believed in the system of slavery used five arguments to defend their position. At first, they argued that Africans were biologically inferior to whites. Governors, state legislators, and even preachers articulated the view that it was necessary to have someone do menial jobs and that blacks were best qualified by biology to perform those services.

Their second argument was that Africans were intellectually inferior to whites and therefore most useful to serve, as Governor Hammond of South Carolina put it, "the mud-sill of society and political government."

Third, they argued, like George S. Sawyer, that Africans were incapable of throwing off "the chains of barbarism and brutality that have long bound down the nations of that race; or to rise above the common cloud of darkness that still broods over them."

A fourth point was that, since Africans were heathens, it was necessary to enslave them to ensure that their souls would be saved and that they would be civilized. Thus, according to this doctrine, permanent enslavement was a good thing for the improvement of Africans.

The fifth point in support of slavery was that it had produced a unique civilization among the whites. The argument was meant to demonstrate that, far from being a bad thing for whites, the slave system was good for whites because they had found time to spend on leisure activities that advanced culture. Each of these arguments was dissected and demolished by the abolitionists. In the end, slavery was shown to be brutal and unjustifiable.

The battle for the hearts and minds of the American people was fierce during the 1840s and 1850s. It did not always remain a battle of words. Many individuals who sought to protect Africans were beaten and killed. Some of the northern whites who wrote editorials in support of abolition and against slavery had their newspaper offices bombed. The Georgia legislature offered $4,000 for the capture of William Lloyd Garrison. Arthur Tappan had $12,000 on his head. Any person found with copies of David Walker's Appeal could be arrested and fined by the authorities.

ABOLITIONISTS

Abolitionists such as Charles Remond, Frederick Douglass, Harriet Tubman, and Sojourner Truth were often joined by white antislavery leaders such as Elijah P. Lovejoy, Wendell Phillips, Lydia Maria Child, John Greenleaf Whittier, and William Lloyd Garrison.

Lovejoy was killed in Alton, Illinois, in 1837 by a white mob who did not like his antislavery articles. Phillips was one of the best orators of his day. He delivered hundreds of speeches against slavery. Whittier, a poet, wrote poems against the injustice and brutality of separating children from parents. "The Farewell" and "The Slave Ships" are two of his best-known works. Lydia Maria Child's *Appeal for That Class of Americans Called Africans* (1833) was the second most important book written against slavery in the United States. David Walker's *Appeal to the Colored Citizens of the World* had appeared in 1829.

Antislavery sentiments stretched from Virginia to Massachusetts and stirred the conscience of many people (figure 6.6). The Quakers had held the first protest in 1789 in Philadelphia's Germantown section (see figure 6.8, page 87). Their spirit spread to other cities. Benjamin Lundy, a Quaker humanitarian who lived in Wheeling, Virginia (now West Virginia), campaigned through his paper "The Genius of Universal Emancipation" for the liberation of the enslaved African. With a similar fervor and unselfishness, William Lloyd Garrison of Boston established *The Liberator* on January 1, 1831, to

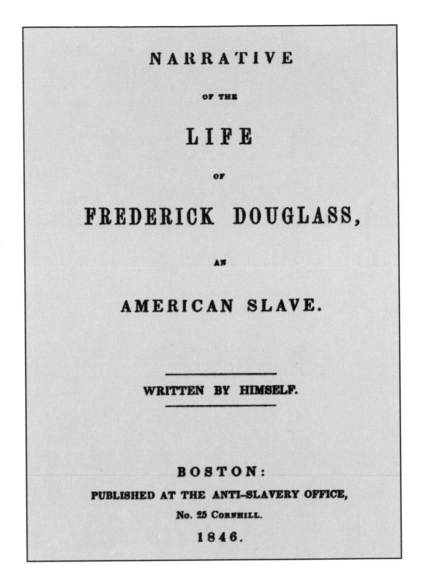

NARRATIVE

OF THE

LIFE

OF

FREDERICK DOUGLASS,

AN

AMERICAN SLAVE.

WRITTEN BY HIMSELF.

BOSTON:
PUBLISHED AT THE ANTI-SLAVERY OFFICE,
No. 25 CORNHILL.
1846.

Figure 6.5 (above). Cover of an autobiography of Frederick Douglass published in 1846 by the Anti-slavery Office located in Boston, Massachusetts.

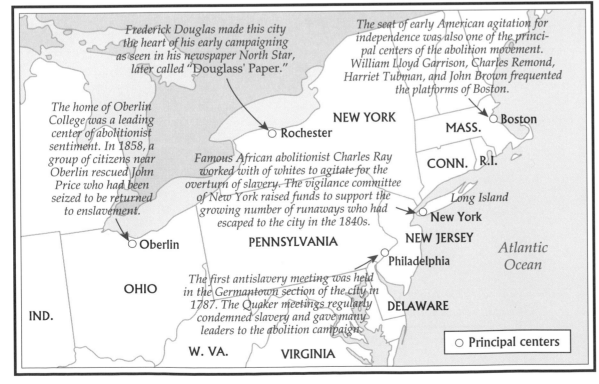

Frederick Douglas made this city the heart of his early campaigning as seen in his newspaper North Star, later called "Douglass' Paper."

The seat of early American agitation for independence was also one of the principal centers of the abolition movement. William Lloyd Garrison, Charles Remond, Harriet Tubman, and John Brown frequented the platforms of Boston.

The home of Oberlin College was a leading center of abolitionist sentiment. In 1858, a group of citizens near Oberlin rescued John Price who had been seized to be returned to enslavement.

Famous African abolitionist Charles Ray worked with of whites to agitate for the overturn of slavery. The vigilance committee of New York raised funds to support the growing number of runaways who had escaped to the city in the 1840s.

The first antislavery meeting was held in the Germantown section of the city in 1787. The Quaker meetings regularly condemned slavery and gave many leaders to the abolition campaign.

NEW YORK
MASS.
CONN. R.I.
Long Island
New York
NEW JERSEY
Atlantic Ocean
Boston
Rochester
Oberlin
PENNSYLVANIA
Philadelphia
OHIO
DELAWARE
IND.
W. VA.
VIRGINIA

○ Principal centers

Figure 6.6. Early antislavery centers of the northeastern United States.

crusade against the evils of slavery. Garrison was one of Lundy's followers and a leader in agitation. Garrison wrote in the first issue of The Liberator: "I will be as harsh as truth and as uncompromising as justice. On this subject I do not wish to think or speak with moderation. . . . I am in earnest—I will not equivocate—I will not excuse—I will not retreat a single inch—and I will be heard."

Denied the right of petition, and refused the use of the U.S. mail by President Andrew Jackson, the abolitionists, African and white, took to the platform with a vengeance. When the New England Antislavery Society was formed in 1832, several Africans were prominent among the organizers. Charles Remond, son of a barber, would become the first popular spokesperson for the African community through his work with the society (see page 79 for text of a Remond speech). One year later in 1833, the American Antislavery Society was formed and counted among its members most of the major African leaders for nearly half a century. It was not dissolved until 1870.

The intensity of the antislavery meetings was such that slavery sympathizers attacked those who supported freedom for Africans. Charles Blockson also tells us in his article "The Underground Railroad," which appeared in the National Geographic in July 1984, that Lucretia Mott, a Quaker minister and leader, drew angry crowds of whites in Norristown, Pennsylvania, when after a major rally against slavery she walked out of the meeting arm in arm with the great Frederick Douglass. Coolheaded members of the African American community protected the antislavery leaders from harm.

Frederick Douglass

Frederick Douglass, born in 1817, lived for ten years as a slave on a Maryland plantation before he was bought by a Baltimore shipbuilder (figure 6.7). Douglass had been in several fights with white overseers during his enslavement and had been severely flogged more than once. In his free time stealing away from his work, Frederick taught himself to read. He escaped to freedom in 1838 and gave himself the name Douglas, adding an extra "s" after a character in the book *The Lady of the Lake*. A precocious young man, he planned his escape with great care.

Douglass lived at first in New Bedford, Connecticut. William Lloyd Garrison gave him some assistance with his education. An avid reader and a fine student of literature, Douglass soon became skilled enough to speak on the abolition of slavery.

In 1841 at an antislavery convention in Nantucket, Massachusetts, Douglass

Figure 6.7. Frederick Douglass (1817–1895). An escaped slave, he became the foremost proponent of the abolitionist movement during the nineteenth century. Credit: The National Archives/Corbis.

spoke with such eloquence and sincerity that he was immediately offered a job as an agent of the Massachusetts Antislavery Society. From that time until the outbreak of the Civil War, Douglass lectured in England and the United States. With £150 raised by his new allies, Douglass purchased his freedom.

His career against every restraint on human beings was noble. He published two newspapers, *The North Star* and *Douglass' Paper*. Both were passionate instruments in the battle against slavery. Later in life he was appointed recorder of deeds in the District of Columbia and then minister to Haiti.

Despite his many personal achievements in government service, editing newspapers and broadsides, public speaking and ceremonial oratory, statescraft and diplomacy, Douglass always felt that the nation never truly understood the deep hurt it had afflicted upon the African people during the enslavement. He was one example of a former slave having accomplished against the odds.

Douglass died in 1895, the year Booker T. Washington made his famous Atlanta compromise speech. He was an

Figure 6.8. Abolitionist rally. Starting with a 1789 Quaker protest in Philadelphia's Germantown section, abolitionist rallies became common place prior to the Civil War. Credit: Gleason's Pictorial Drawing Room Companion/Corbis.

international figure whose work for his own people inspired all people of all races and placed him in a uniquely significant historical position with respect to liberty.

INTENSIFYING THE RESISTANCE

More than 100,000 slaves were lost to the South between 1810 and 1850 through the work of abolitionists and vigilance committees of the North and the determined, heroic efforts of the escaped Africans to remain free (figure 6.8). It is estimated that the total value of the "property" lost topped $30 million and could have been as high as $80 million.

It must be remembered that not all white southerners supported slavery. There was sentiment against it in almost every community, although this opposition rarely expressed itself in unpopular ways. As the South was not solid in its support of slavery, though nearly so, the North was not of a single mind either. In fact, George Whitefield, the famous hellfire evangelist, defended slavery. In Notes on Virginia Thomas Jefferson had voiced the opinion that Africans were by nature inferior to whites. Other southerners took Jefferson's words to support their view of slavery.

The Voice of Charles Lenox Remond

The request which I would make of you is the request of a suffering humanity—the observations which I would direct to you are the observations of justice and truth; and, such being the case, surely there is no Irishman, worthy the name, who will consider that my request is unreasonable, or my observations ill-timed or out of place. The request which I now make, and have often made, is, that those who hear me will forget complexion, and that when the hateful truth is naked to our ears, that slavery exists in America, they will be inclined to consider the subject not as one of color, but of kind—not as one, the merits of which are to be decided by the hue of the skin, but rather one the test whereof should be the nature and character of the being who is enslaved. Enough! he is a man, and so are ye.

The crucial decade of the 1850s brought sectional strife and strain that literally ripped the nation apart before a shot was fired. Lines had been drawn and sides had been taken. Proslavery leaders had become more aggressive in carrying their fight into the territory of the abolitionists. They had stepped up the pursuit of runaway Africans. They sought to strengthen their control over the thought of whites in the South while defending the system of slavery outside. Thus, they murdered whites in Georgia and South Carolina who had committed the crime of "mixing" with Africans. When Amos Dresser went to the South to sell Bibles and got caught by a mob who believed he was stirring up trouble among Africans, he was condemned and then beaten publicly.

The discovery of gold in California and the westward movement of the population meant that the question of slavery in the new territories had to be discussed and decided. What was to be the policy in respect to the state of California? Several options were open to American legislators. They could exclude slavery from the entire area of new territories. They could let the people who populate the areas decide their own future. They could divide the new territories into slave and free. Others insisted that slavery could not be legally excluded from the territories. The antislavery forces began their own offensive. They outspoke and outwrote the South during this period.

The publication of *Uncle Tom's Cabin* in 1852 was a momentous event. Harriet Beecher Stowe's novel sold more than 300,000 copies in the first year. Orations from the book were given in public ceremonies and theaters put on dramatic productions of the work. Never had a book shown to such a wide audience the devastation of enslavement on human beings. Stowe's work detailed the cruelty of the slave owners and overseers in the most brutal form. The book provided a glimpse into the deprivations and pains of Africans under the system of the whip. No longer could the southern plantation owners or their defenders conceal the truth about the horrible institution that was a blight upon the land. Since most whites, even in the South, did not own slaves (although most supported the institution), they had rarely seen it shown in such graphic manner. The dehumanization of Africans by the white slave owners and overseers meant a greater dehumanization of the whites. This one book did more in 1852 to destroy the image of slavery as a necessary evil than all other books and articles combined. The southerners had been dealt a severe blow by *Uncle Tom's Cabin*.

The Compromise of 1850, a temporary solution to the crisis of newly added territories, had left neither the North nor the South satisfied with the national situation over the question of slavery. The compromise had allowed California to enter the nation as a free state; Texas to cede land to New Mexico and be compensated; new territories to be set up without mention of slavery; creation of a tough fugitive slave law; and the prohibition of the slave trade in the District of Columbia.

When Stephen A. Douglas of Illinois introduced the Kansas-Nebraska Act of 1854 to the Senate, it signaled the end of the Compromise of 1850. It called for Kansas and Nebraska to decide the slavery issue themselves. Whigs, Free Soilers, and some Democrats who opposed the act discussed a common strategy that led to the creation of the Republican Party.

THE WOMEN FIGHTERS

When the final epic of the African American people is written, the role of women in the struggle for equality, dignity, and honor will be seen as a centerpiece of the drama. Never content to watch the battles from the sidelines, women have placed themselves in the thick of every contest for human rights ever fought on American soil. Indeed, these women have given the best accounting of themselves one could imagine.

The leadership positions of African American women have often been achieved with great opposition from

Women of History

Sarah Allen, Missionary	1764–1849
Caroline Anderson, Doctor	1849–1919
Janie Barrett, Teacher	1870–1949
Matilda Beasley, Teacher	1834–1903
Ann Becraft, Teacher	1805–1833
Rosa Bowser, Teacher	1885–1931
Sue Brown, Organizer	1877–1941
Mary S. Cary, Abolitionist	1823–1893
Anna J. Cooper, Teacher	1858–1964
Anna Douglass, Abolitionist	?–1882
Susan Frazier, Organizer	1866–1901
Charlotte Grimke, Scholar	1834–1914
Emma Hackley, Artist	1877–1922
Alice D. Nelson, Author	1875–1935
Mary Patterson, Teacher	1840–1894
Mary Peake, Teacher	1823–1862
Frances Preston, Orator	1844–1929
Charlotta Pyles, Abolitionist	1806–1880
Susie Shorter, Writer	1859–1912
Georgia Simpson, Scholar	1866–1944
Amanda Smith, Missionary	1836–1915
May Talbert, Reformer	1866–1923
Susan Vashon, Nurse	1838–1912
Josie Washington, Organizer	1861–1949
Lulu Williams, Reformer	1874–1945

men. Yet the record is clear that the women who have succeeded in establishing themselves in history by virtue of their works have been among the most honored and distinguished African Americans.

Perhaps the greatest African American to have lived is Harriet Tubman. No man or woman has shown any greater commitment to freedom and self-respect, to loyalty and work, to honor and courage, to love and faith than Harriet Tubman.

Tubman was never alone in her hatred of slavery or in her willingness to die for freedom. Open the pages of any book on the African American experience and the names of women leap forward with clarity and definition: Sojourner Truth, Charlotte Forten Grimke, Charity Still, Cornelia Loney, Ann Maria Weems, Leah Green, Frances Hilliard, Maria Jane Houston, Elizabeth Banks, Laura Lewis, Ellen Craft, Mary Ann Shadd Cary, Diana Mills, Mary Cooper, Lydia Ann Johns, and thousands of others who campaigned actively against slavery and oppression by their own individual acts of courage or in preparing the way for others.

Women have contributed to every scene of the African American drama. From the very beginning when the slave ships left the shores of Africa, women demonstrated immense courage in the face of the most brutal and callous rage. When they could no longer take the abuse, some threw their children to the sea; others leaped to the sharks themselves. On board the ships, women led in the comforting of the sick, the care for the dying, and the affection for the parentless. Most of all, they saw visions, gave hope, and dreamed dreams that kept people alive.

Mary Ann Shadd Cary

Mary Ann Shadd Cary was the first black newspaperwoman in the United States. A fierce competitor, believing in her ability and possessing a grand sense of dignity, she became an outstanding educator, writer, lawyer, and antislavery abolitionist. Prior to the Civil War, she appeared on many platforms as a major speaker against the evils of slavery. Her lectures were received warmly because of the logic of her arguments. She was also one of the first women to openly speak up for women suffrage. When the Civil War began, Mary Ann Shadd Cary volunteered as a recruiting officer and held the position of recruiting officer until the end of the war. When she died, she had achieved national recognition for her pioneering efforts as a newspaperperson and campaigner for human rights.

Shadd's example was to inspire a generation of young African American women to become involved in education and information distribution. In fact, of the many women to achieve distinction in this area, Ida B. Wells Barnett and Mary McLeod Bethune became household names.

Mary McLeod Bethune

Mary McLeod Bethune's place in African American history is so monumental that to write of African Americans without her is to leave out a major chapter (figure 6.9). Bethune was born on July 10, 1875, near the small town of Mayesville, South Carolina. Early in life she expressed a desire to be a teacher and spent seven years at the Scotia Seminary in North Carolina. Religion was central to her vision of progress in the African American community. She studied at the Moody Bible Institute in Chicago after leaving North Carolina. She wanted to become a missionary. It was the good fortune of the African American community that her application to the Presbyterian Board of Missions in New York was turned down for an appointment to Africa. When she was unable to secure a post in Africa, she began teaching in the United States.

Figure 6.9. Mary McLeod Bethune (1875–1955). One of the leading figures in the country in the 1930s and the only woman in the unofficial "shadow cabinet" set up by President Franklin Roosevelt. Credit: Corbis-Bettmann.

President Herbert Hoover asked her to come to Washington to attend the White House Conference on Child Health and Protection in 1930. President Franklin Roosevelt asked her to serve on the advisory board of the National Youth Administration (NYA). She was so successful at establishing the foundation of the NYA that President Roosevelt called upon her to set up an Office of Minority Affairs. This was the first time that an African American woman had been granted such a post. Her title was changed to director of the Division of Negro Affairs.

Mary McLeod Bethune was one of the leading figures in the country in the 1930s and the only woman in the unofficial "shadow cabinet" set up by President Franklin Roosevelt. Always devoted to education, Mrs. Bethune founded her own school, the Daytona Educational and Industrial School for Negro Girls, in 1904. In 1926 she oversaw its merger with the Cookman Institute, giving birth to the Bethune-Cookman Institute.

Mary McLeod Bethune died in 1955 at the age of eighty. She had been drawn to the plight of the children of African American builders of the railroads in Florida in 1904. After her death the children of those children contributed a monument to her memory. It was the first monument to an African American or a woman ever built on public lands in the United States. In her life and death, Bethune left a legacy of hope, challenge, faith, and racial dignity.

Sojourner Truth

Sojourner Truth was born about 1798 in Ulster County, New York, to parents who were enslaved (see figure 6.10, page 91). Her childhood experience living in the cold, wet cellar of the home of the family to which she and her parents belonged left indelible impressions on her. She would later recount how her mother taught her the Lord's Prayer and trust in God.

In 1827 New York granted legal emancipation to enslaved Africans, but

Sojourner's owner refused to release her. She escaped but was caught and would have been returned had not a friend agreed to pay for her services for the remainder of the year.

When she decided to leave New York to lecture, she told a friend that her name was no longer Isabella but Sojourner. She lectured everywhere she found people (figure 6.11). Her wit and originality made her a very popular speaker. Sojourner also had the gift of song, and though she had little schooling, she commanded the attention of her audience by the force of her logic and the eloquence of her cadence. As to her name she said, "And the Lord gave me Sojourner because I was to travel up and down the land showing the people their sins and being a sign unto them. Afterwards I told the Lord I wanted another name, 'cause everybody else has two names, and the Lord gave me Truth because I was to declare the truth to the people."

What attracted audiences to Sojourner Truth's lectures was her unassailable honesty, humor, and spirituality. Every speech that she gave resonated

Figure 6.10. Sojourner Truth (1797–1883). Born Isabella Baumfree, she became a preacher and abolitionist as she spread "the truth" across the nation.

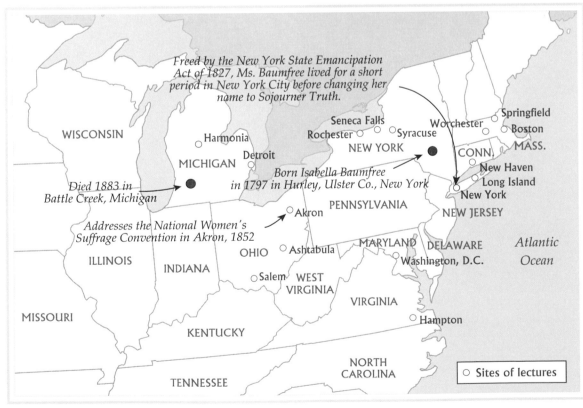

Figure 6.11. The life, travels, and lectures of Sojourner Truth.

with a deep sincerity that reminded listeners of her suffering while demonstrating the strength of character that made her the most sought after female abolitionist of her time. She campaigned for freedom for the enslaved African and when freedom came in 1865 she was 67 years old. Truth fought for women's rights believing that the rights of Africans and the rights of women were natural and God given. Thus, her legacy, written in the hearts of men and women who loved liberty, is one of unfailing struggle against all forms of oppression.

Sojourner Truth was buried in 1883 at the Oak Hill Cemetery in Battle Creek, Michigan, where she settled after the Civil War. She was eighty-five.

Mary Church Terrell

The life of Mary Church Terrell spanned an entire history of struggle. Born in 1863, the year of the Emancipation Proclamation, Terrell died in 1954, the year of the Brown *v.* Board of Education of Topeka, Kansas, decision.

She was born in Memphis, Tennessee, but traveled throughout the world as an activist for African and women's rights. She graduated from Oberlin College and

Figure 6.12. Madame C. J. Walker (1867–1919). Promoted beauty among people of color throughout the world with her own international beauty care business, which especially helped African Americans to project themselves positively.

moved to Washington, D.C., where she was appointed to the school board in 1895. A year later, she became one of the founding members of the National Association of Colored Women.

From the various positions and platforms she occupied, she spoke out fervently against every form of discrimination and segregation. The laws in Washington made segregation legal until 1953. Mary Church Terrell led the campaign to integrate public facilities in the nation's capital. When the Supreme Court finally ruled that public accommodations had to be desegregated in Washington, it was a victory for the many years of battle in which Mrs. Terrell had been engaged. Although Mary Church Terrell had been born of parents who had been enslaved, she never once believed that anyone could enslave her. She was a giant among giants.

Madame C. J. Walker

Born Sarah McWilliams in 1869 in the small town of Delta, Louisiana, the person who was to become the wealthiest woman of her race was orphaned at seven (figure 6.12). She was married at fourteen and widowed at twenty.

She traveled upriver to St. Louis in order to begin life anew and make something out of herself. She secured a job in a laundry and worked to send her daughter to school. Soon after she arrived in St. Louis, she met and married Charles J. Walker. Using his initials, she became Madame C. J. Walker.

It was not long before her various formulas for beauty care began circulating in the African American community. Her innovations in hairstyling made her the virtual leader of African American hair fashions. By 1910, when she had moved to Indianapolis, she had developed an entire line of toiletries and cosmetics for the body and face. With the tremendous surge in African American interest in beauty and fashion, due to the newly gained freedom to decide their own beauty styles, Madame C. J. Walker soon set up Walker beauty parlors across the nation. The results of this activity made her a millionaire. Before her death in 1919 she had become well known for her philanthropy to African American institutions. Her gifts to the National Association for the Advancement of Colored People, the Young Men's Christian Association of St. Louis, Tuskegee Institute, and Mary McLeod Bethune's original school for girls were significant and instructional. Her will required that two-thirds of the profits of her company should be distributed to organizations that worked to improve the welfare of the community.

Rosa Parks

The name Rosa Parks is inextricably connected to the Civil Rights Movement. She gave no resounding speeches, led no massive demonstrations against the citadels of segregation, wrote no petitions, and argued no particular points of law. What she did was simple and electrifying (figure 6.13).

On December 1, 1955, Rosa Parks took a ride on a public bus in Montgomery, Alabama, that was to land her in history as one of the most inspirational leaders of all time. She had entered the bus on her way home just as other passengers had crowded onto the bus. When the bus was filled to capacity, the white bus driver looked back and saw that Rosa Parks was seated in the "white" section of the bus while a white man was standing. As he had probably done many times without incident, the bus driver ordered Mrs. Parks to the rear of the bus. As far as he was concerned, she was breaking the law by sitting where only whites were allowed to sit.

Rosa Parks refused to move and allow the white man to take her seat. Her feet were tired and her soul said she should not move. She remained in her seat. The bus driver was annoyed. He stopped the bus and called the police. They came and arrested Rosa Parks for refusing to give up her seat. She was jailed and brought to trial. This incident caused the entire African American community to rise up as it had never done in any city. No black person rode the Montgomery buses. The boycott that was to be felt around the world was now on. Rosa Parks's courage and fortitude had sparked a movement. The names of the players would rewrite the history of America because of her action. Martin Luther King Jr. and attorney Fred Gray, two young, recent college graduates from northern schools, would join Rosa Parks in the noble cause.

Harriet Tubman

Harriet Tubman, fighter, comforter, confidante, nurse, and hero is without comparison in word or deed (see figure 6.14, page 94).

Harriet Tubman's name is synonymous with the famed escape route called the Underground Railroad. Born in 1820 in Dorchester County, Maryland, she succeeded in escaping from slavery in 1848. Her life as a slave had been difficult, filled with hard work, severe punishment, harassment, verbal abuse, and little joy. Harriet left two brothers and her husband, John Tubman. He had taken money she had saved to purchase her freedom and then had threatened to report her escape attempt to her owner.

Tubman's freedom placed a heavy burden on her because she believed it

Figure 6.13. Rosa Parks was a simple citizen of Montgomery, Alabama, who change the course of African American history by refusing to leave the white seating section of a public bus. Credit: UPI/Corbis-Bettmann.

was necessary to assist others in their escape attempts. Nineteen times between 1849 and 1859 she went south of the Mason-Dixon line to bring Africans to the North. Slaveholders offered $40,000 for her capture. Never captured, Harriet Tubman became one of the leading spirits of the abolition movement. Her hatred of slavery had led her to recruit soldiers for John Brown's raid on Harpers Ferry. Tubman thought of John Brown as a more important emancipator than President Lincoln. During the Civil War she joined the Union Army as a nurse, spy, and scout, applying much of her knowledge of people, places, and terrain.

Two years after the war John Tubman died, and in 1869 Harriet Tubman married Nelson Davis, a Civil War veteran. The remainder of her life was spent in poverty. Although Sarah Bradford wrote and published Tubman's biography and Tubman was able to use some of the money to ease her financial burden, the

Figure 6.14. Harriet Tubman (1820–1913). A freed slave who organized the Underground Railroad, a system for helping Southern slaves escape to the North. Credit: Library of Congress/Corbis.

government did not give her a pension until thirty years after the war. She was awarded $20 per month as a pension. With this money Harriet Tubman ran the Harriet Tubman Home in Auburn, New York, where she died in March 1913.

THE UNDERGROUND RAILROAD

The Underground Railroad is the name given to the various means by which some northerners, black and white, assisted fugitives in finding safe places (see figure 6.15, page 95). Benjamin Brawley says that by the underground system "thousands of people were enabled to get to Canada." The most favored routes were through Ohio and Pennsylvania since the Quaker influence in these two states was very strong and the Quakers had shown an early moral inclination to assist enslaved Africans in escaping bondage.

While various "stations" were established to aid fugitives, the great majority of Africans used their own ingenuity to find their way to safety. This is so despite the fact that Harriet Tubman made nineteen trips to the South to "steal away" 300 enslaved Africans, or the fact that Levi Coffin received nearly 100 slaves per year at his house, or the fact that Thomas Garrett is said to have assisted 2,700 slaves in their search for freedom.

The truth is that the South was without sharp boundaries and in places it was an open sieve where thousands of runaways crossed over and made it to the North. The Mason-Dixon line became the standard boundary between slaveholding and relatively free states. It was in actuality the boundary between Pennsylvania and Maryland that had been drawn by two English surveyors in 1763–1767 to settle a dispute between the Penn and Baltimore families. However, the actual boundary between the slave and free states also followed the Ohio River to the Mississippi and with the exception of Missouri, the 36"30' boundary established by the Missouri Compromise of 1820.

Most Africans who found their way north to freedom did so on the basis of their own intelligence and wit. They were

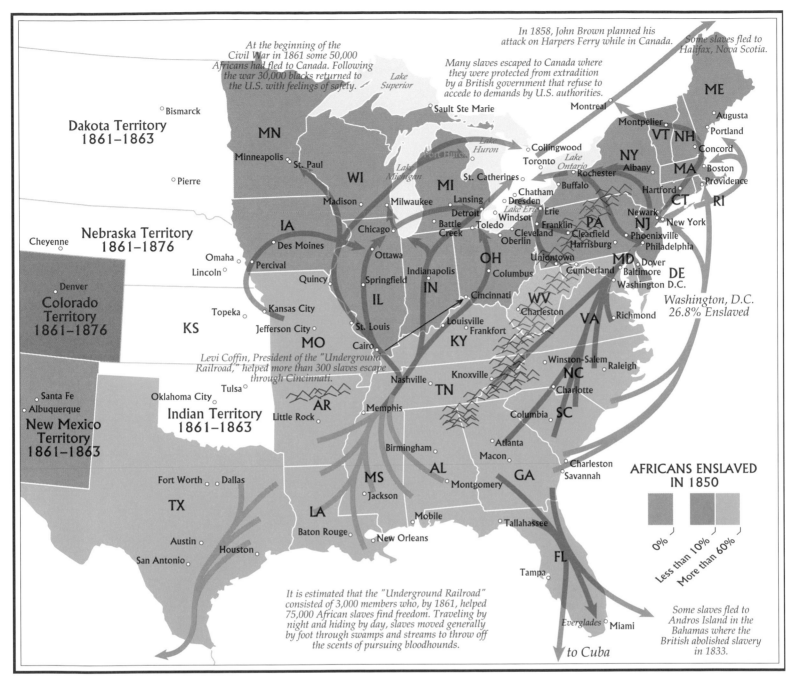

Figure 6.15. Passage to freedom: the Underground Railroad.

not given maps, food, clothing, or friendship. Thousands of these lone and unknown individuals, tired of slavery, organized their own liberation in spite of close supervision by plantation overseers. These unsung heroines and heroes of liberty constituted the largest number of escaping slaves.

Slave escapes have been romanticized because of the famous series of safe houses and way stations that constituted the Underground Railroad. Harriet Tubman was the most knowledgeable conductor on the Underground Railroad. Known for her directness, courage, and leadership, she once pointed a gun at an African reluctant to follow her to freedom and said, "Before I'd see you a slave I'll see you dead and buried in your grave." The man followed her.

Harrowing escapes and daring disguises made for inspiring testimonies. In quaint shanty communities, when the day's work was completed, Africans often gathered to tell the stories of how someone had learned that someone else had "overcome" slavery and eluded the slaveowners.

There was no more revolutionary act a slave could make than taking herself or himself out of the economic system. It meant that the slaveowner was deprived of labor and property, neither of which the African believed the whites rightly owned. Escape routes, though often improvised by virtue of many individual efforts, became indelibly engraved in African history as they were constantly retold when people reached freedom.

William Still's great book *The Underground Railroad* did as much as the actual exploits of the escaped Africans to impress the idea of the Underground Railroad in the minds of the American people. The book was first published in 1872 and was an account of facts, authentic narratives, letters, and other reports of hardships, hairbreadth escapes, and death struggles of the slaves in their efforts for freedom from the horrible bondage.

William Still was for many years one of the principal people connected to the vigilance committee in Philadelphia. He was chairman of the Philadelphia Branch of the Underground Railroad. In that capacity he was personally involved with the attempts of many people to escape and to change their identities. The anti-slavery meeting in Philadelphia asked him in resolution form to record his reminiscences and the experiences he had relating to the Underground Railroad. Still wrote his book in response to that direct request from the society.

In January 1872 he wrote that his book included interesting narratives of the escapes of "many men, women and children, from the prison-house of bondage; from cities and plantations; from rice swamps and cotton fields; from kitchens and mechanic shops; from border States and Gulf States; from cruel masters and mild masters; some guided by the north star alone, penniless, braving the perils of land and sea, eluding the keen scent of the blood-hound as well as the more dangerous pursuit of the savage slavehunter; some from secluded dens and caves of the earth, where for months and years they had been hidden away waiting for the chance to escape; from mountains and swamps, where indescribable suffering from hunger and other privations had patiently been endured."

The escaping African used every bit of ingenuity at his or her disposal. Despite the limited knowledge they often had of the world, they created a system of escape mechanisms that were used by others familiar with the circumstances of slavery. In instances where the enslaved African had responsibility for shipping, they would often box themselves and ship themselves. Whatever was useful for escaping enslavement was used.

According to historian and curator Charles L. Blockson, most Africans hated enslavement and used every means to escape. He tells the story of William and Ellen Craft of Macon, Georgia, who escaped in 1848. The clever William asked his wife, Ellen, who was of a light complexion, to dress as a man with a well-cut suit and a top hat, and he would be her faithful servant. Blockson says that they contrived a broken arm to conceal her inability to write and a bandage for a toothache to conceal her beardlessness. In this manner the couple traveled in sleeping-car quarters to Philadelphia.

Figure 6.16. Dred Scott (1795–1858). Born a slave in Virginia, his owner took him to Missouri, a free state, where Scott argued that he should therefore be freed. This gave rise to the infamous Scott *v.* Sanford case where the Supreme Court ruled that slaves are not regarded as U.S. citizens.

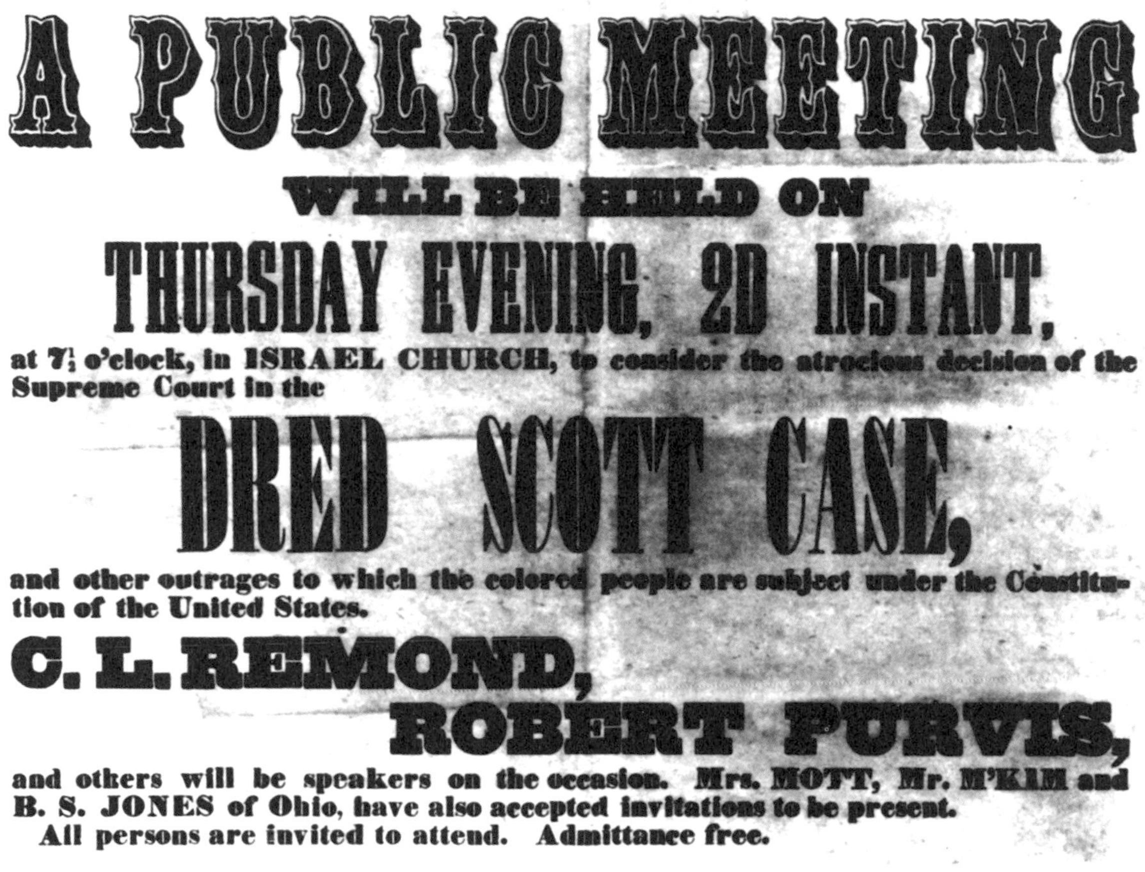

A PUBLIC MEETING

WILL BE HELD ON

THURSDAY EVENING, 2D INSTANT,

at 7½ o'clock, in ISRAEL CHURCH, to consider the atrocious decision of the Supreme Court in the

DRED SCOTT CASE,

and other outrages to which the colored people are subject under the Constitution of the United States.

C. L. REMOND,
ROBERT PURVIS,

and others will be speakers on the occasion. Mrs. MOTT, Mr. M'KIM and B. S. JONES of Ohio, have also accepted invitations to be present.

All persons are invited to attend. Admittance free.

Figure 6.17. Poster announcing a public meeting decrying the Supreme Court decision regarding Dred Scott.

DRED SCOTT

In 1834 a white army officer by the name of Emerson stationed in Missouri decided to move to Illinois. He took with him an enslaved African, Dred Scott (figure 6.16, page 96). Two years later, he moved to Minnesota, again taking Dred Scott with him. In 1838, the white man moved back to Missouri with Dred Scott.

By this time Scott began to raise questions about the legality of his situation. Slavery was illegal in Illinois and Minnesota was a free territory. Scott wanted to know if his residence outside of a slave state made him a free person. Abused and attacked by his owner in 1848, Scott, with the assistance of anti-slavery lawyers, brought a suit against his owner for assault and battery. The circuit court of St. Louis ruled in Scott's favor. The ruling was appealed by Emerson to the state's Supreme Court, which reversed the lower court's decision. In the meantime, Emerson sold Scott to a New York citizen named Sandford. Determined and courageous,

Dred Scott brought suit against Sandford on the grounds that they were citizens of different states. The case reached the U.S. Supreme Court, where a decision was made in 1857 that had far-reaching implications. Essentially, the Supreme Court ruled that Scott was not a citizen of Missouri, or any state, and that as a slave he was only property and that his owner could take property to any place within the jurisdiction of the United States. Ownership of Scott and his family soon passed to a Massachusetts family, and he was liberated.

Freedom's road was often long and arduous for enslaved Africans. Many gained the courage to risk their lives and their loved ones lives to seek freedom. While thousands made it to the "other side of Jordan," others were captured by slave catchers, betrayed by acquaintances, killed by robbers, and captured and reenslaved by whites other than their former masters. Enough Africans were successful, however, to etch this as a heroic period in world history.

"My Lord Gwineter to Rain Down Fire"

7

THE CIVIL WAR

At the beginning of the Civil War the United States was in the midst of a long, uneasy terror caused by the spirit of the slave system. Sapped of much of its moral and spiritual power, the nation increasingly found itself conflicted in its domestic politics.

Africans had spread to every part of the American nation, as free and as slave, by the 1850s. There were Africans in California, some traveling through the treacherous waters of Cape Horn to reach the West Coast, others traveling on land with whites. The South was preeminently the home of the African population by 1860. North Carolina, Georgia, Virginia, South Carolina, and Alabama accounted for more than 75 percent of the total black population.

The southern investment in slaves contrasted with the rising northern investment in machinery; the South tend-

ed toward labor-intensive agriculture and the North became increasingly industrialized. The differential in development meant a widening of the gap between the treatment of Africans in the South and those in the North. Southern blacks experienced the most brutal slavery between 1830 and 1860. This was the period of ultimate terror. It was as if white slave-owners, patterollers, and overseers dreamed of the most horrible means of extracting labor and then used Africans to test their theories of how long a human could live being driven to work harder and harder under the threat of punishment even unto death. Many died. Those who lived blessed the night and dreaded the morning.

As the slave system in the South tightened its reins on the African population, the northern states, because of the needs of industry, gave free blacks more

Figure 7.1. The United States in 1861: states prior to the Civil War.

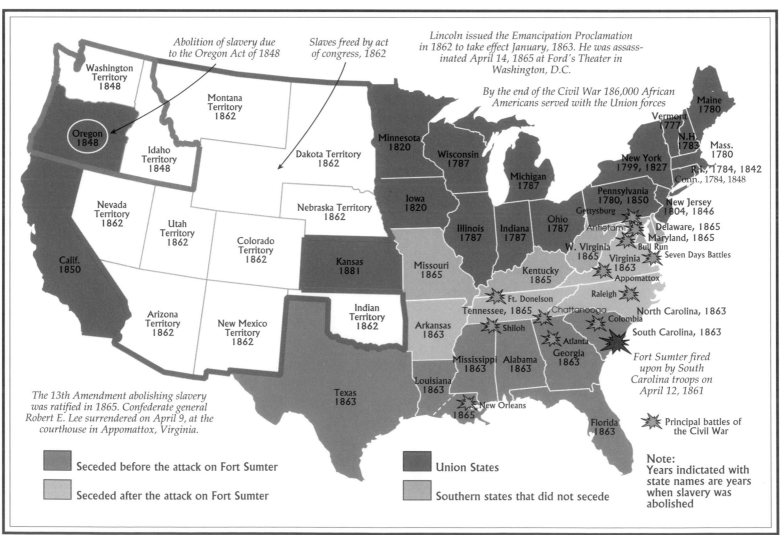

liberties. By 1860, most northern states had discontinued slavery and more and more Africans were being incorporated into the labor force of the industrial revolution.

The testimony of the enslaved people themselves is most chilling. The case of Nancy, a daughter of Cordelia Loney, shows the extent of human suffering and humiliation that was experienced. Cordelia had seen several of her children sold from her without ever once being told that they would be sold. When her mistress got it in her head that she would work Nancy (who had been in ill health since birth) to death, Cordelia knew that she was powerless to help her daughter. The overseer and his wife had tried to convince the mistress of Nancy's ill health. The mistress would not hear of it. She told the overseer in a fit of anger one day to "whip her every day, and make her work or kill her."

When a nephew of the mistress visited the plantation, Nancy was sold to him and taken to New Orleans. Her mother, Cordelia, upon escaping to freedom, said that when she learned that her sick child had been sold, she felt wretched. But she said, "I was not at liberty to make my grief known to a single white soul. I wept and couldn't help it." The stain upon the nation's soul called for cleansing.

The Civil War, the most devastating war ever fought on American soil and the most deadly in terms of individuals killed, was like a giant cleansing of the land. Those who opposed slavery, black and white, joined against it for their own reasons and ushered in a new history without the enslaved.

AFRICANS IN THE CIVIL WAR

Africans participated on both sides of the Civil War, but it was the overwhelming support that the soldiers gave the Union army that helped turn the war in support of the North (see figure 7.3, page 102). The population of the Confederacy in 1861, at the beginning of the Civil War, was only 5,220,000 whites and nearly 4 million Africans. By contrast, the Union states had a population of 22,000,000, and

Figure 7.2. Christian Fleetwood (1840–1914). Civil War Medal of Honor winner for heroism on the battlefield at Chaffin's Farm, September 29, 1863, at the age of 23.

the border states of Maryland, Delaware, Kentucky, and Missouri held 430,000 enslaved Africans, included in the Union numbers. The secessionist states, the Confederacy, mustered in 800,000 soldiers, approximately 15 percent of its white population, compared with the Union's ability to field 1,600,000, about 7 percent of its white population of 21,570,000.

It is generally accepted that the Confederacy was able to fight as long as it did because of the African rear guard who took care of the factories, the loading docks, the farms, and the fortifications and battery emplacements. Africans were pressed into service in the Confederacy as cooks, servants, and medics. Of course, many Africans took the crisis of the Civil War as an opportunity to run away to the Union side. At first the Union army refused to accept runaways into Union camps, not recognizing that the African laborers were in fact making it possible for the Confederacy to continue their struggle. President Lincoln had made it clear to all who consulted him that the war was not being fought to free slaves but to preserve the Union. Thus, Union soldiers

Figure 7.3 (above right). African soldiers serving in the Civil War by state.

Table 7.1 African soldiers serving in the Civil War by state.

Alabama	2,969
Arkansas	5,526
Colorado Territory	95
Connecticut	1,765
Delaware	954
District of Columbia	3,269
Florida	1,044
Georgia	3,486
Illinois	1,811
Indiana	1,537
Iowa	440
Kansas	2,080
Kentucky	23,703
Louisiana	24,052
Maine	104
Maryland	8,718
Massachusetts	3,966
Michigan	1,387
Minnesota	104
Mississippi	17,896
Missouri	440
New Hampshire	125
New Jersey	1,185
New York	4,125
North Carolina	5,035
Ohio	5,092
Pennsylvania	8,612
Rhode Island	1,837
South Carolina	5,462
Tennessee	20,133
Texas	47
Vermont	120
Virginia	5,723
West Virginia	196
Wisconsin	104
Not accounted for by state	5,896
Total	169,038
Casualties	68,179

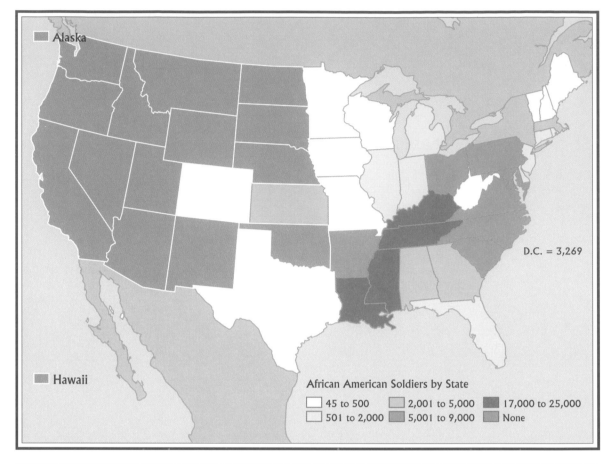

Alaska

Hawaii

D.C. = 3,269

African American Soldiers by State

45 to 500	2,001 to 5,000	17,000 to 25,000
501 to 2,000	5,001 to 9,000	None

Figure 7.4. African American troops to the rescue. Credit: Corbis-Bettmann.

were forbidden to accept runaways into their ranks. Many Africans were returned to their slave plantations under armed guards of the Union army. However, most runaways were returned under flags of truce when Confederate soldiers would come into the Union camps looking for Africans. Union generals gladly surrendered any African that was claimed by the southerners.

Soon the Union army realized that by sending Africans back to the Confederacy they were prolonging the war by giving the South the support it needed for production and maintenance. Furthermore, they understood that if the Union army kept the Africans, many of whom had come to fight against the Confederacy, they could use them in support of their side. A precedent was set on May 24, 1861, by General Benjamin E. Butler of Virginia when he refused to return three runaways to their owner, a Confederate officer. In fact, Butler's reasoning became the accepted logic and law of the Union. He reasoned that since the runaways were possessions of the enemy who represented a foreign government, as articles of war they had to be confiscated once they came under the control of the Union army.

Butler called the Africans who had escaped slavery and been confiscated by the Union army "contraband." On August 6, 1861, the Congress of the United States passed the first Confiscation Act, which allowed the Union army to confiscate the slaves of those owners who were at war with the Union. Not content to watch the war from afar, thousands of Africans flooded the Union camps to fight against the Confederacy and decide their own destiny.

The Pulitzer Prize-winning playwright Charles Fuller has dedicated an entire dramatic series entitled *We* to this important historical situation in the African American experience. The new situation—Africans prepared to die for their freedom—meant a new response from the North. The new attitude on the part of African soldiers also meant that they wanted to be treated fairly in terms

of wages. The situation was to cause the Union army to act with caution regarding the black troops.

The Union army did not respond immediately to the flood of African sentiment about fighting against the Confederacy. Rather, at first, Africans were used in much the same way as they had been used in the Confederate army. Nevertheless, the clamor to engage the enemy increased among Africans, particularly in the North. In Pittsburgh, Philadelphia, Cincinnati, Detroit, Washington, New York, and Boston, Africans rented halls and practiced war drills; some even volunteered to pay their expenses to fight against the South. Artisans of every occupation in the African American community petitioned the government for enlistment. The official policy of the Department of War was that "the Secretary of War has no intention of using colored soldiers." Lincoln's administration wanted to keep the war, as much as possible, "a white man's war" with no reference to Africans. The public knew that this could not be done, and prominent Africans such as John Rock and Frederick Douglass increasingly forced the issue. Eventually, northern sentiment was that it wanted a victory and the recruitment of Africans to the Union army was finally recognized as a key to that victory. Recruitment posters went up in all of the major cities of the North. Philadelphia, Boston, New York, and Rochester were particularly involved in recruitment drives (see figure 7.5, page 104). Both women and men recruiters from the ranks of the abolitionists encouraged Africans to strike their blow for liberty.

In early 1861, the Louisiana Native Guards had been organized as the first regiment formed by free Africans. This regiment had sided with the Confederacy and marched with the state militia in a parade in New Orleans on November 23, 1861. A principal reason free Africans in New Orleans formed their own regiment was to avoid being forced into the Confederacy ranks as common laborers and servants. Others, of course, had a

Figure 7.5. A poster calling colored men to arms.

MEN OF COLOR, TO ARMS! NOW OR NEVER!

This is our Golden Moment. The Government of the United States calls for every Able-Bodied Colored Man to enter the Army for the THREE YEARS' SERVICE, and join in fighting the Battles of Liberty and the Union. A new era is open to us. For generations we have suffered under the horrors of slavery, outrage and wrong; our manhood has been denied, our citizenship blotted out, our souls seared and burned, our spirits cowed and crushed, and the hopes of the future of our race involved in doubts and darkness. But now the whole aspect of our relations to the white race is changed. Now therefore is our most precious moment. Let us Rush to Arms! **Fail Now and Our Race is Doomed** on this the soil of our birth. We must now awake, arise, or be forever fallen. If we value Liberty, if we wish to be free in this land, if we love our country, if we love our families, our children, our homes, we must strike NOW while the Country calls: must rise up in the dignity of our manhood, and show by our own right arms that we are worthy to be freemen. Our enemies have made the country believe that we are craven cowards, without soul, without manhood, without the spirit of soldiers. Shall we die with this stigma resting on our graves? Shall we leave this inheritance of shame to our children? No! A thousand times No! **We WILL Rise!** The alternative is upon us; let us rather die freemen than live to be slaves. What is life without liberty? We say that we have manhood—now is the time to prove it. A nation or a people that cannot fight may be pitied, but cannot be respected. If we would be regarded *Men*, if we would forever **SILENCE THE TONGUE OF CALUMNY**, of prejudice and hate; let us rise NOW and fly to arms! We have seen what Valor and Heroism our brothers displayed at **PORT HUDSON** and at **MILLIKEN'S BEND**; though they are just from the galling, poisoning grasp of slavery, they have startled the world by the most exalted heroism. If they have proved themselves heroes, can not we prove ourselves men? **ARE FREEMEN LESS BRAVE THAN SLAVES?** More than a Million White Men have left Comfortable Homes and joined the Armies of the Union to save their Country; cannot we leave ours, and swell the hosts of the Union, to save our liberties, vindicate our manhood, and deserve well of our Country?

MEN OF COLOR! All Races of Men—the Englishman, the Irishman, the Frenchman, the German, the American, have been called to assert their claim to freedom and a manly character, by an appeal to the sword. The day that has seen an enslaved race in arms, has, in all history, seen their last trial. We can now see that **OUR LAST OPPORTUNITY HAS COME!** If we are not lower in the scale of humanity than Englishmen, Irishmen, white Americans and other races, we can show it now.

MEN OF COLOR! BROTHERS and FATHERS! WE APPEAL TO YOU! By all your concern for yourselves and your liberties, by all your regard for God and Humanity, by all your desire for Citizenship and Equality before the law, by all your love for the Country, to stop at no subterfuges, listen to nothing that shall deter you from rallying for the Army. Come forward, and at once Enroll your Names for the **Three Years' Service.** **STRIKE NOW**, and you are henceforth and forever **FREEMEN!**

stake in the Confederacy itself as slave-owning blacks. As for these southern regiments actually firing a shot, there is no established evidence that they were ever called upon to fight against the Union. In fact, as soon as the Union army gained control over New Orleans, the regiment switched sides and gave its services to the Union.

On the Union side, more than 185,000 Africans eventually fought in the war, setting high marks for valor, courage, and tenacity. Their casualty rate was nearly 37 percent due to the Confederacy's policies of not taking African prisoners. Those who were captured were almost always killed. While the white northerners may have seen the Civil War as a dispute about the integrity of the Union, Africans saw it as their chance to even scores, to liberate themselves, and to prove once and for all that they were prepared to take up arms to defend themselves against those who had exploited their persons and minds. The high casualty rate among African American soldiers was deliberate on the part of the southerners but it also suggested that the northern army used the African troops as vanguard or point troops in dangerous situations.

Opposition to Africans serving in the Union army had created a strong reaction in the African American community.

Table 7.2. Some of the significant Civil War battles engaged in by African regiments.

1. Amite River
2. Appomattox Court House
3. Arkansas River
4. Ash Bayou
5. Ashepoo River
6. Ashwood Landing
7. Athens
8. Barrancas
9. Bayou Bidell
10. Bayou Boeuf
11. Bayou Macon
12. Bayou St. Lewis
13. Bayou Tensas
14. Bayou Tunica
15. Bermuda Hundreds
16. Berwick
17. Big Creek
18. Big River
19. Big Springs
20. Black Creek
21. Black River
22. Boggs' Mill
23. Boyd's Station
24. Boykin's Mills
25. Bradford Spring
26. Brawley Fork
27. Brice's Cross Roads
28. Brigsen Creek
29. Brush Creek
30. Bryant's Plantation
31. Cabin Creek
32. Cabin Point
33. Camden
34. Cedar Keys
35. Chaffin's Farm
36. Charleston
37. Chattanooga
38. City Point
39. Claresville
40. Clinton
41. Coleman's Plantation
42. Columbia
43. Concordia Bayou
44. Cow Creek
45. Cox's Bridge
46. Dallas
47. Dalton
48. Darbytown Road
49. David's Bend
50. Decatur
51. Deep Bottom

52. Deveraux Neck
53. Drewry's Bluff
54. Dutch Gap
55. East Pascagoula
56. Eastport
57. Fair Oaks
58. Federal Point
59. Fillmore
60. Floyd
61. Fort Adams
62. Fort Anderson
63. Fort Blakely
64. Fort Brady
65. Fort Burnham
66. Fort Donelson
67. Fort Gaines
68. Fort Gibson
69. Fort Jones
70. Fort Pillow
71. Fort Pocahontas
72. Fort Smith
73. Fort Taylor
74. Fort Wagner
75. Franklin
76. Ghent
77. Glasgow
78. Goodrich's Landing
79. Grand Gulf
80. Gregory's Farm
81. Haines' Bluff
82. Hall Island
83. Harrodsburg
84. Hatcher's Run
85. Helena
86. Henderson
87. Holly Springs
88. Honey Hill
89. Hopkinsville
90. Horsehead Creek
91. Indian Bay
92. Indian Town
93. Indian Village
94. Island Mound
95. Island No. 76
96. Issequena County
97. Jackson
98. Jacksonville
99. James Island
100. Jenkin's Ferry
101. John's Island
102. Johnsonville
103. Jones' Bridge

104. Joy's Ford
105. Lake Providence
106. Laurence
107. Little Rock
108. Liverpool Heights
109. Madison Station
110. Magnolia
111. Marengo
112. Mariana
113. Marion
114. Marion County
115. Mckay's Point
116. Meffleton Lodge
117. Memphis
118. Milliken's Bend
119. Milltown Bluff
120. Mitchell's Creek
121. Morganzia
122. Moscow Station
123. Mound Plantation
124. Mound Pleasant Landing
125. Mud Creek
126. Murfreesboro
127. Nashville
128. Natchez
129. Natural Bridge
130. New Kent Court House
131. New Market Heights
132. Olustee
133. Owensboro
134. Palmetto Ranch
135. Pass Manchal
136. Petersburg
137. Pierson's Farm
138. Pine Barren Creek
139. Pine Barren Ford
140. Pine Bluff
141. Plymouth
142. Point Lookout
143. Point of Rocks
144. Point Pleasant
145. Poison Springs
146. Port Hudson
147. Powhatan
148. Prairie d'Anne
149. Pulaski
150. Raleigh
151. Rector's Farm
152. Richland
153. Ripley
154. Roache's Plantation
155. Rolling Fork

156. Rooseville Creek
157. Ross Landing
158. Sabine River
159. Salkehatchie
160. Saltville
161. Sand Mountain
162. Sandy Swamp
163. Scottsboro
164. Sherwood
165. Shipwith's Landing
166. Simpsonville
167. Smithfield
168. South Tunnel
169. Spanish Fort
170. St. John's River
171. St. Stephens
172. Steamer Alliance
173. Steamer Chippewa
174. Steamer City Belle
175. Steamer Louts
176. Suffolk
177. Sugar Loaf Hill
178. Sulpher Branch
179. Swift Creek
180. Taylorsville
181. Timber Hill
182. Town Creek
183. Township
184. Trestle
185. Tupelo
186. Vicksburg
187. Vidalia
188. Wallace Ferry
189. Warsaw
190. Waterford
191. Waterloo
192. Waterproof
193. White Oak Road
194. White River
195. Williamsburg
196. Wilmington
197. Wilson's Landing Wharf
198. Yazoo City
199. Yazoo Expedition

Joined by their white allies from the abolition movement, Africans petitioned to be able to fight in the war. Considerable agitation existed in the urban communities of the North for arming Africans. After all, the struggle was about the future of the African in the United States despite the rhetoric about keeping the Union one. William Lloyd Garrison and Wendell Phillips believed that the government was acting in a cruel and unnatural manner by denying Africans the right to demonstrate how much they wanted freedom. Furthermore, northern blacks should have the opportunity to show their southern and enslaved brothers and sisters how much they were willing to give for liberty.

The arguments against Africans fighting came not only from the Lincoln administration, but from several sources. Many white soldiers did not want to see Africans fighting in the war. They reasoned that the Union uniform should be reserved for those whose claim to citizenship was unquestioned. Some even went so far as to voice their opinion that the war was "a white man's war." The president feared that citizens in the border states would object to the arming of Africans to fight whites. He also believed that this action would erode his support in the North. President Lincoln felt that the sentiment against the African in the North, while different from that in the South, would be against arming blacks with Union weapons. It was not until the spring of 1862 that Lincoln, under pressure from the military leaders who had begun to fear that the southerners were growing stronger, agreed to arm Africans.

ROBERT SMALLS

Robert Smalls was born in Beaufort, South Carolina, on April 5, 1839 (see figure 7.6, page 106). Like all enslaved Africans, he was prevented from doing the things he dreamed of doing. He could not gain an education without breaking the law of South Carolina. Others could not teach him how to read or write without breaking the law.

In 1851, Robert Smalls was sent to Charleston and began work as an outfitter for ships. This job allowed Smalls to become very familiar with ships and sailing. According to the record of the House of Representatives, Forty-seventh Congress, second session, Report No. 1887, which placed Smalls on the Retired List of the Navy, he was entitled to retirement because of his valuable service to the country during the Civil War. By 1861, he had become aware and knowledgeable of the steamer that was later to make him famous.

On May 12, 1862, the Confederate steamboat *Planter* had returned to Charleston from an engagement that included moving guns from Cole's Island to James Island. The officers had gone ashore and slept in the city, leaving on board a crew of eight African men. Among them was Robert Smalls, who had earlier been ordered by the Confederates to serve on the naval ship *Planter*. However, on May 13, the brave Smalls, with the contingent of seven other enslaved Africans, decided that he could steer the ship out of Charleston Harbor and surrender it to the Union forces blockading it.

Consulting with his crew, Smalls discovered that five of them wanted to join him. Two remained behind. According to the House of Representatives report, the escape plan was very hazardous. The boat would have to pass beneath the guns of the forts in the harbor. Lack of courage and steadiness or detection by the Confederates would mean certain death.

Every precaution was taken by Smalls. Having made the resolution, he planned the action to the smallest detail. Under his command, wood was taken on the ship, steam was put on, and with her valuable cargo of guns and ammunition intended for a new fortification, Fort Ripley, the *Planter* moved out of the harbor at two o'clock in the morning.

Smalls steered the ship up beyond the North Atlantic wharf, where his wife and two children and eight other people were waiting to embark. These passengers were taken aboard at 3:25 in the morning, May 13.

The perilous journey had begun. There was no turning back. With nine men, five women, and three children, Robert Smalls passed Fort Johnson and blew the usual salute on the steam whistle. He proceeded down the bay. When he had reached the area of Fort Sumter, he stood in the pilot house leaning out the window as the captain had usually done. He even folded his arms in the same manner and wore the same kind of straw hat. The signal that was required to be given as a ship passed out into the sea was blown as coolly as any other captain would have done. Fort Sumter answered by signal, "all right," and the ship headed toward Morris Island, occupied by a light artillery unit, and then beyond the guns of Fort Sumter.

When the Fort Sumter soldiers discovered that the ship was headed for the Federal fleet they signaled to the Morris Island contingent to stop her. But it was too late. The ship had passed beyond the range of the Morris Island guns and was making its way toward the Union vessels. Robert Smalls knew exactly what he was doing. As the ship approached the Union forces, a white flag was displayed, but because it was not seen at first, the Union steamers stood ready to defend themselves. Just as they were about to fire, they noticed the flag of truce.

Smalls was called a "wheelman" because the title of "pilot" was reserved for whites. Nevertheless, the expertise he demonstrated in directing the ship to the Union forces indicated skill, courage, and intelligence. Smalls became one of the first African American naval heroes. The Union army saluted him as a member of the navy with retirement.

JOHN BROWN

John Brown, who was born in Connecticut in 1800, had prepared all of his life to overturn slavery (see figure 7.7, page 108). On October 16, 1859, he seized the arsenal at Harpers Ferry, Virginia. His plan was to make his way into the mountains with his nineteen men and from those fastnesses to sally back and forth to destabilize the slave institutions.

Figure 7.6. Robert Smalls (1839–1916). Named a pilot in the Union navy by President Lincoln, he commanded the *Planter*, he later became the longest serving African-American congressman during the Reconstruction era while representing South Carolina.

John Brown went to Kansas and joined his five sons in a battle against proslavery forces in 1855. On May 24, 1856, he had killed five of his opponents at Pottawatomie Creek, Kansas. The apologists for slavery feared John Brown. He took it upon himself to rid the region of proslavery sympathizers. Later in the year, John Brown's forces repelled a strong Missouri invading force intent on introducing slavery into Kansas territory.

In the spring of 1858, Brown met with a group of white and black abolitionists in Chatham, Ontario, to tell them about his plan to establish an antislavery community and stronghold in the mountains of Virginia and Maryland. He proposed, and the convention of people gathered adopted, a provisional constitution and set of ordinances for the people of the United States. He was elected commander-in-chief of this provisional government. Gerrit Smith and other prominent Boston abolitionists invited him to Boston to present his plans. They also arranged to provide him with funds. Leading African Americans, Harriet Tubman and Frederick Douglass among them, were kept apprised of the movement. Brown had settled in North Elba, New York, an

Figure 7.7. John Brown (1800–1859). Filled with antislavery sentiment, he dedicated his life to freeing slaves. He was hanged after being found guilty of making battle plans to attack the South at Harpers Ferry, West Virginia.

African American community, because he felt comfortable among the exploited and oppressed.

Brown's small cadre of revolutionists captured the Harpers Ferry armory and rounded up about sixty leading citizens as hostages (see figure 7.8, page 109). They were able to hold out during his skirmishes with the local militia, but when a contingent of marines came to the battlefront, Brown had to surrender. He lost two of his sons in the fighting.

Thus, only two days after his seizure of the arsenal in Harpers Ferry, he was wounded, captured, and depressed. Three months later he was hanged for treason, slave insurrection, and murder. His death was an energizing force to the abolitionists. They made memorials to John Brown throughout the land. He was praised as the best America had to offer from the most prestigious pulpits; slave parents taught their children about the deeds of John Brown—he was a hero in his own time.

Some hated him and despised him for standing against slavery. Those who sup-ported the institution of slavery saw John Brown and his spirit as dangerous for the nation. Should the Africans get into their heads that they would follow the pattern set by John Brown, there would be diffi-culty throughout the land. In councils and assemblies in Maryland and Virginia, the slave owners questioned the extent of John Brown's influence. Others passed judgment on his character and his mental stability, going so far as to say that he had become unhinged because of his love for the African people. Of course, John Brown was neither crazy nor a fool. He had spent months, maybe even years, organizing his plot, assessing the kind of support he would receive from the Africans were he to succeed, consulting with the leading abolitionists, and preparing his sons to fight alongside him.

When the war between the states finally began, the Union soldiers used John Brown's name and vision for inspi-ration. He had seen the war coming and had warned that it was impossible to build a nation with one part of it slave and the other part of it free.

Few men have given their lives so freely for the liberation of others. There is perhaps no greater story of sacrifice on the part of a white person during the Great Enslavement than the life story of John Brown, forever enshrined in the best memories of the United States of America.

The Legacy of John Brown

John Brown understood more about the nature of the Civil War (which he never lived to see) than many of those who directed it. President Abraham Lincoln (see figure 7.9, page 110) and his cabinet insisted in all of their documents and speeches that the war was not to be fought over slavery.

Lincoln was not John Brown. While Lincoln opposed slavery in a general way, he did not believe in social or politi-cal equality for Africans. It was therefore important for him to insist that the war was not over slavery. If he had agreed that the war was over slavery, he could have been accused of prosecuting a war

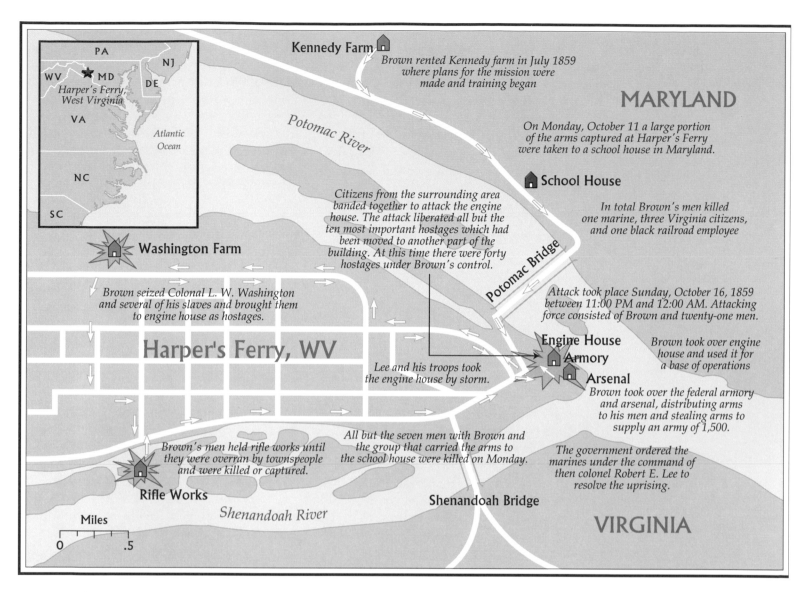

Inset map labels:
PA
NJ
WV MD DE
Harper's Ferry, West Virginia
VA
Atlantic Ocean
NC
SC

Kennedy Farm

Brown rented Kennedy farm in July 1859 where plans for the mission were made and training began

MARYLAND

On Monday, October 11 a large portion of the arms captured at Harper's Ferry were taken to a school house in Maryland.

School House

In total Brown's men killed one marine, three Virginia citizens, and one black railroad employee

Potomac River

Citizens from the surrounding area banded together to attack the engine house. The attack liberated all but the ten most important hostages which had been moved to another part of the building. At this time there were forty hostages under Brown's control.

Potomac Bridge

Washington Farm

Brown seized Colonal L. W. Washington and several of his slaves and brought them to engine house as hostages.

Harper's Ferry, WV

Attack took place Sunday, October 16, 1859 between 11:00 PM and 12:00 AM. Attacking force consisted of Brown and twenty-one men.

Engine House
Armory
Arsenal

Brown took over engine house and used it for a base of operations

Lee and his troops took the engine house by storm.

Brown took over the federal armory and arsenal, distributing arms to his men and stealing arms to supply an army of 1,500.

Brown's men held rifle works until they were overran by townspeople and were killed or captured.

All but the seven men with Brown and the group that carried the arms to the school house were killed on Monday.

The government ordered the marines under the command of then colonel Robert E. Lee to resolve the uprising.

Rifle Works

Shenandoah River

Shenandoah Bridge

VIRGINIA

Miles
0   .5

against whites in support of blacks. Thus, in his official rhetoric he argued that the war was over the Union.

Most African Americans knew that the war was over slavery. The peculiar institution overshadowed all other issues. It stood astride everything. There was no way for the government to avoid slavery as an issue; it would not go away. Lincoln had even thought seriously about colonization as an answer to the issues surrounding the slave question. In 1862, he proposed a gradual emancipation that would have allowed slaveowners to be compensated for enslaved Africans set free under his scheme. The idea was to free Africans and then return them to Africa. Africans in New York, Washington, Baltimore, Boston, and Philadelphia held protest meetings

against this idea, and it never saw the light of day as official policy.

It has been argued that Lincoln believed that if he emancipated Africans in the rebel territories, whites would more easily accept the emancipation were the Africans made to leave the country. As it turned out, when the Emancipation Proclamation was issued on January 1, 1863, it did not have much immediate impact. It actually took the Thirteenth Amendment, which was finally ratified in December 1865, to put teeth in the emancipation.

What the Emancipation Proclamation did was to encourage blacks to enlist in the Union army. Africans had fought in every war before the Civil War but no war was more eagerly fought than this.

Figure 7.8. Sunday, October 16, 1859: John Brown's raid on Harpers Ferry.

PROBLEMS AFTER THE CIVIL WAR

The Civil War came to an end on April 9, 1865, but the misery of Africans did not cease with the end of the enslavement that had lasted nearly 250 years. By December 1865, the Thirteenth Amendment outlawing slavery in any territory and state was made a part of the Constitution, enough states having ratified it. With Abraham Lincoln dead and Andrew Johnson sworn in as president, the four million Africans began to test their new freedom. Thousands wandered the country they had never known looking for lost relatives in counties and states they had only heard about before. The war had dislocated relatives but more freedom gave the African an opportunity to find relatives who had escaped or been sold to different masters prior to emancipation. This was the period of the Great Mourning Treks. Africans worked for wages where the wages were fair but often refused to be treated like slaves now that they were free.

President Andrew Johnson admitted four states back into the Union seven months after he took office in April 1865. This angered some members of Congress who believed that the president ignored reality. Leaders of southern states quickly restored their dominance and introduced a group of laws known as Black Codes to control the freed Africans. These codes granted some rights that were denied under enslavement—marriage, property ownership, and the right to give testimony in court, for example. However, the codes included restrictions that were meant to ensure complete white control over the lives of the freed Africans. The southern courts could take African children who either had parents who could not support them, seemed to be orphaned, or actually were orphaned and assign them to whites. This was a new form of slavery, a way to secure black labor without pay. The Black Codes required Africans to have jobs approved by whites or be arrested, fined, or assigned to jobs with whites who only had to pay whatever fine was assessed against the Africans.

Congress was furious with President Johnson's actions, which were seen as lenient to the South. The state of Georgia had even sent the former vice president of the Confederacy to Congress. In June 1866, Congress passed the Fourteenth Amendment, which extended citizenship and civil rights to Africans. The amendment also reversed the Dred Scott decision of 1857 that had taken away African citizenship prior to the Civil War, and it prohibited certain Confederate officers from holding public office. In February 1866, President Andrew Johnson vetoed a bill passed by Congress to broaden the powers of the Freedmen's Bureau. The bureau of Refugees, Freedmen, and Abandoned Lands had been established on March 3, 1865, for the purpose of resettling and educating rural Africans in the south. However, as early as 1861, four years prior to the end of the Civil War, Lewis Tappan of the American Missionary Association had sent teachers to open the first day school for the freedpersons at Hampton, Virginia. By 1864 the American Missionary Association had sent more than 250 northern teachers to the South.

While the missionary efforts of the Baptists, Methodists, Presbyterians, Congregationalists, African Methodists,

Figure 7.9. Abraham Lincoln (1809–1865). Lincoln was elected as a radical moderate in 1860 arguing that the government had no right to prohibit slavery in the South. Throughout his term in office, Lincoln's policies and philosophies changed as he issued the Emancipation Proclamation in September of 1862, which conferred legal, though not actual, freedom on three-quarters of America's slave population. Actual emancipation came in 1865 with the drafting of the Thirteenth Amendment (see page 124). Credit: Library of Congress/Corbis.

and Friends were enormous, the Freedmen's Bureau was chiefly responsible for starting schools between 1865 and 1870. During the first year of the Civil War, 4,239 schools were established with 9,307 teachers and nearly 250,000 students. Carter Woodson and Charles Wesley wrote in their book *The Negro in Our History* that historians will remember several white teachers saying, "High upon the roll of honor Negroes inscribe as immortal apostles . . . Corey at Virginia Union, Packard and Giles at Spelman, Cravath at Fisk, Ware at Atlanta, Armstrong at Hampton, Graves at Morehouse, and Tupper at Shaw."Africans and their supporters had found the Freedmen's Bureau to be an indispensable ally in the south. President Andrew Johnson did as much as he could to weaken the agency. Thus, his veto of the bill that should have given the Freedmen's Bureau more powers was followed quickly by other presidential actions. Two months later he vetoed a civil rights bill meant to protect African Americans from the restrictions of the Black Codes. Congress repassed both bills within three months over Johnson's veto. Tennessee, the home state of Andrew Johnson, was the only ex-confederate state to ratify the Fourteenth Amendment. The ten other states, at Johnson's suggestion, voted against the amendment.

Radical Republicans controlled the Congress after the 1866 elections, and they dealt severe blows to President Johnson's policies and the ex-Confederates. A series of laws were passed that brought southern white control of government to an end in the South. The Military Reconstruction Acts were put into effect by the summer of 1867. Under these acts the governments in the South set up by President Johnson were dissolved. These governments did not permit blacks to vote, imposed a new kind of slavery through the Black Codes, and failed to protect defenseless Africans who were frequently harassed and killed during the two years of southern white government.

The Military Reconstruction Acts affected the ten states still out of the Union. Tennessee had been allowed to reenter. There were five military districts with a Union general in charge of each district. Twenty thousand soldiers were stationed over the districts to provide security and to assist in law enforcement. The generals were responsible for voter registration. Each state was permitted to return to the Union if it ratified a new constitution, elected a new government under the constitution, and ratified the Fourteenth Amendment.

Six of the ten states returned to the Union by June 1868. The four remaining states became a part of the Union again in July 1870. The last four states had to ratify the Fifteenth Amendment as well since it passed Congress in 1869 and became a part of the Constitution in March 1870. However, now that the states were back in the Union, it did not signify that there was a change of heart regarding the rights and opportunities to be granted to blacks. The new political arrangement would serve as a shield for a continuation of discrimination against Africans. Just as soon as the Union army left and the South became acceptable to the Union, the African Americans became desperate.

The Compromise of 1877, which had seen the North capitulate to the South against the will of the African masses, brought about greater emphasis on self-help, racial dignity, and pride. The programs of the Reconstruction did not cease—there was still interest in political franchise, civil rights, and representation in political bodies. Nevertheless a greater emphasis on education was being shown.

Increasingly, the African community knew that it had been abandoned. In fact, during the Republican national convention held in Louisville, Kentucky, in 1883, the delegates said in part that the laws intended to secure rights for African Americans were nothing but dead letters.

Africans were angered by the lack of federal support for civil rights. At state and regional conventions throughout the North and South, and especially the

South, delegates vowed to use all legal means within their power to secure their rights. They complained about prejudiced judges and juries, short school terms, discrimination in the Republican party, and the convict lease system. In 1885, the people of Baltimore founded the Brotherhood of Liberty with the express purpose of fighting for the just rights of African Americans.

In 1888, more than 350 African Americans met in Georgia to condemn the chain gang, discrimination in public transportation, lynch law, disfranchisement, and general harassment. They supported the temperance issue as well as industrial education.

Two significant conventions were held in 1890. These two conferences represented the best thinking of the time on questions confronting the African American community. T. Thomas Fortune, the newspaper journalist who had become known as an agitator, founded the Afro-American League in Chicago. This was to become one of the principal agencies for dissemination of African American political ideas. A few months later in Washington, D.C., a group of about 500 blacks gathered to establish the American Citizens' Equal Rights Association. J. C. Price was named head of the convention. He served as a leading spokesperson for both organizations until they ceased to function due to internal ideological problems.

INTO BATTLE

Africans have distinguished themselves as soldiers in every war fought by Americans. We shall not recount each campaign but simply convey the extent of the African's nobility and character in military campaigns.

The Boston Massacre occurred on March 5, 1770, when British troops marched down State Street and were confronted by a group of Americans led by Crispus Attucks, a tall, impressive African of ebony complexion. Attucks and three others were killed, the African being the first to die. There is a monument in Boston, the Attucks Monument,

to honor the courage of Attucks. Later, at the Battle of Bunker Hill, Peter Salem showed unusual courage by rushing forward and shooting Major Pitcairn of the British army as he was exulting in his anticipated victory. Also during the Revolutionary War, the man who captured General Prescott was an African named Prince, not the American, General Barton, as often claimed.

The Battles of Mobile and New Orleans

During the battles of Mobile and New Orleans in 1812, African troops distinguished themselves by heroic deeds. Under Andrew Jackson's command at Mobile, some white troops were retreating is disarray until an African named Jeffries saved the day by taking lead of the soldiers and rallying them for the battle. At the battle of New Orleans, Jackson specifically called on the Africans to assist in the struggle against the British. When the battle was over, he thanked the fighters in these words: "Soldiers: from the shores of Mobile I collected you to arms. I invited you to share the perils and to divide the glory with your white countrymen. I expected much from you, for I was not uniformed of those qualities which must render you so formidable to an invading force. . . . I knew that you loved the land of your nativity, and that, like ourselves, you had to defend all that is most dear to man. But you have surpassed all my hopes."

Civil War

The examples of Crispus Attucks, Peter Salem, and Salem Poor in the American Revolutionary War would inspire thousands of African soldiers during the Civil War. Africans fought in the Civil War by state and individual enlistment, the latter being enlistment in which a person simply reported to a Union officer and asked to be signed up. Although this was considered by some officers to be irregular, many black soldiers used irregular measures in order to gain entry into the war. Nearly 170,000 African Americans are accounted for by states as serving in the Civil War, but another

Table 7.3. African American servicemen awarded the Medal of Honor.

U. S. Army

William Appleton	4th U.S. Colored Troops	September 29, 1864	Cited for gallant conduct at New Market Heights, Virginia.
Private William H. Barnes	38th U.S. Colored Troops		Among the first to enter the Confederate works, although wounded, at Chiffin's Farm near Richmond, Virginia.
First Sergeant Powhatan Beaty	5th U.S. Colored Troops	September 29, 1864	Cited for gallantry in action at Chiffin's Farm near Richmond.
First Sergeant James H. Bronson	5th U.S. Colored Troops	September 29, 1864	Cited for gallantry in action at Chiffin's Farm near Richmond.
Sergeant William H. Carney (see figure 7.10, page 114)	54th Massachusetts Colored Infantry		The first African American to win the Congressional Medal of Honor. Carney was cited for valor on June 18 1863, during the Battle of Fort Wagner, South Carolina, in which he carried colors and led a charge to the parapet after the standard bearer had been killed. He was twice severely wounded during this battle.
Sergeant Decatur Dorsey	39th U.S. Colored Troops	July 30, 1864	Cited for valor in the Battle of Petersburg, Virginia. When his regiment was driven back to Union lines, he carried the colors and rallied the men in his unit.
Sergeant Major Christian A. Fleetwood	4th U.S. Colored Troops		Cited for gallantry in action at Chiffin's Farm near Richmond.
Private James Gardiner	36th U.S. Colored Troops		Cited for gallantry in action at Chiffin's Farm near Richmond.
Sergeant James Harris	38th U.S. Colored Troops		Cited for gallantry in action at Chiffin's Farm near Richmond.
Sergeant Major Thomas Hawkins	6th U.S. Colored Troops	July 21, 1864	Cited for valor in the Battle of Deep Bottom, Virginia. Credited with the rescue of his regimental colors.
Sergeant Alfred B. Hilton	4th U.S. Colored Troops		Cited for gallantry in action at Chiffin's Farm near Richmond.
Sergeant Major Milton M. Holland	5th U.S. Colored Troops		Cited for gallantry in action at Chiffin's Farm near Richmond.
Corporal Miles James	36th U.S. Colored Troops		Cited for gallantry in action at Chiffin's Farm near Richmond.
First Sergeant Alexander Kelly	6th U.S. Colored Troops		Cited for gallantry in action at Chiffin's Farm near Richmond.
First Sergeant Robert Pinn	5th U.S. Colored Troops		Cited for gallantry in action at Chiffin's Farm near Richmond.
First Sergeant Edward Radcliff	38th U.S. Colored Troops		Cited for gallantry in action at Chiffin's Farm near Richmond.
Private Charles Veal	4th U.S. Colored Troops		Cited for gallantry in action at Chiffin's Farm near Richmond.

U. S. Navy

Aaron Anderson	serving on the gunboat *Wyandank*	Participated in the clearing of Mattox Creek on March 17, 1865. Cited for carrying out his duties courageously in spite of devastating fire from the enemy.
Robert Blake	serving on the gunboat *Marblehead*	An ex-slave enlisting in the navy after escaping from a Virginia plantation, Blake displayed heroism on the *Marblehead* December 25, 1863.
John Lawson	serving on gunboat *Hartford*	Cited for bravery in the Battle of Mobile Bay on August 5, 1864. After recovering from unconsciousness he continued to perform his duties under heavy enemy fire.
Joachim Pease	serving on gunboat *Kearsarge*	Cited for gallantry in action in the engagement with the Confederate gunboat *Alabama*.

10,000 or so remain unaccounted for in this measure.

The role of African American women in the war was critical to the conduct of the battle on the frontlines. When the "contraband" (i.e., Africans who walked into the Union army camps and were seized from the slaveowners as spoils of war) came to the towns and cities, the African American women served as social welfare experts and supporters. They gathered food, shelter, and clothing for the contraband and prepared them to function in freedom. Some of the women worked in hospitals and in military camps. They moved into liberated areas in the South to help people find jobs and homes. They became school teachers in communities that had 100 percent illiteracy. They organized study groups to teach women and men from the southern plantations how to take care of themselves. The African American women were as active as the men in their sphere of work. No one seemed to wait for others to work; they all had responsibilities.

Like other wars in other places and times, the Civil War served to further liberate African American women. Most women had some degree of training and could teach others how to serve themselves and the nation in a more effective way. By the end of the war in 1865, 10 percent of the total government troops' strength had been supplied by African Americans. Twenty-five percent of the navy's sailors were Africans.

African troops who enlisted in the army were always placed in "colored" regiments. They were in light or heavy artillery, cavalry, infantry, or engineer regiments. Most of these regiments were led by white officers. There were occasional black noncommissioned officers. Among the white officers who became well known for having good commands of African troops were Colonel Robert Gould Shaw of the Fifty-fourth Massachusetts Regiment, Colonel Thomas Wentworth Higginson of the First South Carolina Volunteers, and General N. Banks of the First and Third Louisiana Native Guards.

It should be noted that two regiments of General Butler's Corps d'Afrique were staffed by African Americans. Among the African officers was Captain P. B. S. Pinchback. In addition to Pinchback, who became a politician during Reconstruction, were Major F. Dumas, Captain H. Ford Douglass, Lieutenant W. D. Matthews, and Major Martin R. Delany. These officers served with dignity and honor. The Civil War may have started out as a white man's war, as some of the white officers had claimed, but in the end it was a war for the liberation of the African—and African men and women participated in it fully.

Figure 7.10. Sergeant W. H. Carney (1845–1866). After being cited for valor during the Civil War, he was given the Congressional Medal of Honor on May 23, 1900, making him the first African American to receive such an award.

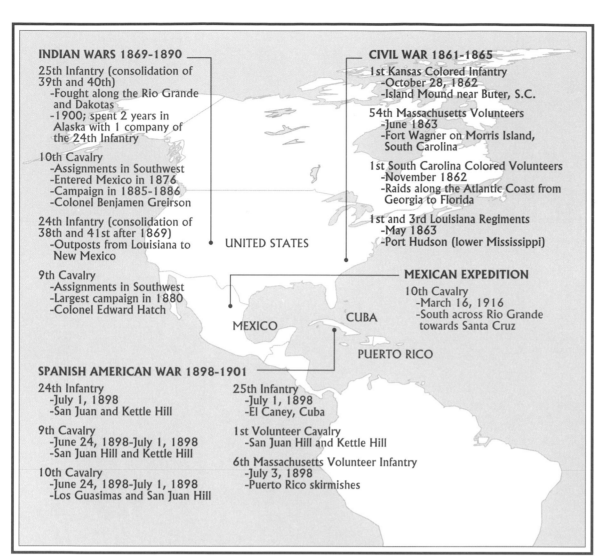

INDIAN WARS 1869-1890

25th Infantry (consolidation of 39th and 40th)
-Fought along the Rio Grande and Dakotas
-1900; spent 2 years in Alaska with 1 company of the 24th Infantry

10th Cavalry
-Assignments in Southwest
-Entered Mexico in 1876
-Campaign in 1885-1886
-Colonel Benjamen Greirson

24th Infantry (consolidation of 38th and 41st after 1869)
-Outposts from Louisiana to New Mexico

9th Cavalry
-Assignments in Southwest
-Largest campaign in 1880
-Colonel Edward Hatch

CIVIL WAR 1861-1865

1st Kansas Colored Infantry
-October 28, 1862
-Island Mound near Buter, S.C.

54th Massachusetts Volunteers
-June 1863
-Fort Wagner on Morris Island, South Carolina

1st South Carolina Colored Volunteers
-November 1862
-Raids along the Atlantic Coast from Georgia to Florida

1st and 3rd Louisiana Regiments
-May 1863
-Port Hudson (lower Mississippi)

UNITED STATES

MEXICAN EXPEDITION

10th Cavalry
-March 16, 1916
-South across Rio Grande towards Santa Cruz

MEXICO   CUBA

PUERTO RICO

SPANISH AMERICAN WAR 1898-1901

24th Infantry
-July 1, 1898
-San Juan and Kettle Hill

9th Cavalry
-June 24, 1898-July 1, 1898
-San Juan Hill and Kettle Hill

10th Cavalry
-June 24, 1898-July 1, 1898
-Los Guasimas and San Juan Hill

25th Infantry
-July 1, 1898
-El Caney, Cuba

1st Volunteer Cavalry
-San Juan Hill and Kettle Hill

6th Massachusetts Volunteer Infantry
-July 3, 1898
-Puerto Rico skirmishes

Figure 7.11. African American military units in campaigns and wars between 1861 and 1901.

Figure 7.12. African American troops returning home after the Civil War. Credit: Library of Congress/Corbis.

"Swing Low, Sweet Chariot"

8

THE PROMISE
OF RECONSTRUCTION

The end of the Civil War brought about in African Americans an incredible thirst for knowledge and information. Rarely in history have a people longed for education as the freed Africans longed. When the words "Freedom has come" were spoken, thousands of Africans began their search for the fountains of knowledge believing that one of the great differences between them and the whites was knowledge.

The response of the Freedmen's Bureau was massive within the context of the times. Riding upon the limited goodwill of the people of the United States, the Bureau set up 4,000 schools, found 9,000 teachers, and taught 250,000 Africans, young and old, how to read and write. At emancipation only one out of every ten Africans could read and write. The widespread assistance of the Bureau was necessary to provide safe and secure conditions for the newly freed Africans.

The narratives of freed Africans tell various stories of generosity and eagerness to learn. In some instances, Africans were taught in schools that had been established on the farms where they worked before and after emancipation. Now more than ever, the institutions of higher learning became more popular. Schools such as Lincoln University, founded in 1854 in Pennsylvania, and Hampton Institute in Virginia attracted large numbers of students from the South. More and more schools were opened for the business of educating the African American population. With an insatiable desire for knowledge, some African Americans spent years securing rudimentary educations in order to serve others as teachers. "Each one teach one" seemed to have been the motto of the day as those who gained the basic education rushed to teach those who had no education. In some instances, teachers were those who had achieved the equivalent of a fifth-grade education. Believing that it was possible to secure the American dream through proper education, African Americans in the South created local organizations and support groups to encourage especially promising students to gain more education. Churches set up educational committees, which, in some instances, became the basis for starting schools and colleges. Seldom have so many churches been committed to the social and educational advancement of the African American. With minimal resources and through hard work and diligence, they created the conditions that elevated a downtrodden community. Consistent to the principles of self-help, these churches and institutions recorded some of the most glorious achievements of the African community.

On the whole, African Americans were not welcomed into the nation's white colleges in the postwar era. Some northern colleges, such as Oberlin, achieved reputations as liberal institutions that welcomed good African American students, but by no means was this welcome universal.

African Americans had the support of numerous northern philanthropic families and institutions. Combined with the support of African American churches, these supporters made a difference.

EXODUS: THERE MUST BE A BETTER PLACE!

The last quarter of the nineteenth century was hell for African Americans in the South and the sentiment of the people often turned to separation, either by leaving the South or by founding separate cities. In May 1879, Africans from throughout the South gathered in Nashville, Tennessee, to discuss the continuing violence against their families. In a report adopted by the body at that convention, grievances and proposed remedies were set forth. Indeed, the convention encouraged people to emigrate to the North and West in search of better living conditions.

Forty thousand Africans went to Kansas in less than two years. Others left the South for Missouri, Indiana, and Colorado. The entire African population in the South was convinced that the whites of the South defeated during the war would take out their frustrations on the Africans remaining in the South after Reconstruction.

In 1877, the Liberian Exodus Joint Stock Company had been formed in Charleston, South Carolina, and had purchased a ship, the *Azor*. Its aim was to send emigrants to Africa, to bring African products to the United States, and to establish a regular steamship line between Charleston and Monrovia, Liberia. Whites, fearful of losing domestic workers, did everything they could to prevent the company's success. The ship had been repaired in Boston, but whites in Charleston induced the custom house officials to pronounce the ship ill prepared until it was refurbished with a copper bottom. When that was accomplished (at an expensive price), not all of the people who held places on the ship were permitted to sail. Through the connivance of the captains and business interests in Charleston, the ship was hijacked and sold in Liverpool even though it had been legitimately purchased by the combined resources of Baptists and Methodists in South Carolina. The United States Circuit Court in South Carolina refused to even entertain a suit brought by the Africans to reclaim their property.

The turbulent road to freedom was often marked by economic, physical, and legal harassment, yet the African American community continued to produce men and women who defied the odds. Those who built towns and cities dreamed of the possibility of living in America free of political and social discrimination. So the towns of Langston, Boley, Nicodemus, and Mound Bayou became metaphors for the search for peace and tranquility in the midst of the racial hatred that existed in the South. The towns were shelters in the storm.

LABOR AND THE NEWLY FREED AFRICAN

The labor movement did not greet the free African with open arms. The relationship between the white worker and the black worker was initially one of bitter suspicion. White workers met in 1866 to form the National Labor Union. This was meant to be the representative union of working people. However, African

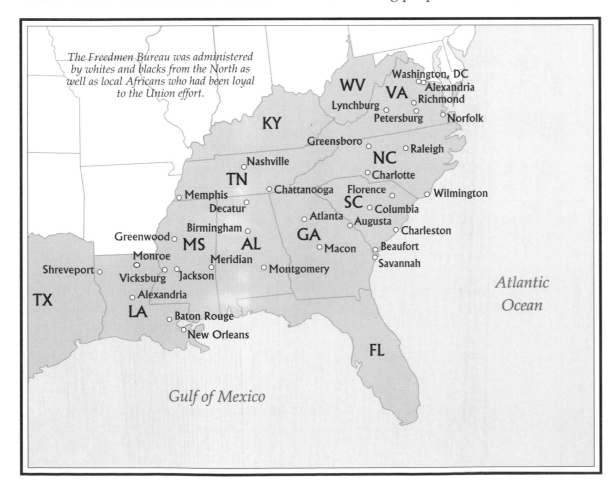

The Freedmen Bureau was administered by whites and blacks from the North as well as local Africans who had been loyal to the Union effort.

Figure 8.1. Post-Civil War chapters of the Freedman Aid Society. The Freedmen Aid Societies were established in the South immediately after the Civil War to assist the African refugees who had been dislocated by the turmoil. Set up by the federal government with an Act to Establish a Bureau for the Relief of Freedmen and Refugees in 1865, the Bureau was part of the War Department. Since the purpose was to provide shelter and food for the refugees, the aid societies were abundant in larger cities of the South.

Americans were never accepted on equal basis with whites in the National Labor Union. White workers felt that the Africans, so recently freed from slavery, did not understand the true principles of labor unions.

In response to the reluctance of white unions to admit them as full members, African American workers met in 1869 to form the National Negro Labor Union with the express purpose of advancing the cause of black workers. It was not until the 1880s that African American workers finally succeeded in having an affiliation with the National Labor Union. In fact, prior to that time, the National Labor Union looked upon the black workers as strikebreakers, willing to work for lower wages than white workers.

The position of the African American worker in the society was not enviable. Used by manipulative employers, the black worker was often forced to work for lower wages in order to have a job at all. Ruthless and unfair bosses fired Africans first and hired Africans last.

African Americans entered every legitimate field of employment soon after slavery. But their futures were uncertain and subject to deceitful practices of more-experienced white businessmen. In Savannah, Georgia, former slaves collected enough money among themselves to capitalize a business for $50,000 that turned out to be of no value when the money disappeared in the white bank and they were unable to collect it. Also in Savannah, Africans tried to run a lumber company in which they had invested $40,000. This business failed as well. In 1865, the black community of Baltimore organized a shipyard, the Chesapeake and Marine Railway and Dry Dock Company, capitalized at $40,000. It went out of existence in 1883. Since the African American community had little expertise in the business world it was prey for many fast-talking white entrepreneurs. The inability of African Americans to control the economics of their own community meant the eventual failure of the social vision of Reconstruction.

THE STARK FACTS ON LYNCHINGS

Cases of Africans being burned at the stake occurred as far back in American history as the early nineteenth century. But the special brutality of the lynchings of blacks was reserved for the period after the Civil War. The decade between 1890 and 1900 was the most dangerous time in the post-Civil War era for an African man to be alive. Nearly 1,700 persons were lynched in that decade as compared to 921 in the decade between 1900 and 1910; 840 from 1910 to 1920; and nearly 400 between 1920 and 1930. Between 1918 and 1927, eleven black women were also lynched, three with child at the time.

Mob violence against blacks continued into the 1980s. The mobs burned victims to death, hanged them and burned their bodies, mutilated them to death by cutting parts of their bodies, drowned them, or dragged the victims through the streets tied to an automobile. Beyond the numbers, which tell their own stories, the aggravated brutality of the murders shouted an irrational hatred of African Americans. The lust for blood and gore, which is not satisfied by recourse to law or by the normal process of men engaged in warfare, drove the mob to the most heinous types of murders.

The states with the most lynchings in the post-Civil War period were also the ones that led in the irrational brutality and mutilation of the bodies of the victims (see figure 8.2, page 121). Texas mobs lynched fifty-five persons during the late nineteenth century; sixteen victims were sadistically murdered. Of thirty-four victims, Arkansas put five people to death during the same period with unusual viciousness. The story is the same for Georgia, Alabama, Mississippi, and Louisiana. Citing figures alone will not give the reader the entire story. Many of the victims were not guilty of the crimes for which they were accused.

The following true story should show a human dimension. Henry Lowry of Nodena, Arkansas, had been held in bondage for a white landowner for more than two years. On Christmas Day 1920, the African American asked the landlord to pay him his back pay. He was cursed and struck by the landlord and shot by the landlord's son. Lowry drew his own gun and shot and killed the landlord and his daughter. He then escaped to Texas, where he was arrested. The governor of Arkansas guaranteed him a fair trial. He waived his rights to remain in Texas and agreed to return to Arkansas. The two officers who went to Texas to bring him back took him through Louisiana and Mississippi. At Sardis, Mississippi, a mob, previously arranged, overpowered the officers, and took Lowry from them and held him to be lynched. The newspapers were urged to print the details of time and place of the lynching. The *Memphis Press* sent a reporter to cover the killing. Ralph Roddy wrote:

> More than 500 hundred persons stood by and looked on while the Negro was slowly burned to a crisp. A few women were scattered among the crowd of Arkansas planters, who directed the gruesome work of avenging the death of O. T. Craig and his daughter, Mrs. C. P. Williamson.
>
> Not once did the slayed beg for mercy despite the fact that he suffered one of the most horrible deaths imaginable. With the Negro chained to a log, members of the mob placed a small pile of leaves around his feet. Gasoline was then poured on the leaves, and the carrying out of the death sentence was under way.
>
> Inch by inch the Negro was fairly cooked to death. Every few minutes fresh leaves were tossed on the funeral pyre until the blaze had passed the Negro's waist. Even after the flesh had dropped away from his legs and the flames were leaping toward his face, Lowry retained consciousness. Not once did he whimper or beg for mercy. Once or twice he attempted to pick up the hot ashes in his hands and thrust them into his mouth in order to hasten death. Each time the ashes were kicked out of his reach by a member of the mob.
>
> As the flames were eating away his

abdomen, a member of the mob stepped forward and saturated the body with gasoline. It was then only a few minutes until the Negro had been reduced to ashes. (White 1969).

Figure 8.2. Post-Civil War lynchings and mutilations.

Roddy's account was like hundreds in the late nineteenth and early twentieth centuries. An African was charged with some crime, sometimes on the slightest evidence, and before he could be brought to trial, a mob had overcome the sheriff, or police, and dragged the victim out to be lynched. So much a part of the reality of the South was lynch law that white families brought their children to see black men lynched. In these moments of deepest pain for the African American community—pain that has never healed—the white mobs found cruel joy. Lynching Africans became a pastime to rival any form of cheap amusement.

It was in times like these that African Americans hated the past and questioned the future. Only faith and hard-won character kept alive the possibilities for redress. Neither lynching nor mob violence could prevent the African American from seeking to secure all of the legal and political rights that were due under law. The Africans lynched for standing up for their rights, for challenging wrong, for protecting their honor and the dignity of their people are the firmest testament to human courage in American history.

Ku Klux Klan

The rise of the South—that is, the white South—was based on the disfranchisement of the African American. All of the guarantees made by the Constitutional amendments were nothing more than high-sounding ideal if they could not bear concrete results. It was difficult for the people who had struggled to be free to see how the federal government could protect them from the anger, bitterness, and wanton harassment of their white neighbors who were intent on trying to prove that they still maintained power over the lives of blacks.

The Ku Klux Klan was the epitome of the violent agents against African American rights. Other groups of whites had organized before the Klan in the South. In Georgia, the Regulators, Black Horse Cavalry, and Jayhawkers were hunting down and shooting blacks in the 1880s. Scores of these organizations appeared all over the South. These were societies with names like the White Line, Knights of the White Camellia, the Pale Faces, White League, Rifle Clubs of South Carolina, and the White Brotherhood. Their aim was to preserve white privilege and reestablish white supremacy in the face of what they saw as the encroachment by African Americans.

The Ku Klux Klan inherited the mantle of the Knights of the Golden Circle, a secret white organization organized before the Civil War to advance southern interests. Its organizers met in Pulaski, Tennessee, in 1866 to form their secret society. The name was formed by combining the Greek ku klos, circle, and the English "clan."

Soon thereafter, the organization adopted the costumes of an African brotherhood with origins in the Moorish conquest of Spain as their official uniforms, long white robes with hooded caps. The Ku Klux Klan was not a funny organization; it was the vanguard of racial attacks against Africans. Carrying out a campaign of whippings, burnings, bombings, and intimidations, the Klan created havoc over much of the United States concentrating particularly in the South (see figure 8.3, page 123 and figure 8.4, page 125). Since the Klan generally did its evil at night, it seemed difficult for authorities to capture and convict them for persecuting Africans.

Fourteenth Amendment

Africans had lived in North America for nearly 250 years before significant numbers of whites even came close to wanting the same things that African Americans wanted for themselves. The Reconstruction period (1865–1877) was one of the most remarkable periods in the history of an oppressed people. Africans who had mostly worked in agriculture also became successful as owners of their own farms; others served in state legislatures and succeeded in passing legislation that guaranteed public education for all children; still others were judges, congressmen, and senators who represented the best interests of their constituents, black as well as white.

The Fourteenth Amendment introduced the word "equal" into the Constitution and the Fifteenth Amendment declared that no person should be denied the vote on account of race, color, or previous condition of servitude (see page 124). This legal foundation for the idea of equality was erected with the full participation of Africans in private and public consultations and assemblies.

However valiant the African American heroines and heroes were in defense of the just right of Africans to be treated fairly and equally in the American society, they did not succeed during Reconstruction. Indeed, Du Bois, the eminent scholar, could write in *The Souls of Black Folk:* "Despite compromise, war, and struggle, the Negro is not free."

Vigorous campaigns against injustice and for equality for all have characterized the legendary struggles of Africans in America. These campaigns have always aimed to make the nation more responsive to the moral dimensions of its own grand vision. Reconstruction, nobly conceived by a few and bitterly opposed by the many, was for all practical purposes a failure. The federal government abandoned the recently freed Africans to conditions defined by white southerners; refused to seriously consider granting them "forty acres of land and a mule"; and consigned the defenseless Africans to a life of sharecropping for whites.

While the myth abounds of a radical reconstruction movement led by Africans to take over the South, this is far from the truth. Only in the state of South Carolina during one session of the lower house did Africans form a majority. During the twelve years of Reconstruction there was neither a black governor nor a black majority on any state board governing hospitals, prisons, or universities. In effect, fear and apprehension of Africans were responsible for much of what whites wrote about Reconstruction. In fact, Africans sought to make America what it has always said it wanted to be, but they were not to succeed. The 1877 Compromise was to lead to the withdrawal of the United States army from the South and the abandonment of the Africans to violent attacks of the Ku Klux Klan. Reconstruction would come to an end and it would be nearly 100 years before another movement to bring equality would emerge; it would then be called the Civil Rights Movement.

PLESSY V. FERGUSON

In the famous case of Plessy *v.* Ferguson in 1896, the Supreme Court was asked by Homer Adolph Plessy to decide the constitutionality of Louisiana's Jim Crow law.

Plessy was arrested for riding in the white section of the railway coach while on a sixty-mile stretch from New Orleans to Covington, Louisiana. His refusal to sit in the Jim Crow section was illegal under Louisiana law, which required "equal but separate accommodations for the white and colored races" in public facilities. The defendant in the case, Ferguson, was the Louisiana judge who conducted the criminal trial. The counsel for Plessy was

Figure 8.3. Ku Klux Klan cross-burning. Credit: Dave G. Houser/Corbis.

Albion W. Tourgee, a white lawyer from upstate New York who had been a judge briefly in North Carolina during Reconstruction. In his brief to the Supreme Court, Tourgee said, "Justice is pictured blind and her daughter, the Law, ought at least to be colorblind." The only dissenting justice, John Marshall Harlan, caught this phrase in his dissent and reduced it to "Our Constitution is colorblind."

The United States Supreme Court declared that the action brought by Plessy was under the provision of the Fourteenth Amendment, which required, according to the court, only that separate accommodations be equal. The Court had sanctioned segregation as the law of the land. This law remained in force for fifty-eight years until 1954.

NEW GOVERNMENTS

The ten occupied southern states registered 700,000 black and 660,000 whites to vote in the elections held in 1867 and 1868. Registration figures indicate that many whites refused to vote although they constituted a majority of the population. Many northerners, whites and some

The Reconstruction Amendments

The 13th, 14th and 15th Amendments were adopted directly following the Civil War and have become known as the Reconstruction Amendments. The main purpose of the Reconstruction Amendments was to acknowledge African Americans as equal citizens of the United States. The first Constitutional action taken to grant African Americans civil rights came with the 13th Amendment. Lincoln's promises of abolishing slavery in his Emancipation Proclamation were finally added to the Constitution in 1865. Three years later, the 14th Amendment extended the rights and liberties of the Constitution to finally include African Americans. In 1870, the Reconstruction Amendments extended another right, this time giving African Americans the opportunity to participate in the democratic election process with the passage of the 15th Amendment.

AMENDMENT XIII

Section 1. Neither slavery nor involuntary servitude, except as a punishment for crime whereof the party shall have been duly convicted, shall exist within the United States, or any place subject to their jurisdiction.

AMENDMENT XIV

Section 1. All persons born or naturalized in the United States, and subject to the jurisdiction thereof, are citizens of the United States and of the State wherein they reside. No State shall make or enforce any law which shall abridge the privileges or immunities of citizens of the United States; nor shall any State deprive any person of life, liberty, or property, without due process of law; nor deny to any person within its jurisdiction the equal protection of the laws.

Section 2. Representatives shall be apportioned among the several States according to their respective numbers, counting the whole number of persons in each State, excluding Indians not taxed. But when the right to vote at any election for the choice of electors for President and Vice President of the United States, Representatives in Congress, the Executive and Judicial officers of a State, or the members of the Legislature thereof, is denied to any of the male inhabitants of such State, being twenty-one years of age, and citizens of the United States, or in any way abridged, except for participation in rebellion, or other crime, the basis of representation therein shall be reduced in the proportion which the number of such male citizens shall bear to the whole number of male citizens twenty-one years of age in such State.

Section 3. No person shall be a Senator or Representative in Congress, or elector of President and Vice President, or hold any office, civil or military, under the United States, or under any State, who, having previously taken an oath, as a member of Congress, or as an officer of the United States, or as a member of any State legislature, or as an executive or judicial officer of any State, to support the Constitution of the United States, shall have engaged in insurrection or rebellion against the same, or given aid or comfort to the enemies thereof. But Congress may by a vote of two-thirds of each House, remove such disability.

Section 4. The validity of the public debt of the United States, authorized by law, including debts incurred for payment of pensions and bounties for services in suppressing insurrection or rebellion, shall not be questioned. But neither the United States nor any State shall assume or pay any debt or obligation incurred in aid of insurrection or rebellion against the United States, or any claim for the loss or emancipation of any slave; but all such debts, obligations and claims shall be held illegal and void.

AMENDMENT XV

Section 1. The right of citizens of the United States to vote shall not be denied or abridged by the United States or by any State on account of race, color, or previous condition of servitude.

blacks, came south to assist the freedpersons. Lawyers, teachers, businessmen, and federal officials, with their carpetbag suitcases (thus the name "carpetbaggers") entered the South to help reconstruct the society. While some opportunists were among them, most were dedicated to improving the educational and economic lot of Africans recently freed.

Among the African Americans elected to office were two who represented the state of Mississippi in the United States Senate. Hiram Revels represented Mississippi for a partial term of 1870–1871 and Blanche Kelso Bruce for a full term of 1875–1881. Twenty blacks were in the U.S. House of Representatives between 1869 and 1901. Scores of blacks served in state legislatures and as state treasurers, lieutenant governors, and school superintendents and clerks. Lieutenant Governor P. B. S. Pinchback served as governor of Louisiana for forty-three days when the governor was removed from office. The only African to serve on a state supreme court was Justice Jonathan Jasper Wright of South Carolina. Although the great majority of Africans were illiterate, those who were elected to high office were usually educated. Senator Revels, for example, had been born free in North Carolina, attended Knox College in Illinois, and had been a school principal in Baltimore before settling in Mississippi. Senator Bruce was born enslaved in Virginia but escaped to Ohio, where he attended Oberlin College before settling in Mississippi. He became a planter, sheriff, state legislator, and county school superintendent. Governor Pinchback was the son of a white father and black mother. Set free by his father, he attended school in Cincinnati but had to withdraw when the white relatives of his father robbed his mother of the property that had been given to her and the ten children she bore for him. Pinchback worked on riverboats, enlisted in the Union army, and rose to captain in the Louisiana Native Guards. Not all of the Africans elected to office had such worldly credentials as these three but they were by no means an illiterate

Figure 8.4. The rise of the Klan: Ku Klux Klan membership, 1925.

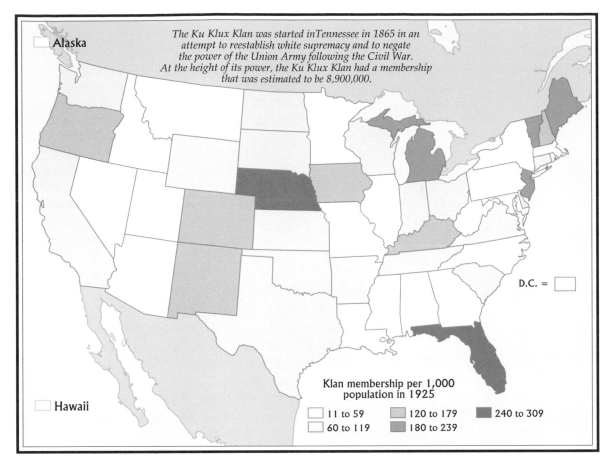

The Ku Klux Klan was started in Tennessee in 1865 in an attempt to reestablish white supremacy and to negate the power of the Union Army following the Civil War. At the height of its power, the Ku Klux Klan had a membership that was estimated to be 8,900,000.

Klan membership per 1,000 population in 1925

| 11 to 59 | 120 to 179 | 240 to 309 |
| 60 to 119 | 180 to 239 | |

group of politicians as depicted in the highly controversial film *Birth of a Nation.*

African Americans went to the polls to vote in elections with tremendous excitement. Having been denied the freedom to vote in democratic elections in a nation that was based upon the idea of democracy, the campaigns and elections were the greatest gifts to a long-mistreated people. Savoring their right to vote, many African Americans risked their lives and futures by going to the polls despite threats and harassments.

Mississippi elected a remarkable group of politicians between 1868 and 1874. In 1868, at a constitutional convention, 16 African Americans and 84 whites had worked out a new constitutional document that included provisions against racial discrimination and property qualifications for juries and suffrage. The state legislature undertook to construct an economic system that would assist in pulling the state out of an economic crisis of the first order. The state

had been virtually wiped out during the Civil War. Perhaps not even Georgia, with General Sherman's March to Atlanta, suffered so much physical destruction as Mississippi. The state still lay in waste when the 40 black and 120 white state legislators took control of both houses in 1872.

The achievements of these reform-minded individuals were stunning under the circumstances. They reorganized the University of Mississippi, created a biracial educational system and voted to finance it, established two schools for African Americans, and set up one university for the training of African American professionals. In this state, one of the most wedded to the slavocracy, public accommodations were opened to all without regard to race or color. So advanced was the state legislature that new facilities for the handicapped were also voted on and funded.

Some of the giants of Reconstruction served here. John K. Lynch served as the speaker of the Mississippi lower house, T.

W. Cardozo was superintendent of education, James Hill was secretary of state, and A. K. Davis was lieutenant governor. Only three African Americans have ever served in the United States Senate, and two were from Mississippi. When Edward W. Brooke (Republican from Massachusetts) was elected in 1966, he joined the limited company of Hiram Revels and Blanche K. Bruce.

Revels's record and qualifications were superior in his day. He had served in the Union army, studied in seminary, and rose to the post of presiding elder in the African Methodist Church before he was elected to the Natchez City Council.

On January 20, 1870, the Mississippi legislature agreed, after petitions from the black community, to elect Revels to fill the unexpired U.S. Senate term of Confederate president Jefferson Davis. Revels was popular among the African American community and was well liked because of his generous nature. At the age of forty-two, Revels became the first African American senator in history. Acceptance by his Senate colleagues was not certain, however.

Pressure from the black community was constant and consistent. Revels was the best person qualified for the post. It took three days of debate over Revels's qualifications to settle the issue. When the election was finally held, the United States Senate voted overwhelmingly to seat the first African American senator. The public galleries broke out in joyous celebrations as Hiram Revels walked down the aisle for his swearing-in ceremony on Friday, February 25, 1870.

Blanche Bruce, Mississippi's second African American U.S. senator, served from 1875 to 1881. He was well educated and possessed impressive oratorical skills. Bruce had served in a number of government posts in the state of Mississippi prior to becoming a senator. He was sergeant-at-arms of the state senate, tax assessor for Bolivar County, and sheriff. He also served as superintendent of public schools. By the time of his 1874 election, Bruce owned a 1,000-acre farm.

Bruce was known as a spokesperson

for African Americans. He also made his mark in the Senate in support of the rights of other oppressed groups. He introduced numerous bills intended to improve the lives of African Americans; he castigated the United States for its treatment of the Native Americans; and he gave speeches against the bill that restricted Chinese immigration. Bruce was one of the most respected members of the Senate. He was proposed for the vice presidency in 1880. He withdrew in favor of Chester A. Arthur, who later became president. Bruce was eventually appointed registrar of the United States Treasury by President James A. Garfield.

GRANDFATHER CLAUSE

As soon as the Union Army withdrew from the South, the life and liberty of African Americans were at risk. Southern states found ways to render the thirteenth, fourteenth, and fifteenth amendments useless. The Fifteenth Amendment (1870) said "the right . . . to vote" could not be taken away because of "race, color, or previous condition of servitude." However, each of the southern states, led by Mississippi and South Carolina, devised novel responses to African American citizenship and voting rights. Most states employed three devices to eliminate African American voters from the polls: criminal convictions, poll taxes, and literacy tests. The state of Mississippi changed its constitution in 1890 to bar any person "convicted of bribery, burglary, theft, arson, obtaining money or goods under false pretenses, perjury, forgery, embezzlement or bigamy" from voting. To deprive Africans of the right to vote, the white officials often arrested blacks and convicted them of offenses to remove them from the voting rolls. Whites who actually committed such offenses were overlooked.

In addition to the criminal offense device, the states required a poll tax to be paid usually nine months before the election. Thus, the tax had to be paid in February if the election was held in November. The voter had to bring the receipt indicating payment to the polling place. Many African Americans were unable to pay the poll tax, which was cumulative: if a voter wanted to vote the poll tax for previous years had to be paid as well. Many more individuals, due to living conditions, were unable to keep the receipts for nine months. These receipts were often lost or misplaced between February and November. A potential voter who had no criminal record, who had paid the poll tax, and who kept the receipt still faced an additional test. The person would have to demonstrate that he could read and interpret sections of the state constitution. Many educated African Americans were denied the right to vote because the registrar was the sole judge.

Whites who may have lost their right to vote if the same rules were applied to them escaped disfranchisement because of laws the southerners referred to as "grandfather clauses." Louisiana passed such a law in 1898 when it became the third state to change its constitution to keep African Americans from voting. The Louisiana law read in part: "No male person who was on January 1st, 1867 or at any date prior thereto, entitled to vote . . . and no son or grandson of any such person . . . shall be denied the right to register and vote." Since blacks could not vote until after March 2, 1867, the law was discriminatory against virtually every African American in the state. Other states passed similar laws.

Some Key Cases of Racial Equality

The following cases represent a small number of Supreme Court decisions that have aided in the African American struggle for equality. Three of the cases showed the continual racism of the South. In Patterson v. Alabama, nine African American boys were found guilty of rape by an all-white jury while receiving an inadequate defense. They "committed no crime other than being black." In Smith v. Allwright, the state of Texas denied African Americans the right to vote in primaries, a direct violation of the 15th Amendment. Interracial marriages became the topic of the 1967 case Loving v. Virginia. A majority of white Americans (72% of Southern whites) were against "white-black unions," and sixteen states prohibited them.

The case of Brown v. Board of Education is perhaps the most important court decisions regarding African Americans. "Separate but equal" in education came to an end, and soon the idea of desegregation was expanded to housing and employment. Summaries of these cases follow.

Patterson v. Alabama (1931). The "Scottsboro Case" as it was called resulted in a strong decision from the Supreme Court that the denial of African Americans from a jury list resulted in the denial of a fair trial.

Smith v. Allwright (1944). This civil rights victory invalidated the intentional exclusion of African Americans from Texas's all white primary on the grounds that primaries are central to the electoral process. Whites had argued that the Democratic party was a private organization and thus exempt from the Fifteenth Amendment.

Brown v. Board of Education of Topeka, Kansas (1954). One of the most widely applauded decisions of the Supreme Court. The Court overruled the "separate but equal" doctrine announced in its infamous 1896 Plessy v. Ferguson decision and declared segregated schools unconstitutional.

Loving v. Virginia (1966). A civil rights landmark because it invalidated the antimiscegenation laws of Virginia and fifteen other states, which made it illegal for African Americans and whites to marry. The Supreme Court ruled that criminal bans on interracial marriage violated the Fourteenth Amendment's equal-protection clause and the freedom to marry, which the Court declared to be "one of the basic

"Now Ain't Them Hard Trials"

9

A New
Repression Cometh

In reaction to the end of Reconstruction, many southern states enacted repressive legislation with the aim of disfranchising Africans. By 1879, many African people felt compelled to leave the South. The years from 1890 to 1910 became the anvil upon which the rights and the spirits of Africans were severely crushed.

Africans had gone through cruel political repression and oppression from the very origins of the English settlements. However, free Africans had been able to vote in every one of the thirteen states except Georgia and South Carolina. In 1792, the state of Delaware enacted the first legislation against free Africans voting. This was followed by Maryland, Virginia, and other states. Finally, in 1814, Connecticut legislated against free Africans voting. By the time of the Civil War, called by some the "Uncivil War," only five states in New England and, under certain limitations, the state of New York allowed free Africans to vote.

The war brought new realities to the South. Indeed, the consequences were to be found in the Thirteenth Amendment to the Constitution, which abolished slavery, the Fourteenth Amendment, which gave citizenship to formerly enslaved Africans, and the Fifteenth Amendment, which protected the right to vote.

Yet the southern reaction to Reconstruction, with its mixture of achievements and failures largely due to Africans' lack of education, harassment by whites, and inadequate financing, was swift and brutal. All over the South in the decade from 1870 to 1880, white thefts, assaults, intimidations, suppression of ballot boxes, removal of polls to secret places, false certifications, and lynchings conspired to deny the African the right to vote.

The white northerners became interested in material advantages in the South and left the Africans to the conscience of the white southerner. In little or no time the evil peonage system was put into effect. Peonage meant that an African could be arrested for the smallest offense, and in many cases people were arrested for no offense and made to work for white landowners and businessmen. This outgrowth of the convict lease system continued many of the labor traditions of the plantation era.

Sharecropping was introduced to ensnare the labor of Africans who had committed no offenses but who were needed by white landowners to sow and harvest their crops. When Africans became satisfied with their share of the share system and sought to leave the farms, whites enacted new laws to make it technically illegal for an African to leave the employ of a white. In effect, slavery under the guise of a share system deprived Africans of labor and profits and threatened their lives.

LYNCHINGS

The lynchings of Africans in the South became one of the greatest blots on American society starting at the end of the nineteenth century (see figure 9.1, page 131). In 1872, twelve Africans were lynched; twenty years later the number had reached 255. Benjamin Brawley claims that "within a period of thirty five years not less than 3,200 Negro men and women were lynched within the boundaries of the United States, and sometimes the burning or mutilation of the victims was savage in its brutality" (Brawley 1924). (See figure 9.2, page 132.)

Whites could not exploit African labor without depriving Africans of their political rights and denying them justice in the courts. Thus, the South promulgated everywhere the idea of African inferiority and established that idea by providing inferior services and wages. Prisons proliferated to "break" the Africans who refused to bow to inferior treatment. In every sector of society—education, economics, and law—the Africans were given less and treated harshly. Whites became alarmed at the human being their policies had created. Simultaneously, whites feared and envied the freedom, virility, passion, and temperament of the African.

By 1893, white mobs lynched an African a day. Crime against a white

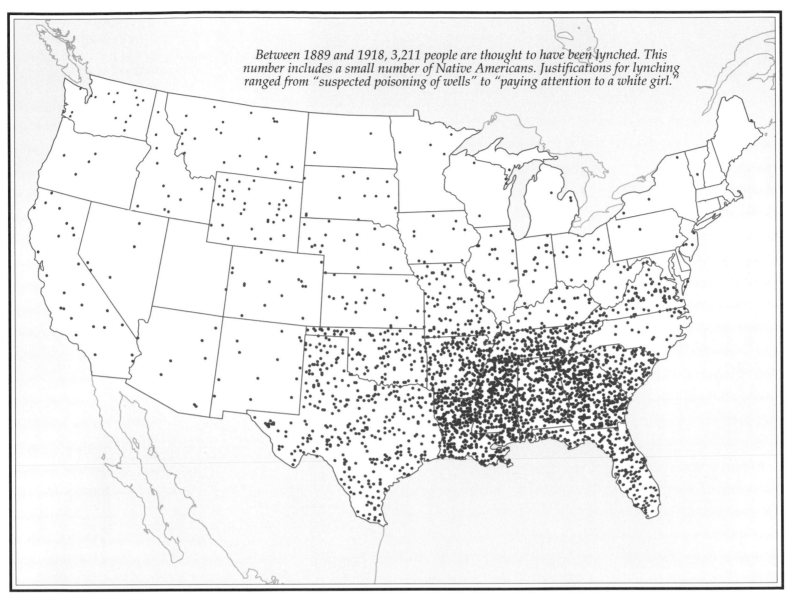

Between 1889 and 1918, 3,211 people are thought to have been lynched. This number includes a small number of Native Americans. Justifications for lynching ranged from "suspected poisoning of wells" to "paying attention to a white girl."

Figure 9.1 (above). Thirty years of lynchings: 1889 to 1918.

Table 9.1. Lynchings, 1889–1918.

State	Count	State	Count	State	Count
Alabama	276	Louisiana	313	Ohio	12
Alaska	4	Maine	1	Oklahoma	96
Arizona	8	Maryland	4	Oregon	4
Arkansas	214	Massachusetts	0	Pennsylvania	4
California	26	Michigan	4	Rhode Island	0
Colorado	18	Minnesota	4	South Carolina	120
Connecticut	0	Mississippi	373	South Dakota	13
Delaware	1	Missouri	81	Tennessee	196
Florida	178	Montana	22	Texas	335
Georgia	386	Nebraska	17	Utah	0
Idaho	11	Nevada	4	Vermont	0
Illinois	24	New Hampshire	0	Virginia	78
Indiana	19	New Jersey	3	Washington	16
Iowa	8	New Mexico	13	West Virginia	11
Kansas	22	New York	3	Wisconsin	4
Kentucky	27	North Carolina	22	Wyoming	34
		North Dakota	2		

**Figure 9.2 (above).
Lynching in the south.**

woman was the reason most frequently given as to what justified the lynching. However, Brawley says that "this did not figure in more than 30 percent of the cases recorded" over a thirty-year period. The most common reason seems to have been murder growing out of disputes over wages.

The situation did not moderate when the United States entered World War I. When the war was over and African American soldiers came home, they were met with the same segregation and racism they had left behind. *Crisis Magazine*, published by the National Association for the Advancement of Colored People, spoke for the returning soldiers in one of its editorial pages: "This country of ours, despite all its better souls have done and dream, is yet a shameful land. It lynches. . . . It disfranchises its own citizens. . . . It encourages ignorance. . . . It steals from us. . . . It insults us. . . . We return. We return from fighting. We return fighting. Make way for Democracy! We saved it in France, and by the Great Jehovah, we will save it in the U.S.A., or know the reason why."

In no nation had the systematic plunder of homes and the atrocious victimization of relatively defenseless people been prosecuted so vigorously before. It would be forty years before the Germans under the Nazis carried out their wanton attacks on the Jewish people. However,

**Figure 9.3 (near right).
Lucy Stone (1818–1893).
She traveled from town to town as an abolitionist lecturing against slavery and arguing for equality among all men and women.**

**Figure 9.4 (far right).
Lucretia Mott
(1793–1880). Helped to organize the Philadelphia Female Anti-Slavery Society of which she was president for many years. She argued for equal rights among men and women and all races.**

in a rash of irrationality the white mobs of the South attacked any African who expressed the desire or showed the will to act independently of whites. It was a time of great distress in the land. Two individuals, Booker T. Washington and Ida B. Wells Barnett, stepped into the spotlight to condemn the abuse of the justice system and the insanity of hangings, mutilations, and live burnings of African people. Together they made the prohibition of lynching one of the most important topics of the early twentieth century.

BOOKER T. WASHINGTON

Booker T. Washington sat astride African American politics, social interactions, and education for an entire generation (figure 9.5). The ramifications of his achievements were felt in every sector of the American society. Washington was the first "Negro spokesman" after Reconstruction. Born in West Virginia during the reign of slavery, he was educated at Hampton Institute and later founded Tuskegee Institute in Alabama. From this past, Booker T. Washington emerged as a national leader with a reputation far beyond the hamlet of his birth.

Washington was greeted by kings, queens, and presidents as the African American leader. Washington was consulted whenever anyone sought facts or opinions on questions related to African Americans. Consequently, his impact on African American education was impressive. During the Washingtonian era, it seemed little Tuskegees were being established everywhere, would-be African American leaders or educators modeled their styles after him, and major philanthropists endowed him with financial support for his institution.

His philosophy, stated in several books and hundreds of speeches, was straightforward: education of the hands and hearts for work and discipline was more important than political or social rights. This philosophy often threw him into conflict with African Americans from the North, such as W. Monroe Trotter and W. E. B. Du Bois. They believed that

political and civil rights were necessary to assure that whatever economic gains were achieved would be secured. Du Bois, for example, contended the right of African Americans to vote was fundamental to a democratic society.

Even more, Washington took strong exception to the Ku Klux Klan and was active in the antilynching campaign, giving his support to Ida B. Wells Barnett in her pursuit of a law against the lynch mob. Despite his detractors on many issues, Washington pressed ahead on creating a population of Africans in the South who would be self-sufficient and economically capable. Failure to recognize the intractability of racism in the South and throughout the nation and failure to adequately prepare students to resist the intellectual and cultural attacks on Africans may have been his most serious flaws. Nevertheless, African American education cannot be discussed in any meaningful way without comment on Booker T. Washington, who died in 1915.

Figure 9.5. Booker T. Washington (1856–1915). Born a slave, he became an educator, statesman, and a civil rights leader. He felt that African Americans needed to be better educated and more self-reliant in order to gain economic and moral advancement. Credit: Corbis-Bettmann.

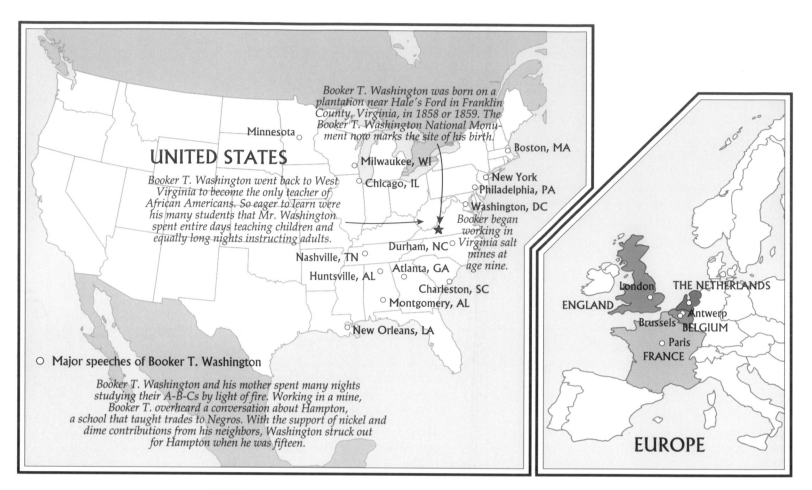

Booker T. Washington was born on a plantation near Hale's Ford in Franklin County, Virginia, in 1858 or 1859. The Booker T. Washington National Monument now marks the site of his birth.

UNITED STATES

Booker T. Washington went back to West Virginia to become the only teacher of African Americans. So eager to learn were his many students that Mr. Washington spent entire days teaching children and equally long nights instructing adults.

Minnesota ○

○ Milwaukee, WI
○ Chicago, IL

Boston, MA ○

○ New York
○ Philadelphia, PA

○ Washington, DC

Booker began working in Virginia salt mines at age nine.

Durham, NC ○

Nashville, TN ○

○ Atlanta, GA

Huntsville, AL ○

○ Charleston, SC
○ Montgomery, AL

○ New Orleans, LA

○ Major speeches of Booker T. Washington

Booker T. Washington and his mother spent many nights studying their A-B-Cs by light of fire. Working in a mine, Booker T. overheard a conversation about Hampton, a school that taught trades to Negros. With the support of nickel and dime contributions from his neighbors, Washington struck out for Hampton when he was fifteen.

London ○
ENGLAND

THE NETHERLANDS

○ Antwerp
Brussels ○ BELGIUM

○ Paris
FRANCE

EUROPE

Figure 9.6 (above). Speeches of and events in the life of Booker T. Washington.

Figure 9.7 (right). Travels of Booker T. Washington throughout the eastern United States.

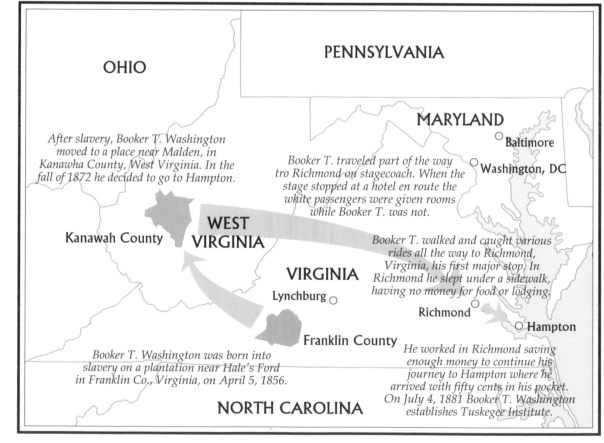

OHIO

PENNSYLVANIA

MARYLAND

○ Baltimore

After slavery, Booker T. Washington moved to a place near Malden, in Kanawha County, West Virginia. In the fall of 1872 he decided to go to Hampton.

○ Washington, DC

Booker T. traveled part of the way tro Richmond on stagecoach. When the stage stopped at a hotel en route the white passengers were given rooms while Booker T. was not.

WEST VIRGINIA

Kanawah County

Booker T. walked and caught various rides all the way to Richmond, Virginia, his first major stop. In Richmond he slept under a sidewalk, having no money for food or lodging.

VIRGINIA

Lynchburg ○

Richmond ○

○ Hampton

Franklin County

Booker T. Washington was born into slavery on a plantation near Hale's Ford in Franklin Co., Virginia, on April 5, 1856.

He worked in Richmond saving enough money to continue his journey to Hampton where he arrived with fifty cents in his pocket. On July 4, 1881 Booker T. Washington establishes Tuskegee Institute.

NORTH CAROLINA

IDA B. WELLS BARNETT

Born in Holly Springs, Mississippi, in 1862, Ida B. Wells began to teach in a country school at the age of fourteen (figure 9.8). Moving to Memphis in 1884, she continued to teach while attending Fisk University in Nashville during the summer. Due to a lawsuit involving her refusal to give up her seat in a railroad car designated for "whites only," Wells lost her teaching job and subsequently turned to journalism. For a time she wrote for a local Afro-American weekly, *Living Word,* and in 1891 she became co-owner and editor of the Memphis weekly, *Free Speech.* A year later, after she revealed in print who was responsible for the lynching of three Memphis Afro-Americans, a mob of whites demolished her printing press and office. Wells fled to New York City—where she was hired by an Afro-American weekly—and launched into an antilynching campaign. The antilynching cause took her on lecture tours across the country and to England twice. Later Wells settled in Chicago and in 1895 she married Ferdinand L. Barnett. In

Figure 9.8 (left). Ida B. Wells Barnett (1864–1931). She was one of a small number of women in the South to call attention to lynchings of African Americans and campaign for them to end.

Figure 9.9 (below). Speeches of and events in the life Ida B. Wells Barnett.

Ida B. Wells married militant race leader Ferdinand Barnett in Chicago and went on to become chair of the Anti-Lynching Bureau of the National Afro-American Rights League.

New England

Boston, MA

Rochester, NY

Chicago Philadelphia, PA

Nebraska Springfield, IL

California Washington, DC

East St. Louis, IL

Kansas Cairo, IL

Missouri Knoxville, TN

Little Rock, AR Memphis

Ida B. Wells Barnett was born in 1862 in Holly Springs, Mississippi.

Ida B. Wells Barnett worked as a teacher in Memphis, Tennessee where she compiled the first statistical phamplet on lynching called the Red Record.

○ Major speeches of Ida B. Wells Barnett

Ms. Wells Barnett became part owner and editor of the Memphis Free Speech. After exposing the facts behind the lynching of three African American business men, the paper was demolished by hoodlums in May, 1892.

Chicago, she contributed to newspapers and periodicals and also founded and headed the Ida B. Wells Club. In 1898, Wells led a delegation to President William McKinley to protest lynchings, and that same year she became the secretary of the national Afro-American Council. Some ten years later Wells founded the Negro Fellowship League. In 1913, she was appointed adult probation officer in Chicago, and two years later she was elected vice president of Chicago's Equal Rights League.

The state of Tennessee has recognized Ida B. Wells Barnett as one of its leading historical figures in communication. Few states can boast of someone as bold and brave as Ida B. Wells Barnett. In her prime she fought against all anti-African people, convinced that the African American people needed to defend themselves. She had been blessed with the ability to write and felt that it was her responsibility to take on the challenge of eradicating ignorance but most of all saving the innocent lives of African American people who were lynched as a matter of amusement. Never fearful of her own life (though she was placed in some difficult situations), Barnett could

only think of the mutilated bodies of black men and women that she had seen in the South. These sights alone were enough to give her all of the courage and boldness she needed.

The combination of the enterprising and courageous Ida B. Wells Barnett and Booker T. Washington was a powerful union of spirit and purpose. They both worked to get an antilynching bill passed. The difficulty this bill met in the United States Congress demonstrated the plight of the African American. With no one really defending the rights of the African, the antilynching law was certain never to see the light of day during the height of lynch law in the South. The lobby against the law was very strong and numerous attempts were made to force the Congress to abandon discussion of it. By now the Ku Klux Klan had grown to an organization of more than 100,000 white-hooded knights. They had made more than 200 appearances and seemed to flourish in the South and North Central States.

THE GRIMKES

The African American people have been tremendously tested by the circum-

Figure 9.10 (near right). A. H. Grimke (1849–1930). A lawyer, editor, politician, and civil rights leader who started the first African-American newspaper in New England while protesting all forms of discrimination and segregation.

Figure 9.11 (far right). F. J. Grimke (1850–1937). A clergyman and civil rights advocate who sided with the philosophy of W. E. B. Du Bois, he preached moral excellence as the way to achieve social and spiritual salvation.

stances of living in the United States. Yet in every generation there have been men and women who have taken up the task of fighting against injustices. The Grimke family was famous for its commitment to truth. In fact, Angela and Charlotte both had a compelling interest in demonstrating that Africans were not inferior to whites. Charlotte's journals are revelations of intense commitments to justice.

Strong convictions led Angela Grimke to write poetry and Charlotte Forten Grimke to write essays. The Grimkes were stalwarts against any kind of discrimination. An important aspect of the sense of eventual victory over segregation was the African American's vital belief that conditions can get better. With this faith the justice pioneers could go from victory to victory with confidence.

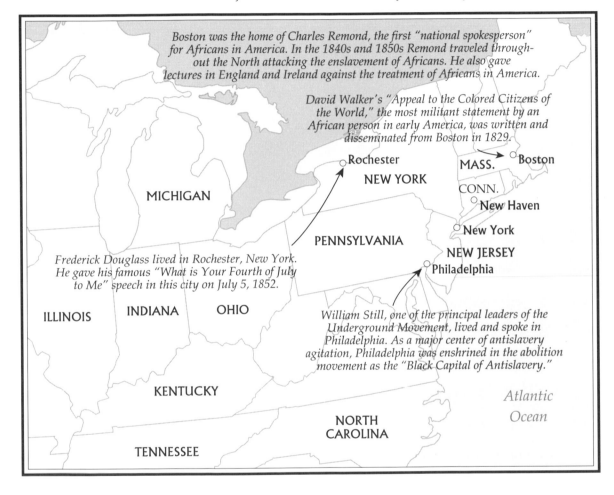

Figure 9.12. Early African orators and writers.

Boston was the home of Charles Remond, the first "national spokesperson" for Africans in America. In the 1840s and 1850s Remond traveled throughout the North attacking the enslavement of Africans. He also gave lectures in England and Ireland against the treatment of Africans in America.

David Walker's "Appeal to the Colored Citizens of the World," the most militant statement by an African person in early America, was written and disseminated from Boston in 1829.

Frederick Douglass lived in Rochester, New York. He gave his famous "What is Your Fourth of July to Me" speech in this city on July 5, 1852.

William Still, one of the principal leaders of the Underground Movement, lived and spoke in Philadelphia. As a major center of antislavery agitation, Philadelphia was enshrined in the abolition movement as the "Black Capital of Antislavery."

MICHIGAN

Rochester

NEW YORK

MASS. Boston

CONN.

New Haven

New York

NEW JERSEY

Philadelphia

PENNSYLVANIA

ILLINOIS INDIANA OHIO

KENTUCKY

NORTH CAROLINA

TENNESSEE

Atlantic Ocean

"And Still We Rise"

10

IN DEFIANCE
OF SEGREGATION

The achievements of African Americans in the arts, education, science, business, religion, and industry have been extraordinary within the historical realities of enslavement, segregation, and discrimination. Up from the valley of despair, African Americans have erected the banners of hope and human will in many different arenas. What is America without the names and accomplishments of Paul Robeson, Katherine Dunham, John Biggers, Elizabeth Catlett, Billie Holiday, Max Roach, Wynton Marsalis, John Coltrane, Duke Ellington, Sammy Davis Jr., Josephine Baker, Alvin Ailey, Pearl Primus, James Brown, Aretha Franklin, Michael Jackson, Miles Davis, Stevie Wonder, Ira Aldridge, Bill Cosby, Sidney Poitier, and Harry Belafonte? It is impossible to think seriously about literature without considering the significant works of Ralph Ellison, Toni Morrison, Langston Hughes, Alice Walker, Sonia Sanchez, Charles Fuller, Toni Cade Bambara, Gloria Naylor, Rita Dove, Mari Evans, Gwendolyn Brooks, August Wilson, Ed Bullins, James Baldwin, Richard Wright, Paul Laurence Dunbar, Carlton Molette, Sterling Brown, Zora Neale Hurston, Langston Hughes, Paul Carter Harrison, John Edgar Wideman, and Imamu Baraka.

In every field of human endeavor, African Americans have made lasting impressions. The moral stand taken by scholars, artists, writers, and educators has been based upon the social and political order in America. As Martin Luther King Jr. reminded his African American audiences, "We are in America, and we are in America to stay." King was giving voice to the generally accepted belief that the vast majority of African Americans will always be domiciled in the United States. In taking a stand to participate in the American arena, African Americans have fought in all of the wars, made contributions in every sphere, and sought to make the dream of equality a reality within the American society.

No intellectual, social, or political idea has escaped the thinking of the best minds of the population regarding the plight and condition of African Americans. The personalities who have given their intellectual resources to the problems confronting African Americans are a veritable panoply of brilliant and articulate leaders: Charles Remond, David Walker, Nat Turner, Frederick Douglass, Anna Julia Cooper, Henry Highland Garnet, T. Timothy Fortune, R. C. Benjamin, George T. Downing, Ida B. Wells, Mary Ann Shadd Cary, Marcus Garvey, A. Philip Randolph, Roy Wilkins, Mary McLeod Bethune, W. E. B. Du Bois, Malcolm X, and Adam Clayton Powell are just a few of the courageous men and women who have sought to make America responsive to the needs of the African American population.

The two social and political champions of the twentieth century, the fountains from which all other thinkers drank, were supported by the growing disenchantment among Africans in the urban areas of the North. Thus, Marcus Garvey and W. E. B. Du Bois found the source of their inspiration among the northern communities, each finding a different group of northerners for his power base. On the other hand, Booker T. Washington had already established himself as the agrarian apostle, believing that it was better for African Americans to perfect the working with hands in order to control industry and agriculture.

Garvey arrived in the United States in 1916, a year after Washington's death (see figures 9.2 and 9.3, page 143). He had admired him from afar and hoped to appeal to the same common people as Washington. Du Bois, college educated and erudite, found that he could best serve by continuing the line of thinking he had embarked on during Washington's lifetime.

MOVING ON UP

The generation of African Americans who lived in the first quarter of the twentieth century experienced a period of severe discrimination and injustice. With hardly any support from the federal government, they struggled to maintain homes and institutions under extreme conditions. White control of the South, sanctioned by the federal government, meant that Africans were not legally protected from the most overt kinds of racism. Any white person could insult any black person with impunity. By the turn of the century, the segregation mode introduced as custom in the South had attained legal status almost everywhere in the region. Africans suffered most from the inequities of the justice system.

The fact that the South had lost the war created a strong residual element of irrational hatred for Africans. Since the whites could not punish the federal government, they could certainly punish African Americans at will and dare the federal government to interfere with their states' rights to treat Africans any way they pleased. Furthermore, having lost free African labor, the whites resented the fact that they now had to pay Africans for work that was once done by enslaved Africans. So the justice system was the stage for southern victories over northern sentiments. For instance, even though the Supreme Court ruled that blacks had to be allowed on juries, it almost never occurred.

The structure of racial segregation did not develop immediately after Reconstruction but was gradually put in place by a series of complicated laws and maneuvers that had the effect of totally reducing the African to a slave within the framework of law. Much like apartheid was to become in South Africa, segregation in the South made everything legal. Prohibition against the African community was sanctioned by the law of the city or state. It was illegal for Africans to sleep in the same house with whites. It was illegal for Africans to attend theaters with whites, and so forth. Severe penalties would be exacted from Africans who violated the laws that had been set up to enforce segregation; many Africans paid the penalty of death for dignity.

In 1901, Congressman George White delivered his farewell address to Congress by saying that it was in behalf "of an outraged, heart-broken, bruised and bleeding, but God-fearing people,

faithful, industrious, loyal people—rising people, full of force." It would be more than a quarter of a century before an African would again serve in the Congress. Oscar De Priest, a Republican, would be elected congressman from Chicago in 1928, the first African American to be elected from a northern state.

Conditions became so desperate in the early part of the twentieth century that white philanthropists held several meetings of leading Africans to discuss the problems confronting the African American community. In 1904, John D. Rockefeller began donating large sums to train teachers for the African American community. During the next year, Andrew Carnegie called a meeting of black leaders, including Booker T. Washington and W. E. B. Du Bois.

The proposals from that conference included a resolution to press for absolute civil, political, and public equality. Du Bois was clearly in conflict with Washington's more conciliatory method. Thus, when the Niagara Movement was formed in 1905 with a representation that included twenty-nine militant African American intellectuals from fourteen states, it was in clear opposition to Booker T. Washington. When members of this group later formed the National Association for the Advancement of Colored People in 1909, Washington voiced his opposition.

The NAACP charter was signed by several prominent individuals including Du Bois, Jane Addams, John Dewey, Willam Dean Howells, and Lincoln Steffens. Signers of the NAACP charter understood the fragile nature of the African's life in the United States. They knew that despite the political rights that Africans were supposed to have in the North, these rights were often unavailable. Some states did not permit Africans to vote in the same manner as whites until the Fifteenth Amendment had been passed. Now in the twentieth century there were rights that had to be reinforced and tried on a regular basis before they became acceptable to white northerners. Political rights, shaky as they may have been in some northern states, were not quite as difficult to attain as civil rights. Segregated riding coaches persisted into the twentieth century in some northern communities; residential segregation was still practiced; and Africans could often be discriminated against in public accommodations in northern cities. As soon as African Americans began to hold posts in city governments and on the judiciary in the north, political rights led to some limited protection for civil rights. What the mass of Africans discovered was that laws on the books did not necessarily mean better living conditions. Outright public hostility toward Africans often carried more weight than the law. If white citizens rose up against the granting of some right to Africans, many times the right was rescinded.

Economically, the African American worker at the turn of the century was inheriting the whirlwind generated by the anti-African hostility of the post-Reconstruction period. Industrial employers in both the North and the South were discriminatory. Labor unions were hardly any different at the time. Africans were either not hired or if hired given the worst jobs in terms of condi-

tions and pay. Many of the craft unions exercised exclusionistic principles that kept blacks from well-paying positions. Instead of protecting all workers, the early unions protected positions for white men only. Actually, the hostility toward African workers was one of the chief reasons for the decline in the number of skilled Africans in the crafts. During the Great Enslavement, the majority of craftsmen in many areas were African. Blacksmiths, carpenters, plasterers, and other tradespeople during the enslavement were most often Africans. This did not change drastically until the post-Reconstruction period, when many immigrants from Europe began to arrive and take the skilled jobs blacks had held.

W. E. B. Du Bois

Du Bois's name is synonymous with the best in African American scholarship. No intellectual of his day ranks with him, although giants lived among the people: Woodson, Locke, Hurston, Brawley, Frazier. His intellectual life stretched from 1889 to 1963 and covered some of the most momentous times of our history.

Great Barrington, Massachusetts, is rather inauspicious in African American history except for the fact that it is the birthplace of Du Bois (figure 10.1). That alone has distinguished this tiny village in Massachusetts. From Great Barrington, Du Bois traveled to Fisk, Harvard, and Berlin for his education. Fisk infused the young Du Bois with the love of learning and gave him a lifetime commitment to the uplift of his people. Harvard and Berlin introduced him to the great minds of the European world and showed him how to secure his own place. When he received his doctorate in 1897, he had established himself as a scholar. His dissertation, "The Suppression of the African Slave Trade," is one of the most widely known dissertations in history.

Du Bois left African Americans with legacies of intellect, activism, and devotion to cause. He wrote more than 2,000 documents including books, articles, pamphlets, plays, poetry, manifestos, and protest essays. Like Imhotep, the first

Figure 10.1. W. E. B. Du Bois (1868–1963). An influential author and civil rights leader, he felt that African Americans needed to develop their own aesthetic and cultural values before they could gain true equality. Credit: Corbis-Bettmann.

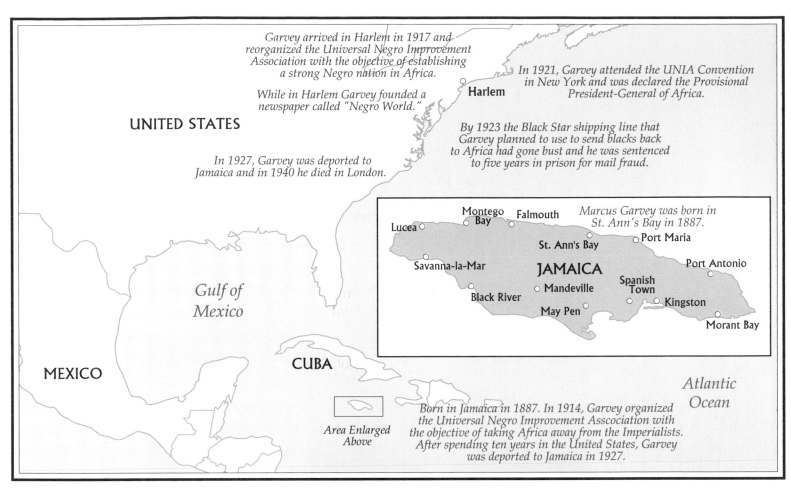

Garvey arrived in Harlem in 1917 and reorganized the Universal Negro Improvement Association with the objective of establishing a strong Negro nation in Africa.

While in Harlem Garvey founded a newspaper called "Negro World."

In 1921, Garvey attended the UNIA Convention in New York and was declared the Provisional President-General of Africa.

UNITED STATES

In 1927, Garvey was deported to Jamaica and in 1940 he died in London.

By 1923 the Black Star shipping line that Garvey planned to use to send blacks back to Africa had gone bust and he was sentenced to five years in prison for mail fraud.

Harlem

Montego Bay   Falmouth   Marcus Garvey was born in St. Ann's Bay in 1887.

Lucea

St. Ann's Bay   Port Maria

Savanna-la-Mar   JAMAICA   Port Antonio

Gulf of Mexico

Mandeville   Spanish Town

Black River   May Pen   Kingston

MEXICO   CUBA

Morant Bay

Atlantic Ocean

Area Enlarged Above

Born in Jamaica in 1887. In 1914, Garvey organized the Universal Negro Improvement Asscociation with the objective of taking Africa away from the Imperialists. After spending ten years in the United States, Garvey was deported to Jamaica in 1927.

multidimensional African intellect, Du Bois's intellectual output established him as a twentieth-century icon in history, sociology, and political science. An activist from his student days, he remained committed to erasing color discrimination until his death in Ghana in August 1963. As one of the founders of the National Association for the Advancement of Colored People, he promoted the campaign against racial discrimination for nearly fifty years as an active editor for the organization's *Crisis Magazine.*

Du Bois taught at Wilberforce University in Ohio and Atlanta University and was a visiting professor at dozens of universities around the world. Yet no major American university ever offered him a permanent post! The University of Pennsylvania made him an assistant (not assistant professor) while he wrote the monumental *The Philadelphia Negro.* Undaunted by racism, Du Bois kept the flame of his activism burning against all forms of discrimination. His devotion to cause meant that he

Figure 10.2 (above). 1887 through 1940: the life of Marcus Garvey.

Figure 10.3. Marcus Garvey (1887–1940). Born a West Indian, he dedicated his life to the "uplifting" of all Black people throughout the world, stating that they needed to form their own nations and institutions to be truly independent. Credit: Underwood & Underwood/Corbis-Bettmann.

applied discipline to every activity in the interest of African American rights.

The Great Depression

The economic collapse that hammered the United States during the 1930s struck the African American community, already at the lowest rung of the American economic ladder, with the most brutal blow. African American unemployment figures escalated far beyond their already high percentages during the Depression. By 1935, one-sixth of the people on relief were African Americans, who constituted about one-tenth of the total United States population. Being the last worker to be hired and the first to be fired, the African American could count on being out in the cold as the Great Depression bore down on the land.

President Roosevelt skillfully negotiated the social and economic interests of the African American community. The alphabet soup agencies—WPA, Works Progress Administration; CCC, Civilian Conservation Corps; and NYA, National Youth Administration—were strongly urged to hire African Americans as consultants and advisors. Wage differentials based on race were forbidden and the administration pursued a generally sensitive policy toward African Americans. The masses of the African population became Roosevelt New Deal Democrats and ended the dominance of the Republicans in African American politics.

In 1931, the nation followed the famous Scottsboro trial in the newspapers and on the radio. Nine African American youths were framed in Alabama. They were accused of attacking two white female hoboes. They were finally freed. By 1933, Franklin Delano Roosevelt had felt the outrage of the African American community and moved to hire several people, including the great Mary McLeod Bethune, as a "black Cabinet." Events that would remain in the annals of American history—such as Arthur Mitchell's election to Congress from Chicago as the first African American Democratic Congressman in 1934; Joe Louis's defeat of James J.

Braddock in 1937; William Hastie's appointment as a federal judge in the same year; and Marian Anderson's appearance before 75,000 at the Lincoln Memorial—could only add to the drama of the era.

Harlem Renaissance

An incredible aura of confidence and creativity occurred in the northern cities as African Americans journeyed to the urban areas during the 1920s. In New York City, the black population produced artists, writers, musicians, orators, dramatists, and entertainers of such great talents and with so much authenticity that the period was called the Harlem Renaissance. In fact, this period in American history was not only significant for the African American community but for the regeneration and rejuvenation of the entire scope of American art and entertainment. Lasting into the 1940s, the Harlem Renaissance was localized in New York, but its impact was far-ranging. Displaying the cultural and creative abilities of the African American community, writers and artists from various parts of the nation descended upon Harlem. Indeed, the name of the community was synonymous with all that was best in the African American population. Small communities in many cities identified themselves as Harlem. There were Harlem cookies, Harlem books, Harlem behaviors, and Harlem attitudes. Harlem was in vogue. Around the world, people heard the name of Harlem and it was no longer the Dutch city that people thought of but the American community made famous from the richness of its culture.

The best of the poets, the jazz and blues classicists, the choreographers and dancers with something new to demonstrate, and the plastic artists and dramatists who wanted to show the world what the African American had achieved in the art world since the emancipation came to this community by the droves. This was an upbeat time, the people were optimistic, the rhetoric was visionary, and the streets were lively. The literature of the period was varied and diverse. Langston

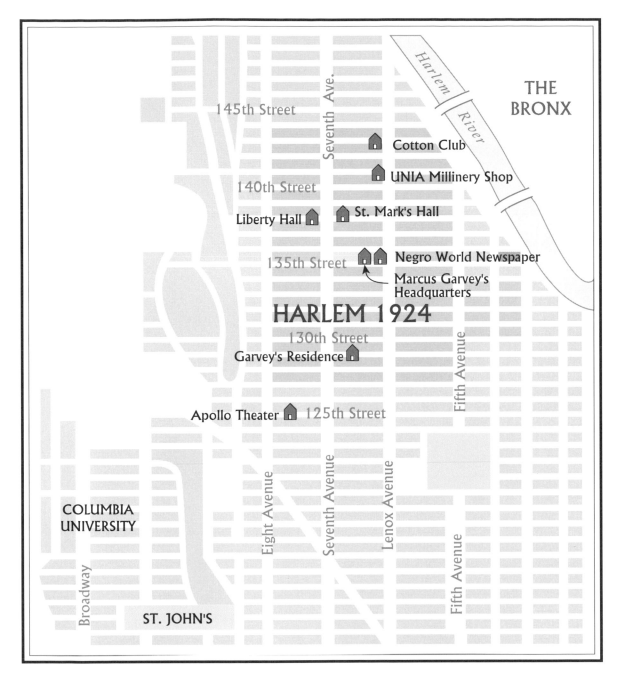

Figure 10.4. African Americans in Harlem in 1924.

Hughes and Zora Neale Hurston would be the king and queen of the parade of excellence and their dynamic voices would inspire numerous other poets and writers. Arna Bontemps, Sterling Brown, Robert Hayden, Owen Dodson, Margaret Walker, and Melvin Tolson would enter this chapter of the creative genius of the African Americans either as members of the Harlem community or contributors to its intellectual power. They drew their inspiration from earlier writers such as Countee Cullen, Claude McKay, James Weldon Johnson, Alain Locke, and Benjamin Brawley.

Although the Harlem Renaissance has been discussed in relationship to the influence it had on many white patrons and indeed their influence on the artists and writers of this period, most scholars believe that the Harlem cultural revolution was the single most important movement in the African American art community before the Black Power movement of the 1960s. Numerous books have appeared since the Harlem Renaissance that attest to the making of the critical and creative movement that pushed African American art to the forefront of the American cultural stage.

Figure 10.5 (near right). A. Phillip Randolph (1889–1979). Continually sought equal rights and labor opportunities; organized the Brotherhood of Sleeping Car porters and later arranged the first union contract between a white owner and Black laborers in 1937.

Figure 10.6 (far right). Lena Horne (1917–). Became the first African-American woman in American films to be fully supported by her studio as she appeared in musical scenes.

Figure 10.7 (near right). Langston Hughes (1902–1967). Considered one of the best writers of the twentieth century, he wrote many poems and novels with African Americans as his main characters. Credit: Library of Congress/Corbis.

Figure 10.8 (far right). Paul Robeson (1898–1976). Extremely intelligent and athletic, he gained popularity as an actor on stage because of his wonderful singing ability.

Among the names that should be on the tongues of every American child and certainly names that should be known by all African people are Paul Laurence Dunbar, one of the greatest dialect poets of all time, and Gwendolyn Brooks, the first African American poet to receive a Pulitzer Prize for poetry. They framed the Harlem Renaissance, Dunbar coming just before it, and Brooks coming just after it.

The character of a people is often reflected in the work of their writers. Arna Bontemps was a poet, novelist, and short-story writer whose career spanned the Harlem Renaissance and the early years of the Black Arts Movement. In 1925 he wrote "Golgotha Is a Mountain" and received the Alexander Pushkin Award for the poem. Two years later he received first honors in the *Crisis Magazine* contest for "Nocturnes at Bethesda." Among his novels are *Black Thunder, God Sends Sunday*, and *Drums at Dusk.*

Maya Angelou was born in St. Louis in 1928 (figure 10.10). She has lived in Acrra, Ghana, and London, England. She studied African dance with Pearl Primus in the 1950s. Angelou is a multitalented writer whose works (which were inspired by her own personal history) have created an entirely new biographical genre. Her international fame rests on her major work, *I Know Why the Caged Bird Sings.*

Zora Neale Hurston is by all accounts one of the most important figures in African American letters. She was born in 1903 in Eatonville, Florida. Hurston is the most dominant female figure in the Harlem Renaissance era. Her legacy is seen today in the writing of Toni Morrison, Alice Walker, Toni Cade Bambara, Kristin Hunter, Gloria Naylor, and Marita Golden. The elements of the Harlem Renaissance period that opened the way for a new interpretation of the African American reality were a commitment to understanding the historical and cultural values that had produced resilience, practical expression of the poetic and narrative qualities of the culture, and a full recognition of the emotional and rational attributes of a people who had raised themselves above the

Figure 10.9. Joe Louis (1914–1981). On June 22, 1937, he won the world's heavyweight championship of boxing and held the title longer than anyone else in boxing history (25 fights over 11 years, 8 months, and 7 days). Credit: Library of Congress/Corbis.

Figure 10.10. Maya Angelou (1928–). She has become one of America's most visible African American writers gaining popularity with autobiographies describing her experiences with racism in the South. Credit: UPI/Corbis-Bettmann.

Figure 10.11 (near right).
Ruby Dee (1923–). Born Ruby Ann Wallace, she became an actress with a long, solid career where she often portrayed helpful, understanding wives; later married actor Ossie Davis. Shown here, tear in eye, listening to Jesse Jackson. Credit: Jacques M. Chenet/Corbis.

Figure 10.12 (far right).
Pearl Primus (1919–). Born in Trinidad, she moved to New York City and became a successful dancer in 1944. Her travels throughout the South and her experiences with sharecroppers greatly influenced her choreography.

Figure 10.13 (near right).
Richard Wright (1908–1960). In the 1940s, he set the standard for modern prose writers while using his own life experiences to demonstrate racial inequality in the United States.

Figure 10.14 (far right).
Count Basie (1904–1984). "The man who put the 'swing' in the Swing era." He assembled the Count Basie Orchestra, which performed with many popular vocalists.

Figure 10.15. Jackson State University. From top left: Arna Bontemps, Melvin Tolson, Jacob Reddick, Owen Dodson, Robert Hayden. From bottom left: Sterling Brown, Zora Neale Hurston, Margaret Walker, Langston Hughes.

conditions of oppression. It was a self-assertive age, a time of concrete response to the many dimensions of life in the urban communities of the North. But this response, dynamic and spontaneous at first, became in the lengthening years of the Renaissance a more deliberate response. One reason for this type of response had to do with the popularity of the earlier voices, such as Countee Cullen, Claude McKay, and Alain Locke. They made it possible for the voices of Langston Hughes, Arna Bontemps, and Zora Neale Hurston to be more deliberate in their creative responses to the circumstances they encountered later.

Commercial success had a lot to do with this inasmuch as they also had sponsors who were capable of giving them money to produce shows, read poetry, write books, or go on trips to investigate cultural and historical phenomena related to African people. Thus, the elements that were responsible in the first place for the outbursts of intellectual and creative energies that were dubbed the Harlem Renaissance were essentially superseded by new circumstances. This did not mean that the Renaissance had lost its character; it only meant that the writers of the era were becoming more capable of determining what needed to

be said to different audiences. Quite frankly, the Harlem Renaissance prepared the way for other movements in the African diaspora—the Negritude movement in France, the Indigenist movement of Haiti, Abdias do Nascimento's Negro Theatre movement of Rio de Janeiro, and the Afro-Cuban Movement of Nicolas Guillen.

THE GREAT WARS
OF THE TWENTIETH CENTURY

More than 700,000 African Americans registered for the armed forces on July 5, 1917. Before the end of World War I more than 2,290,500 men and women had enlisted; 400,000 of those had been called into active service. According to John Hope Franklin, the eminent historian, 32 percent of blacks who registered were accepted while only 26 percent of whites were accepted due to discrimination against blacks in the matter of exemptions (see *From Slavery to Freedom*, New York: Vintage, 1966, pp. 455–70).

One of the sharpest blows to the African American population was the retirement of the highest-ranking black officer, Colonel Charles Young, due to high blood pressure. Colonel Young rode his horse from Ohio to Washington, D.C., to demonstrate his health, but to no avail.

The retirement board was not convinced that he was physically fit and did not rescind his retirement. African Americans took up the challenge of commissioned officers as a civil rights campaign. Congress created schools to train white officers but not black officers. A delegation of distinguished citizens led by Joel Spingarn appealed to the military authorities to make the training of African American officers one of their priorities. The military establishment was unconvinced. Subsequently, agitation grew at Fisk, Howard, Tuskegee, Atlanta, and Lincoln as well as some other colleges. Soon thereafter, General Leonard Wood met with Joel Spingarn and asked him to secure the names of 200 African Americans of college status willing to become officers. The Central Committee of Negro College Men was established at Howard University and within ten days it had gotten the names of 1,500 men who wanted to become army officers. A sustained campaign, supported by the NAACP and other organizations, was mounted to get Congress to act. Finally, the camp, segregated from the white training camps and isolated from the black communities, was established in Fort Des Moines, Iowa. On October 15, 1917, 639 men received their commissions.

To further combat German propaganda circulating in the United States about America's alleged plan to use black soldiers as cannon fodder, Emmett J. Scott, who had been Booker T. Washington's secretary for eighteen years, was made special assistant to the U.S. secretary of war, Newton Baker.

Nevertheless, during World War I no African Americans served in the Marine Corps, and in the navy they served only in the most menial jobs. The army permitted African Americans in every section except aviation. All other units were open: African Americans could serve in units such as engineering, infantry, cavalry, signal corps, hospital corps, field artillery, intelligence, adjutants, chaplains, and mechanics. The army of the early twentieth century was segregated and the positions opened to blacks were limited; yet African American resistance to discrimination in the army was sustained and persistent.

African Americans serving in the armed forces faced daily threats, insults, and harassments. In Charlotte, North Carolina, where 10,000 African Americans were stationed, only a table outside a YMCA frequented by white soldiers was available for African Americans to use to write letters. The military police attacked African American soldiers at will, and white officers assigned them to the most difficult, hazardous labor battalions even though they had qualified for posts requiring higher skills. Under such circumstances it was difficult to keep up morale for fighting for one's country. However, convinced that it was necessary to demonstrate once more the African's persistence, few men gave up under the oppressive conditions.

In September 1917 some of the men of the Twenty-fourth Infantry became embroiled in a general riot with whites in Houston, Texas. Numerous and repeated insults were hurled at the African American soldiers by the white civilians. The commanding officer disarmed the soldiers, fearing that they might be provoked into using their weapons to defend themselves. The soldiers refused to provide opportunity for the citizenry to attack them with civilian weapons and managed to retain some weapons of their own. Seventeen whites were killed in the ensuing battle. Thirteen soldiers were hanged for murder and mutiny and forty-one sentenced to life in prison. With no pretense of a fair trial, the government came down on the side of white racism and against the honest self-defense of its own African soldiers. The trial and case linger in the African American psyche as one of the greatest examples of American injustice. The thirteen soldiers have never been forgotten and now they are martyrs to the cause of dignity. The Pulitzer Prize-winning dramatist Charles Fuller captures the poignancy of these issues in his powerful play *The Brownsville Raid*. In 1973, Representative Augustus E.

Hawkins, Democrat from California, sponsored a bill in the U.S. Congress directing the secretary of defense to rescind the effect of the dishonorable discharges of the Brownsville soldiers. Meanwhile, Army Secretary Robert Froehlke ordered the charges dropped and the dishonorable discharges changed to honorable discharges.

When the opportunity came to distinguish themselves on the war front, the African Americans did not wane. The 369th United States Infantry arrived in France in early 1918. By April of the same year, they had moved to the front lines of the fighting, exactly one year to the day after the American government had declared war on Germany.

Few men have fought more bravely. They took Champagne and for a few months held almost 20 percent of the territory occupied by American forces. The 369th was then moved into the direct path of the German offensive at Minaucourt and bore the heaviest part of the offensive. But they did not budge. By the end of the war they had received numerous awards and recognitions. They were the first allied unit to reach the Rhine River. They never lost a man to capture. They never lost a trench. They never lost a foot of territory. Furthermore, the historic 369th served in active combat as a unit of a foreign army longer than any other American unit in battle; the brave men fought for 191 continuous days on the front line. The Germans called them the "Hell Fighters" and the entire regiment won the French government's Croix de Guerre. One hundred seventy-one individuals were cited with the Croix de Guerre and Legion of Honor for exceptional gallantry.

In addition to the Hell Fighters of the 369th, the Eighth Illinois Infantry, renamed the 370th United States Infantry when it reached France, the 371st Infantry, which was organized at Camp Jackson, South Carolina, the 372nd Infantry, composed of African American national guardsmen, all fought in France. The 370th, equipped with French weapons, served in Mihiel and the Argonne Forest by September 1918. The 270th had begun a campaign from the area around Mont de Tombes and Les Tueries to pursue the Germans out of France and into Belgium. Twenty-one men received the Distinguished Service Cross, one received the Distinguished Service Medal, and sixty-eight were awarded some grade of the Croix de Guerre. The 370th was involved in the last battle of the war, attacking and capturing fifty German supply wagons and their crews half an hour after the armistice went into effect.

The 371st Infantry Regiment arrived in France in April 1918. It was attached to the French 157th Division, the famous "Red Hand." The 371st held the front at Avocourt and later at Verriores for three months. In the September offensive, the 371st took several German posts near Monthois. They captured German prisoners, weapons, a munitions depot, and several railroad cars. For this brave action the entire regiment was decorated by the French government. Three officers won the Legion of Honor, 123 won the Croix de Guerre, and 26 won the Distinguished Service Cross.

The 372nd was a combination of national guardsmen from several states and the District of Columbia. It also reached France in April 1918. In May, this regiment took over the defense of the West Argonne sector. For three months the 372nd came under intense shelling, but by September the regiment was in hot pursuit of the enemy. The French general Moreau decorated the regiment's colors after German surrender in November.

Every African American fighting unit paid a heavy price. The Germans dropped leaflets on the soldiers of the 92nd Division stating that the United States was a racist nation that would never give Africans equal opportunity or justice even if they fought for the Americans. Not one African American deserted to the German side, although every African American recognized the social and political situation in the United States.

America presented the African American soldier with racism, discrimination, and indignity. Yet most of the military men and women subscribed to the eventual overthrow of American injustice. They were fighting men and women whose purpose was to demonstrate the commitment and loyalty of the African American to the United States. The persistent failure of the American society to reward the heroism of African Americans after World War I became a sad reminder of the truth in the German propaganda. Of course, as time would prove, the African Americans understood much more about the nature of racism than the Germans thought. When World War II started and German racism against Jews, the Roma, and Africans became clear, the German actions were validation of the suspicions of the African American soldiers of World War I.

Many African Americans distinguished themselves in every war fought by the United States. A few reached high positions in the military during the world wars. Others achieved fame during the Korean and Vietnam wars. The names of the heroes of battle are like diamonds studded in the center of every page of American warfare: Peter Salem, Salem Poor, Christian Fleetwood, Dorie Miller, Benjamin O. Davis, Chappie Tames, Colin Powell, and hundreds of others.

Figure 10.16. General Benjamin O. Davis (1877–1970). In the course of a fifty-year military career, he became the first African American to become a general in the United States army. Credit: UPI/Corbis-Bettmann.

Figure 10.17. General "Chappie" James (1920–1978). The first African-American four-star general in United States military history; as a member of the Air Force he was an ace pilot during the Korean War.

COLIN POWELL

General Colin Powell was born in New York City of hardworking Jamaican immigrants in 1937 (figure 10.18). He grew up poor in the Bronx and attended public schools in New York City, the City College of New York, and graduated with a major in Geology in 1958. Subsequently he entered George Washington University and received an MBA.

At City College he signed up for the ROTC and when he graduated he received a commission as an army Second Lieutenant. His career was meteoric in the military training school and he succeeded as an officer. Powell saw combat in two tours of Vietnam, became chief aide to Casper Weinberger, and then served as national security advisor under President Reagan. He played a role in the American deployments in Panama and the Persian Gulf. By 1989, he had been appointed by President Bush to the Chair of the Joint Chiefs of Staff, the highest military rank ever attained by an African American. He was decorated with numerous United States medals including the Bronze Star Medal and the Purple Heart.

After the Persian Gulf War General Powell became a national hero. He was known for a candid, straightforward, blunt-talking style that made him a magnetic personality to many people. Encouraged by friends to run for the highest office in the nation, General Powell considered the idea and rejected it, preferring in the middle 90s to enjoy his role as a charismatic leader.

Figure 10.18. Colin Powell, Chairman of the Joint Chiefs of Staff, poses with Desert Storm troups in Saudi Arabia. Credit: Senior Airman Rodney Kerns, USAF.

"Great Day, Great Day, the Righteous Marching"

11

THE ERA OF
DEMONSTRATIVE PROTEST

The inexorable movement toward justice and equality in American society was made so because of the sparks of genius that ignited the flames of an inextinguishable warrant for righteousness. First among the many who lit the fires of resistance and stoked the embers of consciousness was Dr. Martin Luther King Jr.

MARTIN LUTHER KING JR.

Martin Luther King Jr. epitomized the decade of the Civil Rights Movement (figure 11.1). Two events may be said to have contextualized the decade. One event, Brown *v.* Board of Education of Topeka, Kansas, occurred in 1954 as a decision by the Supreme Court (see page 127); the other, the Civil Rights Act of 1964, was an action of the Congress of the United States.

The electric nature of the protests and demonstrations led by King and his Southern Christian Leadership Conference colleagues such as Jesse Jackson (see figure 11.2, page 157) stole much of the limelight from the aging National Association for the Advancement of Colored People and the Urban League, both of which had been content to rely on legal solutions and economic answers to the problems confronting African Americans. King's movement had the moral authority of the Christian church and the labor leaders and the international community behind it. He transcended the narrow legal confines of the American judiciary and raised a higher level of questions about the possibilities of human beings living together in a free and open society.

Martin Luther King symbolized an entire era of civil protest in the United States. Valiant and eloquent, he was the consummate field marshal on the battlefield of justice. African Americans saw in King the long-awaited promise of the deliverer who would put before the courts and officials the numerous grievances of an oppressed, segregated, and passionate people.

There were several events that propelled King to the forefront of the Civil Rights Movement. In the first instance, the 1954 Supreme Court decision found that segregated schools were inherently unequal, thus reversing a half-century of tradition and law that had begun with Plessy *v.* Ferguson. This prepared the way for numerous challenges to segregation, the practice of separating the races and giving African Americans the least desirable part of the separation. In 1955, Rosa Parks refused to get up from her seat on a Montgomery bus because she was tired, an action that initiated the Montgomery bus boycott. Martin Luther King became the chief spokesperson and leading strategist of the boycott. Alongside Fred Cray, then a young attorney, King developed a civil rights mode of operation that would culminate in many successors.

Throughout the South, segregation was confronted as never before. It was the age of heroes and heroines. Courageous African American elementary and high school students marched into hostile educational institutions with only their faith that justice would be victorious on their side. President Dwight Eisenhower ordered U.S. troops into Little Rock, Arkansas, to enforce court-ordered desegregation in 1957. Three

Figure 11.1. Martin Luther King Jr. (1929–1968). Using nonviolent protests and passive resistance, he was the driving force in gaining equal rights for African Americans during the Civil Rights Movement that began in the 1950s. Shown here, arm-in-arm with the Reverend Ralph Abernathy, King marches in protest through the streets of Chicago. Credit: UPI/Corbis-Bettmann.

years later, four North Carolina college students began a lunch counter sit-in at a department store. The movement swept across the entire nation as African Americans demanded to be served as any other citizens would be served.

King mounted scores of protests in small and large cities; freedom riders tested desegregation laws and were mobbed in 1961 by groups in Birmingham, Alabama; James Meredith was guarded by U.S. marshals as he became the first African to enroll at the University of Mississippi in 1962. By 1963, civil rights protests had reached their peak and thousands of people had been arrested and jailed and scores of people murdered in the quest for freedom. The 1963 March on Washington brought more than 200,000 people together at the Lincoln Memorial to demand jobs and civil rights legislation. It was Martin Luther King's and the Civil Rights Movement's finest hour.

August 28, 1963, was memorable because of King's eloquent "I Have a Dream" speech. This was the high point of national consciousness about racial inequality. The Civil Rights Movement was united as never before. From this time forward, legislators began a campaign to place civil rights on the legislative agenda of the United States. King emerged from this speech as the moral voice of a nation. The United States would never be the same and the meaning of America would be stretched to include more people. By the time of his assassination in 1968 Martin Luther King Jr. had become the moral icon of a generation. His death elevated him even more to a position of national hero.

Out of this movement came new coalitions, new arguments for justice, new approaches to racism, and new methods for negotiating with recalcitrant administrations. Released at this time also were energies that led to more militant and insistent calls for revolution and change in the way the nation conducted social and political business. The voices of Huey P. Newton, Maulana Karenga, Bobby Seale, Stokely Carmichael, Eldridge Cleaver, and Angela Davis were

raised in new lines of argument. They were young voices, the children of Malcolm X, who would be heard in the corridors of power and whose words would be repeated in the pulpits.

Malcolm X, like Martin Luther King, was a pivotal figure in the movement for equal rights and opportunities for African Americans. Malcolm X was as much an authentic hero as Martin Luther King. He was as responsible as anyone for the Black Power Movement because he was the spiritual force behind it. Stokely Carmichael, the national chairperson of the Student Nonviolent Coordinating Committee (SNCC), may have shouted the words "black power" in 1966, which he had heard in Adam Clayton Powell's speech at Howard University, but it was Malcolm X's day.

The Black Power Movement was not a sudden departure from the Civil Rights Movement, but rather it was a carefully developed strategy that had its roots in the philosophy of the cultural national-

Figure 11.2. Jesse L. Jackson (1941–). Among the leadership of the Southern Christian Leadership Conference (SCLC) was Jesse Jackson, shown here, years later with Butch Johnson. Starting as a Baptist minister, Jackson founded PUSH (People United to Save Humanity) in the early 1960s. Later, he founded the Rainbow Coalition, which provided a platform from which Jackson mounted a strong bid for the Democratic presidential nomination in 1984. Credit: Jacques M. Chenet/Corbis.

Figure 11.3. The funeral of Martin Luther King followed his assassination on April 4, 1968. The facts of the events surrounding the assassination are now in question. Three days following the murder, Coretta Scott King, pictured here with entertainer Harry Belafonte, takes her place in front of marchers led by Reverend Ralph Abernathy SCLC's appointed successor to King. Credit: Flip Schulke/Corbis.

Figure 11.4. Malcolm X (1925–1965). Often seen as a controversial civil rights leader, he preached self-help, self-defense, and a strong education as the primary ways to win equality for African Americans. Credit: UPI/Corbis-Bettmann.

ists. Chief among these individuals was Malcolm X, a follower of the Honorable Elijah Muhammad of the Nation of Islam. It was the nationalists' philosophies of self-help, self-interested policies, no-nonsense politics, and strong cultural values that made the call for black power so natural during the 1960s. It expressed faith in the ability of African Americans to act for themselves. The refrain was interpreted by many Americans as a separatist call. White groups that had given support to civil rights organizations began to question whether they should continue to do so. Some dropped their support and criticized black leadership for not calling for sanctions against Carmichael and the Black Power leaders. Maulana Karenga of the US movement and Huey Newton of the Black Panthers occupied central places in the evolution of ideas that were found in both King's and Malcolm X's doctrines.

MALCOLM X

Malcolm X did not attend the March on Washington. He was at the height of his personal charisma as a national leader and stood out as the only visible African American leader who refused to meet President John Kennedy. Malcolm X believed that the president was not doing enough to advance the rights of Africans. He expressed the belief that the United States should have protected working-class Africans in the South from the Ku Klux Klan. His positions on issues had been formed by the discipline of the Nation of Islam.

Malcolm X was born Malcolm Little in Omaha, Nebraska (figure 11.4). He lived in Detroit, Boston, and New York. He converted to the Islamic teachings of the Honorable Elijah Muhammad while in prison. When he came out of prison in the 1950 he became an ardent follower of and the leading evangelist for the Nation of Islam. In 1964, Malcolm X broke with the Nation of Islam and Elijah Muhammad to form his own organization, the Organization of Afro-American Unity.

The strength of Malcolm X's appeal was his simple, unrelenting logic. Few

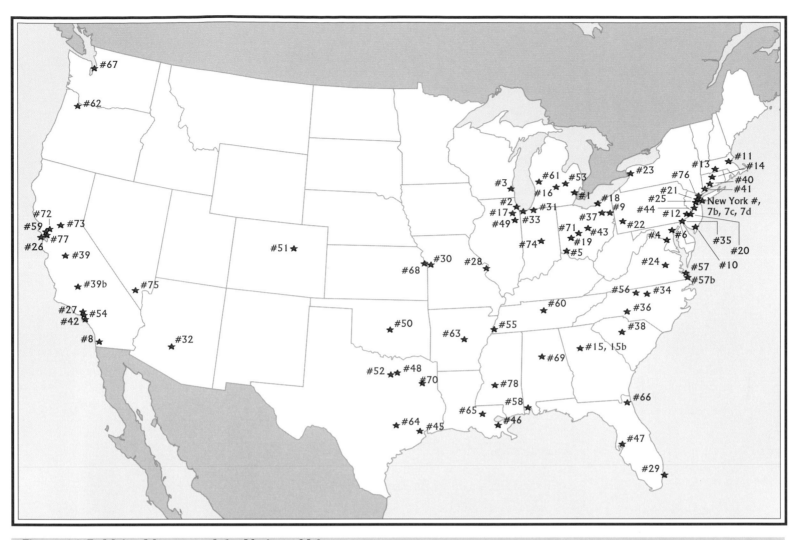

Figure 11.5. Major Mosques of the Nation of Islam.

1. Detroit, MI
2. Chicago, IL
3. Milwaukee, WI
4. Washington, D.C.
5. Cincinnati, OH
6. Baltimore, MD
7. New York, NY
   (a) Harlem
   (b) Corona
   (c) Brooklyn
   (d) Bronx
8. San Diego, CA
9. Youngstown, OH
10. Atlantic City, NJ
11. Boston, MA
12. Philadelphia, PA
13. Springfield, OH
14. Hartford, CT
15. (a) Atlanta, GA
    (b) Atlanta, GA
16. Lansing, MI

17. Joliet, IL
18. Cleveland, OH
19. Dayton, OH
20. Camden, NJ
21. Jersey City, NJ
22. Pittsburgh, PA
23. Buffalo, NY
24. Richmond, VA
25. Newark, NJ
26. San Francisco, CA
27. Los Angeles, CA
28. St. Louis, MO
29. Miami, FL
30. Kansas City, MO
31. South Bend, IN
32. Phoenix, AZ
33. Gary, IN
34. Durham, NC
35. Wilmington, DE
36. Charlotte, NC
37. Akron, OH

38. Columbia, SC
39. (a) Fresno, CA
    (b) Bakersfield, CA
40. New Haven, CT
41. Bridgeport, CT
42. Long Beach, CA
43. Columbus, OH
44. Trenton, NJ
45. Houston, TX
46. New Orleans, LA
47. Tampa, FL
48. Dallas, TX
49. Kankakee, IL
50. Oklahoma City, OK
51. Denver, CO
52. Fort Worth, TX
53. Flint, MI
54. Compton, CA
55. Memphis, TN
56. Winston-Salem, NC
57. (a) Norfolk, VA

   (b) Portsmouth, VA
58. Prichard, AL
59. Pittsburg, PA
60. Nashville, TN
61. Grand Rapids, MI
62. Portland, OR
63. Little Rock, AR
64. Austin, TX
65. Baton Rouge, LA
66. Jacksonville, FL
67. Seattle, WA
68. Kansas City, KS
69. Birmingham, AL
70. Tyler, TX
71. Springfield, OH
72. Richmond, VA
73. Sacramento, CA
74. Indianapolis, IN
75. Las Vegas, NV
76. Patterson, NJ
77. Oakland, CA

speakers could match his control of the idioms and tropes that represented the culture of African American people in urban communities. He had mastered the best elements of the culture and could bring them to bear on the most complex issues facing the African community. Ossie Davis said of Malcolm X, "He was our manhood." He spoke the words that were on the minds and in the hearts of thousands of downtrodden and exploited Africans. His eloquence was not the eloquence that comes from reading high-sounding books or studying the figures and metaphors of the ancient writers and speakers, but one solidly based in the folkways and cultural styles of the people to whom he addressed his words.

His message made people feel that he was genuinely concerned about the issues to which he gave voice. Malcolm X could not be questioned on ethical and moral grounds without responding with precise arguments. He understood the nature of his leadership role and acted it with tremendous fidelity to his movement.

Malcolm X understood what many of the professors analyzing his words and writings did not understand. He knew that the principal struggle was for the minds of the African American people. Few scholars and writers accepted his analysis while he was alive. In fact, Archie Epps questioned whether Malcolm X understood that it was irrelevant that Africans had had civilizations hundreds of years ago. What one sees is that Malcolm X was far beyond his detractors in his analysis of the conditions of blacks in America. What he was saying in his speeches was that the conquest of the mind is necessary before you can have the proper conquest of material conditions. His life was committed to substance in the midst of a society committed to symbol. There was no empty rhetoric in his soul, no carnal imagination, no evil spirit, just simple, direct, committed logic in support of the best values and traditions of a society founded on revolution and change. This meant that he had to attack the false signs and images that paraded as justice and righteousness. His intent was to love in a cleansing manner. He erected no great monuments to piety, but he played in the same arena of civil and human relations as the great thinkers of any age.

His chief gift to the nation was the common sense of his oratory. He understood reality at a time when others were dealing in platitudes. He spoke not to some theoretical audience but to his own people. In the best traditions of oratory and rhetorical theory, Malcolm X was a master because when he spoke his audiences felt that they could have given the same speech had they the ability and the courage.

Coupled with this unusual gift of oratory was his sincerity. There has rarely been an African American leader who conveyed more honesty than Malcolm X. Those who heard him knew exactly what he meant because in the manner of his speaking he told them what he meant.

MAULANA KARENGA

The philosopher Maulana Karenga created the Kwanzaa holiday as a celebration of joy in 1966 (see figure 11.6, page 161). The seven principles of family-hood—umoja, unity; kujichagulia, self-determination; ujima, collective work and responsibility; ujamaa, cooperative economics; nia, purpose; kuumba, creativity; and imani, faith—are the centerpieces of the celebration. Kwanzaa begins on December 26 and lasts for seven days. One candle is lit on each of the seven days and one of the principles is discussed. Among the items necessary for the Kwanzaa celebration are the kinara, candleholders; mkeke, mat; kikombe, the cup; and various hand-made gifts.

During the 1960s Maulana Karenga was a doctoral student at the University of California, Los Angeles, when he conceived of the organization US for the liberation of the minds of African Americans. He believed it was impossible to discuss political or economic liberation until there had been psychological liberation. The US movement maintained a consistent policy of teaching African

American cultural values, and its Kawaida (custom and tradition) philosophy gave birth to numerous student groups around the nation. Karenga's movement included the writers Imamu Baraka and Haki Madhubuti, both of whom established institutions based on the Kawaida philosophy. Kawaida's appeal was both intellectual and political.

HUEY P. NEWTON AND BOBBY SEALE

Huey P. Newton and Bobby Seale were the cofounders of the Black Panther Party in Oakland, California (see figures 11.7, 11.8, and 11.10, page 162 and figure 11.11, page 163). The party had a ten-point program that included the freeing of all political prisoners, the feeding of schoolchildren, and the removal of the police from the African American community. A key component of the Black Panther Party was self-defense for the African community. They argued that it was as American as the Constitution for a person to defend himself or herself.

THE GROWTH OF ISLAM

Islam's greatest growth among African Americans was generated in the twentieth century by six charismatic readers: Noble Drew Ali, Master Wallace Fard Muhammad, Honorable Elijah Muhammad, Malcolm X, Wallace D. Muhammad, and Louis Farrakhan. Each leader attracted new adherents and taught Islam as an alternative to the Christian religion. Noble Drew Ali came to Newark, New Jersey, from North Carolina and founded the Moorish Science Temple in 1913. He established temples in Philadelphia, New York, Baltimore, Boston, and Chicago. In 1929, Ali died in Chicago while still trying to institutionalize the Moorish Science Temple. His success had been encouraging, and soon after his death W. D. Fard (or Master Wallace Fard Muhammad) appeared in Detroit as the reincarnation of Noble Drew Ali. He set up temples of Islam in Detroit and Chicago, attracting many followers from the Garvey Movement as well as from Ali's Moorish Science Movement. Serving as a lieu-

Figure 11.6. Maulana Karenga (1941–). A prominent advocate for Black Power, he is a Black aestheterian and activist in institutionalizing Kwanzaa to bring about unity, positive thinking, and common values among African Americans.

tenant to Master Wallace Fard Muhammad, a young Georgian, Elijah Poole, studied Islam and African American nationalism and became the heir to the movement when Master Wallace Fard Muhammad mysteriously disappeared in 1934. As Elijah Muhammad, he became sole leader of the Nation of Islam and began to build the organization into a national presence. Elijah Muhammad's son Wallace D. Muhammad and Louis Farrakhan were to emerge as inheritors of Elijah's legacy. Malcolm X, assassinated in February 1965, had been the most eloquent and skillful orator for the Nation of Islam prior to being censored and suspended in November 1963 by Elijah Muhammad for saying after President John Kennedy's death that "the chicken had come home to roost," which he later explained meant that the climate of violence had led to the killing of the president.

The Nation of Islam started as a nationalist organization but evolved into a religious organization. With mosques around the country, the religion attracted many young men who saw it as the most active force in the nation. The Nation of Islam's appeal seemed to be in the directness of its message, the discipline of its followers, and the political consciousness of its adherents. This is different from the organization under the leadership of

Figure 11.7 (near right). Huey Newton (1942–1989). Cofounder of the Black Panther Party with Bobby Seale; felt the use of violence was the only way to defeat racism and inequality in America. Credit: UPI/Corbis-Bettman.

Figure 11.8 (far right). Bobby Seale (1936–). Cofounder of the Black Panther Party, which aimed to protect residents of the ghetto against police brutality and to ensure equal rights by militant means. Credit: Ted Streshinsky/Corbis.

Figure 11.9 (near right). Kawame Toure (Stokely Carmichael) (1941–). A member of the militant SNCC who organized Southern African Americans to vote and protest. Pictured here speaking in Mississippi, Carmichael coined the slogan "Black Power." Credit: Flip Schulke/Corbis.

Figure 11.10 (far right). Black Panthers hold a vigil for comrade Eldridge Cleaver. Credit: UPI/Corbis-Bettmann.

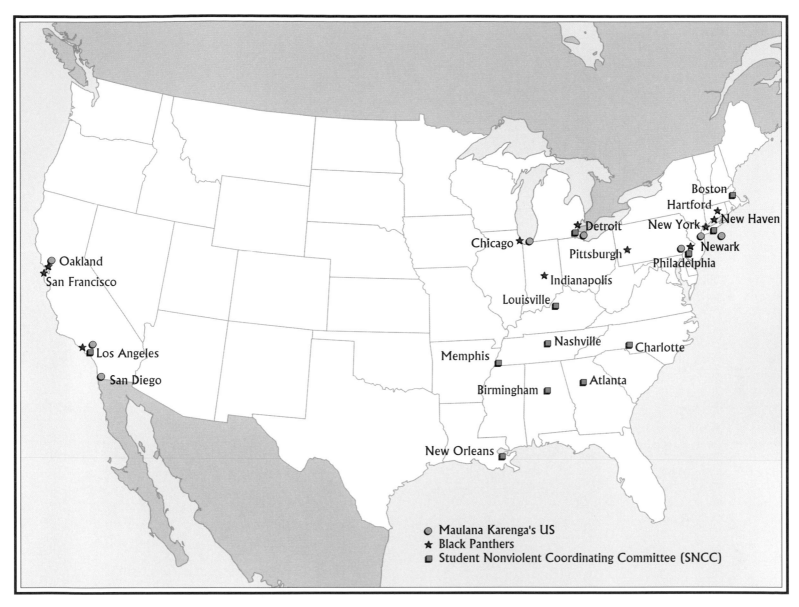

Figure 11.11. Principal chapters of US, Black Panthers, and SNCC.

Elijah Muhammad. Under his leadership, the organization disavowed any political ambitions or involvement in religion. The Honorable Elijah Muhammad taught that the government of the United States should have nothing to do with the Nation of Islam and that the Nation of Islam should have nothing to do with the United States of America.

THE MOMENTUM OF HISTORY

History is made by the interactions of dynamic themes and vigorous individuals. When one charts the history of the African American people it is obvious that the energetic entry of creative and politically active individuals has had a tremendous impact on the nature of the

nation. Their names should never be forgotten and any atlas of the history and culture of the African American people must record their works.

Carter G. Woodson

The "father of African American history" is what many of his peers called Carter G. Woodson (see figure 11.12, page 164). He did more than anyone to institutionalize the teaching and study of the history of African Americans. Although W. E. B. Du Bois is considered by many to be the greatest intellectual of his time, Woodson was undoubtedly the most unswervingly committed historian.

Woodson was born in New Canton, Virginia. in 1875, and educated at Berea

Figure 11.12. Carter Woodson (1875–1950). An early pioneer in writing about African-American history and in educating other African Americans about their past.

Figure 11.13. Walter F. White (1893–1955). Became assistant secretary in the NAACP's New York office in 1918 and was a major voice against lynchings in the South.

Figure 11.14. Thurgood Marshall (1908–1993). Argued and won several cases in front of the Supreme Court dealing with the separate but equal clause found in the Plessy decision; became the first African-American Supreme Court justice in 1967.

College, the University of Chicago, Harvard University, and the Sorbonne. His major achievements include the creation of the Association for the Study of Negro Life and History in 1915, the Journal of Negro History in 1916, the Associated Publishers in 1921, and the book *The Miseducation of the Negro.* African American history, which is a part of African American studies, owes a great debt to Woodson.

Walter White

Walter White (figure 11.13) was the secretary of the NAACP during its most courageous period. Born in 1893, White died in 1955 after being one of the most stalwart champions of African American rights. He published several books against lynching. His most famous work was *Rope and Faggot: A Biography of Judge Lynch.* He also wrote two earlier novels, *Five in the Flint* and *Flight.* The NAACP awarded him the coveted Spingarn Award in 1937.

Thurgood Marshall

Thurgood Marshall, Supreme Court Justice, was born on July 2, 1908, in Baltimore, Maryland (figure 11.14). He attended Lincoln University and Howard University Law School. Marshall graduated from Howard at the top of his 1933 class. His career as an attorney was to span the civil rights era. His career with the NAACP was the most distinguished in its legal history. He was named national special counsel in 1938 and handled all cases that dealt with the constitutionality of African American rights. He was appointed to the job of director-counsel of the Legal Defense and Educational Fund in 1950. In this position, he played a key role with a team of lawyers in arguing the now famous Supreme Court case on school desegregation (Brown *v.* Board of Education of Topeka, Kansas).

Marshall also figured in the decisions requiring the admission of qualified African Americans to the University of Texas Law School and the right of Texas blacks to vote in the Democratic primaries. In 1961 he served on the federal bench as circuit judge for the Second Circuit.

The pinnacle of his distinguished career in law came in 1967 when he was asked by President Lyndon B. Johnson to serve on the Supreme Court. Thurgood Marshall always had strong sentiments in support of human rights and justice. He once criticized the nation for not understanding the role blacks played in expanding justice.

Lorraine Hansberry

Lorraine Hansberry was born in 1930 and died in 1965 (figure 11.15). Within the short span of her lifetime she made dramatic history, becoming the first African American dramatist to win the New York Drama Critics Circle Award in 1959.

Her play *A Raisin in the Sun* became an international success. It was the first major play by an African American to appear on Broadway. Hansberry, originally from Chicago, had written the play while she lived in New York. A second play, *The Sign in Sidney Brustein's Window*, was about the western intellectual's preoccupation with reflection rather than action.

Gwendolyn Brooks

Gwendolyn Brooks received the Pulitzer Prize for poetry in 1950 for her book Annie Allen. She was born in 1912 in Topeka, Kansas (figure 11.16). Her family moved to Chicago when she was still very young. In 1945, she completed a book called *A Street in Bronzeville*. This book brought her to the attention of the country as *Mademoiselle* named her one of the ten outstanding American women. Brooks has received numerous awards including being the national poet laureate at the Library of Congress. Her name is synonymous with the best tradition of African American letters.

Her books include *Bronzeville Boys and Girls, Maud Martha, The Bean Eaters, In the Mecca, Riot, Family Pictures, Beckonings, Aloneness, Primer for Blacks*, and *To Disembark*. She has written many other books and articles and is the major African American poet since Langston Hughes.

Figure 11.15. Lorraine Hansberry (1930–1965). Triggered controversy with her play *A Raisin in the Sun* that sparked a new era for the role of the Black artist in the Civil Rights Movement.

Figure 11.16. Gwendolyn Brooks (1917–). Her poetry has been said to be "a commitment to social justice" for African Americans in the tradition of other African-American artists as she communicates brotherhood and love.

Figure 11.17. Whitney M. Young Jr. (1921–1971). As the Executive Director of the National Urban League, he felt a demonstration was needed to improve the economic and social conditions of African Americans, therefore aiding M. L. King Jr. in 1963 with the March on Washington.

Figure 11.18. Constance Baker Motley (1921–). A lawyer and the first African-American woman elected to the New York State Senate in 1964, she campaigned for civil rights in housing, education, and employment.

She has been a strong supporter of young writers, giving useful advice and keen criticism. Brooks represents the bridge between the Harlem Renaissance and the Black Arts Movement, becoming in her own poetry and style the embodiment of the best traditions of both. In her judgment, the 1960s had much more promise for the liberation of art than did the Harlem Renaissance.

Whitney Young

Whitney Young was the executive director of the National Urban League from 1961 to 1971 (figure 11.17). He was born in Kentucky in 1922 and drowned while swimming in Lagos, Nigeria, in 1971. An indefatigable worker and a serious campaigner for African American rights in the field of economics and housing, Whitney Young was one of the major civil rights leaders during the 1960s.

He served as dean of the School of Social Work at Atlanta University from 1954 to 1961. He wrote several books on racism including *To Be Equal* and *Beyond Racism*. While serving as dean of social work at Atlanta University, he was elected to the post of president of the National Association of Social Workers. He was called upon to serve on seven presidential commissions as well as the boards of some major American corporations and foundations. His work in the urban communities also enabled him to be involved with organizations such as the Urban Coalition, Urban Institute, and the Rockefeller Foundation.

Constance Baker Motley

Constance Baker Motley became the first African American female federal judge in 1966 when she was appointed to the U.S. District Court for Southern New York by President Lyndon Johnson (figure 11.18). Motley worked for the NAACP while she was still a student at Columbia. She had argued nine successful cases before the Supreme Court before she left her position with the NAACP. In 1982, she was named chief judge of the United States Court of Appeals for the Second Circuit, which covers New York City.

Jackie Robinson

Jackie Robinson was born in Cairo, Georgia, on January 31, 1919. He was raised in Pasadena, California, and attended the University of California, Los Angeles. After a stint in the army as a lieutenant during World War II, Robinson returned to the states hoping to become a physical education teacher. He chose to play baseball with the Black Baseball League in order to sharpen his skills. In 1945, Branch Rickey of the Brooklyn Dodgers assigned him to the Montreal Royals to be groomed for the major leagues. At the time Robinson was playing for the Kansas City Monarchs.

On April 10, 1947, the Brooklyn team announced that it had purchased Robinson's contract. A day later Jackie Robinson began his career in the major leagues. He retired in 1956 after compiling an outstanding record as a hitter, base stealer, and fielder. He had been cited for being the Most Valuable Player in 1949, had played on one world championship team, and had stolen home base nineteen times, once during a world series game. He died in 1972 in Stamford, Connecticut, a legend in his own time.

Ella Fitzgerald

Ella Fitzgerald has been called the greatest female jazz artist. She was born in 1918, discovered in 1934 after an amateur contest, and made her first recording in 1935. Since that time Ella Fitzgerald's name has become synonymous with jazz interpretation. Musicians honor her for her ability to use her voice as an instrument. She improvised with the greatest of ease in the midst of all kinds of tunes. Few jazz artists are so universally acclaimed as she was.

Carl Rowan

Carl Rowan held two important posts in the U.S. government (see figure 11.21, page 168). He was ambassador to Finland in 1963 and later was the director of the United States Information Agency. He was born in Ravenscroft, Tennessee, on August 11, 1925, and at the age of nineteen became one of the first fifteen

Figure 11.19. Jackie Robinson (1919–1972). Became the first African-American Major League Baseball player in 1947, sparking the racial integration of all professional sports. Credit: Corbis-Bettmann.

Figure 11.20. Ella Fitzgerald (1918–1996). Pictured in her early years, the luminous Ella Fitzgerald became world famous for her mastery of "scat" singing, a technique in which the singer improvises and uses nonsense syllables. Her style was eventually imitated by other jazz vocalists. Credit: Corbis-Bettmann.

Figure 11.21. Carl Rowan (1925–). Considered the most influential African American journalist for the past four decades while describing African Americans quest for equality in America and throughout the world.

African Americans commissioned by the navy. Rowan attended Tennessee State University, Oberlin College, and the University of Minnesota, where he majored in journalism.

Carl Rowan became a much sought-after feature writer and journalist once he entered the profession. Along the way he wrote several books, including *South of Freedom, Go South in Sorrow, The Pitiful and the Proud, Wait Till Next Year,* and others.

Elliot Percival Skinner

Elliot Percival Skinner, like Carl Rowan, was an appointee under the Johnson administration, to a government post. Skinner, the leading scholar on the Mossi culture of Burkina Faso (Upper Volta), was appointed to the ambassadorship because of his expert knowledge of the history and culture of the Mossi people. Dr. Skinner is the Franz Boas Professor of Anthropology at Columbia University. He has been one of the principal Africanists, writing and teaching on Africa for the past thirty years.

Kariamu Welsh Asante

Kariamu Welsh Asante, the winner of numerous creative arts awards from the National Endowment of the Arts and the New York State Council of the Arts, Pew Foundation, and the John Guggenheim Foundation, was invited by Prime Minister Robert Mugabe of Zimbabwe in 1981 to organize the National Dance Company of Zimbabwe (figure 11.22). As one of the first African Americans to live in post-independence Zimbabwe, she made the National Dance Company one of the most internationally successful companies on the continent. The Umfundalai dance technique, which she created to identify African dance movements, is now used throughout the African dance community.

One senses the tremendous energy of a resourceful community in the achievements of African Americans. The singular brilliance of the expressive culture of African Americans is seen in the dance, such as the Umfundalai technique of

Figure 11.22. Kariamu Welsh Asante (1949–). Professor of African American studies at Temple University who has received several dance and choreography fellowships and two Fullbright Awards to work in the National Dance Company of Zimbabwe.

Kariamu Welsh Asante, or the interpretative style of Ray Charles's music. The dramatists August Wilson and Charles Fuller's (figure 11.23) concentration on what African American historical experiences are and ought to have been is of the same fabric with Ralph Ellison's (figure 11.25) insights into the nature of being among African Americans. On the other hand, someone like Muhammad Ali (figure 11.24) was the audacious presentation of the soul. He was always, as a public figure, present, real, engaged and engaging.

There is, in every aspect of the American society, the presence and voice of the African, thinking, working, creating, inventing, performing, expressing all of the pathos and hope of a unique historical experience.

Figure 11.23. Charles Fuller (1939–). "One of the most contemporary American theater's most forceful and original voices," who explored human relationships between African Americans and whites through his stage work.

Figure 11.24 (far left). Muhammad Ali (1942–). More than just one of the greatest heavyweight boxers of all time, he was a political voice who stood for equality among all and the end of American involvement in the Vietnam War.

Figure 11.25 (near left). Ralph Ellison (1914–1994). Teacher and writer who gained popularity with his only novel, *Invisible Man*, which tells the story of a Southern African-American youth and his fight against white oppression.

"Before This Time Another Year"

12

THE TRANSFORMING OF AMERICA

The social and economic condition of African Americans has never been in parity to the state of the American nation. Indeed, the quest of the African in America from the beginning until now has been the acquisition of a social and economic status similar to that of Americans of European descent. The unequal origin of these populations, one white and free and the other black and enslaved, has made this quest elusive even at the end of the twentieth century.

Since the 1960s, numerous achievements have been made in politics, but the economic and social conditions of African Americans have remained constant. While it is possible to boast of hundreds of elected officials at the municipal, state, and national levels, the shift in the American economy that has caused numerous industrial manufacturing jobs to leave the urban North has added severe pressures on African American families. The number of African Americans in corporate positions is far greater now than thirty years ago, yet the intense poverty faced by the masses of African Americans has been unrelenting. Facts such as these demonstrate the seemingly intractable nature of the depressed social and economic situation.

If social and economic conditions have presented the nation with frustratingly difficult problems, the passage of the Civil Rights Restoration Act of 1988 over a presidential veto, the passage of enforcement amendments to the Fair Housing Act of 1968, and the two candidacies of Jesse Jackson for nomination to the highest office in the land have kept alive the spirit of struggle and the vision for a more equitable society. With more than 6,000 elected officials, African Americans are in a much better position than ever to make a difference in the moral and political climate of the nation. In 1990, the late David Richardson, Pennsylvania state representative and national leader of African American state representatives, said, "The social and economic conditions will only get better as the ethical climate gets better. That is one of the main jobs for state legislators and other national leaders." All major indicators of the economic, social, and political climate in the nation suggest that unless Americans collectively remove the stones from the path of progress, the nation will never live up to its noblest aspirations.

The National Urban League has called for Parity 2000, a vision that by the year 2000 the private and public sectors of the American society achieve equity in education, training, hiring, health, and housing. Judging from the statistical information reported in this volume, such a goal is useful as a point of departure for a vision of the future, but it will take concrete moral and financial commitments to correct the wrongs perpetrated on the African American population that began with the Great Enslavement.

Two hundred and fifty-eight years after the establishment of Jamestown, Virginia (1607–1865), Africans were finally emancipated from bondage. During this period white Americans had every advantage afforded to them by the laws of the country. The two hundred and forty-six years Africans worked for free, from 1619 to 1865, were years in which the wealth accumulated by the white population grew at an enormous rate. Cities were built, fortunes were made, and property was acquired while Africans waited for the day when America would pay its great debt of freedom and prosperity.

BLACK COLLEGES

The primary educational delivery capability of the historically black colleges and universities was underscored in 1990 when Walter Annenberg donated $50 million to The United Negro College Fund. Since the middle of the nineteenth century, when Lincoln University and Cheyney University were established, the historically black colleges and universities (HBCU) have had a profound impact on the quality of the African American professional classes. From 1852 to 1954, these colleges essentially kept African Americans in the professional ballgame (see figure 12.1, page 173). Without them the condition of blacks in America would

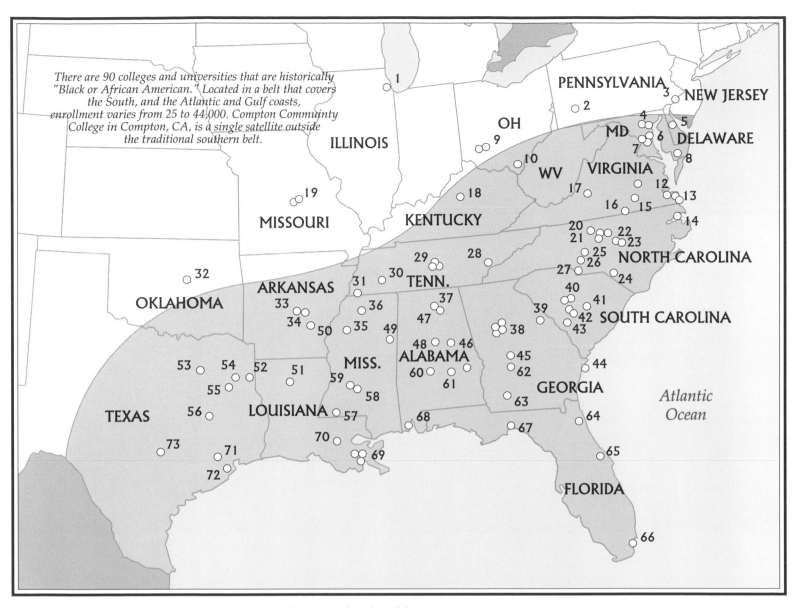

Figure 12.1. Traditional African-American colleges and universities.

	College or University	Location	Highest degree conferred	Control	Percent African American	Enrollment
1.	Olive-Harvey College	Chicago, IL	Associate	Private	96	8,314
2.	Lincoln University	Lincoln, PA	Master's	Public	98	1,250
3.	Cheyney State College	Cheyney, PA	Master's	Private	95	1,666
4.	Coppin State College	Baltimore, MD	Master's	Public	86	2,448
	Morgan State University	Baltimore, MD	Doctorate	Public	92	3,982
5.	Delaware State College	Dover, DE	Baccalaureate	Public	55	2,389
6.	Bowie State College	Bowie, MD	Master's	Private	72	3,074
7.	University of District of Columbia	Washington, DC	Baccalaureate	Private	81	11,869
	Howard University	Washington, DC	First Professional/Doctorate	Private	85	10,756
8.	University of Maryland-Eastern Shore	Princess Anne, MD	Master's	Public	72	1,316
9.	Central State University	Wilberforce, OH	Baccalaureate	Public	84	2,779
	Wilberforce University	Wilberforce, OH	Baccalaureate	Private	99	739
10.	Rio Grande College	Rio Grande, OH	Baccalaureate	Private	88	1,709
11.	Virginia Union University	Richmond, VA	First Professional	Private	98	1,200
12.	Hampton Institute	Hampton, VA	Master's	Private	92	5,147
13.	Norfolk State College	Norfolk, VA	Master's	Private	88	7,721
14.	Elizabeth City State University	Elizabeth City, NC	Baccalaureate	Private	80	1,583
15.	Virginia State College	Petersburg, VA	Master's	Public	92	3,891
16.	Saint Paul's College	Lawrenceville, VA	Baccalaureate	Private	97	736
17.	Virginia Seminary	Lynchburg, VA	Master of Divinity	Private	95	50
18.	Kentucky State University	Frankfort, KY	Baccalaureate	Public	42	2,105
19.	Lincoln University	Jefferson City, MO	Baccalaureate	Public	26	2,478

Figure 12.1. Traditional African-American colleges and universities (con't).

	College or University	Location	Highest degree conferred	Control	Percent African American	Enrollment
20.	Winston-Salem State University	Winston-Salem, NC	Baccalaureate	Public	82	2,358
21.	Bennet College	Greensboro, NC	Baccalaureate	Private	98	549
	North Carolina Agricultural & Technical State University	Greensboro, NC	Master's	Public	90	5,991
22.	North Carolina Central University	Durham, NC	Master's/First Professional	Public	83	4,552
23.	Saint Augustine's College	Raleigh, NC	Baccalaureate	Private	98	1,671
	Shaw University	Raleigh, NC	Baccalaureate	Private	98	1,473
24.	Fayetteville State University	Fayetteville, NC	Baccalaureate	Private	74	2,679
25.	Livingstone College	Salisbury, NC	Baccalaureate/First Professional	Private	98	642
26.	Barber-Scotia College	Concord, NC	Baccalaureate	Private	98	441
27.	Johnson C. Smith University	Charlotte, NC	Baccalaureate	Private	99	1,165
28.	Knoxville College	Knoxville, TN	Baccalaureate	Private	98	680
29.	Fisk University	Nashville, TN	Master's	Private	98	650
	Meharry Medical College	Nashville, TN	First Professional/Doctorate	Private	76	751
	Tennessee State University	Nashville, TN	Master's		62	7,012
30.	Lane College	Jackson, TN	Baccalaureate	Private	99	1,310
31.	LeMoyne-Owen College	Memphis, TN	Baccalaureate	Private	98	906
32.	Langston University	Langston, OK	Baccalaureate	Private	75	3,532
33.	Philander Smith College	Little Rock, AR	Baccalaureate	Private	89	582
	Shorter College	Little Rock, AR	Two Years	Private	80	100
34.	University of Arkansas-Pine Bluff	Pine Bluff, AR	Baccalaureate	Public	83	3,531
35.	Coahoma Junior College	Clarksdale, MS	Two Years	Public	98	614
36.	Rust College	Holly Springs, MS	Baccalaureate	Private	98	919
37.	Alabama Agr. & Mech. College	Huntsville, AL	Master's	Public	85	3,800
	Oakwood College	Huntsville, AL	Baccalaureate	Private	99	1,075
38.	Atlanta University/Clark College	Atlanta, GA	Doctorate	Private	93	3,292
	Morehouse College	Atlanta, GA	Baccalaureate	Private	99	2,387
	Morris Brown College	Atlanta, GA	Baccalaureate	Private	90	1,300
	Spelman College	Atlanta, GA	Baccalaureate	Private	99	1,757
39.	Paine College	Augusta, GA	Master's	Private	90	708
40.	Allen University	Columbia, SC	Master's	Private	99	25
	Benedict College	Columbia, SC	Baccalaureate	Private	99	1,616
41.	Morris College	Sumter, SC	Baccalaureate	Private	99	796
42.	Claflin College	Orangeburg, SC	Baccalaureate	Private	99	791
	South Carolina State College	Orangeburg, SC	Baccalaureate	Public	92	4,781
43.	Voorhees College	Denmark, SC	Master's	Private	98	616
44.	Savannah State College	Savannah, GA	Master's	Public	79	1,824
45.	The Fort Valley State College	Fort Valley, GA	Master's	Public	89	1,735
46.	Talladega College	Talladega, AL	Baccalaureate	Private	98	560
47.	Miles College	Birmingham, AL	Baccalaureate	Private	99	680
48.	Stillman College	Tuscaloosa, AL	Baccalaureate	Private	98	791
49.	Mary Holmes College	West Point, MS	Two Years	Private	99	622
50.	Mississippi Valley State University	Itta Bena, MS	Master's	Public	98	2,396
51.	Grambling State College	Grambling, LA	Master's	Public	89	6,205
52.	Wiley College	Marshall, TX	Baccalaureate	Private	98	417
53.	Southwestern Christian College	Terrell, TX	Two Years	Private	92	240
54.	Jarvis Christian College	Hawkins, TX	Baccalaureate	Private	98	466
55.	Texas College	Tyler, TX	Baccalaureate	Private	98	450
56.	Paul-Quinn College	Waco, TX	Baccalaureate	Private	93	509
57.	Alcorn State University	Lorman, MS	Master's	Public	96	2,600
58.	Jackson State University	Jackson, MS	Master's	Public	95	6,030
59.	Tougaloo College	Tougaloo, MS	Baccalaureate	Private	93	7,988
60.	Selma University	Selma, AL	Baccalaureate	Private	98	220
61.	Alabama State University	Montgomery, AL	Master's	Public	98	44,000
62.	Tuskegee Institute	Tuskegee, AL	Master's/First Professional	Private	82	3,095
63.	Albany State College	Albany, GA	Baccalaureate	Public	85	1,893
64.	Edward Waters College	Jacksonville, FL	Baccalaureate	Private	96	671
65.	Bethune-Cookman College	Daytona Beach, FL	Baccalaureate	Private	96	1,888
66.	Florida Memorial College	Miami, FL	Baccalaureate	Private	81	2,321
67.	Florida Agr. & Mech. College	Tallahassee, FL	Master's	Public	81	5,949
68.	S. D. Bishop State Junior College	Mobile, AL	Two Years	Public	67	1,857
69.	Dillard University	New Orleans, LA	Baccalaureate	Private	94	1,340
	Southern University in New Orleans	New Orleans, LA	Baccalaureate	Public	95	2,729
	Xavier University of Louisiana	New Orleans, LA	Master's	Private	88	2,207
70.	Southern University and Agricultural & Mechanical College	Baton Rouge, LA	Master's/First Professional	Public	96	9,811
71.	Prairie View Agricultural & Mechanical University	Prairie View, TX	Master's	Public	81	57
72.	Texas Southern University	Houston, TX	First Professional/Doctorate	Public	93	7,447
73.	Huston-Tillotson College	Austin, TX	Baccalaureate	Private	90	50
74.	Compton Community College	Compton, CA	Associate	Public	89	4,700

have been even more dismal. But these colleges and universities produced an educated cadre committed to service and enlightenment. Out of this commitment came lawyers, doctors, teachers, and preachers who would keep the condition of the race uppermost in their minds.

Initially, Lincoln University and Hampton College were founded to serve both Native Americans and African Americans. The Native Americans who attended both these schools often came from homes and communities closely related to the African population.

Although these HBCUs play a decreasing role in educating the black population, the better institutions continue to attract high-quality students from throughout the African world. More than 80 percent of all African Americans in higher education are at predominantly white institutions. Some of these institutions, such as Wayne State University, Temple University, City College, and California State University, Dominguez Hills, have percentages of African American students above the percentage of blacks in the national population. In some instances, major urban institutions have populations of African American students beyond the total numbers for some historically black colleges in their region.

Nevertheless, the reputation for quality remains strong at Tuskegee, Fisk, Lincoln, Hampton, Morehouse, Howard, and Spelman. These schools have experienced a resurgence in student interest since the 1980s. What this means is that the African American community has found a tremendous need for these colleges. Bill and Camille Cosby donated $20 million to Spelman College in 1988. Lincoln University in Pennsylvania is reported to have inherited art worth more than $500 million. Born in separatism forced by segregation, these colleges have achieved their prestige because of their commitment to teaching, humanity, and progress.

Graduate Programs

Eight universities in the United States offer graduate degrees in African

American studies either through interdepartmental programs or in departments. Temple University in Philadelphia, the University of California, Berkeley, and the University of Massachusetts are the only comprehensive African American studies programs in the nation with doctorates in the field of African American studies. With three degrees—B.A., M.A., and Ph.D.—and a large international student body from Africa, Europe, Asia, South America, and North America, Temple remains the principal center of graduate education in African American studies.

In addition to Temple, Massachusetts, and UC, Berkeley, three other U.S. educational institutions offer M.A. degree programs in African American studies: Ohio State University, Cornell University, and the State University of New York at Albany. Yale University, the University of California, Los Angeles, and the University of Wisconsin, Madison, offer interdisciplinary and interdepartmental programs.

More than 200 universities and colleges offer degrees at the B.A. level. Among the most significant departments, in addition to those that offer graduate programs, are the University of Wisconsin, Milwaukee, Brown University, Indiana University, California State University, Long Beach, California State University, Northridge, and Kent State University. These schools offer strong curricula and have consistently had dedicated faculty and students. They serve large and diverse constituencies.

The departments and programs in African American studies are direct outgrowths of the pioneering work of educators such as Carter G. Woodson, W. E. B. Du Bois, Charles Johnson, Alain Locke, and Mary McLeod Bethune.

MEDICINE

The people of Africa brought to America much of the accumulated medicine of the continent. Indeed, African medicine at the time of the European slave trade was equal to if not superior to medicine in Europe. Many healers knew the medicinal value and curative proper-

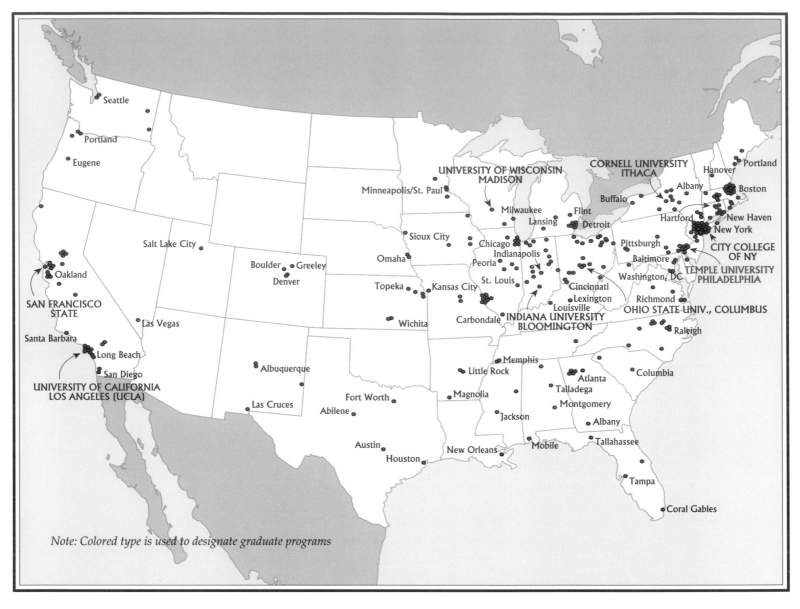

Note: Colored type is used to designate graduate programs

Figure 12.2. Departments or programs in African-American studies.

ties of numerous herbs, minerals, and plants as well as surgical and rehabilitative procedures inherited from thousands of years of practical experience.

Root medicine became a prominent aspect of African American life during and after slavery. Practitioners, whether of the conjuring, the herbalist, or the spiritualist tradition, occupied prominent places in the community. Various therapies utilized in Africa were used in America. For example, the vaccination of smallpox was introduced into the American colonies by an African named Oneissimus. In 1740, an African who had escaped was identified as being able "to bleed and draw teeth." In 1751, another African, Cesar, was credited with discov-

ering a cure for rattlesnake bite. Santomee was trained in Holland and practiced medicine among the Africans, Dutch, and English in New York.

James Derham was the first African American trained as a physician. During the 1780s he established one of the largest followings in New Orleans. Derham was an astute observer of the traditional African healers and took this tradition into consideration in some of his own practices. Among the physicians of the nineteenth century were James Still, David Ruggles, William Wells Brown, and Martin Delaney. Eight African physicians served the army medical corps in the Civil War: John V. DeGrasse, C. B. Purvis, A. Tucker,

William Powell, John Rapier, William Ellis, A. R. Abbott, and A. T. Augusta. The famous African nationalist John S. Rock was a lawyer but also a physician.

Medical schools were opened at Howard in Washington, D.C., and Meharry in Nashville, Tennessee, in 1872. Six other medical schools opened but soon closed due to lack of finance, inadequate equipment and supplies, and local resistance. The three principal medical colleges established by African Americans are Howard University Medical School, Meharry Medical College, and Morehouse College of Medicine. Despite the fact that these colleges have been chronically underfunded, they have continued to produce the greatest number of African American physicians and medical scientists.

At the beginning of the twentieth century, four African American physicians were considered the outstanding medical innovators: Daniel Hale Williams, who performed the first open-heart surgery in history; George Cleveland Hall, surgeon who developed diagnostic techniques that were used by his peers; Nathan E. Mossell, founder of the Frederick Douglass Hospital in Philadelphia; and Auston M. Curtis, a colleague and protégé of Dr. Daniel Williams in Chicago. In the latter part of the twentieth century, the names of Louis T. Wright, antibiotic aureomycin; William Hinton, Hinton test for syphilis; Jane Cook Wright Jones, chemotherapy; Ulysses Grant Dailey, International College of Surgeons founder-fellow; Charles Drew, blood plasma; W. Montague Cobb, anatomist; Arthur Lee, cardiac surgery; Louis Sullivan, U.S. Secretary for Health; and numerous others must be added to the list.

CHARLES RICHARD DREW
AND THE AMERICAN BLOOD BANK

Charles R. Drew, M.D., was born in Washington, D.C., on June 3, 1904 (see figure 11.4, page 178). He attended and graduated from Dunbar High School, lettering in four sports. An athletic scholarship and part-time work as a waiter assisted him through Amherst College in

Massachusetts, where Drew, an outstanding athlete, won letters and an award for excellence in five sports.

He graduated from Amherst in 1926 and entered McGill University School of Medicine two years later. In Montreal he rapidly demonstrated his brilliance as a student. Because of his discipline and enthusiasm for science, he was invited to work as an assistant on a blood research project. Although he trained in surgery, he never lost sight of his first love: blood research. His persistence in this field of research led to the significant discovery of the techniques for separating and preserving blood and advancing work with blood plasma. This discovery would revolutionize the storage of blood and blood transfusions and make it possible to establish a blood bank. Thus, when Drew completed his research and established and opened the first blood bank, he became one of the most distinguished scientists of his day. Already holding the M.D., in 1940 he became the first African American to earn the Doctor of Science in Surgery.

The importance of Charles Drew's research was underscored by the fact that Europe was at war and thousands of soldiers who would have been considered mortally wounded prior to Dr. Drew's

Figure 12.3. Lincoln College, Lincoln, Pennsylvania.

Figure 12.4. Charles Drew (1904–1950). Developed techniques for separating and preserving blood, including advanced work in the field of blood plasma, that aided in saving numerous lives during World War II.

discoveries were saved. In 1941, the American Red Cross appointed Drew director of its first blood bank. When Pearl Harbor was attacked by the Japanese, Drew was able to provide blood plasma for Americans who were wounded during the surprise attack.

However, the American Red Cross decided to use blood from white donors only for wounded members of the military, insisting that they did not want to mix the blood of African Americans with white blood. Drew was enraged. He resigned from his position over the unscientific position of the American Red Cross, saying, "The blood of individual human beings may differ by blood type groupings, but there is absolutely no scientific basis to indicate any difference according to race."

Fortunately, he was named head of the Department of Surgery, chief surgeon at Freedman's Hospital, now Howard University Hospital in Washington, D.C. He continued to distinguish himself as a practical scientist. On April 1, 1950, he was fatally injured in a car accident in North Carolina, two months before his forty-sixth birthday. It was reported that

Drew bled to death because the "white" hospital would not admit him. Ironically, the surgeon, scientist, and scholar whose life's work was devoted to saving others was denied access to the methods and procedures that he invented and that could have saved his own life.

INVENTORS

From medical science to gas masks African Americans demonstrated the same inventiveness that Charles Drew had come to manifest in his career. African Americans found two factors were important to their work as inventors: necessity and freedom. The inventions found in this section represent a few of the practical inventions created by African Americans. Freedom meant that creative individuals could have their works patented. During the Great Enslavement any objects invented by an enslaved person was owned by the enslaver. No one knows how many inventions were developed by blacks but credited to white inventors during the Great Enslavement. Just by examining the profusion of inventions patented by Africans in the period 1871–1900, one gets the idea that this creativity did not start with the emancipation.

More than 300 patents were recorded during the twenty-nine-year period mentioned above. Many of these patents were being developed during the Great Enslavement and were only revealed when slavery had ended. Artisans and toolmakers were often allowed to tinker in their owners' work sheds. Blacksmiths particularly were responsible for fashioning new inventions in order to make the work on the farms easier. Sometimes one enslaved person would take an idea to a blacksmith and ask him if he could create something to perform a certain task. When they were able to accomplish these creative feats to lessen the drudgery of their work, they felt some satisfaction.

The inventive spirit that poured forth after the Civil War and during Reconstruction must be considered remarkable for a number of reasons. For the most part, the African American population was illiterate; few men or women could read or write. Yet within a few years of emancipation inventors were capable of seeking their own patents. Many of the inventors used others to secure their patents for them. In some cases, unscrupulous lawyers and friends took advantage of the ignorance of the African American inventors and claimed the inventions as their own. Incidents such as this occurred often enough to make inventors cautious about their ideas. In fact, many African Americans, instead of securing the patents for themselves, sold the patents to entrepreneuring whites—who then made money on the inventions of Africans. The case of Garrett A. Morgan is one of the most celebrated examples of an African selling his invention or idea to whites who went on to reap great financial benefits from the idea. Morgan was born in 1877 and lived until 1963. He was an exceptionally bright inventor, creating several products of benefit to society.

Morgan's gas inhalator was shown to be effective against smoke when he rescued several men in Cleveland while wearing the inhalator. Hundreds of orders came in for the inhalator from fire companies throughout the United States. When southerners found out that the inventor was an African, they often canceled their orders. In World War I, the gas inhalator was transformed into a gas mask.

Unwilling to take a chance that prejudice against his race would thwart his aims to market his most famous technological invention, Morgan sold his automatic traffic light invention to the General Electric Company for $40,000.

ARTISTS, ACTORS, AND PERFORMERS IN THE TRADITION

When the word is spoken in the context of African Americans it arouses excitement and promise. From the performing arts to the plastic arts, the number of African Americans that can be classified as artists or who classify themselves as such is staggering given the population. Painters, poets, entertainers,

Table 12.1. Selected inventions by African Americans, 1871–1900.

Ashbourne, A. P.	Biscuit cutter	November 30, 1875
Bailey, L. C.	Folding bed	July 18, 1899
Beard, A. J.	Rotary engine	July 5, 1892
Beard, A. J.	Car-coupler	November 23, 1897
Becket, G. E.	Letter box	October 4, 1892
Bell, L.	Locomotive smokestack	May 23, 1871
Benjamin, M. E.	Gong and signal chairs for hotels	July 17, 1888
Binga, M. W.	Street sprinkling apparatus	July 22, 1879
Blackburn, A. B.	Railway signal	January 10, 1888
Blair, Henry	Corn planter	October 14, 1834
Blair, Henry	Cotton planter	August 31, 1836
Boone, Sarah	Ironing board	April 26, 1892
Brooks, C. B.	Street-sweeper	March 17, 1896
Brown, O. E.	Horseshoe	August 23, 1892
Burr, J. A.	Lawn mower	May 9, 1899
Butts, J. W.	Luggage carrier	October 10, 1899
Carter, W. C.	Umbrella stand	August 4, 1885
Church, T. S.	Carpet beating machine	July 29, 1884
Cook, G.	Automatic fishing device	May 10, 1899
Cooper, J.	Elevator device	April 2, 1895
Cornwall, P. W.	Draft regulator	February 7, 1893
Cralle, A. L.	Ice-cream mold	February 2, 1897
Davis, W. R., Jr.	Library table	September 24, 1878
Dorticus, C. J.	Machine for embossing photos	April 16, 1895
Elkins, T.	Refrigerating apparatus	November 4, 1879
Flemming, F., Jr.	Guitar (variation)	March 3, 1886
Grant, G. F.	Golf tee	December 12, 1899
Gregory, J.	Motor	April 26, 1887
Headen, M.	Foot power hammer	October 5, 1886
Jackson, B. F.	Gas burner	April 4, 1899
Latimer and Nichols	Electric lamp	September 13, 1881
Marshall, T. J.	Fire extinguisher (variation)	May 26, 1872
McCoy, E.	Lubricator for steam engines	July 2, 1872
Spears, H.	Portable shield for infantry	December 27, 1870
Sutton, E. H.	Cotton cultivator	April 7, 1878
Woods, G. T.	Electromechanical brake	August 16, 1887
Woods, G. T.	Railway telegraphy	November 15, 1887
Woods, G. T.	Induction telegraph system	November 29, 1887
Woods, G. T.	Overhead conducting system for electric railway	May 29, 1888
Woods, G. T.	Electromotive railway system	June 26, 1888
Woods, G. T.	Railway telegraphy	August 28, 1888

dancers, choreographers, musicians, comedians, sculptors, actors, and composers are gathered in the African American population at a higher percentage of the work force than in the general population. There is a belief that the person who brings joy and happiness to others sits closest to heaven.

Avery Brooks, the actor of stage and film, once spoke about his gift in terms of it being an attribute that comes with the territory of his family and his culture. He did not go to school to learn to sing; he sings. Music and dance, always part of the African culture, have remained the chief components in the drama of African American artists. This is true whether an artist conceptualizes movies as Spike Lee does or paints as John Biggers paints. Dance and music are the elementary bases of the cultural approach. Thus, the poets, choreographers, and sculptors deal with the complexities of the music and dance idioms in the African American culture. From the earliest days of the African Company in 1821 and Henry Brown's African Grove in 1825 to the current time, African Americans have provided America with some of the most memorable occasions in entertainment. This expertise is known not only in the United States but all over the world, even in Africa itself. Pearl Primus established the National Dance Company of Liberia and Kariamu Welsh Asante established the National Dance Company of Zimbabwe. Other African American choreographers and artists have introduced African American culture and art to international audiences. This is particularly true with musicians.

Artists

Henry Ossawa Tanner

Henry Ossawa Tanner was born in Pittsburgh in 1859. He chose painting as a career during a time when it was difficult for an African American to make a living as an artist. After he attended the Pennsylvania Academy of Fine Arts, he discovered that he could not make a living unless he taught art and took photographs on the side.

Tanner's most famous work is called The Banjo Lesson (1890). Unable to make the kind of impact he wanted to make in the art field in the United States, Tanner went to France in 1891, where he concentrated on religious themes. At the time of his death in 1937 he had attained the stature of being the most respected black artist of his day.

Edmonia Lewis

Edmonia Lewis was the first African American woman to be considered an artist. She was also the first woman in America to be recognized as a sculptor.

She was born in 1845 in upstate New York. She was educated at Oberlin College in Ohio, which was the first college to admit women on a nonsegregated basis. Edmonia Lewis was extremely interested in European classical subjects while at Oberlin. As soon as she left school she moved to Boston, where she did a bust of Robert Could Shaw, the commander of the first African American regiment from the state of Massachusetts during the Civil War. Lewis left the United States for Rome in 1865. She became a leading artist in Italy and when she returned to the states she was commissioned to do many works. She died in Rome in 1890.

Lois Mailou Jones

Lois Mailou Jones is one of the greatest African American artists of the twentieth century. Born in 1905 in Boston, Jones was educated at the Boston Museum School of Fine Arts and Designers School.

She has become famous for the diversity of her art. She started as a fashion artist with award-winning textile and design illustrations. In 1930, she became a professor at Howard University, teaching courses in design and watercolor painting. Jones interprets the African world from the background of her experiences in many cultures. She explores with sensitivity the depth and power of the compelling forces of color and shapes in the African American worldview.

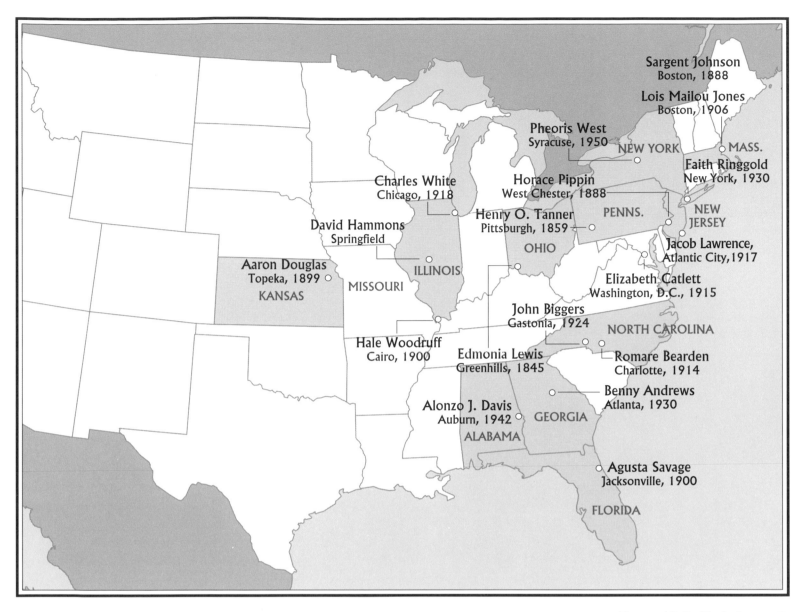

Figure 12.5. Birthplaces of major African-American artists.

The following labels appear on the map:

Sargent Johnson
Boston, 1888

Lois Mailou Jones
Boston, 1906

Pheoris West
Syracuse, 1950

NEW YORK

MASS.

Faith Ringgold
New York, 1930

Charles White
Chicago, 1918

Horace Pippin
West Chester, 1888

PENNS.

NEW JERSEY

Henry O. Tanner
Pittsburgh, 1859

David Hammons
Springfield

OHIO

Jacob Lawrence,
Atlantic City, 1917

Aaron Douglas
Topeka, 1899

ILLINOIS

MISSOURI

Elizabeth Catlett
Washington, D.C., 1915

KANSAS

John Biggers
Gastonia, 1924

NORTH CAROLINA

Hale Woodruff
Cairo, 1900

Edmonia Lewis
Greenhills, 1845

Romare Bearden
Charlotte, 1914

Alonzo J. Davis
Auburn, 1942

GEORGIA

Benny Andrews
Atlanta, 1930

ALABAMA

Agusta Savage
Jacksonville, 1900

FLORIDA

Musicians

SAMMY DAVIS JR.

Sammy Davis Jr., "the world's greatest entertainer," died in 1990. Davis was born in New York City on December 8, 1925. He began appearing on stage at the age of four. His uncle, Will Mastin, had a trio that included Sammy Davis Sr. and Sammy Davis Jr.

During World War II, Davis joined the army and wrote and directed plays for the entertainment of the troops. When he returned to civilian life, he was able to secure an engagement in Hollywood. Davis became popular across the nation after his Hollywood stint. He recorded numerous hit tunes and was famous for his many talents as a singer, actor, dancer, mimic, and musician. Sammy Davis Jr. was the complete entertainer.

ARETHA FRANKLIN

Aretha Franklin was born in 1942 (see figure 12.7, page 183). She immersed herself in the spirituals and gospels that were popular in her father's church in Detroit. By the time she signed a contract with Atlantic Records, she had already become a major figure in the gospel-singing world. But it was not until she started singing rhythm and blues that she became a superstar. Her albums have sold millions of copies around the world with her special blend of gospel sounds and blues cadences. She has appeared in film, entertained in Europe and Asia, and launched several artistic ventures of her own. Called by her contemporaries "the modern queen of soul," Aretha Franklin is a musician of superior ability.

DUKE ELLINGTON

Duke Ellington is believed to be the single most impressive figure in modern American music (see figure 12.8, page 183). Unquestionably he contributed more to jazz than any other composer. He is responsible for writing more than 500 compositions, some of them standards in the field.

He was born in 1899 in Washington, D.C., to a well-to-do family. Because of his artistic gifts, he was given a scholarship to the Pratt Institute of Fine Arts in New York. However, he decided to play local music engagements instead. To support himself between engagements he painted signs and houses. Soon he was doing well enough with music to forgo his painting. Some people believe that he would have become a fairly successful artist had he continued in that genre. As it turned out, Ellington did not do so badly in music.

Gaining fame from his tours with such greats as Fats Waller and Sonny Greer, Duke Ellington worked to establish the jazz discipline. A five-year stint at the Cotton Club from 1927 to 1932 cemented his talents and his reputation in the field of African American music. He made many records from the Cotton Club and became a prominent figure in the jazz world. Other bandleaders used

Figure 12.6. Centers and artists of influence: African-American music.

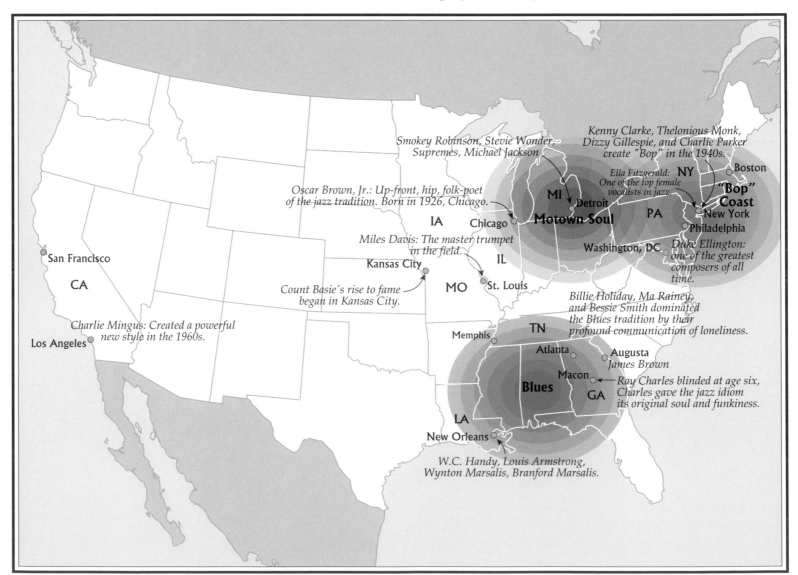

Ellington as their lodestone. His genius was so vast and so creative that he moved the world of jazz in any way he wanted. While other musicians and bandleaders may have been satisfied with remaining a fixture at the Cotton Club, the Duke took his show on the road and found more success than he had ever dreamed possible. His collaborations with Cootie Williams, Barney Bigard, and Johnny Hodges established the style of jazz orchestrations for the next twenty-five years. Among his contributions to the field of jazz were practical as well as theoretical items. For example, Ellington was the first musician to gain more than the three-minute limit on the length of commercial records. He was also the first to use scatting as a jazz instrument. The best musicians of the time played with his band. Oscar Peterson, Ben Webster, Ray Nance, and Harry Carney were just a few of the giants of the business who played with Duke's band.

DIZZY GILLESPIE AND CHARLIE PARKER

The cofounders of the innovative jazz movement known as bebop were Dizzy Gillespie (figure 12.9) and Charlie Parker (see figure 12.10, page 184). The creations of these two musical geniuses continue to direct the field of jazz. Gillespie, a master trumpeter, was an arranger and writer. Charlie Parker was a gifted saxophonist. The combination of Gillespie and Parker was electric for jazz. After the death of Charlie Parker in 1955, Dizzy Gillespie went on to become the major interpreter of the bebop school of jazz.

Gillespie was born in 1917 in North Carolina. He moved to Philadelphia and later joined with Fletcher Henderson and others in small orchestras. By the time he joined Cab Calloway and Mercer Ellington, he had perfected his bebop experimentation and his name was sealed in history.

Charlie Parker (1920–1955) was a saxophonist of incredible talent. He was born in Kansas City, Kansas, on August 29. He died of a drug overdose at age thirty-five. Parker lived fast, marrying at sixteen and becoming a father at seven-

Figure 12.7. Aretha Franklin (1942–). Labeled a modern day "queen of soul," Franklin emerged as a musical force throughout the world. Winning numerous Grammy Awards for her pop music, she performs at President Bill Clinton's inauguration in this photograph. Credit: Neal Preston/Corbis.

Figure 12.8 (left). Duke Ellington (1899–1974). Gained respect of fellow musicians because of his work as a jazz orchestra leader and is considered to have made the greatest contribution to jazz music in the United States. Credit: Underwood & Underwood/ Corbis-Bettmann.

Figure 12.9. Dizzy Gillespie (1917–1993). Grammy award-winning career jazz musician who played the trumpet; he is credited for the development of the jazz genre of bebop around 1940.

THE TRANSFORMING OF AMERICA   183

Figure 12.10 (above). Charlie Parker (1920–1955). Parker's innovations in rhythm and harmony continue to be a part of most jazz musicians today. Here, Parker jams with Lester Young. Credit: UPI/Corbis-Bettmann.

Figure 12.11 (right). Michael Jackson (1959–). Known for his incredible dancing style, he sang lead vocals for the original Jackson 5 before launching his solo career that included the 40-million-selling album *Thriller* in 1983. Credit: Neal Preston/Corbis.

Figure 12.12 (below right). John Coltrane (1926–1967). Innovator on tenor sax who played with Dizzy Gillespie, Miles Davis, and Thelonious Monk prior to originating controversial sound defying easy categorization. Credit: UPI/Corbis-Bettmann.

teen. By the age of twenty he was on his way to New York, where he played with Earl "Fatha" Hines, Billy Eckstine, Cootie Williams, and Dizzy Gillespie. Parker's gift of musical genius immortalized his name and his nickname, "Yardbird."

JOHN COLTRANE

John Coltrane left his mark on the tenor saxophone in such a way that it is impossible to discuss the instrument without reference to him (figure 12.12). Coltrane spent many years developing his style and technique in Philadelphia. His early work in the jazz idiom was with Miles Davis, Thelonius Monk, and Dizzy Gillespie.

Coltrane was the epitome of tenor saxophone innovators. His music was often considered harsh and different, but it became the standard by which younger saxophonists judged themselves. No presence in jazz saxophone was as dominating as that of John Coltrane during his short life. His experimentation, particularly alongside Thelonius Monk, has been compared with the innovation of Gillespie and Parker. At his death in 1967, Coltrane was already a historical figure.

LOUIS ARMSTRONG

Louis Armstrong was born on July 4, 1900 (see figure 12.13, page 185). By his death in 1971, he had become one of the best-loved people on earth. As a child of fourteen, Armstrong was arrested in New Orleans for firing a pistol. He was sent away to the boys' home where he learned to play the cornet. When he was released from the home, Armstrong knew what he wanted to do for a living.

King Oliver, who had played in the Kid Ory Band, left for Chicago in 1919 and Louis Armstrong was given his place in the band. When he went to Chicago in 1922 to join King Oliver, he was well on his way to international fame. Oliver and Armstrong perfected duets that engaged them in counterpoint with each other. The audiences loved their performances. Armstrong also worked with Fletcher Henderson and Erskine Tate. Through all of his engagements he continued to

exhibit tremendous charisma as a performer. He traveled the world as an ambassador of jazz.

When he performed solo, as he did on many occasions, he elevated jazz in the minds of many listeners because of his skill and his ability to engage the audiences. Louis "Satchmo" Armstrong was one of the greatest performers to have lived in the twentieth century. He performed in films and plays and as a soloist. In the 1930s he toured Europe with Bing Crosby to rave reviews for his artistry. He died in his sleep in 1971.

B. B. KING

B. B. King's influence in the blues world is without comparison (figure 12.14). In the 1960s and 1970s he became the most celebrated blues musician of all time. No other blues artist has sold as many records as B. B. King. He was born in Indianola, Mississippi, in 1925. From the humble beginnings of a black child in Mississippi during the period of Mississippi's worst outbreak of violence against blacks, B. B. King rose to become the most famous name in blues.

B. B. King gained international recognition after he made a tour of Europe and appeared on numerous television shows. Neither Billie Holiday, Big Bill Broonzy, Bessie Smith, nor Leadbelly came close to the popularity of this versatile guitarist.

BILLIE HOLIDAY

Billie Holiday dominated the vocal tradition in blues in ways that neither Bessie Smith nor Ma Rainey was ever able to do (figure 12.15). She was referred to by Lester Young as "Lady Day" because of her style and charisma. Born in Baltimore in 1915, Holiday moved to New York when she was still a young girl. In Harlem she began to sing at various nightclubs to the thrill of her audiences. In 1934, she made her first recording with Benny Goodman.

Billie Holiday's most famous records were "Strange Fruit" and "God Bless the Child." In both of these classic recordings she conveyed the universal sense of loneliness that has become so much a part of

Figure 12.13. Loius Armstrong (1900–1971). One of America's most beloved entertainers. Born on the Fourth of July, Loius Armstrong's influence throughout jazz is unmistakable and enduring. Credit: Corbis-Bettmann.

Figure 12.14. B. B. King (1925–). King is one of the most successful artists in the history of the blues. His career started at the age of 14 after purchasing a guitar for eight dollars with money he earned working in the cotton fields.
Credit: Hulton-Deutsch Collection/Corbis.

Figure 12.15. Billie Holiday (1915–1959). Nicknamed "Lady Day," she was part of the great blues singing tradition and through her music she depicted the harsh and cruel reality of Southern lynchings. Credit UPI/Corbis-Bettmann.

the African American's ethos—a deep, personal, and collective longing for a place, some place, far away from here.

Legendary Soul and Hip Hop Transitions

In the two decades between 1970 and 1991 a revolution occurred in African American music. While the traditional artists of rhythm and blues and jazz continued to fill the nightclubs, the soulful singing of Otis Redding, Gladys Knight and the Pips, Aretha Franklin, Sam Cooke, Jerry Butler, James Brown (see figure 12.18, page 188), Al Green, Wilson Pickett, the Temptations, the Ojays, Dionne Warwick, Smokey Robinson and the Miracles, and Diana Ross made a world of difference in the mass arena of music. They had the beat of the community in their hands and voices, and the list of artists who knew how to touch the noblest elements in the African American spirit was long. The Jacksons, Michael and Janet, continued their own success story as international stars into the 1990s.

Yet the musical movement was not to remain immersed in the traditions; it was to give way to the hard-driving, staccato verbal styles of the hip-hop age in a new transition. New artists with a heritage in the urban centers of the Northeast and West brought the oral tradition to a new level. The names of the artists, Public Enemy, LL Cool J, KRS-One, Rakim, De La Soul, A Tribe Called Quest, Queen Latifah, Ras Kass, Kam, Sister Souljah, Bahamadia, and Lauryn Hill, appealed to an entirely new generation of hip hoppers. Some encouraged an image of irreverence and so Tupac Shakur, Biggie Smalls, Scarface, Master P, Ice Cube, Ice Tea, and Snoop Doggy Dog became household names for the waywardness of a certain element in the African American community.

Key producers, such as Sean "Puffy" Combs, Kenneth Edmonds, and Russell Simmons, attempted to rescue the music and bring it to a wider audience. Executives such as Dyana Williams of the International Association of African American Music have worked to define the direction of the powerful musical tra-dition. They have continued the tradition started by the earlier generations of musicians, organizers, cultural interpreters, and music producers. And the transitions that came to the earlier generation are sure to come to the present one, but for now the beat goes on with a steady cadence.

The list of musicians is endless: Paul Robeson, Grace Bumbry, Ray Charles (see figure 12.17, page 187), Samuel Coleridge-Taylor, Margaret Bonds, Duke Ellington, Count Basie, Leontyne Price, Martina Arroyo, Ted McDaniel, Frank Foster, David Baker, Marian Anderson, Michael Jackson (see figure 12.11, page 184), Stevie Wonder, and Andre Watts.

THE MOVIE INDUSTRY

The portrayal of African Americans in the popular media in the United States has always been caught on the cross of expediency. White filmmakers and producers have not seen the African American audience as primary in the presentation of images and symbols. Therefore, the images of the African American that appear in the movies are more often than not images that are comfortable to whites. Inherent in the presentation of images of Africans that are comfortable to whites is the contradiction that they will not be positive, real, or utilitarian images to blacks.

The movie industry has had this problem since 1915, when *The Birth of a Nation* was presented to the public. D. W. Griffith was considered among the most innovative filmmakers of the period, and he is still revered as one of the great minds of the film industry. He established the pattern that was to be followed by successive filmmakers and producers in Hollywood.

The movie was a hit with white audiences, but it was negative about Africans. Blacks in this film were portrayed by whites in blackface. The image Griffith presented of the African American was of a scared, laughing, clowning, benevolent fool. Furthermore, African Americans during Reconstruction were shown as corrupt, vile, licentious vil-

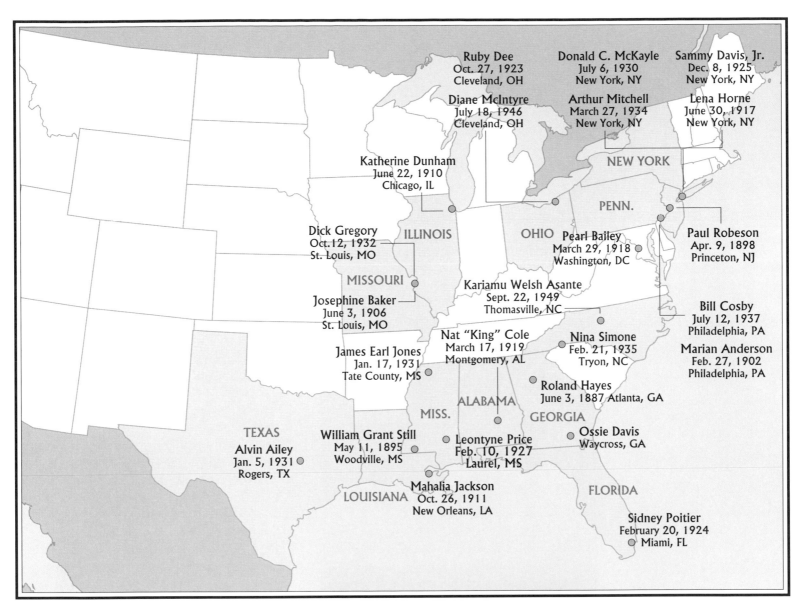

Figure 12.16 (above). Birthplaces of influential performing artists.

lains. It is not difficult to see how these images could be rejected by blacks. While whites may have gained laughter from the portrayals, blacks saw them as one more attempt to destroy the self-esteem of African Americans. Thus, the complexity of the expediency question was thrown into relief for succeeding generations of white movie makers. Griffith made another film, *One Exciting Night,* in 1922 that further underscored his negative portrayal of Africans. Apologists for Griffith often cite the film *Intolerance* as his attempt to counter the stereotypes he had created about the African. At the height of the southern attacks on Africans, the presentation of these negative images simply added fuel to fires of hatred already burning.

Figure 12.17. Ray Charles (1933–). After an attack of glaucoma in 1939, he was left completely blind but overcame this tragedy to become one of the best musicians in the pop and soul industry. Credit: Miroslav Zajic/Corbis.

The image of Africans as savages and barbarians was presented in other movies. Thus, early movies such as *Hallelujah* and *Hearts in Dixie* served to create the most appalling images of African Americans. It is true that these images were found in the literature and popular culture of the society, but the movie industry gave a legitimacy to them that has continued to the present time.

Black exploitation films popular in the 1970s as a reaction to the interest in African images were almost universally sadistic, macho, and violent. However, blacks flocked to these films because Hollywood was providing images of blacks that, while not flattering, were action oriented, and brimming with popular culture. The movies of the 1970s exploited the African American audience but provided no real substance in terms of its concerns and interests. The films of this period were financially successful until the audience grew weary of the same formula of beautiful women and men who were sexy savages, killing each other for drugs. When the industry regained its financial footing, the making of movies with a specifically black interest again disappeared.

The rise of Spike Lee as a filmmaker in the 1980s created a stir in Hollywood because for the first time a filmmaker seemed to have the heart and soul of his black audience in mind as he made his films. Spike Lee spoke of his work as Afrocentric in the sense of the African American being a subject rather than a marginal object. Such a revelation may well continue to activate the best filmmakers in African American culture.

Sidney Poitier

Sidney Poitier was the most dominant African American film actor for a generation (figure 12.19). He was born in Miami on February 20, 1927. His family raised him in the Bahamas until he was fifteen years old. At that time he returned to Miami and finally caught a freight train to New York. Once he arrived in New York he secured employment as a dishwasher at a restaurant. When the war came, Poitier enlisted and served for four years.

As soon as he got out of the army he headed for New York again. This time he auditioned for the American Negro Theatre Company. He was eventually allowed to work for the company but had to take acting and diction lessons.

Figure 12.18. James Brown (1932–). Has become one of the most exciting and flashy singers by infusing gospel music and funk in his own way, which has inspired many of today's musical artists. Credit: Neal Preston/Corbis.

Figure 12.19. Sidney Poitier (1927–). Considered to be the most important African-American actor ever to appear in American motion pictures, he changed Hollywood's image of Black America. Credit: UPI/Corbis-Bettmann.

His first film was the 1950 film *No Way Out*. In succession he made about ten films during the decade of the 1950s. He starred in *A Raisin in the Sun* both on Broadway and in the film version. In 1965 Poitier received the Oscar for his performance in *Lilies of the Field,* the first African American to receive the award for a starring role. He had been nominated earlier for the award for his performance in *The Defiant Ones.*

Paul Robeson

Paul Robeson was born in Princeton, New Jersey, on April 9, 1898 (see figure 10.8, page 146). Robeson rose to become one of the best-known African Americans in history. He went to Rutgers University on a football scholarship and won letters in every sport in which he participated, establishing a record for the university. Not only was he a world-class athlete but he also gained Phi Beta Kappa honors for his academic achievements.

Because of his thirst for knowledge, he enrolled in Columbia Law School and obtained a law degree in 1923. He made his professional debut as an actor in 1922 in *Taboo*. His most famous roles were in *The Emperor Jones* and *Othello.*

Paul Robeson was a living legend. He traveled to many countries, singing and acting and demonstrating the versatility and depth of African American culture. He spoke Spanish, French, German, Russian, Chinese, and Gaelic. He was a political activist as well as a scholar and actor. Wherever he saw oppression and human exploitation, he spoke out against it. His career suffered as a result, but Robeson was true to his commitments in support of human rights.

AFRICAN AMERICAN WRITERS

African American writers have become major interpreters of the contemporary and historical scene. The most important American writers of this era cannot be discussed without the naming of African Americans. Toni Morrison had become one of the most significant novelists at the onset of the 1990s. Her works continue to thrust her into the forefront

of the genre. She is joined by Paule Marshall, Alice Walker (see figure 12.25, page 192), and Gloria Naylor as major figures in the literature of the novel. In drama, the playwrights Charles Fuller and August Wilson must be considered two of the best of the last two decades. Other writers include John A. Williams, Mari Evans, John Edgar Wideman, Sonia Sanchez (see figure 12.25, page 192), Ntozake Shange, Ismael Reed, David Bradley, and Marita Golden.

Margaret Walker

Margaret Walker was born on July 7, 1911, in Birmingham, Alabama. She published her famous poem "For My People" in 1942. She received a fellowship to study at the University of Iowa. Her most famous novel is *Jubilee*. She has written other works including an intellectual and analytical biography of Richard Wright.

John A. Williams

John A. Williams was born in Jackson, Mississippi, in 1925 (see figure 12.20, page 190). He is considered one of the best contemporary novelists. Williams has consistently made innovations in the novel form while maintaining a strong identification with his audience. Convinced that he should write for his audience, his most famous works are *The Angry Ones, The Man Who Cried I Am, Click Song, Sissie,* and *Sons of Darkness.*

Richard Wright

Richard Wright was the first major African American novelist to gain wide acceptance for his work (see figure 10.13, page 148). His work is still seen as the measure of many other writers. He had a significant influence on the manner in which Ralph Ellison (see figure 11.25, page 169) and James Baldwin (see figure 12.24, page 192) articulated their views of African American reality. Wright's major works are *Native Son* and *Black Boy.*

Zora Neale Hurston

Zora Neale Hurston was a consummate writer who used her experiences and those of her people as the materials

Figure 12.20. John A. Williams (1925–). Described as a controversial independent thinker, Williams was born in jackson, Mississippi. In addition to his many award winning publications is a 1970 work called The King God Didn't Save which lamented the alleged "failure" of Dr. Martin Luther King.

Figure 12.21. Zora Neale Hurston (1903–1960). Having been born in an all-Black town, the experiences there heavily influenced her work and aided her in becoming a master of folklore.

Figure 12.22. Toni Morrison (1931–). In her writings she is committed to the freedom of Blacks in America and across the world; she uses African-American women as symbols to show the African-American struggle against racism and sexism.

for her novels and essays (figure 12.21). Her most famous novel, which is now considered a classic, is *Their Eyes Were Watching God.* She also wrote anthropological essays and folklore as well as an autobiography.

Toni Morrison

Toni Morrison emerged in the 1970s and 1980s as an authoritative African American novelist (figure 12.22). Born in Lorain, Ohio, on February 19, 1931, Morrison has seen her influence grow with each novel. Among the novels that have gained her international recognition are *The Bluest Eye* (1970), *Sula* (1973), *Song of Solomon* (1977), *Tar Baby* (1981), and *Beloved* (1987), for which she won the Pulitzer Prize. In 1998 she published *Paradise* in the same tradition of rich dialogue and narrative. She has explored childhood madness, the estrangement of friends, fables of eroticism, and myths of discovery and power, enslavement, and the supernatural. Morrison is recognized as one of the most influential writers of the twentieth century.

Frances Ellen Harper

Born of free parents in 1825 in Baltimore, Frances Ellen Harper was educated in Baltimore at a school run by her uncle. Born Frances Watkins, she married Fenton Harper in 1860. A volume of her verse, *Poems on Miscellaneous Subjects* (1857), sold 10,000 copies in the first five years following publication. Her other works include *Sketches of Southern Life* (1872) and *Moses: A Story of the Nile* (1869). The most popular black poet of her time, she raised the question of whether Afro-American authors should dwell on their own racial problems or address such wider issues as temperance.

MUSIC AND DANCE

Olaudah Equiano wrote in The Interesting Narrative of the Life of Olaudah Equiano (1789) that in Africa "every great event . . . is celebrated in public dances, which are accompanied with songs and music suited to the occasion." Among African Americans the

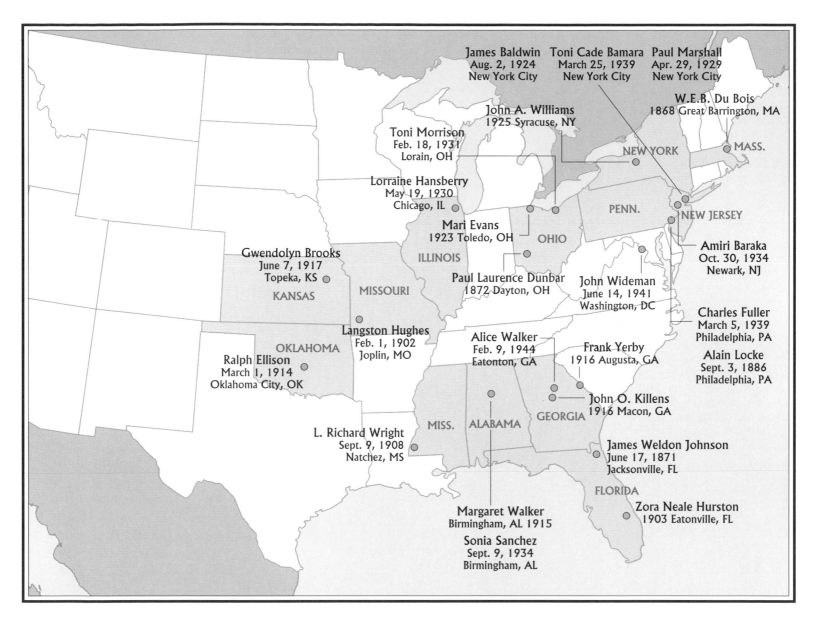

Figure 12.23. Birthplaces of major African-American writers.

dance remains a principal medium of expression. The exclamation "Let's party" is synonymous with "Let's dance." This expressive modality, combining party and dance, has precedents in Africa with the words "music" and "dance." In many West African languages, to say "music" is to mean dance as well. To conceive of music without the dance is almost impossible.

The spirituals represent the most fundamental epic of the African American people. Collectively, the more than 1,000 songs growing from the deepest emotional wellsprings of a patient, optimistic, persistent, long-suffering, strong, joyous, hard-working, clever, religious, creative, sorrowful, happy people are the intense

testaments of nobility. They are the noble statements of a gifted people, infused with dignity and strength under duress, these songs voice the majestic grandeur of victory over oppression. They possess an exalted sentiment that never falls below the line of greatness. Whether you hear "Go Down Moses" or "Walk Together, Children," you will feel the same sense of grandeur.

Those who created these master songs did so despite the fact that they had come from various parts of the continent of Africa. In the crucible of slavery were Yoruba, Ibo, Hausa, Fulani, Akan, Ewe, Ga, Wolof, Touculeur, Mande, Sherbro, Luba, Kuba, Dan, Douala, Ibibio, Edo, and more than 100 other ethnic groups.

Figure 12.24. James Baldwin (1924–1987). Became one of the most prominent African-American intellectuals of the 1950s and 1960s as a writer-activist wanting to confront racism and "illuminate the dream of the disenfranchised."

Figure 12.25. Alice Walker (1944–). A novelist, short-story writer, educator, and editor, she sends the message that African-American women need to recover their heritage in order to experience spiritual health and overcome racism and sexism.

Figure 12.26. Sonia Sanchez (1934–). Poet, playwright, and educator who wrote about the social and psychological inequality of African Americans while promoting African-American studies in schools.

Over a 250-year period these songs constituted the most elegant statement of a people's relationship to the universe and one another. In the music of the spiritual one finds the total embodiment of the African soul in response to the alien conditions of a new land, a new language, and a new religion. Indeed, the spirituals serve as calling cards to the world, a signature attesting to the uniqueness of African Americans' historical experiences in America: "Go down Moses, way down yonder in Egypt's land, tell ole Pharaoh to let my people go." With a limited knowledge of Africa and a rich imagination applied to the stories from the Jewish Bible, African Americans translated so much of the Judeo-Christian legacy into specific situations: "You got to walk that lonesome valley. You got to go there by yourself. Ain't nobody here can go there for you," all in reference to suffering in America.

The instruction was definite, the commitment personal. Ultimately, each person had to go through whatever "valley" of life alone. Often, when parents would witness their children sold away from the plantation where they had been born, they would retire to their shacks and sing in the most mournful tones, "You got to walk that lonesome valley."

These songs make the African American's spiritual world. They frame the mythical ideas that inform the epic journey of the people in a strange land. What the early Africans attempted to do in the cotton and tobacco fields with these songs was to record, if not on paper with pen, in the hearts of the people with pathos, the meaning of the enslavement and the emancipation from it. The songs grew out of religious sentiment, perhaps in some instances incomplete Christian references, but certain and meaningful African religious ideas and patterns of living. Thus, they held the African's commitment to family, to children, to mother, to the earth, to the water, particularly the river, and to hope. In fact, hope as faith was the central element in many of the earlier songs. The Africans could not live under the Great Enslavement without some hope, some possibility of liberation, some balance in God's system of justice.

Du Bois, in his wisdom, called these master songs the sorrow songs because they recorded the sufferings and pains of an enslaved people. Always, however, these songs introduced an element of victory over despair. The people danced.

THE LAW

The condition of Africans in America has always been consecrated by law, regardless of the political era. Thus, under enslavement the federal and state laws defined the limits of African freedom. Despite the social, theological, and economic reasons given for enslavement, the ultimate grounds of the American case against Africans were the system of laws effected to define the African's place. Much like the situation of blacks in South Africa during most of the twentieth century, Africans in America experienced legal imprisonment.

During enslavement many issues were raised that had to be adjudicated by law. In fact, the draconian system of laws often created ambiguity even in the minds of the enslaved. The Dred Scott case and the subsequent decision of 1857 ostensibly nullified the power of Congress to prohibit slavery in the territories. The Supreme Court, under Chief Justice Roger B. Taney, followed the lead of many lower courts on African rights. Indeed, in 1849 the Massachusetts Supreme Court had upheld Boston's right to keep schools segregated. Although this was later struck down by the Massachusetts legislature, the Boston case would be cited in many subsequent court cases.

It would take the civil rights era to usher in the new dispensation. Lawyers such as Thurgood Marshall and Fred Gray made legal history. Gray, a young attorney in Montgomery, was considered alongside Martin Luther King Jr. a leader of the Montgomery bus boycott. A skillful attorney, Gray, like King, was in his twenties when the boycott was introduced. A graduate of Case Western Reserve School of Law in Cleveland,

Figure 12.27. Toni Cade Bambara (1939–). A freelance writer and lecturer who is also a civil rights leader; she became directly involved with writing about the cultural and sociopolitical problems of urban communities in the 1960s.

Figure 12.28. John Henrick Clarke (1915–1998). Called the Dean of African American Historians, he is welcomed to Temple University by Molefi Kete Asante.

Figure 12.29. Amiri Baraka (1934–). A leading Black nationalist, playwrite, and director who wrote about angry African Americans with an affirmation of Black life. Credit: UPI/Corbis-Bettmann.

THE TRANSFORMING OF AMERICA   193

Ohio, Fred Gray had always wanted to provide legal services for those who could least afford them. Montgomery gave him service and national prominence. Influenced by the courage and genius of the NAACP's lawyers, particularly Thurgood Marshall, Gray was a southern example, much like Medgar Evers, of the will to challenge racism and segregation in his own chambers.

With reference to the wrongs inflicted on and the injuries received by the African American community in Montgomery and other cities in Alabama and the rest of the South, the young lawyers of the Southern Christian Leadership Conference preached a religion of equality, civil rights, justice, and peace. They gained political insight, educational experiences, and practical skills that were to be used in many venues during the Civil Rights Movement. These local attorneys assisted the legal battle for civil rights by defending demonstrators in court.

CIVIL RIGHTS/UNIONISM

By 1963, more than 100 of the then 130 affiliate chapters of the AFL-CIO had pledged to abolish racially segregated chapters, accept all eligible applicants regardless of race, color, or creed, and work for nondiscrimination agreements in all contracts made with management. This did not mean that all of the local affiliates were successful in transforming themselves.

Segregation was a matter of practice and custom in the U.S. federal government, and agencies often found themselves searching out their own racial contradictions. Through all of this, the African American community kept up its campaign to desegregate American society beginning with the government.

Nearly 300,000 African Americans worked for the U.S. government in 1963, representing a total of approximately 13 percent of all government employees. Most of these employees were in blue-collar jobs, and those in white-collar jobs were concentrated in the four lowest grades. Nevertheless, some African Americans pointed to the percentage of the government labor force as indicative of achievement during a time when African Americans were only 11 percent of the national population.

As in other periods of American history, so it was in the 1950s and early 1960s, the bulk of the black population was untouched by the government hiring statistics. For example, in 1963, the year of the March on Washington, 12 percent of the African American population was unemployed as compared to 5.6 percent of the whole population.

The 1960s were to be turbulent and dynamic years. The condition of African Americans at the start of the 1960s was severe to say the least. Segregated housing was still the custom of the land. This meant an intensification of all of the social problems that come with high density enforced by the iron hand of practice: overcrowded schools, poor health, high insurance rates, deterioration of housing stock, and juvenile delinquency.

Protests and petitions were developed and executed in an effort to force real estate firms and banks to discontinue discriminatory practices. The more than 1,400,000 African Americans who had migrated to the North in the 1950s served a catalytic role in many of the protests in the North. Thus, North and South, the movement for freedom and justice was joined and in the 1960s the nation was one massive cauldron of shifting ideologies and structural transformations.

The NAACP had introduced a wide range of lawsuits contesting discrimination on the basis of race in every public sector. Rivalry between leaders of the civil rights organizations produced attacks on segregation on the economic, legal, and social fronts. Leaders of the NAACP, the Congress of Racial Equality, and the Urban League were joined by the Southern Christian Leadership Conference and the Student Nonviolent Coordinating Committee as the big five of the Civil Rights Movement. Supported by the labor movement, they produced the dramatic 1963 March in Washington.

James Weldon Johnson

By the 1950s, the NAACP had demonstrated its ability to attract some of the lost intelligent activists of the century. Alongside Du Bois and Walter White, James Weldon Johnson (figure 12.31) was a stalwart in every campaign for respect and dignity. He joined the staff of the NAACP in 1916, two years before Walter White, and established himself as one of the leading promoters of the organization. Johnson, along with his brother Rosamond, wrote the "Negro National Anthem," which begins "Lift every voice and sing." Johnson's place in the annals of African American history is singularly enshrined in protest against injustice and in the defense of freedom.

Allensworth: The Philosopher's Town

Having shown extraordinary industry in overcoming the deficiencies of the previous condition of servitude, Africans at the turn of the twentieth century felt the stings of discrimination and prejudice meant to force them into political, economic, and social subjugation through segregation laws. Numerous individuals—determined to establish new possibilities—built schools, institutions, businesses, and towns. One of the most remarkable characters in this period was Colonel Allen Allensworth, the founder of Allensworth, the only African American town ever built in California.

Allen Allensworth was born in Louisville, Kentucky, on April 7, 1842. He showed early evidence of resistance to a system that would not allow him to learn to read. At the age of twelve he was sold for teaching himself to read and write. His slave owner thought he would become uncontrollable and create dissension among other Africans. As soon as he was twenty-one years of age, Allensworth fled slavery and became a member of the United States army. His experience in the Union army served as a basic lesson in the future of America, as Africans would use their experience to create opportunity for others.

After the Civil War, Allensworth worked in the commissary of the St.

Louis Navy Yard until he could save money for a business. In 1867, he entered the restaurant business with his brother. Eager to better his living conditions, he took advantage of the Eli Normal School's program to improve his education. He studied the Bible and the ministry. By 1871, Allensworth was an ordained preacher for the Fifth St. Baptist Church. Six years later he married the talented pianist Josephine Leavell, who was also a school teacher. They had two daughters, Nellie and Eva.

The United States army had four black regiments in the 1880s and none of them had a black chaplain. Allensworth appealed to President Grover Cleveland

Figure 12.30 (above left). Jesse Jackson, Leon Sullivan, and Louis Farrakhan at an African American Summit in Gabon, West Africa. Credit: David Barnes.

Figure 12.31 (lower left). James Weldon Johnson (1871–1938). Intellectual who played a key role in the civil rights movement as a teacher, poet, critic, diplomat, and NAACP official. Became popular as a lyricist and is especially known for the poem "Lift Every Voice and Sing," often called the Black national anthem.

to appoint him chaplain for the African soldiers. This request was granted on April 1, 1886, and Allensworth was made chaplain of the Fourteenth Infantry with the rank of captain. He later reached the rank of lieutenant colonel. He served the army until 1906 and upon his retirement took his family to settle in Los Angeles.

Since Allensworth had become a leading orator for self-help programs of economic empowerment, he was ready in 1908 to put his philosophy to practice.

William Payne, a young teacher, was to become Allensworth's chief supporter when the colonel proposed a race colony. Payne had received some education at Denison University in Granville, Ohio, and was a gifted teacher. Unable to acquire a job in public education in Pasadena, Payne combined his talents and resources with those of Allensworth. They persuaded several others to join their efforts to establish a colony. Dr. Peck, an African Methodist Episcopal minister; Mr. Palmer, a Nevada miner;

Figure 12.32. Dr. Martin Luther King speaking at Mississippi rally. Credit: Flip Schulke/Corbis.

and Mr. Mitchell, a Los Angeles realtor, joined to form the California Colonization and Home Promotion Association.

The organization selected an area around a depot connecting Los Angeles and San Francisco on the Santa Fe rail line. The depot, called Solito, was renamed Allensworth. It began a thriving community of farmers, artisans, and teachers. Allensworth had its own post office, school, drugstore, livery stable, machine shop, and hotel. Plans to build a vocational school on the philosophy of Booker T. Washington were developed, but the state legislature refused to support the idea.

The Allensworth Progressive Association was the governing body of the town. The officers were elected and held town meetings to foster full participation by all residents. The town became a school district in 1912, incorporating thirty-three square miles. In 1914, the town was made a judicial district, and two residents, Oscar Overr and William H. Dotson, became the first black men in California history to hold elected offices as justice of the peace and constable, respectively. Colonel Allensworth was killed in Los Angeles in 1914 when he stepped off a streetcar and was struck by a motorcyclist.

Despite the lack of water and constant legal battles with the Pacific Farming Company (the land development company responsible for delivering water to the town), Allensworth survived until 1966, when suspiciously high levels of arsenic were found in the town's well water. The town became a state historical site on May 14, 1976.

THE AGE OF GLORY

Martin Luther King Jr. gave his famous "I Have a Dream" speech at the Lincoln Monument in Washington, D.C., on August 28, 1963. Four young African American girls were bombed to death in a Birmingham, Alabama, church during the same year. The battle lines were clearly drawn, and segregationists intensified their campaign to enforce the laws of violence and terror. They were met with the tenacity and courage of scores of young leaders: Julian Bond (figure 12.33) , Robert Moses, James Forman, Charles Blackwell, Dona Richards, Fannie Lou Hamer, Cornelia Gray, and an army of volunteers. The movement was larger than anyone. It could not be stopped because the moral outrage was so vast and monumental that the society was carried toward a new destiny. As the Yoruba say, "Eshu was having his own way and that was that."

James Chaney, Michael Schwerner, and Andrew Goodman were murdered in Philadelphia, Mississippi, in 1964. The federal government arrested nineteen whites for various charges but not murder. Among those arrested were the sheriff and deputy sheriff of Neshoba County. Robert Moses emerged as one of the chief organizers of the Student Nonviolent Coordinating Committee. He helped to fashion a regional network linking the civil rights workers with resources and volunteers. James Forman assumed a leadership role in the struggle by asserting a militant stand against Christians who supported segregation. Julian Bond led the demonstrations against segregated lunch counters in Atlanta, Georgia. Dona Richards left the University of Chicago and went south during the summer of 1964. She registered voters under the freedom registration program. As a result, the Freedom Democratic Party was firmly established and founded upon voter's strength. Fannie Lou Hamer, Cornelia Gray, and others traveled to Atlantic City to the Democratic National Convention of 1964. The case of the Freedom Democratic Party was placed before the Credentials Committee of the Democratic Party. The new party claimed that the Mississippi Democratic Party had discriminated against African Americans and was therefore not the legitimate representative of the state of Mississippi. Hamer refused to accept a compromise and is projected into history because of her eloquent defense of principle and morality. Her tone was firm because it was based upon the concrete work she had done

Figure 12.33. Julian Bond (1940–). First became known as a civil rights activist by cofounding the Student Nonviolent Coordinating Committee (SNCC); later he was elected to the Georgia legislature but not seated because of his anti-Vietnam War ideals. The Supreme Court soon allowed him to take over the position anyway. Credit: Library of Congress/Corbis.

with the organizers of the Freedom Democratic Party.

The names of the martyrs were read in churches: Medgar Evers, Jimmie Lee Jackson, Viola Liuzzo, James Reeb, Chaney, Schwerner, and Goodman. Organizations worked around the clock to defeat the racists who attempted to block the Civil Rights Movement through fear tactics.

James Farmer of the Congress of Racial Equality (Core) became a visible symbol of leadership, breaking with the more moderate position of the leadership of other civil rights organizations to join with the Southern Christian Leadership Conference and the Student Nonviolent Coordinating Committee for more direct action. CORE became a dynamic ally of the civil rights movement, helping to shape and direct its course. The leadership of the NAACP and Urban League was supportive but noncommittal on the value of direct action to achieve effective progress for the African American community. Nevertheless, they were supportive of the general aims of the movement.

Roy Wilkins, the leader of the NAACP (see figure 12.34, page 198), and Whitney Young, leader of the Urban League, had always seen themselves as

Figure 12.34. Roy Wilkins (1901–1981). Reported on acts of violence against African Americans that took place for no other reason than the color of skin and African ancestry. Credit: Library of Congress/Corbis.

the legitimate heirs to the protest tradition. They had become suspect to the leaders of SNCC, CORE, and VISTA because of the slow pace at which they moved for legitimate redress of grievances. Both were stalwarts of the struggle in much the same way as A. Philip Randolph, the father of the modern protest, had been during his active days. They believed that legal remedies were permanent remedies.

Like the rest of the nation, the civil rights community was stunned by the creativity, courage, and boldness of the students in the movement. The Freedom Riders and volunteers for the freedom registration campaigns had focused national attention so keenly on the grievances of the African American people that it was only a matter of time before racial segregation as a system crumbled.

Figure 12.34. Million Man March, Washington, D.C., October 16, 1995. Held for African American men to unite and work to end violence, drugs, and other social problems experienced by African Americans. Credit: David Barnes.

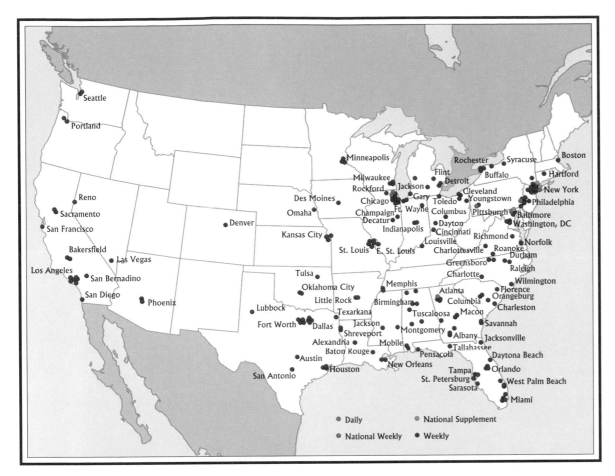

**Figure 12.35.
Locations of African
American newspapers.**

Seattle
Portland
Minneapolis
Rochester Syracuse Boston
Milwaukee Flint Buffalo Hartford
Rockford Jackson Detroit
Reno Des Moines Chicago Gary Cleveland Youngstown New York
Sacramento Omaha Ft. Wayne Toledo Pittsburgh Philadelphia
San Francisco Champaign Columbus Baltimore
Denver Decatur Dayton Washington, DC
Kansas City Indianapolis Cincinnati Richmond Norfolk
Bakersfield Louisville Roanoke
Las Vegas St. Louis E. St. Louis Charlottesville Durham
Los Angeles Greensboro Raleigh
San Bernadino Tulsa Charlotte Wilmington
San Diego Oklahoma City Memphis Atlanta Florence
Phoenix Little Rock Birmingham Columbia Orangeburg
Lubbock Texarkana Tuscaloosa Macon Charleston
Fort Worth Jackson Montgomery Savannah
Dallas Shreveport Albany Jacksonville
Alexandria Mobile Tallahassee
Baton Rouge Pensacola Daytona Beach
Austin New Orleans Orlando
San Antonio Houston Tampa West Palm Beach
St. Petersburg
Sarasota Miami

● Daily   ● National Supplement
● National Weekly   ● Weekly

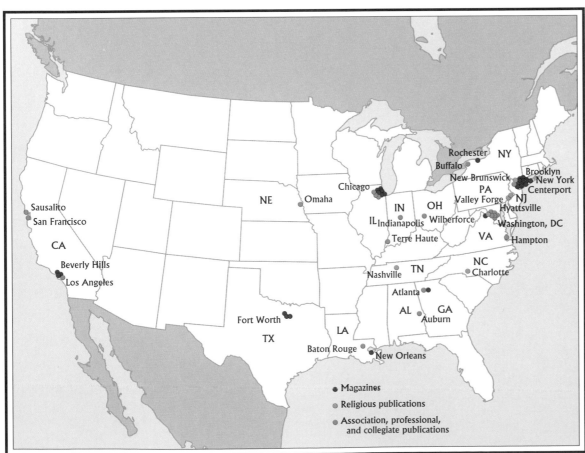

**Figure 12.36.
Locations of African
American magazines
and periodicals.**

Rochester NY
Buffalo New Brunswick Brooklyn
Chicago PA New York Centerport
NE Omaha IN OH Valley Forge NJ
IL Indianapolis Wilberforce Hyattsville
Sausalito Terre Haute Washington, DC
San Francisco VA Hampton
CA NC
Beverly Hills Nashville TN Charlotte
Los Angeles
Atlanta
AL GA
Fort Worth Auburn
TX LA
Baton Rouge
New Orleans

● Magazines
● Religious publications
● Association, professional,
   and collegiate publications

THE TRANSFORMING OF AMERICA   199

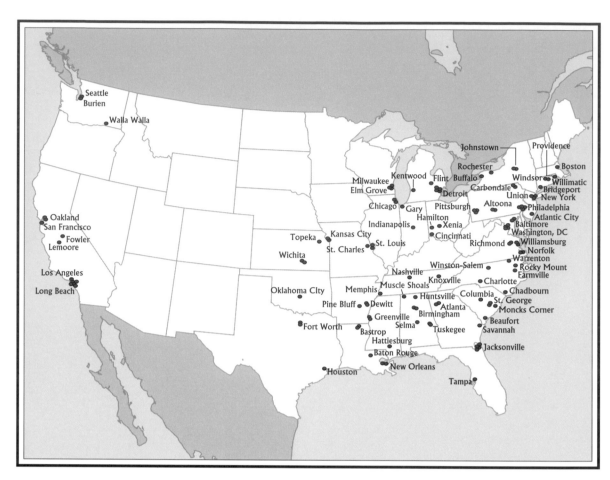

Figure 12.37. Locations of African American radio stations.

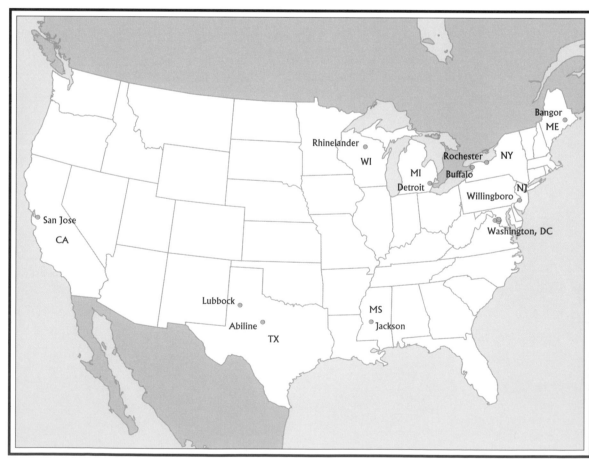

Figure 12.38. Locations of African American television stations.

"Didn't My Lord Deliver Daniel"

13

SOCIAL AND
ECONOMIC REALITIES

African Americans were predominantly a rural and southern people until the great urban migration of the World War II era. During the 1940s and 1950s thousands of African Americans moved to the major northern urban centers to seek better jobs and more equitable living conditions, free from racial prejudice.

The great cities of the North that had attracted escaped Africans during the Great Enslavement in the nineteenth century now provided opportunities for southern blacks to begin life anew in the middle of the twentieth century. Cities such as Chicago, New York, Philadelphia, and Detroit became magnets for entire southern communities. Patterns developed in the migration: Georgians and Carolinians would travel to Philadelphia and New York; Alabamians, Mississippians, and Louisianians to Detroit and Chicago; and Arkansans and Texans to Los Angeles, Oakland, and San Francisco. Residual migrations to Boston, Milwaukee, and Portland-Seattle often occurred. In some instances, family members would gain employment and then send for other family members, relatives, and friends.

What attracted African Americans most was the freedom from anti-African sentiment. This was translated in practical terms such as the ability for people to secure employment without regard to race. The lure of economic prosperity, political enfranchisement, and social mobility were magnets for the young men and women. The elderly were often left on the farms, as the young people went off to the North to work and perhaps send for their parents and grandparents once they were firmly established.

The North did not hold all good fortune. In fact, residential segregation in the North was frequently the rule. Much like the African American communities in the South, the segregated northern communities were centers of commerce and culture. Harlem in New York, South Street in Philadelphia, Woodlawn in Detroit, Southside in Chicago, and Hough in Cleveland were written into the African American imagination as places of high style, fashion, music, art, culture, religion, and commerce. The evolution of the African American communities from southern and rural to northern and urban has occurred since 1945.

POPULATION STATUS

In 1998, African American population is estimated to be 34.5 million—about 12.8 percent of the total U.S. population. By the year 2000 the African American population is projected to be over 35.4 million, making the African population in the United States the fifth largest African population in the world after Nigeria, Brazil, Egypt, Ethiopia, and Congo. The African population in the United States is larger than the black population of South Africa and Ghana combined.

The African American population is larger than the populations of all European nations except Russia, Ukraine, France, Germany, Poland, the United Kingdom, Spain, and Italy. Actually since 1980 the African American population has grown faster than either the total American population or the white population. The increase has been an average of 1.5 percent per year between 1980 and 1994, compared with 0.9 percent for the white population and the total population. This has been so despite a much more liberal immigration rate of Europeans than Africans to the United States.

By March 1994 more than 18 million or 55 percent of all African Americans lived in the South, 17 percent in the Northeast, 20 percent in the Midwest, and 8 percent in the West. According to the latest national census (1990), the ten cities with the largest concentrations of African Americans are New York, Chicago, Detroit, Philadelphia, Los Angeles, Houston, Baltimore, Washington, Memphis, and New Orleans. Other cities with significant populations of African Americans in the hundreds of thousands include Atlanta, Oakland, and St. Louis (see table 13.1, page 205).

For cities under 100,000 population, East St. Louis, Illinois, with a 98.1 African American percentage of the total population, and Gary, Indiana, with 80 percent, are the generally accepted leaders in terms of African American population concentrations in established cities.

Houston, Baltimore, Washington, Memphis, and New Orleans, all southern cities, are among the eleven cities with the largest numbers of African Americans. However, only three northern cities—Detroit, Philadelphia, and Chicago—are among the cities with the largest African American percentages of their total populations. Southern cities remain more heavily African American than northern cities. While the top five cities with the largest populations of African Americans are in the North, the cities with the highest percentages of African Americans tend to be in the South. Outside of the five largest American cities, with the exception of Los Angeles, the cities with the heaviest concentrations of African Americans are in the South.

The African American population grew by 12.3 percent between 1990 and 1994. This remarkable leap in population is higher than the national rate of 6.6 percent. (The growth rate of African Americans is not as high as that for the Spanish-speaking population.) Increasingly, the African American community must be seen as one of the most urban ethnic groups in the United States since most of the growth is in the cities.

Seven states have African American populations of more than 20 percent (see figure 13.1, page 233). These states are southern and predominantly rural. These states are Mississippi (35 percent), South Carolina (30 percent), Louisiana (29 percent), Georgia (27 percent), Alabama (26 percent), Maryland (23 percent), and North Carolina (22 percent).

In addition to the population domiciled in the United States, there are an additional one million African Americans abroad, mainly in cities in Africa and Europe. Enriched by the presence of Africans from Haiti, Jamaica, Costa Rica, Panama, Belize, the Antilles, Cuba, Puerto Rica, El Salvador, Ethiopia, Liberia, and other nations, the African American community has become one of the most richly diverse ethnic groups in the United States.

DISTRIBUTION OF THE POPULATION

Distribution of the African population in the United States is historically and

Table 13.1. Fifty U.S. cities with the largest African American populations and the percentage of each city's total population that is African American, 1990.

Rank	City	Total African Americans	Percent African American
1	New York, New York	2,102,512	28.7
2	Chicago, Illinois	1,087,711	39.1
3	Detroit, Michigan	777,916	75.7
4	Philadelphia, Pennsylvania	631,936	39.9
5	Los Angeles, California	487,674	14.0
6	Houston, Texas	457,990	28.1
7	Baltimore, Maryland	435,768	59.2
8	Washington, District of Columbia	399,604	65.8
9	Memphis, Tennessee	334,737	54.8
10	New Orleans, Louisiana	307,728	61.9
11	Dallas, Texas	296,994	29.5
12	Atlanta, Georgia	264,262	67.1
13	Cleveland, Ohio	235,405	46.6
14	Milwaukee, Wisconsin	191,255	30.5
15	St. Louis, Missouri	188,408	47.5
16	Birmingham, Alabama	168,277	63.3
17	Indianapolis, Indiana	165,570	22.6
18	Oakland, California	163,335	43.9
19	Newark, New Jersey	160,885	58.5
20	Jacksonville, Florida	160,283	25.2
21	Boston, Massachusetts	146,945	25.6
22	Columbus, Ohio	142,748	22.6
23	Cincinnati, Ohio	138,132	37.9
24	Kansas City, Missouri	128,768	29.6
25	Charlotte, North Carolina	125,827	31.8
26	Nashville-Davidson, Tennessee	118,627	24.3
27	Richmond, Virginia	112,122	55.2
28	San Diego, California	104,261	9.4
29	Norfolk, Virginia	102,012	39.1
30	Buffalo, New York	100,579	30.7
31	Fort Worth, Texas	98,532	22.0
32	Miami, Florida	98,207	27.4
33	Baton Rouge, Louisiana	96,346	43.9
34	Pittsburgh, Pennsylvania	95,362	25.8
35	Louisville, Kentucky	79,783	29.7
36	San Francisco, California	79,039	10.9
37	Mobile, Alabama	76,407	38.9
38	Rochester, New York	73,024	31.5
39	Oklahoma City, Oklahoma	71,064	16.0
40	Tampa, Florida	70,131	25.0
41	Jersey City, New Jersey	67,864	29.7
42	San Antonio, Texas	65,884	7.0
43	Toledo, Ohio	65,598	19.7
44	Denver, Colorado	60,046	12.8
45	Long Beach, California	58,761	13.7
46	Austin, Texas	57,868	12.4
47	Raleigh, North Carolina	57,354	27.6
48	Sacramento, California	56,521	15.3
49	Virginia Beach, Virginia	54,671	13.9
50	Akron, Ohio	54,656	24.5

economically based. Indeed, the reasons are interrelated in all cases. The states with the highest percentages of African Americans are all former slaveholding states. Three of those states—Mississippi, South Carolina, and Louisiana—have percentages of 35, 30, and 29, respectively. Along with Georgia (27 percent), Alabama (26 percent), Maryland (23 percent), North Carolina (22 percent), and Virginia (18 percent), these states constitute the heart of the region of the old slavery economy. And while there has been a profound shift in population to the urban areas, the rural southern states remain firmly entrenched as the heart of the African American community.

States with the lowest percentages and lowest numbers of Africans have had less economic attraction and less historical connection with the African American labor pool. Therefore, Vermont, Montana, Maine, Idaho, South Dakota, and North Dakota have limited populations of Africans. Another clue that the presence of large numbers of Africans in the South is due to history and economics rather than to climatic factors or distance away from the population centers of the South is the relatively strong showing of the state of Alaska, which has a larger percentage of African Americans than states such as Minnesota, Oregon, New Mexico, Washington, Arizona, Rhode Island, Nebraska, and West Virginia. While the total number of Africans in the Alaskan population is not large, only about 14,000, the figure constitutes a larger percentage of that state's total population than is the case in nineteen other states including Hawaii. Rather than climate or proximity, economics and the promise of independence and opportunity have been the factors that lured African Americans to Alaska. Many families experience Alaska first as military employees and then remain as permanent residents.

Washington, D.C., is more than 65 percent African American. African Americans often refer to the city as Bannekerville, in honor of Benjamin Banneker, one of the surveyors who laid out the city. The history of Washington's concentrated African American population can be traced to the Emancipation Proclamation and the African's response to the Union government. Africans, literate and nonliterate, converged on Washington and became home buyers and civil servants. Most African Americans in Washington are employees of the federal agencies or the district's government. This fact led the great Arkansas blues singer Huddie Ledbetter to write a song popular in the 1940s and 1950s that said, "Washington, D.C., is a bourgeois town." With a larger percentage of Africans than any major metropolitan area except Detroit, Washington, D.C., contains all of the cultural achievements, social dislocations, intellectual dynamism, and political action to be seen elsewhere in the African American community.

POPULATION TRENDS

The African American population is a youthful one compared to the national median age. For all races and both sexes the median age is 33.9. However, for African Americans it is 28.4 as compared with 36.5 for whites. Furthermore, the African American male has the lowest median age by race, 26.6, and the African American female at 29.9 has a lower median age than the white female at 37.5. White females tend to live longer, and black males tend to have shorter life spans. Overall, the general African American population remains the youngest of the American ethnic communities (see table 13.2, page 207).

Not only is the African American ethnic group made up of a young population, it is profoundly urban. Less than one-fifth of the African American population is considered rural, whereas two generations ago more than four fifths of the population was classified as rural. Most of the rural population is concentrated in the South with its longer history of enslavement of Africans for agricultural work. Family farms not confiscated from Africans after the fall of Reconstruction now account for a greater proportion of African Americans in the rural areas than remnants of sharecropping. Owning property during the slave period was impossible for most Africans, but for freedpersons it was possible although extremely difficult because of the unusually high prices asked from freedpersons for farm land. Farms purchased from whites during the late nineteenth and early twentieth century gave southern and mostly rural African Americans a stake in the productive sector with which they were most familiar.

VIOLENCE AND MIGRATION

The Ku Klux Klan's attacks on African American property owners and voters in the South at the beginning of the twentieth century drove thousands of farm families away from the South, and their property was often lost to whites. Failure of the U.S. government to protect African Americans during Reconstruction meant that many people were beaten, harassed, and killed. Those able to retain their property often fled to the North and left older family members as caretakers. Nevertheless, the violence left a heavy debt on the people remaining in the South because they had to deal with the attitudes of white southerners who harbored fears and insecurities around black landowners and therefore threatened them with retaliation if they sold their produce in the common markets. If they grew cotton, they were not supposed to receive the same price as the white farmer. If they grew potatoes, they had to almost give away their produce in order for them to continue farming. Most African Americans ended up as subsistence farmers rather than as commercial farmers.

POPULATION CHANGE

The African population of the United States will increase by 1 percent as the white population decreases by 5 percent by 2010. This means that the U.S. population will become increasingly colored, although it will remain overwhelmingly white. In 1980, "other" as a category made up 2 percent of the population. This category is usually checked by those persons not willing to indicate race or

Age Group	All races	White	African American	Percent African American
Total	265,284	219,749	33,503	12.6
Under 5	19,286	15,289	2,948	15.3
5 to 9	19,441	15,361	3,093	15.9
10 to 14	18,981	15,077	2,905	15.3
15 to 19	18,662	14,838	2,904	15.6
20 to 24	17,560	14,010	2,593	14.8
25 to 29	19,007	15,340	2,601	13.7
30 to 34	21,361	17,477	2,810	13.2
35 to 39	22,577	18,697	2,834	12.6
40 to 44	20,816	17,384	2,481	11.9
45 to 49	18,436	15,643	1,997	10.8
50 to 54	13,934	11,952	1,413	10.1
55 to 59	11,362	9,763	1,163	10.2
60 to 64	9,999	8,652	995	10.0
65 to 69	9,892	8,667	929	9.4
70 to 74	8,778	7,844	704	8.0
75 to 79	6,873	6,198	526	7.7
80 to 84	4,557	4,150	320	7.0
85 to 89	2,394	2,182	170	7.1
90 to 94	1,024	923	82	8.0
95 to 99	286	254	27	9.4
100+	57	47	8	14.0
Median age	34.6	35.7	29.5	

ethnicity or for whom no specific category is included. By 2010 that figure will be 5 percent.

Interestingly, the African population growth will derive from birthrate while growth in the "other" category will result largely from immigration. Immigration from Africa to the United States is negligible in the statistics, accounting for less than 1 percent of all immigrants to the United States. Although migration from the Caribbean and South America has increased in the past few years, the African American population remains remarkably uniform since there has been less ethnic infusion. Having originated in the seventeenth century with more than 90 percent of its families able to count back at least six generations, the African American population is quintessentially connected to the history of America. African Americans have been historically connected to the Native American population since the origin of the enslaved population. New groups of Native American/Africans have recently been discovered in the southern states. With the possibility of new concepts of race emerging in the next century, the African American population will more than likely define itself as a cultural rather than a

Table 13.2. Resident population by race and age group and the percent of each age group that is within age range, 1996.

racial group, much like the Hispanic grouping, which is composed of many different ethnic and racial groups. Already Africans from national origins in other parts of the Americas such as Costa Rica, Haiti, Panama, Brazil, Venezuela, Trinidad, El Salvador, Colombia, the Dominican Republic, and Jamaica join persons from the African continent to enrich and enlarge the African American community.

GROWING CITIES AND AREAS

With the exception of the states of California and Texas, the great centers of African American population tend to be east of the Mississippi River. This has been true throughout history, and the trend seems to hold for the future. If there is to be significant shift in population it will probably be among regions in the eastern part of the nation rather than among continents.

There is a real possibility, if current trends continue, that the population will flow from the northern urban communities back to the southern small towns. During the past fifty years there was a decidedly one-way flow of migration from the South to the North. This southward trend started in the 1970s and seems to be continuing at the present time because of the elimination of most discrimination and the opportunity for better jobs in the South.

CRUDE BIRTHRATE

While the data show that the African American birthrate has declined since 1960, it remains higher than the U.S. average and the white average. However, birthrate for the African American community appears to be headed in the direction of the national average. As one can see, the crude birthrate for African American women between the ages of 15 and 44 dropped from more than 150 live births per 1,000 women in 1960 to below 80 in 1994 (see figure 13.2, page 209).

The implications of this dramatic shift in the birthrate for African American women are not easy to determine. It seems certain that the trend toward hav-

ing fewer children will continue into the near future with uncertain consequences. While the white live birthrate also declined during the twenty-five-year span, the rate of decline was less dramatic than that for African American women. This could mean that more African American women and men are using some form of contraceptive than in previous years, male sperm count is declining, or families are deciding to delay children until their financial situations are more secure. Other, more personal and private, reasons may also exist. (See figure 13.3, page 233 for state birthrates for African American women.)

CRUDE DEATH RATE

West Virginia had the highest crude death rate in the nation during the 1980s and into the early 1990s. In a state with only 65,051 Africans Americans, 923 died according to the 1980 census. This represented 1.4 percent of the population. By contrast, Hawaii, with a population of 17,364, recorded only 2 deaths in 1981.

A number of factors may account for the high death rate in West Virginia. The most obvious has to do with the age of the population. While Hawaii tends to attract younger African Americans (i.e., those who remain in Hawaii after serving in the military), West Virginia has a higher percentage of older African Americans. In general, West Virginia may hold a hazard for the population due to cases of black lung disease among men who work in the coal mines. Furthermore, the industry of West Virginia has tended toward the labor-intensive machine industry as opposed to the more information and service economy of Hawaii. It should also be pointed out that the age of West Virginia's African American population is not inconsequential in the determination of the health of the community.

BIRTHS TO SINGLE PARENTS

Nearly one million children were born to single parents during 1990. More than half that number were born to white mothers, a little less than half were born to blacks. Statistics show that African

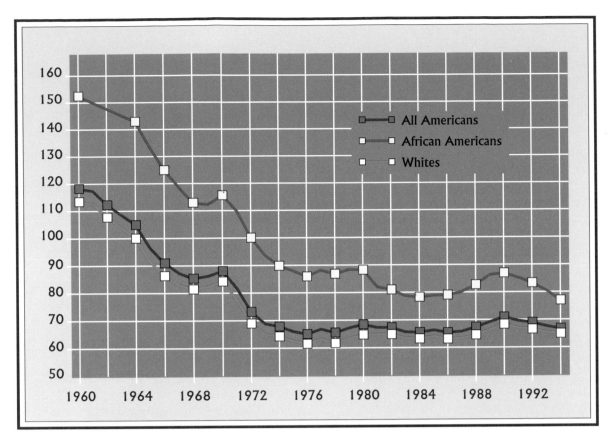

Figure 13.2. Number of births per 1,000 women aged 15 to 44 years, 1960–1994.

American children are more than three times as likely to have a single parent than white children. A child born to a single parent is likely to have fewer life chances than a child born to two parents. This is true in several aspects of the child's life. The most significant aspect is economic support. A child born to a two-parent family will most likely have the financial support needed to do well in school, compete in team or group activities, take vacations, and find amusement. On the other hand, a child born in a single-parent family will find it more difficult to find the resources necessary for effective learning opportunities. This is not to say that a child will not learn or succeed in a single-parent family; obviously this cannot be true since we have thousands of examples where people do succeed. It is essentially the advantage that having a two-parent family may give a child. It is not always the case that a child from a two-parent family has an advantage; a lot depends on the child and the parents. Yet the material conditions for children in single-parent homes is likely to make them less competitive.

In 1996 six states and the District of Columbia had a stunning 75 percent or more births to single parents. Births to unmarried parents in Wisconsin was 82.9 percent percent in 1996. This percentage was followed by the District of Columbia with 79.9 percent; Pennsylvania with 78.4 percent; Illinois with 77 percent; Michigan with 76.6 percent; Nevada with 76.6 percent; and Ohio with 76.5 percent (see figure 13.4, page 234).

INFANT MORTALITY

Infant mortality is one of the standard measures for determining the health of a community or nation. The infant mortality rate in the United States remains higher than that in other industrial countries. The rate for African Americans is more than twice what it is for the white population. (See figure 13.5, page 234 for state infant mortality rates for African American women.)

The death rate of black children in infancy approaches that of underdeveloped nations. Large urban cities have become the tombs of many African American infants.

States such as Illinois (23.3) and Michigan (23.7) represent giant industrial states—relatively rich regions of the country—yet they have infant mortality rates like those of poor southern states. This is due to poor health care in the large, poor urban communities.

HEALTH

While the data show that the African American family is decreasing in size, the state of African American health seems to be increasingly jeopardized. From the time of the Great Enslavement, when the health of the enslaved person was looked at only in terms of economic considerations, to the present time, where the cost of health care has placed most medical care, without insurance, beyond the reach of the great majority of African Americans, health is a serious but costly business in the black community.

African Americans still have one of the highest mortality rates of any ethnic or cultural group in the United States. As socioeconomic levels decline, mortality rates increase. The condition of African American health is directly related to poverty factors such as the lack of medical care for children and poor nutrition. Added to these factors are the unequal access to medical care and discriminatory delivery of the care when it is available.

Unquestionably there has been a gradual improvement in the health of African Americans since the Great Enslavement. During this same period, the health of black women has improved over that of black men. Actually it is possible to speak of a convergence in the life expectancies of African American women and white women in the twentieth century. The picture is bleaker for African American men.

MORTALITY AND MORBIDITY

Like the infant mortality rate, the death rate for African American men is the highest in the United States (figure 13.6). A significant portion of the statistics regarding the high death rate of black males is based upon intentional-injury statistics. The rate at which African American males kill each other in violent confrontations has alarmed all health workers. A culture of machismo has evolved where the threat of violence often means that the challenge for violence must be met with violent acts.

The risks associated with violent death seem to be psychological and cultural. A young African American male with poor self-esteem and from the lowest socioeconomic level is much more likely to be at risk than other members of the black community. Add to these factors the lack of information and knowledge about African cultural values and the chances are great that the person will end up in a violent confrontation that might mean his death or the death of someone else. Homicide remains the leading cause of death for black males between fifteen and thirty-four.

Other leading causes of death in the African American community are heart disease, malignant neoplasms, cerebrovascular disease, chronic obstruction, and pulmonary diseases (see table 13.3, page 211). Within the past ten years AIDS has spread within the African American community. There is no effective vaccine or cure for the disease; yet enough information is available about the disease that it can be prevented. Most African Americans tend to get infected through the sharing of needles used for the injec-

Figure 13.6. Death rate per 100,000 people in the United States, 1995.

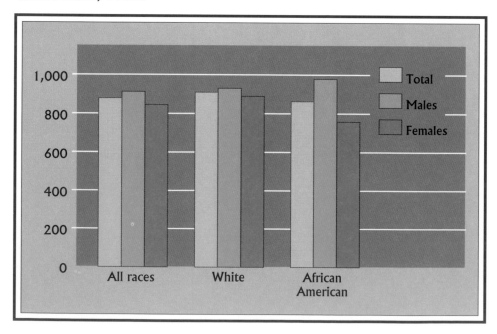

Both sexes	Number	Rate
All causes	286,401	864.2
1 Diseases of the heart	78,643	237.3
2 Malignant neoplasms, including neoplasms of lymphatic and hematopoietic tissues	60,603	182.9
3 Cerebrovascular diseases	18,537	55.9
4 Human immunodeficiency virus infection	17,139	51.7
5 Accidents and adverse effects	12,748	38.5
6 Homicide and legal intervention	10,783	32.5
7 Diabetes mellitus	10,402	31.4
8 Pneumonia and influenza	7,803	23.5
9 Chronic obstructive pulmonary diseases and allied conditions	6,667	20.1
10 Certain conditions originating in the perinatal	4,962	14.9

Male		
All causes	154,175	980.7
1 Diseases of the heart	38,389	244.2
2 Malignant neoplasms, including neoplasms of lymphatic and hematopoietic tissues	32,880	209.1
3 Human immunodeficiency virus infection	12,875	81.9
4 Homicide and legal intervention	8,847	56.3
5 Accidents and adverse effects	8,834	56.2
6 Cerebrovascular diseases	8,011	51
7 Diabetes mellitus	4,110	26.1
8 Pneumonia and influenza	4,019	25.6
9 Chronic obstructive pulmonary diseases and allied conditions	3,917	24.9
10 Certain conditions originating in the perinatal period	2,731	17.4

Female		
All causes	132,226	759
1 Diseases of the heart	40,254	231.1
2 Malignant neoplasms, including neoplasms of lymphatic and hematopoietic tissues	27,723	159.1
3 Cerebrovascular diseases	10,526	60.4
4 Diabetes mellitus	6,292	36.1
5 Human immunodeficiency virus infection	4,264	24.5
6 Accidents and adverse effects	3,914	22.5
7 Pneumonia and influenza	3,784	21.7
8 Chronic obstructive pulmonary diseases and allied conditions	2,750	15.8
9 Nephritis, nephrotic syndrome, and nephrosis	2,243	12.9
10 Certain conditions originating in the perinatal period	2,221	12.7

Table 13.3. Deaths and death rates for the ten leading causes of death for African Americans, 1995.

tion of illicit drugs. Women may pass the disease to their children through pregnancy. Substance abuse constitutes an enormous health care problem as well.

CHANGE IN FAMILY SIZE

While the African American family has decreased in size since 1970, the average African American family remains larger than the average white family. Such is the case despite the increasing gap in economic capability among among families. To a great extent, the data suggest a legacy from the days of plantations and agriculture, when it was economically profitable to slave owners and therefore economically necessary for African families to have large families. Statistics show that rural families and poor families tend to have more children than urban and middle-class families.

African American families are getting smaller. Indeed, the percentage of families with no children grew in 1985 to reach more than 40 percent for the first time since 1970. In addition, families with one or two children increased, while families with three and four children decreased. The decreasing numbers of children in the African American family is probably linked to the rise of two-job families. Parents are finding it more difficult to fulfill the responsibility of

their professions or jobs and to raise families at the same time. With more women entering the workplace and the men already working out of the home, there is no one left to mind the children.

FAMILY CHARACTERISTICS

African American women and men marry at about the same rate across the nation. However, in a few states the rate is slightly different for both sexes. The highest rate of marriage for both women and men is found in the southeastern United States and the mountain states. On the average there are more than 30 marriages per 1,000 persons in those two regions. This may be the result of strong religious sentiments or social traditions. Women tend to marry more often in Alabama than men. Men tend to marry at a higher rate than women in Oregon. In other regions of the country the rate of marriage for men and women tends to be nearly equal.

Data show that African American family size is steadily declining. As late as 1970, the average household had more than 4 people; now it is down to about 3.5 (figure 13.7). Economic pressures on the family unit have played important roles in convincing families to reduce the number of children. Economic vulnerabilities created by the lack of protection for health emergencies or accidents or other calamities are only a few of the reasons given for minimizing the risk to the family by limiting its size. The relative risks of economic catastrophe affect the way adults view their family possibilities. Thus, family size is most often related to aspirations.

CHANGE IN FAMILY STRUCTURE

While the African American family has decreased in size, it has also taken on other characteristics. There is a growing trend of females heading households. While most families are still maintained by males, female-headed families concern social researchers because of the economic implications of such a structure. Women who work tend to make less money than men who work, and

Figure 13.7. Number of children under 18 years of age living in African American households, 1980–1995.

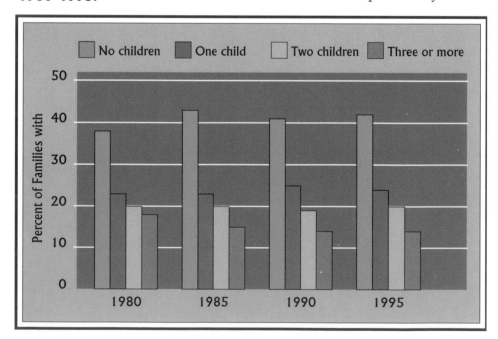

therefore the family will normally be economically penalized for having a female head (figure 13.8).

Whether or not these women have informal support systems will determine to what extent children in such families suffer from lack of care and concern. Informal support networks such as mutual help linkages with other women are often well developed over a period of years. These households may not be as isolated as one may think. Relatives and close family friends often provide the backbone of the network. Such informal networks have strong implications for the practical and material comfort of the family. These networks may provide food, shelter, money, and services.

Some women have also found these networks useful for child care if they have to run errands or go somewhere. In addition to exchanging child care, the women often share commodities. An informal sisterhood is usually formed where services and goods are given to each other on an ask-and-give basis. Informal networks such as these can help to overcome economic insecurity and social vulnerability. One other benefit of these informal linkages is psychological and affective. Women are able to share with each other their problems and gain support in the raising of their children. These spiritual bonds are central to many of the informal networks.

African American Income

Nowhere in the United States is the median African American household income equal to that of white households. In most cases the comparison highlights the vast economic gap that has existed between Africans and whites since the founding of the nation. The Midwest and Northeast have the greatest distinctions. In 1995 in the Midwest, for example, whites have a median income of $32,149 while African Americans in the region have a median income of $16,755. Whites in the Northeast have a median income of $35,262 compared to the African American family median of $20,678. (See figure 13.9, page 235 for

African American median family income for nine regions within the United States in 1996.)

Because African American family income is substantially lower than incomes for white families in every region of the United States, the purchasing power of the average African American family is well below that of the white family. In addition to the income gap is the estate wealth gap that makes the white family income more elastic than the African American family income. Two families, one African American and the other white, with the same salary cannot be equated when the white family's accumulated wealth in stocks, bonds, land, inherited position, and so forth, often far exceeds that of the African American family.

The 1997 Statistical Abstract reported that in 1995 for the first time the number of African American females in the workplace surpassed that of African American males. There were 38,000 more females working than males in that year. The trend continued into 1996, when there were 239,000 more African American females than males working. This trend is noteworthy given family structure which is based in many cases on single-parent household heads.

Figure 13.8. Change in wage earners in African American families, 1980–1993.

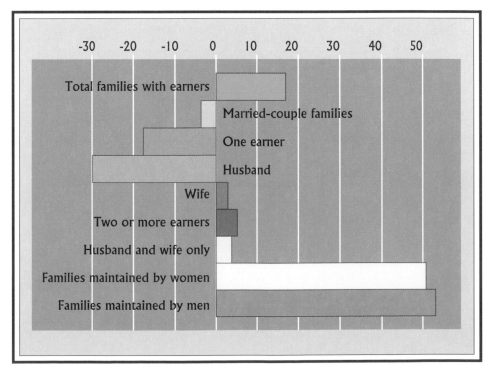

FAMILIES IN POVERTY

African Americans living in Louisiana and Mississippi are more likely to be below the poverty level than African Americans living in other states. Almost every index of the quality of living is worse in Louisiana and Mississippi. Both states are agriculturally based and have limited industrial diversification.

These two states are not alone in large populations of poor blacks. While pover-ty is more pronounced in Louisiana and Mississippi, no state where there is a sizable population of African Americans can speak with confidence about the character of the economic status enjoyed by its black citizens.

EDUCATION

There are nine major cities in which the school population is predominantly African American: Chicago, Detroit, Philadelphia, Houston, Baltimore, Washington, D.C., Memphis, New Orleans, and Atlanta. Many of these school districts have become majority black for two reasons. First, the population of the white residents tends to be older than that of the black residents. Second, and important, where there are children many of the whites choose to send their children to private or religious schools. Thus, even in cities where the overall population is still predominantly white, the school districts have become increasingly African American (see figure 13.10, page 235 and table 13.4 for African American school enrollments in the United States in 1995).

In these cities the schools with the highest percentage of low-income students tend to do poorest on standardized tests in reading and mathematics. Thus, the correlation between poverty and low test scores reveals a persistent problem in the education of African American children. High-poverty schools in which students and parents as well as teachers and counselors must deal with numerous nonacademic issues tend to thwart academic achievement. Of course, this is true whether or not the children happen to be black. Most school districts reflect a close relationship between economic class and academic achievement.

New developments such as the rise of independent black schools and the charter school movement have made it possible for parents to select from a wide range of Afrocentric schools for the education of their children. These schools, such as the Marcus Garvey Shule in Los Angeles, the Sankofa School in Lansing, Michigan, and the Paul Robeson School

Table 13.4. Enrollment in public elementary and secondary schools by race and state, fall 1995.

	White	African American
Alabama	62.1	36.0
Alaska	63.7	4.6
Arizona	56.9	4.3
Arkansas	73.9	23.6
California	40.4	8.8
Colorado	72.5	5.5
Connecticut	72.0	13.5
Delaware	64.7	29.4
District of Columbia	4.0	87.6
Florida	57.5	25.3
Georgia	58.2	37.8
Hawaii	22.9	2.6
Idaho	88.4	0.6
Illinois	63.6	21.1
Indiana	85.6	11.1
Iowa	92.7	3.3
Kansas	82.6	8.5
Kentucky	89.1	9.8
Louisiana	51.0	46.0
Maine	97.3	0.8
Maryland	57.5	35.0
Massachusetts	78.5	8.2
Michigan	76.4	18.4
Minnesota	87.4	4.8
Mississippi	47.7	51.0
Missouri	81.7	16.1
Montana	87.5	0.5
Nebraska	87.2	5.9
Nevada	66.5	9.8
New Hampshire	96.7	0.9
New Jersey	62.5	18.5
New Mexico	39.5	2.4
New York	56.9	20.2
North Carolina	64.6	30.7
North Dakota	90.8	0.8
Ohio	82.2	15.3
Oklahoma	69.4	10.5
Oregon	85.3	2.6
Pennsylvania	80.6	14.0
Rhode Island	78.9	7.0
South Carolina	56.3	42.1
South Dakota	83.7	0.9
Tennessee	75.3	23.1
Texas	46.4	14.3
Utah	90.4	0.7
Vermont	97.3	0.7
Virginia	66.6	26.5
Washington	78.3	4.7
West Virginia	95.2	4.0
Wisconsin	83.2	9.4
Wyoming	89.3	1.0

in Detroit, are examples of the emphasis on quality and centeredness going on in numerous schools in the nation. Most of the schools tend to be elementary and middle schools; there are fewer than ten high schools that call themselves Afrocentric schools. Horace Mann High School in Gary, Indiana, is one of the best examples of what a school can do by centering the child.

Although there has been a continuous rise in the number of school years completed by African Americans since the end of World War II, the number of school years completed still lags behind the general population (see figure 13.11 and 13.12, page 216 for school completion rates). In effect, the legacy of slavery, discrimination, and poverty affects the opportunities and motivation of African Americans, even though there remains a strong education ethic within the community. Between 1940 and 1986 there was almost a ninefold increase in the number of African Americans completing four or more years of high school. This phenomenal rate of increase had a lot to do with the more open societies in the North during the war years and the substantial reliance of African American parents on education to secure children an opportunity for blunting racism.

College attendance also increased over this period of time: from 1.3 percent having completed four or more years of college in 1940 to 10.9 percent by 1986. The biggest gains were made between 1940 and 1970, when the political and social mood of the nation encouraged the admission of African Americans into predominantly white colleges. Heretofore, the 100 or so African American colleges had educated more than 90 percent of the African American population. With the Civil Rights Movement of the 1950s and 1960s, the expansion of educational opportunity emerged as a cardinal component of social progress. Autherine Lucy's integration of the University of Alabama, James Meredith's integration of the University of Mississippi, and Charlayne Hunter's integration of the University of Georgia meant that the

A young African American at the Horus Temple in Edfu, Egypt. Numerous African American families are rediscovering all of Africa.

A beautiful African American woman, Dollis Lambert, of Costa Rican origin celebrating the Kwanzaa Holiday.

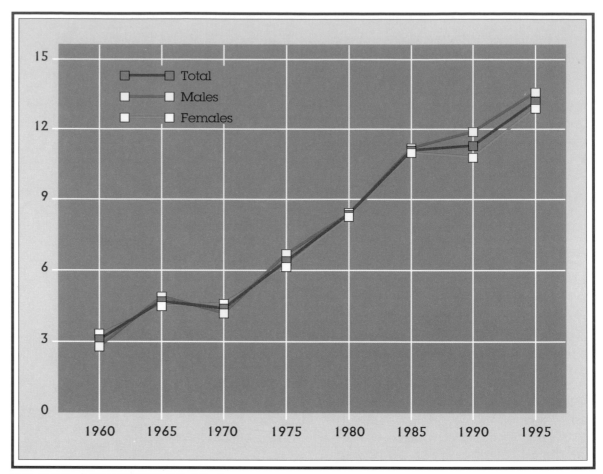

Figure 13.11. The percent of African Americans who have completed four years of college or more, 1960–1995.

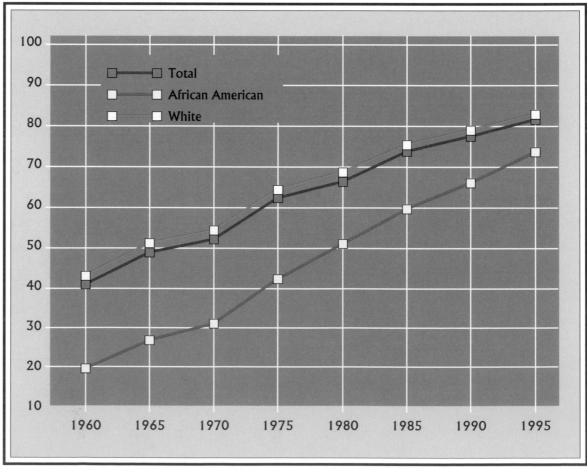

Figure 13.12. The percent of people 25 years of age or older who have completed four years of high school or more in the United States, 1960–1995.

walls of segregation were breached in the deepest parts of the American South. College became more accessible to individuals living at home or in close proximity to major colleges. African Americans took full advantage of these opportunities in the 1960s and 1970s.

Among the issues concerning education that confronted African Americans during the past twenty years are fairness in testing, equity in opportunity, curricula changes, and Afrocentric models and examples at every grade level in public schools and in colleges. These issues will continue to be discussed.

Between 1990 and 1998, numbers of African American students attending higher educational institutions increased. This increase was felt by most major institutions, although the historically black colleges and universities continued to be the main educators of professionals. Both graduate and undergraduate enrollments were up during the decade. During recent years, however, with the sustained assault on the multicultural work of the schools, the attack on affirmative action, and the conservative posture of the government, the nation has seen a dwindling of support for the African American student.

African Americans are now more likely to have earned a high school diploma than in 1980. In 1994, 73 percent of African Americans adults over 25 years of age had a high school diploma. This proportion is up from 51 percent in 1980. The growth rate was similar for men and women.

In addition, 13 percent of the African American population over 25 years of age had a bachelor's degree or higher, an increase from 8 percent in 1980. The corresponding figures for whites were 23 and 18 percent.

ILLITERACY

During Reconstruction, thousands of Africans rushed to schools to learn how to read because they felt they could not be proper citizens without the ability to read and interpret the basic documents of the society. Now, however, although there has been a continuous rise in the number of school years completed by African Americans, there is still a large population of functionally illiterate individuals. This means that they are unable to read the newspaper, to read captions on the television, to answer mail, to read street signs, and to sign checks.

States with the highest illiteracy rates are also the poorest states. They are also the states with the greatest incidents of racial discrimination. Both whites and blacks in the South tend to be illiterate at higher rates than the national average. This means that either the school system has failed these individuals or that it never was given a chance.

Many southerners often preferred to send their children to work rather than to school. Individuals without a basic education are handicapped in society because society is based on reading and writing. Any person unable to read or write, therefore, becomes a negative statistic in a region's attempt to raise the standards of its people.

Illiteracy among African Americans in large urban states approaches the rates in the southern states, but there is a difference. The African Americans who live in the central cities of New York, Chicago, Detroit, and Philadelphia are at the greatest risk. They tend to have more functional illiteracy than African Americans who live in the Plains States or the West.

VOTING PRIVILEGES

By 1998 there were more than 7,500 African American elected officials, covering every state with the exceptions of Idaho, Montana, and North Dakota. Predictably, the states with the highest percentages of African Americans of voting age population tended to have the largest numbers of African American elected officials (see figure 13.13, page 236). The District of Columbia, with 65.6 percent of African Americans of the voting age population, had 244 African American elected officials as of 1988. The fact that the district is a city, with limited opportunities compared to a state (e.g., there is no district legislature), suggests that were the district to become a state, the number of African Americans elected would be larger than in any of the present states. Excepting the District of Columbia, by 1990 the largest number of African American elected officials were (predictably) found in Mississippi with 578, Louisiana with 524, Georgia with 458, Illinois with 443, Alabama with 442, and North Carolina with 428. (Also see figure 13.14, page 236 for eligible African American voters by state.)

AFRICAN AMERICAN BUSINESSES

The 1990s was a period of unprecedented boom in American history, and many African Americans shared in the rewards of a growing economy. Between 1987 and 1992 the number of African American-owned businesses in the United States increased by 46 percent, increasing from 424,165 to 620,912. Furthermore, receipts for all African American firms increased by 63 percent, from $19.8 billion in 1987 to $32.2 billion in 1992. Yet the average amount of receipts, $52,000, still lagged behind the average receipts, $193,000, for all U.S. firms in 1992.

President Bill Clinton, the only Democrat since Franklin Roosevelt to serve two terms, campaigned on a promise to "grow the economy." Many of the measures he took reflected long-standing Republican values but had a mass appeal among Democrats who saw a chance to support human values as well as economic prosperity.

New businesses were created by African Americans at a phenomenal rate, and many of these businesses were related to the electronics industry. Where African Americans had held managerial level appointments in electronics company, many of them assisted the companies in maximizing their profits. Others left those companies to form their own companies. So rapid was the expansion in the 1990s that a good number of businesses went out of business, having been acquired by other electronic businesses. What the activity in this area showed was that African American entrepreneurs

were involved as leaders in a number of successful African American electronic businesses. Others continued to operate large franchises, to engage in the stock market, and to consolidate their holdings in real estate and service-industry businesses. Publishers such as Kassahun Checole of Africa World Press, Haki Madhubuti of Third World Press, and Paul Coates of Black Classic Press continue to move toward sufficiency.

FAMILY INCOME

Despite enormous gains in African Americans' life chances, economic opportunities, and educational possibilities, the economic position of African Americans remains fragile when considered alongside that of white Americans. It is estimated that in 1996 at least 31 percent of the African American population had incomes below the poverty line while only 11 percent of white families lived below the poverty line (see figure 13.15, page 219). By 1996 the African American families living below the poverty line had decreased to 27 percent. The implications for education, material possessions, quality of shelter, and cash for investments are profound and have a major impact on the nature of the African American family's ability to achieve success in the American economy.

When one adds to this the fact that African Americans normally have more children than the white population and the fact that family size has a lot to do with the poverty rate, one can see the explosive nature of the impoverished condition of the African American families. For example, in 1985 17 percent of all African American families had three or more children while only 10 percent of white families had three or more children. Since poverty involves issues of life and death—well-being, disease, education, ignorance—one can easily see how it would create chaos in the family structure. The white infant mortality rate was 10 per 1,000 live births in 1983, while at the same time the African American infant mortality rate was 19 per 1,000 live births. By 1990 the white mortality rate had been reduced to 7.7 per 1,000 births and the African American rate to 17 per 1,000 births. Today, the rate is most likely reduced even more, but the gap between the African American and white American population remains the same.

Poverty is a persistent problem in the American economy, and it continues to affect a greater part of the African American community than the white community. Actually, by 1985 43.5 percent of all African American children lived in poverty and 34 percent of all African American families lived in poverty. However, between 1993 and 1994, poverty rates dropped for African Americans from 33.1 percent to 30.6 percent and for whites from 12.2 percent to 11.7 percent. While it is probably true that poverty among African Americans and whites fell over a thirty-year period, the poverty rate for African Americans has remained consistently about three times greater than white poverty.

AFRICAN AMERICAN EMPLOYMENT

Employment percentages in various sectors have always been different for African Americans than for whites in the United States. The patterns of employment are determined historically. The data represented in the following illustrations show African Americans, whites, and others employed in certain sectors. The charts illustrate the percentage of African American or white workers employed in particular economic sectors; they do not illustrate the percentage of African Americans in the total economic sector itself.

Clearly, while African Americans share in some of the same employment interests as whites, the percentages of the African American population engaged in certain economic sectors differ greatly from those of the white population. For example, a larger percentage of the African American population than of the white population is employed in the professional public administration sector. More than a quarter of all African Americans who are employed are in the professions or public administration sector. By contrast, the largest percentage of employed whites is in the wholesale and retail sector. The employed African Americans are much more likely, therefore, to be employed as directors, man-

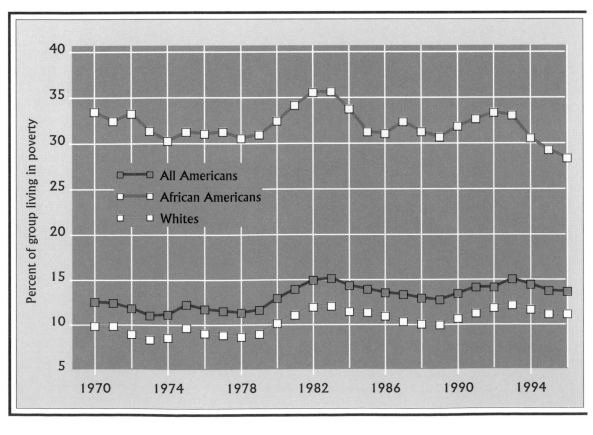

Figure 13.15. The percent of people living in poverty by race, 1970–1996.

Figure 13.16.
The percent of a state's labor force that is African American, 1995.

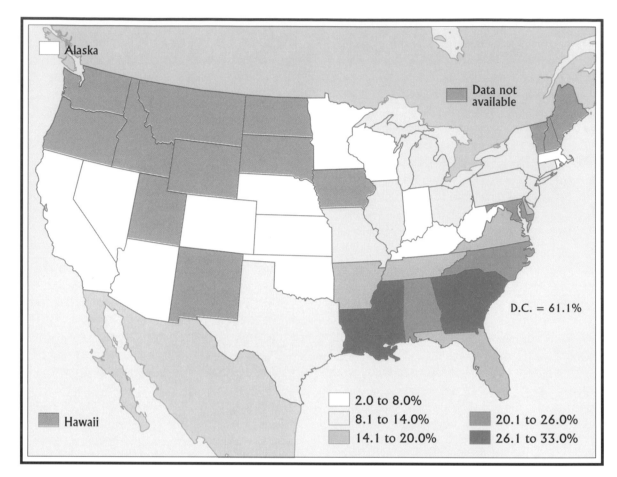

agers, teachers, educators, lawyers, medical practitioners, and institutional administrators than as business persons. The predominant employer in the professions and public administration is the federal government. A considerable number of African Americans have been employed by major municipal governments since the 1960s.

The southeastern United States has the highest percentage of African Americans in the labor force (figure 13.16). Nineteen percent of the workforce in that area is black. Out of more than sixteen million laborers in the region, just over three million are African Americans. Due to the great disparity in wages between blacks and whites, African Americans do not share 19 percent of the income of the region.

As demonstrated in the map, the West North Central, Mountain, New England, and East North Central states have the lowest percentages of African Americans in the labor force. Those regions also have the lowest percentages of blacks in the population.

Historically, the South Atlantic region has always led in the percentage of African Americans in the labor force. Because of the higher concentration of enslaved Africans in the region before emancipation, the result is a more intensive black labor force in the region.

During the 1950s the Honorable Elijah Muhammad, a nationalist leader, argued that the southern states should become a new African American nation because of the heavy presence of African Americans. However, the strong concentration of African Americans in the labor force in the region is not one of diversity. The vast majority of the laborers are in agriculture and light manufacturing. The high technology fields of space science, information processing, biomedicals, and telecommunications often found in the "sunbelt" do not now employ a large percentage of African Americans. This is a situation that is likely to change as the available white labor force becomes smaller due to low birthrates. Already acute shortages of skilled persons in the high technology fields are threatening the United States' position as a world leader in technological innovation. The African American labor pool in the southern region will have to be trained for the new roles in this field.

African American males are employed at a higher percentage of the potential labor force in the West South Central states—notably Texas, Oklahoma, Louisiana, and Arkansas—than in any other region. Ninety-one percent of the African American males in the labor force were employed in 1980. Lowest percentages of employed males were recorded in the East North Central and West North Central regions, respectively. This contrasts with the African American female employment figures, of which the East South Central and East North Central states had the lowest and second lowest percentages.

Black males have historically found employment as ranchers, oil riggers, and farmhands in the Southwest. Females have not found the area to be as attractive for their employment. On the other hand, females do exceptionally well in the Mountain region, New England, Pacific, and West South Central regions. The Mountain region posted 94 percent of its African American females as employed—out of a labor force of thirty-eight persons, thirty-six women were working.

Labor force represents only those individuals who are eligible and seeking jobs. Persons may not be counted in the labor force for various reasons, (e.g., military, prison, or medical disabilities). Thus, to say that 91 percent of African American males in the labor force in the West South Central region is employed is not the same as saying that 91 percent of the African American males in the region are employed.

African Americans in Industries

The distortions of racial history in the United States are shown in the employment of African Americans in various sectors. Cleavages of race have affected the patterns of employment. The percentage of African Americans employed in the professions and public administration is higher than the percentage of other Americans employed in that sector (see table 13.5, page 222). Lawyers, accountants, and managers constitute a large part of this sector. Only in the East South Central region does the percentage of whites and others employed in the professions and public administration approach the figures for African Americans.

Most of the African American growth in this sector occurred during the civil rights era and represented the federal government's response to increased demands for integration of African Americans into the society. In the 1950s and 1960s, employment for African American graduates in the professions was limited due to racial discrimination. The federal government and its various agencies hired many of the college graduates who were blocked from entering the corporate world. Thus, during the 1960s the U.S. government became the largest employer of African American lawyers. In some ways, the U.S. government relieved the pressure building among professionals who could not find employment in the private sector by increasing African American employment in the public sector.

In the South, while a large percentage of whites were also employed in the public sector, their employment was initially related more to state governments than to the federal government. By 1980, however, African Americans had entered many of the state jobs in the South as a result of the voting rights laws. Although whites still dominate the professions and public administration in the South, the percentage of the white population employed in that sector has decreased since the 1980s while African American employment in the sector has increased.

Outside the South, African American professionals participate in the professions and public administration at an even higher percentage of the working population. In New England, nearly 36 percent of the African Americans working are employed in the professions or public administration sector. This compares with 25 percent of the working whites in the region who are employed in the professions and public administration.

Only in the South, with its historical concentration of African Americans, is there a sizable wholesale and retail workforce. Yet in no region of the South does the percentage of regional employment of African Americans in wholesale and retail trade top 15 percent. Largely because of the businesses established in the African American community to cater to personal service needs of the community, the percentage of employment in retail and wholesale trade is greater than in any other region.

Most of the African American businesses in the South are located in the urban centers of Atlanta, New Orleans, Houston, San Antonio, Memphis, Little Rock, Nashville, Louisville, Birmingham, and Dallas. Smaller cities such as Macon, Charleston, Augusta, Chattanooga, Jackson, and Montgomery, as well as

scores of other communities, have basic businesses such as grocery stores, funeral homes, restaurants, and beauty and barber shops. Some agricultural regions have wholesale businesses engaged in selling farm produce (e.g., pecans, vegetables, livestock).

The percentage of African American employment in transportation, communication, and utilities (TCU) is generally higher than the percentage for whites and others. This is not the case, however, in the East South Central and the South Atlantic regions. In both of those regions whites have a slightly higher percentage of employed people working in the TCU sector. In the East South Central region, 7.4 percent of whites and others are employed in the TCU sector while only 6 percent of African Americans are so employed. The figures are slightly different in the South Atlantic region, where the percentage is 7.4 for whites and others and 7.2 for African Americans.

Most African Americans who work in this sector are found in warehousing, the U.S. Postal Service, services incidental to

Table 13.5. Employment for all Americans and African Americans by occupation (in thousands), 1996.

Occupation	Total employed	Percent African Ameircan	Number African Ameircans	% African Ameircan Population
Managerial and professional specialty	36,497	7.4	2,701	7.9
Executive, administrative, and managerial	17,746	6.9	1,224	3.6
Professional specialty	18,752	7.9	1,481	4.3
Technical, sales, and administrative support	37,683	10.3	3,881	11.4
Technicians and related support	3,926	9.4	369	1.1
Sales occupations	15,404	7.9	1,217	3.6
Administrative support, including clerical	18,353	12.5	2,294	6.7
Service Occupations	17,177	17.2	2,954	8.7
Private households	804	1.7	14	0.1
Protective service	2,187	13.1	286	0.8
Service except private household and protective	14,186	17.2	2,440	7.2
Precision production, craft, and repair	13,587	7.9	1,073	3.2
Mechanics and repairers	4,521	7.4	335	1.0
Construction trades	5,108	7.5	383	1.1
Extrctive occupations	130	6.0	8	0.0
Precision production occupations	3,828	9.0	345	1.0
Operators, fabricators, and laborers	18,197	15.3	2,784	8.2
Machine operators, assemblers, and inspectors	7,874	15.2	1,197	3.5
Transportation and material moving occupations	5,302	14.6	774	2.3
Handlers, equipment cleaners, helpers, and laborers	5,021	16.4	823	2.4
Farming, forestry, and fishing	3,566	3.9	139	0.4
Farm operators and managers	1,314	0.5	7	0.0
Forestry and logging occupations	108	5.2	6	0.0

transportation, and sanitary services. While African Americans can also be found as pilots for major and minor airlines, radio and television broadcasters, and utility engineers, numbers are comparatively small.

The percentage of African Americans employed in the manufacturing sector is generally less than for whites and other Americans employed in that sector. Out of nine national regions, African Americans are employed in a greater percentage of the working population in manufacturing in only two regions, the Mid-Atlantic and West North Central. In one other region, the South Atlantic, the percentage of African Americans working in manufacturing is about the same as that for whites and other Americans. Actually, in the Mid-Atlantic region there is a larger percentage of the African American population working in manufacturing (20.4 percent) than whites and others (18.3 percent). Likewise, in the West North Central region the African American percentage of the population in manufacturing is 22.9 and the percentage of whites and others 20.3; however, in the South Atlantic region the African American percentage is 23.7 and the white and others is 24.7.

The other six regions show a much higher percentage of white and other workers who are employed in the manufacturing sector. African Americans are employed in higher percentages of the working population in those areas of the country where textile-mill products are made—the area from Georgia to Virginia, which also constitutes the tobacco region. Since textile workers and tobacco workers are usually on the low end of the pay scale, employers in the textile or tobacco manufacturing area tend to employ persons from the area of the product. This is particularly true in the South, where the workforce, black or white, is not necessarily highly educated. Furthermore, the pattern of giving African Americans low-paying jobs means that a larger concentration of African American workers might be found in manufacturing in these regions.

The greatest disparity in terms of percentage of workers by region and race is in the Mountain region, where 28 percent of the white and other population is employed in manufacturing while only 6.1 percent of African Americans in that region is employed in manufacturing. Whites in the Mountain region have a long history of work in logging and millwork. African Americans in that region are much more likely to be in other employment sectors such as the professions and public administration.

In no region of the country does the percentage of African American workers in the finance, insurance, and real estate sector exceed 10 percent of the working population. Nevertheless, the percentage of African Americans working in finance, insurance, and real estate is nearly the same as it is for white and other workers. However, unlike the whites working in finance, insurance, and real estate, African Americans are more likely to be in the lower echelons of the sector. For example, the numbers of African Americans in this sector reflect the large numbers of African Americans who work as bank tellers and clerks as well as the numbers who are insurance salespersons. One is less likely to find African Americans in the management levels of finance, insurance, and real estate.

African American laborer in Baltimore shipyard. Credit: Library of Congress/Corbis.

The South Atlantic and East South Central regions—the traditional Deep South—has the lowest percentages of African Americans employed in the finance, insurance, and real estate sector. This pattern, illustrated where the percentage of African Americans employed in this sector in the South Atlantic (2.9 percent) and East South Central (2.7 percent), is related to the history of discrimination against African Americans in employment in such areas as banking, credit agencies, savings and loan associations, and investment companies. As late as the 1950s in Georgia, Alabama, and South Carolina, African Americans were employed in banking institutions only as messengers and maintenance workers. The 1980 census data indicate that the South remains the area least likely to employ African Americans in finance and banking.

Agriculture and Africans were bound together in America for nearly 250 years. Indeed, from 1619 to 1865 the African was the principal instrument in the development of American agriculture. In every aspect of the industry, from clearing the forests, plowing the land, tilling the soil, planting the seeds, harvesting the crops, and taking them to market, the African was nearly indispensable. Even after the Emancipation Proclamation, Africans were sharecroppers on land throughout the southern states. The migration to the North, the Great Flight, depleted the farms of African American workers beginning in the 1940s. Even the recent reversal of African American migration has not meant a return to agriculture.

The percentage of white and other workers in agriculture is larger than that for employed African American workers in every region. The region with the largest percentage of employed African Americans in agriculture remains the South Atlantic region of the country. Despite the fact that this region is the farm belt for the African American population, only 3.8 percent of African Americans were employed in the agriculture sector according to the 1980 census. The percentage of white and other work-ers employed in the agriculture sector is also relatively small. With the exception of the 0.9 percent in the West North Central region, the percentage of all Americans in agriculture has steadily decreased over the past four decades.

Nearly a quarter (22 percent) of the employed African Americans in the Mountain region are in business, repair, and personal service. This percentage represents the largest percentage of African Americans in this sector for any region. The African American population in the Mountain region is both a newly established and independent one. Therefore, a higher percentage of that relatively small population has found it necessary to find business or personal service employment. In every region of the nation, however, the percentage of African Americans employed in the business, repair, and personal service sector is higher than that for whites and others. The lowest percentage (6.7 percent) of African Americans employed in this sector is located in the East North Central region, but only 5.9 percent of whites and others in that region is employed in the sector.

Although African Americans are represented more than whites and others in this sector, it does not mean that the benefits of business have accrued to African Americans. Many of the jobs in this sector occupied by African Americans are the menial and lower-paying positions. Furthermore, the sector comprises those working for themselves and those working for others.

Only in the West South Central region does the percentage of employed African Americans represent about the same as that of whites and others in the construction sector. The New England region has the lowest percentage (1.8 percent) of African Americans in the construction sector. The history of African Americans in the construction industry begins in the earliest urban areas of the country, where laborers were used to build houses, stores, and government buildings. Furthermore, just as the Chinese laborers became famous for their heroic work on the railroads of the West, so the African Americans had lent manual labor to the construction of the rail system in the eastern half of the continent. John Henry, the "steel drivin' man," gained his reputation from the participation of African Americans in constructing the railways of the East.

Trade guilds and unions often control entry into the construction sector. Thus, unless African Americans have workers who will apprentice them, they may never gain access to the trades. Construction remains one of the most financially rewarding fields for those without college or high school certification. Of the total white working population in the South Atlantic region, 8.6 percent are employed in the construction industry as compared with 6.7 percent of the African American working population. Most of the whites employed in the construction industry in this region, like the African Americans, are not college graduates.

The percentage of the African American population engaged in the entertainment and recreation sector is largest in the mountain region. The 3.7 percent of the African American working population employed in the entertainment and recreation sector in the Mountain region is directly linked to the Nevada entertainment industry, which includes Reno-Lake Tahoe-Las Vegas. In those areas, the high percentage shows the historic presence of African Americans in entertainment. In fact, the percentage of African Americans employed in this sector is the highest of any region for African Americans or whites. The only other region where the percentage of African Americans in entertainment exceeds that of whites and others is the West North Central region (African Americans 1.4 percent; whites, 0.6 percent), where the city of Chicago anchors a strong African American presence in entertainment and recreation. There is a comparable percentage of African American and white populations employed in entertainment and recreation in the East South Central region. In

both cases, only 0.6 percent of the populations are so employed.

Included in the percentages for African Americans and whites are professional athletes. Although the numbers are relatively small, athletes represent a sizable proportion of the African Americans in entertainment and recreation. While African Americans employed in this sector are highly visible because of media exposure and public appearances, they do not constitute a major segment of the employed African American population. Indeed, the percentages of African Americans employed in every other sector, with the exception of mining, are larger than the percentage in entertainment and recreation.

Only in the westernmost states does the percentage of African Americans employed in the mining industry exceed or equal that of whites and others. The percentages of African Americans and whites in mining are equal in the Pacific region, where percentages of employed persons in the sector are 0.4 percent for each group. The percentage of employed African Americans (7.3 percent) compared to whites and others (3.7 percent) in the mining sector represents available opportunities for African Americans. Of course, in absolute terms there are far more whites in the mining industry than African Americans. In the other regions, the white and others percentages are at least double the percentages of African Americans employed in the sector. Since the numbers of African Americans living in the Mountain region is very small, the overall percentage of African Americans working in mining is exceptionally minuscule.

AFRICAN AMERICAN PROFESSIONALS

The percentage of African Americans in professional occupations is smaller than the national percentage of workers in similar positions (see table 13.6, page 226). In no region of the nation is the percentage of African Americans in managerial positions more than 7 percent of the population of African American workers. By contrast, the percentage of managers among the general population is not less than 8 percent in any region. Indeed, 11 percent of all workers in the Pacific region are managers. Only 6.8 percent of African Americans are managers in the same region. The Pacific region boasts the largest percentage of African American managers vis-à-vis the labor force.

The East South Central and the West South Central regions have the lowest percentages of African American managers, 2.7 percent and 3.7 percent, respectively. This contrasts with the overall percentages in the East South Central with

8.1 percent and the West South Central with 9.2 percent.

There are several ways to explain the situation faced by the African American worker; however, each explanation is rooted ultimately in the legacy of racial discrimination. African Americans were generally denied access to mentoring, refused entry into certain training programs, and hired at entry-level positions. The "revolution" of the 1960s changed many of the discriminatory practices of the past and prepared the way for more access. However, the residual effects of historical discrimination continue to the present day and account for the low percentage of African Americans in managerial positions.

The separation of African Americans and whites in the workplace was common prior to the Civil Rights Movement of the 1950s and 1960s. In those days, African American professionals had few jobs in the North and fewer in the South. Learning to live with black professionals was one of the most difficult lessons whites had to learn in order to change their attitudes about African Americans. The lessons have not been fully learned in some quarters even now, but the situation is far different and more equitable than it has ever been.

The exclusion of African American professionals from many companies was demanded by white workers. This had been the pattern since the early twentieth century when white unionists struck several companies to prevent them from hiring black workers. At another level, many white professionals let it be known that they would not work with black professionals. The fear and hatred of the black worker was often irrational. There was, in fact, no basis for workers' apprehensions about working with black workers. However, the stereotypes they had received from education, parents, peers, and friends prepared them for the most horrible experience should they be required to work with African Americans.

This problem did not escape the federal government. Hundreds of white workers protested when President

The new African American professional (right). American astronaut Guion Bluford, Jr., Ph.D (Colonel, USAF). Credit: NASA.

Table 13.6 (below). Total Americans employed in the professional field and the percent that are African American, 1996.

	Total Americans employed (000s)	% African American
Professional specialty	18,752	7.9
Architects	160	2.7
Engineers	1,960	4.2
Mathematical and computer scientists	1,345	7.2
Natural scientists	536	3.3
Health diagnosing occupations	960	3.7
Health assessment and treating occupations	2,812	8.7
Teachers, college and university	889	6.5
Teachers, except college and university	4,724	9.8
Librarians, archivists, and curators	202	8.0
Social scientists and urban planners	438	9.0
Social, recreation, and religious workers	1,332	17.1
Lawyers and judges	911	3.4
Writers, artists, entertainers, and athletes	2,188	6.0
Public relations specialists	150	13.0
Announcers	62	13.1
Athletes	85	5.6

Truman sought to change the racist nature of the workplace at the federal government. Some whites resigned rather than work with Africans. Truman had also attacked racism in the armed forces. He appointed two commissions to study racial matters. This was the first time that a president had taken (what was considered at the time) such a bold step. The President's Committee on Civil Rights denounced racial discrimination and called for the elimination of segregation in American life. In 1950, three years after the first committee, Truman appointed another committee on Equality of Treatment and Opportunity in the Armed Forces. They named their report Freedom to Serve, taking a cue from the first committee's document In Search of These Rights.

One committee's report gave the government the reasons it needed to attack racism on all fronts. Truman gave the first presidential speech on civil rights in the history of the nation in February 1948. It was after that speech that he decided to go with the second committee and to eventually bring down the barriers to black army personnel.

These were not easy battles to fight, neither for African Americans nor for the president. How must one feel when a colleague feels such great revulsion in working with you that he would rather quit his job than work with you? Nothing could be so compelling in its correctness than the end to racial discrimination, color prejudice, and religious intolerance.

WAGES FOR AFRICAN AMERICAN WORKERS

The gap between the white worker's wages and those of the African American worker steadily increases (table 13.7). The gap between whites and blacks has become an ocean of difference in terms of the estate wealth of the white family and the African American family.

Since the 1960s, the wages between different classes within the black community have shown a severe split between those who "can" and those who "cannot." Incomes grew fast in the 1960s, but the 1970s brought a slowdown. Reductions in poverty rates slowed, and African Americans were the victims of the slowdown. Nearly one-third of black families remained below the poverty line when President Reagan instituted his economic policies. A number of scholars such as Joseph Feagin and Sidney Wilhelm have argued that the conditions of blacks got worse in the 1980s precisely because of the policies of the Reagan administration.

Whatever the case, the fact is that the wages of the black worker began to drop more and more behind that of the white worker. Earnings inequality has certainly increased since the early 1970s. Forty percent of blacks and 20 percent of whites earn less than $10,000. Nearly half of the black male population earned less than $10,000 in 1984. The percentage of black

	Number of workers (in thousands)				Median weekly earnings (dollars)			
	1985	1990	1995	1996	1985	1990	1995	1996
All workers	77,002	85,804	89,282	90,918	343	412	479	490
Male	45,589	49,564	51,222	51,895	406	481	538	557
Female	31,414	36,239	38,060	39,023	277	346	406	418
White	66,481	72,811	74,874	76,151	355	424	494	506
Male	40,030	42,797	43,747	44,428	417	494	566	580
Female	26,452	30,014	31,127	31,724	281	353	415	428
African American	8,393	9,820	10,596	10,871	277	329	383	387
Male	4,367	4,983	5,279	5,316	304	361	411	412
Female	4,026	4,837	5,317	5,555	252	308	355	362

Table 13.7. Total number of workers and median weekly earnings by race and gender, 1985–1996.

families with incomes less than $10,000 increased from 26.8 to 30.2 percent between 1970 and 1984.

Twenty-two percent of white men earn more than $50,000. The number of black men earning more than $50,000 is 8.8 percent. Furthermore, the gap is widening between whites and African Americans. (See figure 13.17 for African Americans in various wage categories.)

There is a divergent experience among upwardly mobile blacks and those who have dropped out of school or who have turned to drugs. While middle-class blacks are much better off than blacks of lower social class status, neither group approaches the white group in terms of earnings. In fact, middle and upper-class blacks have never been able to maintain wage parity with middle and upper-class whites.

Black college graduates did manage to see a rise in their earnings percentage

Figure 13.17. African American income in various categories, 1970 to 1995.

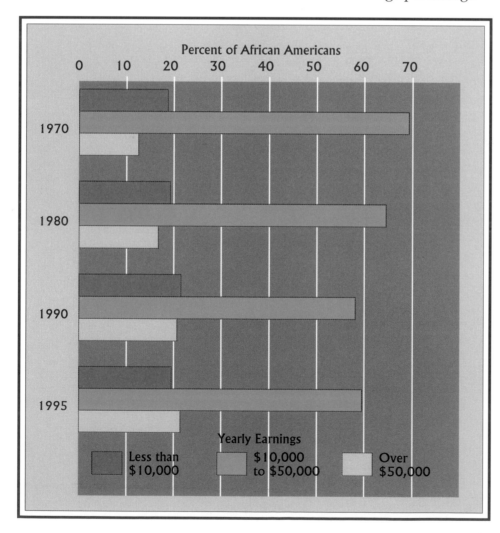

relative to those of whites by about 6 percent over wages in 1979. Despite the gains that African Americans have made at the middle-class levels, the level remains far behind that of whites. The most well heeled African Americans had a hard time meeting the standards of the Bureau of Labor Statistics for income needed to maintain middle-class living standards for a family of four. About 24 percent of African American families were considered middle class in 1979 as compared with 50 percent of white families. By 1988, this figure had climbed to 30 percent for blacks and more than 61 percent for whites.

Wage disparity will probably remain a factor in the economic underdevelopment of the African American community for the foreseeable future. Manning Marable has based his book *How Capitalism Underdeveloped Black America* on the premise that African Americans are controlled through structural economic conditions—that is, in terms of the structural elements of the overall American economy where African Americans remain among the last to be brought into the economic sector and the first to be fired or downsized because of a lack of seniority. Manning sees this situation as part of the structure of racism in the economy (*Essay from the Grass Roots,* Boston: South End Press, 1980).

EMPLOYMENT/UNEMPLOYMENT

The Bureau of Census has been keeping employment and unemployment records since 1940. A person is said to be in the workforce when that person is either employed or unemployed but has sought a position within the past six months. The employment rate is the ratio of people employed to the total number of people in the workforce. The unemployment figure for African American males ages 17 to 24 is 26.1 percent, a staggering (see table 13.8, page 229). With such a high unemployment rate, there are many young men who remain idle and therefore susceptible to the street life. In addition to the economic disaster unemployment brings to the African American community, such a high rate of unemployment also brings an awesome social price. This means that these young men have no money coming in from a legitimate job. They are therefore available for jobs that may be antisocial and against the best interests of the community. Young females are not far behind the males. With 22.7 percent unemployment among teenage and young adult women, it is not difficult to see how poverty becomes a way of life.

The unemployment rates remain higher for African Americans than for whites across the nation. In every region of the country the rate of unemployment in the African American community is twice or more as high as it is for whites. In the states where total unemployment is less than 4 percent—Minnesota, 3.7 percent; Nebraska, 2.6 percent; North Dakota, 3.3 percent; South Dakota, 2.9 percent, Utah, 3.6 percent, and Wisconsin, 3.7 percent—the African American population is relatively small. Yet among these states with populations large enough to report African American statistics, the unemployment rate of African Americans is just as bad or worse than in other regions of the country. For example, in Wisconsin the African American unemployment rate is 10 percent. This is not much different from Minnesota with an African American unemployment rate of 10.7 percent. Nebraska carries an African American unemployment rate of 7.5 percent. These statistics suggest that the tripling formula, where African American unemployment can be predicted to be about three times what it is in the white population, remains intact.

African Americans have always worked. Slavery was full employment. But it is not just work or a job that inspires human beings. People need work that fulfills their human spirits. During World War II, almost 9 out of 10 men aged 25 to 54 had good, solid jobs. This was true whether they were black or white. In the last few years, however, the situation has grown ominous because blacks are not employed at the previous rates. Quite a number of individuals have

totally dropped out because they lack the interest and/or motivation to work. The proportion of African American men and women who work has fallen to one of the lowest points in history. Normally we could speak of black women doing better than the black man, but not in this case. Unemployment among women and men together show the cruel truth of the African American condition. Unemployment has hovered around twice what it is for the white population.

The highest percentages of black unemployment seem to be in the states of Louisiana and West Virginia (see figures 13.18 through 13.21, pages 237 and 238). Both of these states have lost some of their industrial bases in recent years. Louisiana and West Virginia are also relatively poor states in the union. West Virginia uses the coal mines as its principal resource. Since many of the coal mines have closed down, the miners are out of work. In Louisiana, the oil boom was to place the state on the top of the oil world. Money was to be bountiful. Under those conditions the state would find jobs for whites as well as hire African Americans for the surplus jobs. The collapse of the oil market sent the state tumbling. It was not a rich state to begin with, and the fact that it had to recover losses in other budgets meant that there was no money to encourage the hiring of African Americans. Among African American men in Louisiana the most drastic decline in the number of jobs has come since the decline in the oil market. A combination of factors contributed to this state of affairs. In the first place, nonparticipation in the workforce is a relatively new phenomenon; it has often been referred to as the "underclass" among other things. By

Age group	Male	Female
All African Americans	11.1	10.0
16 to 19	36.9	30.3
20 to 24	19.2	18.4
35 to 34	10.1	11.0
35 to 44	7.8	6.9
45 to 54	6.3	3.8
55 to 64	5.1	3.8
65 and over	5.0	5.6

Table 13.8. African American unemployment by age group and sex, 1995.

this name, the writers intend to suggest that the people so named do not fit neatly into a little category in the economics books. Most of the people in this category have been men. But women have begun to get their share of the headaches and problems that come with being alone, destitute, and illiterate.

Historically, more African American women have had to work outside than white women. From the days of slavery, the African American woman was given a job. Yet by the 1980s white women had surpassed the black women in numbers of women hired at the top levels of many corporations and agencies.

Income Differences

There has always been a vast difference in the income wealth of African American and white American families. For instance, in 1985 only 7 percent of African American families received an income of more than $50,000 while 20 percent of white families were in the upper middle-class range of more than $50,000; and by 1990 32.5 percent of white families made over $50,000 in income while only 14.5 percent of all African American families made that much money, usually as a result of the husband and wife working.

In 1990 only 3.4 percent of African American males made more than $50,000 annually while 12.1 percent of white males made more than $50,000. In the case of the white male, he was more often than not the solewage earner for the family. The fact that both the African American male and female had to work also had implications for the care and supervision of children.

As of 1990 African American females made a median annual income of $19,134 while white women made $21,555. For African American males the figure was $22,628 while for white males it was $30,953. According to Statistical Abstracts, no. 721, p. 462, in 1991 the median family income in constant dollars was $21,548 for African Americans and $37,783 for whites. The Center for Popular Economics (CPE), 1995,4.5, stat-

ed that in 1992 27 percent of white households had incomes of over $50,000 compared with only 12 percent of African American and 15 percent of Latino households.

Social organization of the family is one of the fundamental characteristics of income generation in the American economy. For example, women are universally paid less wages than men, although there has been some gain in the last ten years. Yet the fact remains that women are still likely to make less income than men in every category and in all racial and ethnic groups. Since a large number of African American households are headed by women, there is quite a negative impact on the wealth of the families headed by women compared to those headed by men. There has been a steady decline in the number of African American families headed by men since 1960, and this decline reflects on the ability of the family to compete favorably in total earnings with other American families. For instance, in 1960 22 percent of African American families were headed by women, yet twenty-five years later in 1985 that figure had changed to 44 percent. In 1993 the number of African American families headed by women had grown to 47 percent. The percentage figures for the white family during the same years are 9 percent, 13 percent, and 14 percent, respectively. Even though the number of white families headed by females continues to increase, the number is nowhere near the number of black families headed by females.

A number of reasons have been advanced for this situation in the African American community. Employment opportunities have always had a profound impact on the African American family due to the fact that African American men have had the most difficulty in finding employment in the American economy. Families are negatively influenced in many ways when males, normally expected to be providers, cannot find work. Absentee fathers have become one of the greatest dangers threatening the African American family. However, another and perhaps more serious reason for the lack of men in the family is the overwhelming numbers of African American males who have been criminalized by the political, economic, and social system, according to historian Charshee McIntyre. In her book *The Criminalizing of a Race,* McIntyre maintains that the black male population is arrested and imprisoned at a far greater rate than white males. This is a prime reason, therefore, for black male absence from the home. Absent and unable to provide any income for the family, the black male, because he does not participate in the household as a wage earner, endangers the economic status of the family.

ECONOMIC PROSPECTS

By all accounts the situation in employment has remained dismal for African Americans in all regions of the United States (table 13.9). This has been a persistent problem from the end of the Great Enslavement, when forced black employment was nearly 100 percent. After Reconstruction, there was a continuing effort to overcome discrimination in employment so that black employment reflects the general situation in the nation. Of course, in 1986 only 6.8 percent of whites were unable to find employment whereas 14.8 percent of African American workers were unsuccessful in finding work. If one were to examine the teenage rate of employment for ages 16 to 19 in the same year, one would find that the white teenagers' rate of employment was 85 percent compared to the African American teenagers' 64 percent employment. It has grown worse since that time. It is reported that in 1992, while white teenagers were unemployed at a rate of 17.1 percent, African American teenagers were unemployed at 39.8 percent. Records for 1998 are not sufficiently clear to report in this volume, but it appears that the years of economic growth during the Clinton administration may have changed the percentages favorably for all racial groups. Nevertheless, we can predict that the disparity between whites and blacks contin-

Region	Total	Male	Female
United States	1,538,000	762,000	777,000
New England	38,000	16,000	22,000
Middle Atlantic	248,000	134,000	114,000
E. North Central	240,000	121,000	119,000
W. North Central	54,000	28,000	26,000
South Atlantic	434,000	203,000	232,000
E. South Central	158,000	82,000	76,000
W. South Central	205,000	96,000	109,000
Mountain	17,000	8,000	9,000
Pacific	143,000	74,000	69,000

Table 13.9. African American unemployment by region, 1995.

ues until now. There does not seem to be any programmatic modification or social change that can eradicate this large gap between the white and black populations, a gap that we have inherited from the days of the enslavement.

Attacks on affirmative action, the last in a list of programs suggested by political administrations to deal with the inequities brought from enslavement, means that there will be a further postponement of the settling of the debts of the past. In the meantime, the African American community has begun to practice economic self-help, group solidarity, and resilient independence in a productive way. Throughout the United States in local communities there are many nonprofit organizations as well as some informal organizations devoted to economic recovery and advancement. The disparity between the African American and white family in terms of wealth, net wealth, capital, and business assets continues to widen the gap between blacks and whites, rich and poor.

MILITARY SERVICE

Throughout the history of the United States, African Americans have been employed in military service. Currently, 22.2 percent of the approximately 1.8 million enlisted personnel are African American. African Americans total 6.7 percent of the 300,000 military officers. Included below are brief descriptions of contributions made by African Americans in wars and U.S. military campaigns. Maps of African American campaigns can be found on page 115 (figure 7.11) and page 239 (figure 13.22).

Revolutionary War, 1775–1781

Africans participated in the most famous battles of the American Revolution: Ticonderoga, Lexington, Concord, and Bunker Hill. Five thousand Africans fought in every service of the colonial military. Often the memory of these brave soldiers died quickly. Barred from the regular forces and militias of states in the new nation, Africans were rarely seen as a part of historical of American forces.

Three Africans distinguished themselves in this conflict although hundreds fought against the British. Crispus Attucks was one of the first martyrs to American independence. Peter Salem and Salem Poor were cited for gallantry.

War of 1812

When the war ended, one of every six sailors in the U.S. navy was African. William Brown was cited for courageous service.

Battle of New Orleans (1815)

British were defeated by two battalions that included Africans. Several African soldiers were cited for gallant actions.

Civil War

Africans fought in 200 battles and won twenty medals of honor.

Spanish-American War

Four African units went to Cuba commanded by Major Charles Young, the highest-ranking African American officer of that time.

World War I

More than 400,000 African soldiers served in the U.S. army during this war.

Needham Young and Henry Johnson of the 93rd Infantry 369th Regiment became the first Americans to receive the French Croix de Guerre.

World War II

Dorie Miller was the first hero at Pearl Harbor on December 7, 1941, when he shot down six Japanese Zeros with a machine gun he had never used before. He was awarded the Navy Cross. Before the end of the war, three other Africans had won the Navy Cross. More than one million Africans entered the United States armed forces. Seven thousand served as officers; four commanded merchant marine ships; and Colonel Benjamin O. Davis flew sixty missions.

Korean War

In 1950, the U.S. army was racially integrated and the eighty-one-year-old all-African 24th Infantry was the first to be integrated. Two African Americans received the Congressional Medal of Honor

Vietnam War

Fifty-nine blacks were awarded the Congressional Medal of Honor by 1969; nineteen of them awarded during the Vietnam War.

Persian Gulf War

General Colin Powell was appointed chairman of the Joint Chiefs of Staff by President George Bush in 1989, becoming the first American of African origin to hold that title. In his position, General Powell was the top military leader of the United States and prosecuted the Persian Gulf War as leader of the American forces.

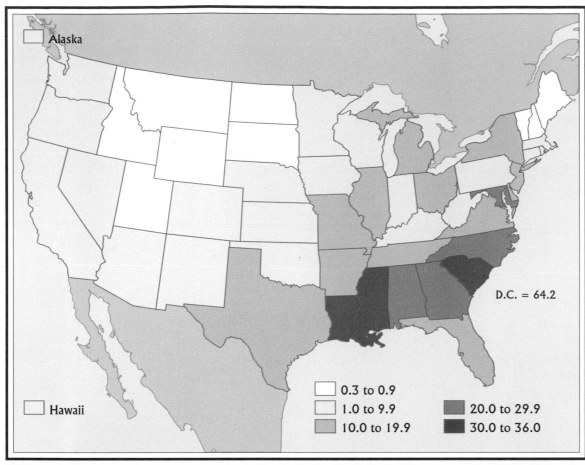

**Figure 13.1.
African American
population as a percent of
the total U.S. population,
1994.**

Legend:
- 0.3 to 0.9
- 1.0 to 9.9
- 10.0 to 19.9
- 20.0 to 29.9
- 30.0 to 36.0

D.C. = 64.2

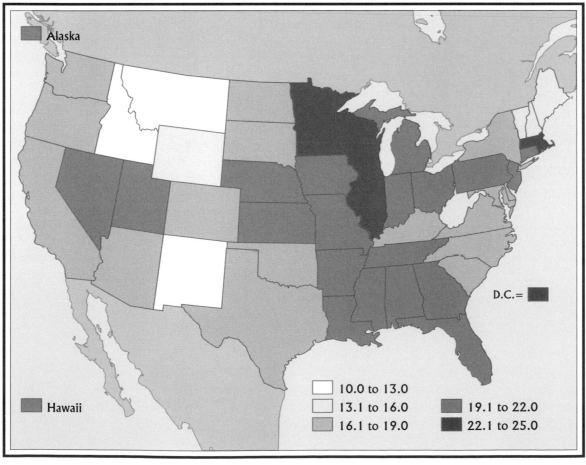

**Figure 13.3.
African American birthrate
(rate per 1,000 African
Americans), 1994.**

Legend:
- 10.0 to 13.0
- 13.1 to 16.0
- 16.1 to 19.0
- 19.1 to 22.0
- 22.1 to 25.0

D.C. =

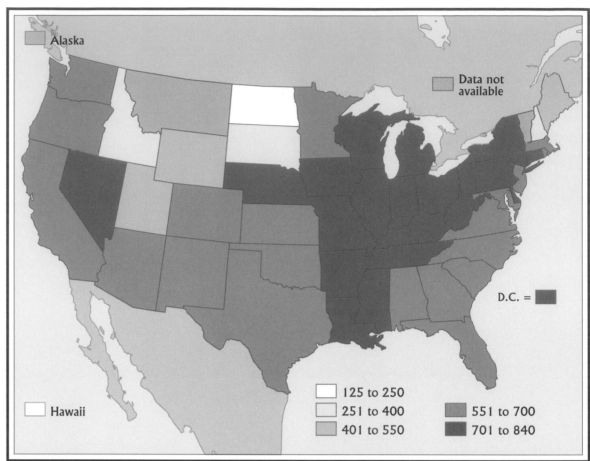

Figure 13.4.
Single parent births per 1,000 live births for African Americans, 1996.

Alaska

Data not available

D.C. = ▮

125 to 250
251 to 400
401 to 550
551 to 700
701 to 840

Hawaii

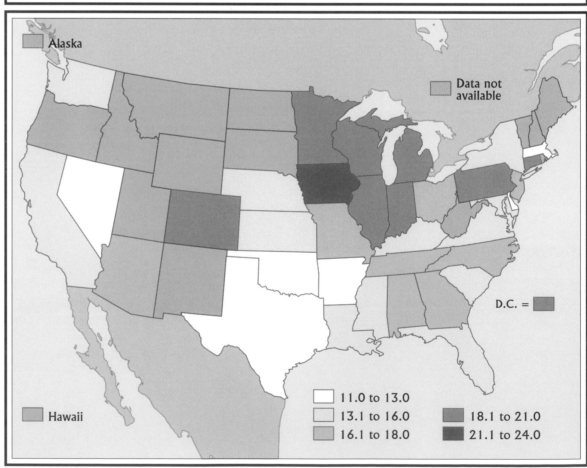

Figure 13.5.
African American infant mortality rate, 1994.

Alaska

Data not available

D.C. = ▮

11.0 to 13.0
13.1 to 16.0
16.1 to 18.0
18.1 to 21.0
21.1 to 24.0

Hawaii

234   SOCIAL AND ECONOMIC REALITIES

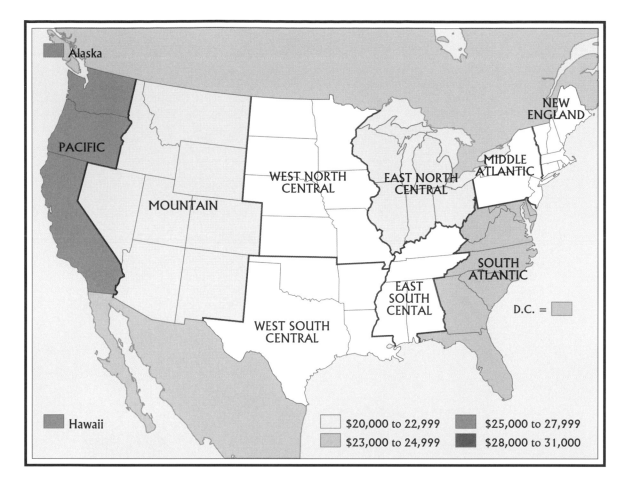

Figure 13.9.
African American median family income (in dollars) by region, 1996.

Alaska

PACIFIC

MOUNTAIN

WEST NORTH CENTRAL

EAST NORTH CENTRAL

NEW ENGLAND

MIDDLE ATLANTIC

SOUTH ATLANTIC

EAST SOUTH CENTRAL

WEST SOUTH CENTRAL

D.C. =

Hawaii

☐ $20,000 to 22,999	▨ $25,000 to 27,999
▨ $23,000 to 24,999	■ $28,000 to 31,000

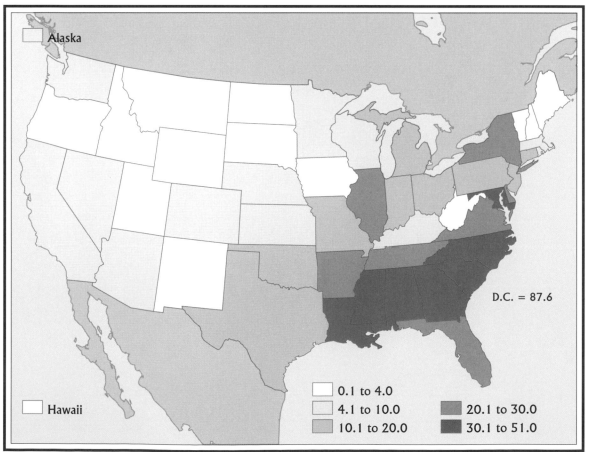

Figure 13.10.
Percent of school enroll-ment that is African American, Fall 1995.

Alaska

D.C. = 87.6

Hawaii

☐ 0.1 to 4.0	
☐ 4.1 to 10.0	▨ 20.1 to 30.0
▨ 10.1 to 20.0	■ 30.1 to 51.0

SOCIAL AND ECONOMIC REALITIES   235

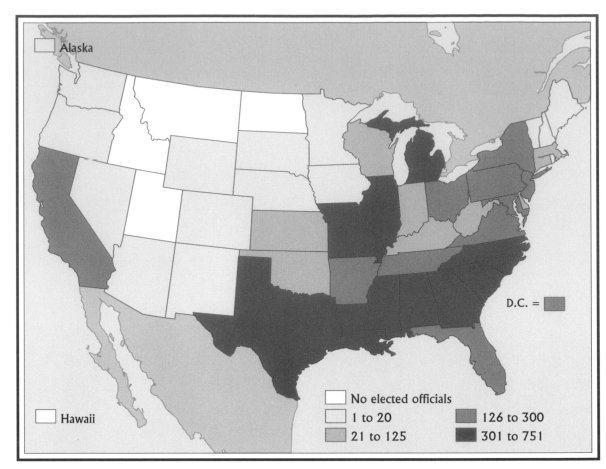

Figure 13.13.
Total number of African American elected officials in each state, 1993.

No elected officials
1 to 20
21 to 125
126 to 300
301 to 751
D.C. =

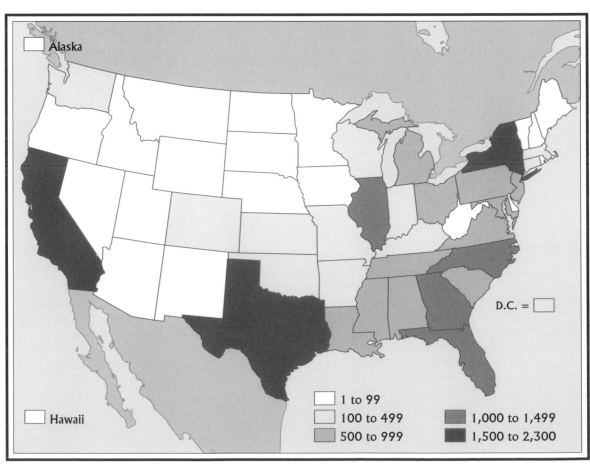

Figure 13.14.
Number of African Americans eligible to vote in November, 1996 (in thousands).

1 to 99
100 to 499
500 to 999
1,000 to 1,499
1,500 to 2,300
D.C. =

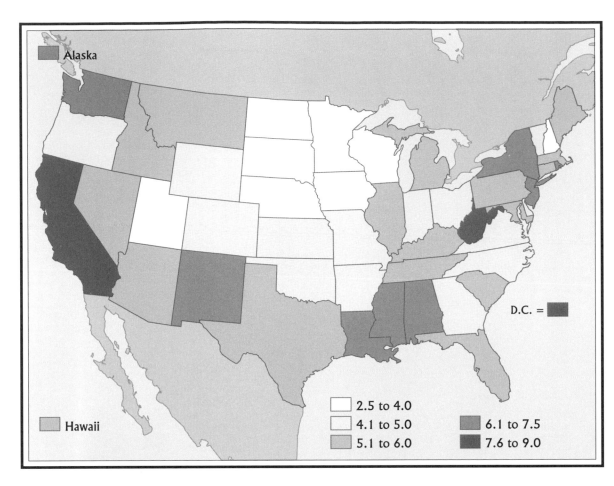

Figure 13.18.
Unemployment rate for all Americans, by state, 1995.

2.5 to 4.0	
4.1 to 5.0	6.1 to 7.5
5.1 to 6.0	7.6 to 9.0

Alaska

Hawaii

D.C. =

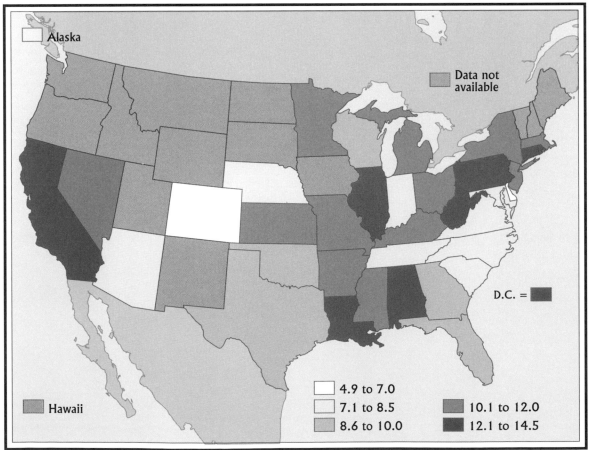

Figure 13.19.
Unemployment rates for all African Americans by state, 1995.

4.9 to 7.0	
7.1 to 8.5	10.1 to 12.0
8.6 to 10.0	12.1 to 14.5

Alaska

Data not available

Hawaii

D.C. =

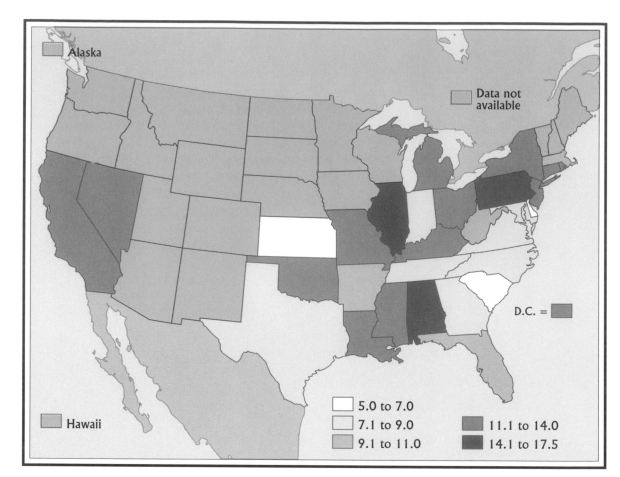

**Figure 13.20.
Unemployment rate for
African American males,
1995.**

5.0 to 7.0

7.1 to 9.0

9.1 to 11.0

11.1 to 14.0

14.1 to 17.5

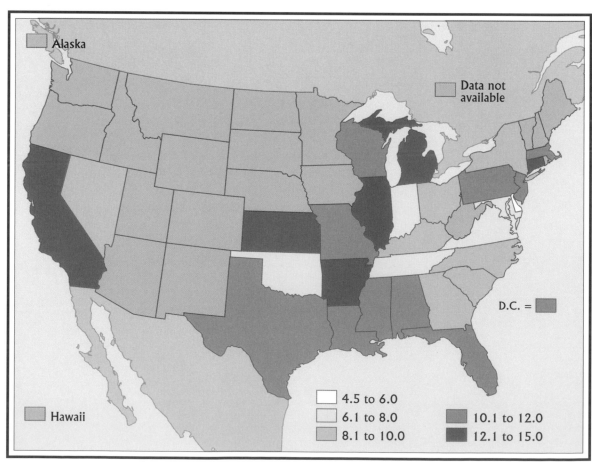

**Figure 13.21.
Unemployment rate for
African American females,
1995.**

4.5 to 6.0

6.1 to 8.0

8.1 to 10.0

10.1 to 12.0

12.1 to 15.0

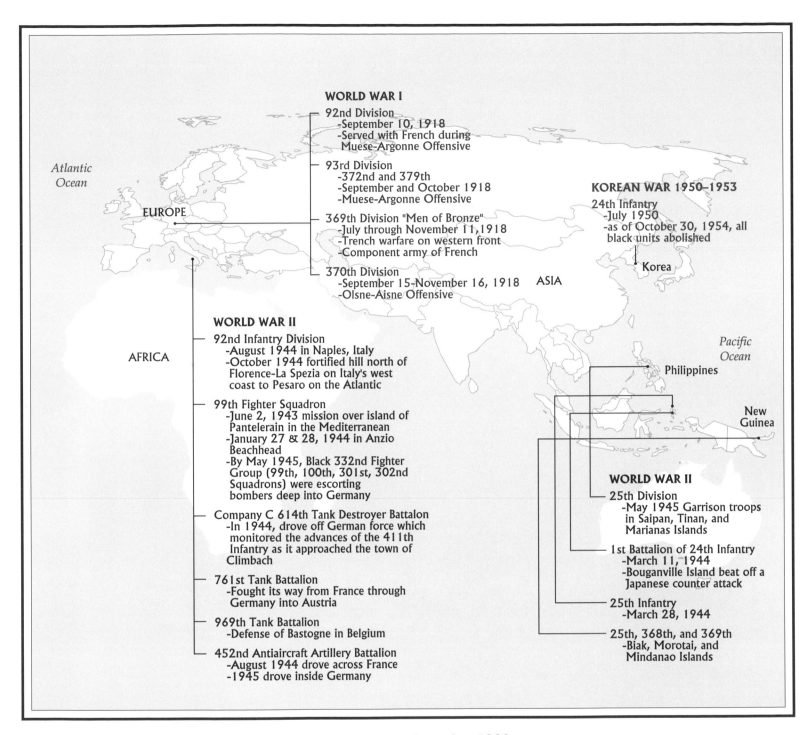

WORLD WAR I

92nd Division
-September 10, 1918
-Served with French during
 Muese-Argonne Offensive

93rd Division
-372nd and 379th
-September and October 1918
-Muese-Argonne Offensive

369th Division "Men of Bronze"
-July through November 11,1918
-Trench warfare on western front
-Component army of French

370th Division
-September 15-November 16, 1918
-Olsne-Aisne Offensive

KOREAN WAR 1950–1953

24th Infantry
-July 1950
-as of October 30, 1954, all
 black units abolished

WORLD WAR II

92nd Infantry Division
-August 1944 in Naples, Italy
-October 1944 fortified hill north of
 Florence-La Spezia on Italy's west
 coast to Pesaro on the Atlantic

99th Fighter Squadron
-June 2, 1943 mission over island of
 Pantelerain in the Mediterranean
-January 27 & 28, 1944 in Anzio
 Beachhead
-By May 1945, Black 332nd Fighter
 Group (99th, 100th, 301st, 302nd
 Squadrons) were escorting
 bombers deep into Germany

Company C 614th Tank Destroyer Battalion
-In 1944, drove off German force which
 monitored the advances of the 411th
 Infantry as it approached the town of
 Climbach

761st Tank Battalion
-Fought its way from France through
 Germany into Austria

969th Tank Battalion
-Defense of Bastogne in Belgium

452nd Antiaircraft Artillery Battalion
-August 1944 drove across France
-1945 drove inside Germany

WORLD WAR II

25th Division
-May 1945 Garrison troops
 in Saipan, Tinan, and
 Marianas Islands

1st Battalion of 24th Infantry
-March 11, 1944
-Bouganville Island beat off a
 Japanese counter attack

25th Infantry
-March 28, 1944

25th, 368th, and 369th
-Biak, Morotai, and
 Mindanao Islands

Atlantic Ocean

EUROPE

AFRICA

ASIA

Korea

Pacific Ocean

Philippines

New Guinea

Figure 13.22. African American troops in U.S. wars and campaigns after 1900.

DATES TO REMEMBER

1311   Abubukari II, Emperor of Mali, sends more than 100 long fishing boats across the Atlantic.

1312   Abubukari II surrenders his throne to Mansa Musa and sails across the Atlantic.

1488   Africans in Ghana, West Africa, greet Columbus when he visits El Mina Fortress.

1594   Ahmed Baba, last vice chancellor of the University of Sankore in Timbuktu, is arrested during the defeat of the Songhay armies by the invading Moroccans.

1619   Twenty Africans arrive at Jamestown, Virginia, aboard a Dutch ship, the first Africans to enter an English colony.

1634   The first African child is born in the Jamestown Colony and is named William by officials of the Anglican Church.

1651   Anthony Johnson, an African from Jamestown, is given a land grant of 250 acres in Northampton County, Virginia.

1676   Africans take a leading role in Bacon's Rebellion in Virginia.

1688   Quakers in Philadelphia make the first formal protest against enslavement of Africans.

1712   Africans revolt against enslavement in New York City, killing nine whites.

1739   Violent African revolt in Stono, South Carolina. Thirty white slave owners and overseers are killed.

1741   Africans in New York City set numerous fires, leading to panic, confusion, and increased tension between enslaved Africans and whites. Nearly 30 Africans are executed for participation in the general insurrection.

1760   Jupiter Hammons, a New York African, publishes the poem "An Evening Thought: Salvation by Christ, with Penitential Cries," becoming the first published African in North America.

1770   During a demonstration on March 5, Crispus Attucks, a Boston dockworker, is gunned down by British soldiers, becoming the first person to give his life for the American cause.

1775   African soldiers fight on the side of the Americans at the Battle of Bunker Hill. At the battles of Concord and Lexington a few distinguish themselves as Minutemen, Pomp Blackman, Samuel Craft, Caesar, John Ferrit, Lemuel Haynes, and Peter Salem among them. Africans also fight on the side of the British, who represent the colonial government. Many of their descendants leave for Nova Scotia after the American Revolution.

Prince Hall forms African Lodge No. 1, establishing the Masons among the black population.

1776   The Americans declare independence from England while retaining enslavement of Africans.

1777   Vermont becomes the first territory to abolish the enslavement of Africans.

1783   Massachusetts abolishes the enslavement of Africans.

1787   The Northwest Ordinance prohibits slavery in the Northwest Territories.

Richard Allen and Absalom Jones organize the Free African Society in Philadelphia.

The American Constitution is approved and extends slavery in the slaveholding states for another 20 years.

1793   Richard Allen founds Mother Bethel African Methodist Episcopal Church in Philadelphia.

1800   Gabriel Prosser organizes a massive slave uprising involving nearly 1,000 Africans in Richmond, Virginia. The revolt is betrayed, and 16 Africans, including Prosser, are hanged.

1804   Ohio enacts "Black Laws" preventing the movement of free Africans in the state.

1807   The European slave trade on the high seas is to end; however, the importation of Africans continues until 1859.

1811   Africans revolt in Louisiana.

1812   Africans comprise nearly 20 percent of the United States navy during the War of 1812 against the British. Some accept the British offer for freedom and escape to Nova Scotia, Jamaica, and eventually Sierra Leone.

1816   Wealthy whites form the American Colonization Society to repatriate free and intransigent Africans to Africa.

1817   Africans in Philadelphia under the leadershp of John Russwurm and Samuel Cornish form a powerful and united opposition to the American Colonization Society.

1821 Thomas L. Jennings becomes the first African in North America to receive a patent for an invention, a dry-cleaning system.

1822 Denmark Vesey, an African from the Virgin Islands, organizes a revolt against slavery in Charleston, South Carolina. The plans are discovered and 35 Africans, including Vesey, are executed.

1827 John Russwurm and Samuel Cornish publish Freedom's Journal, the first African-owned newspaper in the United States.

1829 David Walker, a Bostonian, writes the provocative and militant Appeal to the Colored Citizens of the World.

1830 First national convention of African Americans is held in Philadelphia. Purpose of the meeting is to assess conditions of Africans until 1864.

1831 Nat Turner leads the most successful slave insurrection in the United States. Nearly 60 whites are killed in Southhampton County, Virginia.

1843 Henry Blair receives a patent for a corn planter.

1839 Sengbe, called Cinque, leads a revolt aboard the ship Amistad.

1841 Africans revolt aboard the ship Creole and flee to the Bahamas.

1842 Henry Highland Garnet calls for enslaved Africans to revolt at a meeting in Buffalo, New York.

1843 Sojourner Truth starts her travels and lectures against slavery.

1847 Frederick Douglass publishes his paper, North Star.

Joseph Robert Jenkins of Virginia becomes the first president of independent Liberia.

1848 Harriet Tubman escapes from enslavement in Maryland.

1852 Institute for Colored Youth, forerunner of Cheyney University, founded in Philadelphia.

1853 William Wells Brown publishes first novel, Clotel, by an African.

James Augustine Healy becomes the first ordained African Catholic priest. Becomes head of Georgetown University in 1874.

1854 Ashmun Institute, first African college, is formed; renamed Lincoln University in 1866.

1857 Dred Scott decision denies African rights by law, declaring that Africans are not and cannot be citizens of the United States and that slavery cannot be barred from the western states.

1859 John Brown leads a band of 12 whites, including 4 of his sons, and 5 Africans in a raid on the United States arsenal at Harpers Ferry, Virginia, in order to start a revolt against slavery.

The last slave ship, Clothilde, brings Africans to Mobile, Alabama.

1860 South Carolina secedes from the Union, followed in 1861 by the other states that were to comprise the Confederacy.

1861 Confederates attack Fort Sumter, South Carolina; Civil War begins.

1863 President Lincoln signs the Emancipation Proclamation freeing Africans in those states that had rebelled against the federal government. Africans are not freed in states still under federal control.

White officer, Robert Gould Shaw, leads the all-black fighting unit the 54th Regiment of Massachusetts on a suicide mission against Fort Wagner in Charleston, South Carolina.

1864 New Orleans Tribune becomes first black daily newspaper in the South.

1865 John S. Rock, Boston attorney, becomes the first African admitted to practice before the Supreme Court.

General Robert E. Lee surrenders on April 8, ending the Civil War.

Nathan B. Forrest organizes the Ku Klux Klan.

1866 Fisk University opens.

1867 Congress divides the Confederacy into military districts and requires them to approve the right of Africans to vote.

1958 Howard, Morehouse, and Talladega colleges established.

Fourteenth Amendment ratified.

1869 Ebenezer Don Carlos Bassett is first African diplomat, minister to Haiti.

1870 Hiram Rhodes Revel elected to fill unexpired term of former Confederate president, Jefferson Davis, to become U.S. senator from Mississippi, the first African American to sit in the U.S. Senate.

Richard Greener of Philadelphia graduates from Harvard.

Fifteenth Amendment ratified.

1871 Fisk Jubilee Singers begin national tour.

1872 Charlotte E. Ray becomes the first African American woman lawyer, graduating from Howard University.

Pinckney B. S. Pinchbeck becomes acting governor of Louisiana upon the impeachment of the incumbent.

1876 Edward Boucher obtains doctorate from Yale. Elected to Phi Beta Kappa, he is the first African American to receive an advanced degree from an American university.

Frederick Douglass becomes marshall of the District of Columbia.

Henry Flipper becomes the first African American to graduate from the United States Military Academy at West Point.

1878 Lewis Latimer works with Hiram Maxim on invention of the incandescent electric light.

1879 Pap Singleton leads hundreds of Africans from the South to Kansas and Oklahoma.

1880 Burrett Lewis becomes the first black jockey to win the Kentucky Derby.

1881 Booker T. Washington opens Tuskegee Institute in Alabama.

1883 Spelman College opens.

1884 *Philadelphia Tribune* becomes first weekly newspaper.

1892 Ida B. Wells campaigns against lynching.

1893 Daniel Hale Williams performs the first open heart surgery in Chicago.

1895 W. E. B. Du Bois becomes the first African American to obtain a doctorate from Harvard.

1896 Plessey v. Ferguson case establishes "separate but equal" doctrine on which segregation is based.

1903 W. E. B. Du Bois publishes *Souls of Black Folks.*

1905 Niagara Movement organized to fight for social and civil justice, forerunner to National Association for the Advancement of Colored People.

Robert Sengstacke Abbot starts the *Chicago Defender.*

1907 Alain Locke of Philadelphia, a Harvard graduate, becomes first African American Rhodes Scholar.

1909 Du Bois and others found the National Association for the Advancement of Colored people on the hundredth anniversary of birth of Abraham Lincoln.

Matthew Henson becomes the first man to reach the North Pole.

1910 Jack Johnson becomes the heavyweight champion of the world.

1915 Carter G. Woodson institutes the Association for the Study of Negro Life.

1917 United States enters the Great European War; 300,000 Africans serve.

1919 Eighty-three African Americans are lynched during the "Red Summer of Hate" as the Ku Klux Klan holds 200 meetings throughout the nation.

1920 Marcus Garvey convenes an international gathering of Africans in Harlem under the banner of the Universal Negro Improvement Association and African Communities League.

1921 The Harlem Renaissance begins.

Saide Tanner Mossell Alexander earns a doctorate from the University of Pennsylvania.

1922 Dyer antilynching bill is passed in the U.S. House of Representatives but is defeated in the Senate.

1923 GeorgeWashington Carver receives the Spingarn Medal for distinguished service.

Garrett A. Morgan invents the traffic light.

1924 A. Phillip Randolph organizes the Brotherhood of Sleeping Car Porters union.

1931 Elijah Muhammad founds the Nation of Islam.

1935 Mary McLeod Bethune forms the National Council of Negro Women.

1936 Jesse Owens captures four gold medals at the Berlin Olympics, stunning Adolf Hitler and the German people.

1937 Joe Louis becomes the heavyweight boxing champion of the world.

William H. Hastie is the first African American to be appointed a federal judge.

1938 Crystal Bird Fauset is the first African American legislator; she is elected to the Pennsylvania House of Representatives.

1939 Eleanor Roosevelt resigns from Daughters of the American Revolution when they prevent contralto Marian Anderson from singing in Constitution Hall.

1940 Richard Wright's *Native Son* published.

1941 Scientist Charles Drew

develops techniques to separate and preserve blood. He organizes the first blood bank.

1944 Adam Clayton Powell Jr. elected to U.S. House of Representatives from Harlem.

1945 More than one million African Americans are inducted into the armed forces by the end of World War II.

1947 Jackie Robinson joins the Brooklyn Dodgers baseball team.

1949 Wesley Brown becomes the first African American to graduate from the United States Naval Academy at Annapolis.

1953 Father Divine acquires the huge Woodmont mansion on Philadelphia's mainline for his Peace Mission Society.

1954 U.S. Supreme Court decision in the Brown v. Board of Education of Topeka, Kansas, says separate but equal doctrine is invalid.

1955 Emmett Till, a 14-year-old Chicagoan, is kidnapped and lynched in Mississippi.

Rosa Parks, a civil rights worker, is arrested for refusing to give up her seat on a bus to a white man in Montgomery, Alabama, launching the Civil Rights Movement.

1959 Dr. Martin Luther King Jr. organizes the Southern Christian Leadership Conference.

1960 Students at North Carolina A&T stage the first sit-ins in segregated stores and restaurants.

Wilma Rudolph wins gold medals in the 100-meter run, 200- meter run, and 400-meter relay at the Rome Olympics.

1962 James Meredith fights to enter the University of Mississippi; federal troops are ordered to protect him.

1963 Medgar Evers is assassinated.

More than 250,000 march on Washington and hear Martin Luther King Jr.'s "I Have a Dream" speech.

1964 Dr. King wins Nobel Prize for Peace.

Malcolm X assassinated.

Civil Rights Act passed.

1965 Uprising in Watts section of Los Angeles, California, after police kill black motorist; 35 people are killed.

1966 Bobby Seale and Huey Newton found Black Panther Party in Oakland, California.

Stokley Carmichael, later called Kwame Toure, is elected head of Student Nonviolent Coordinating Committee.

Maulana Karenga founds US organization on the basis of kawaida principles and it becomes the first human rights organization to recognize the need for cultural reconstruction of the African American people.

Edward Brooke, a Massachusetts Republican, becomes the first African American elected to the Senate since Reconstruction.

Robert Weaver becomes the first African American appointed to the presidential cabinet when he is made head of the Department of Housing and Urban Development.

1967 Thurgood Marshall is appointed to the Supreme Court, the first African American elevated to that position.

1968 Shirley Chisholm becomes first African American woman elected to U.S. House of Representatives.

1969 Molefi K. Asante and Robert Singleton found the Journal of Black Studies.

1970 James Williams receives a doctorate in engineering from Cambridge University.

1972 National Black Political Convention takes place in Gary, Indiana.

1973 Coleman Young is elected mayor of Detroit.

1974 Henry Aaron of the Atlanta Braves hits home run number 715, becoming major league baseball's all-time home run leader.

1975 General Daniel C. James of the air force becomes the first African American four-star general.

ABC's adaptation of Alex Haley's book *Roots* draws the largest television audience of any program in history.

1978 Muhammad Ali becomes the first person to win the heavyweight boxing championship three times.

1979 Franklin Thomas is named Ford Foundation president, the first black to head a major foundation.

Arthur Lewis is awarded the Nobel Prize for Economics.

1982 Charles Fuller wins Pulitzer Prize for Drama for *A Soldier's Story.*

Michael Jackson's album *Thriller* becomes biggest-selling record of all time.

1983 Lt. Colonel Guion Bluford becomes the first African from the United States in space; the

Afro-Cuban Arnaldo Tamayo preceded him.

Alice Walker becomes the first African American woman to win the Pulitzer Prize for Fiction with the book *The Color Purple.*

1984 Jesse Jackson, head of Operation PUSH, makes a bid to become the Democratic nominee for president.

1985 Eddie Robinson, football coach of Grambling University, becomes the winningest coach in history.

1986 Astronaut Ronald McNair is killed in the explosion of the space shuttle Challenger along with 6 other astronauts.

1987 Mae Carol Jemison becomes the first African American female astronaut.

Playwright August Wilson wins Pulitzer Prize for *Fences;* will win again for *The Piano Lesson.*

1988   Toni Morrison wins Pulitzer Prize for her novel Beloved.

Temple University becomes the first university to offer the Ph.D. in African American studies.

1989 David Dinkins elected first African American mayor of New York City.

Douglas Wilder of Virginia becomes first African American elected to governorship.

Representative William Gray, Democrat of Pennsylvania, is named house majority whip.

Ronald H. Brown elected chairman of Democratic National Committee.

General Colin Powell is named

chairman of the Joint Chiefs of Staff, the highest military position after the president.

1991 Clarence Thomas is confirmed for the Supreme Court despite charges of sexual harassment by Anita Hill.

1993 President Bill Clinton appoints 5 African Americans to his cabinet: Michael Espy, agriculture; Ronald Brown, commerce; Hazel O'Leary, energy; Jesse Brown, veteran affairs; and Jocelyn Elders, surgeon-general.

Toni Morrison wins Nobel Prize for Literature.

1994 Beverly J. Harvard becomes the first African American woman to head a major urban police department when she accepts the post in Atlanta, Georgia.

1995 The NAACP board of directors elects Myrlie Evers chairperson and Congressman Kweisi Mfume as executve director and national president.

More than one million Afrcan Americans march on Washington, DC, and listen to minister Louis Farrakhan outline an African agenda.

1997 Phile Chionesu and Barbara Smith of Philadelphia organize one million African American women on the Benjamin Franklin Mall.

Tiger Woods becomes the first African American to win the Masters golf tournament.

1998 Franklin Raines becomes head of Fannie Mae, the largest diversified financial company in the world.

SELECTED REFERENCES

General Reference Books

The Arts and Civilization of Black and African Peoples. Lagos, Nigeria: Centre for Black and African Arts and Civilization, 1986.

Asante, Molefi Kete. *African American History: A Journey of Liberation.* Maywood, NJ: Peoples Publishing Group, 1996.

____. *The Afrocentric Idea.* Philadelphia: Temple University Press, 1998.

The Black Resource Guide, 1988–89. Washington, DC: R. Benjamin Johnson and Jacqueline Johnson, 1989.

Bogle, Donald. *Blacks in American Films and Television: An Encyclopedia.* New York: Garland, 1988.

Davis, Marianna. *Contributions of Black Women to America.* Columbia, SC: Kanday, 1982.

Ebony: Pictorial History of Black America. Nashville: Ebony, 1971.

Evans, Mari, ed. *Black Women Writers (1950–1980): A Critical Evaluation.* Garden City, NY: Doubleday, 1984.

Harris, Middleton. *The Black Book.* New York: Random House, 1974.

The History of the African American People: The History, Traditions, and Culture of African Americans. Detroit: Wayne State University Press, 1995.

Hughes, Langston, and Milton Melter. *A Pictorial History of the Negro.* New York: Crown, 1956.

Josey, E. J., and Ann Allen Schockley, eds. *Handbook of Black Librarianship.* Littleton, CO: Libraries Unlimited, 1977.

____, and Marva L. DeLoach, eds. *Ethnic Collections in Libraries.* New York: Neal Schuman Publishers, 1983.

Karenga, Maulana. *Introduction to Black Studies.* Los Angeles: University of Sankore Press, 1995.

Kellner, Bruce, ed. *The Harlem Renaissance: A Historical Dictionary for the Era.* Westport, CT: Greenwood, 1984.

Low, M. Augustus, and Virgil Clift, eds. *Encyclopedia of Black America.* New York: Neal Schuman Publishers, 1983.

Miller, Randall M., and John David Smith, eds. *Dictionary of Afro-American Slavery.* New York: Greenwood, 1988.

Morrison, Donald G. *Black America: A Comparative Handbook.* 2d ed. New York: Paragon House, 1989.

Nunez, Benjamin. *Dictionary of Afro-Latin American Civilization.* Westport, CT: Greenwood, 1980.

Palmer, Colin. *The First Passage; Blacks in America, 1502–1617.* New York: Oxford University Press, 1995.

Ploski, Harry, and A. James Williams. *The Negro Almanac: A Reference Work on the Afro-American.* 4th ed. New York: Wiley, 1983.

Rollock, Barbara. *Black Authors and Illustrators of Children's Books; A Biographical Dictionary.* New York: Garland, 1988.

Shockley, Allen. *Afro-American Women Writers, 1746–1933: An Anthology and Critical Guide.* Boston: G. K. Hall, 1989.

Smith, Jessie Carney, ed. *Images of Blacks in American Culture: A Reference Guide to Information Sources.* New York: Greenwood, 1984.

Smythe, Mabel M., ed. *The Black American Reference Book.* Englewood Cliffs, NJ: Prentice-Hall, 1976.

The State of Black America, 1989. New York: National Urban League, 1989.

U.S. Bureau of the Census. *County and City Data Book, 1983.* 10th ed. Washington, DC: Government Printing Office, 1983.

U.S. Bureau of the Census. *State and Metropolitan Data Book, 1982: A Statistical Abstract Supplement.* Washington, DC: Government Printing Office, 1982.

U.S. Bureau of the Census. *Statistical Abstract of the United States.* Washington, DC: Government Printing Office, 1879–1990, annual.

Van Chi-Bonnardel, Regine. *The Atlas of Africa.* New York: Free Press, 1073.

Bibliographies and Indexes

Allen, Walter R., ed. *Black American Families, 1965–1984: A Classified Selectively Annotated Bibliography.* Westport, CT: Greenwood, 1986.

Brignano, Russell. *Black Americans in Autobiography: An Annotated Bibliography of Autobiographies and Autobiographical Books Written Since the Civil War.* Rev. ed. Durham, NC: Duke University Press, 1984.

Campbell, Dorothy W. *Index to Black American Writers in Collective Biographies.* Littleton, CO: Libraries Unlimited, 1983.

Center for Afroamerican and African Studies, The University of Michigan. *Black Immigration and Ethnicity in the United States: An Annotated Bibliography.* Westport, CT: Greenwood, 1985.

Chapman, Dorothy Hollis. *Index to Poetry by Black American Women.* New York: Greenwood, 1986.

Davis, Lenwood G. *The Black Family in the United States: A Revised Updated Selectively Annotated Bibliography.* New York: Greenwood, 1986.

____, and George Hill. *A Bibliographical Guide to Black Studies Programs in the United States: An Annotated Bibliography.* Westport, CT: Greenwood, 1985.

____. *Blacks in American Armed Forces 1776–1983.* Westport, CT: Greenwood, 1985.

Davis, Nathaniel. *Afro-American Reference: An Annotated Bibliography of Selected Resources.* Westport, CT: Greenwood, 1984.

de Lerma, Dominique-Rene. *A Bibliography of Black Music.* Vols. 1–4. Westport, CT: Greenwood, 1981–85.

Ferry, Margaret. *The Harlem Renaissance: An Annotated Bibliography and Commentary.* New York: Garland, 1982.

Herod, Augustina, and Charles C, Herod. *Afro-American Nationalism: An Annotated Bibliography of Militant Separatist and Nationalist Literature.* New York: Garland, 1986.

Hill, George H. *Black Business and Economics: An Annotated Bibliography.* New York; Garland, 1985.

Hyatt, Marshall. *The Afro-American Cinematic Experience: An Annotated Bibliography.* Wilmington, DE: Scholarly Resources, 1983.

Johnson, Frank J. *Who's Who of Black Millionaires.* Fresno, CA: 1984.

Joyce, Donald. *Blacks in the Humanities, 1750–1984, A Selected Annotated Bibliography.*

Westport, CT: Greenwood, 1985.

Matney, William C., ed. *Who's Who Among Black Americans.* 5th ed. Northbrook, IL: 1988.

McPherson, James M., ed. *Blacks in America; Bibliographical Essays.* Garden City, NY: Doubleday, 1971.

Michael, Colette V. *Negritude: An Annotated Bibliography.* West Cornwall, CT: Locust Hill Press, 1988.

Momemi, Jamshid A. *Demography of the Black Population in the United States: An Annotated Bibliography with a Review Essay.* Westport, CT: Greenwood, 1983.

____. *Housing and Racial/Ethnic Minority Status in the United States: An Annotated Bibliography with a Review Essay.* Westport, CT: Greenwood, 1982.

Newman, Richard. *Black Access: A Bibliography of Afro-American Bibliographies.* Westport, CT: Greenwood, 1984.

Page James A., and Jae Min Roh. *Selected Black American, African and Caribbean Authors. A Bio-Bibliography.* Littleton, CO: Libaries Unlimited, 1985.

Sims, Janet. *The Progress of Afro-American Women: A Selected Bibliography and Resource Guide.* Westport, CT: Greenwood, 1980.

Skowronski, JoAnn. *Black Music in America. A Bibliography.* Metuchen, NJ: Scarecrow, 1981.

Smith, Dwight L., ed. *Afro-American History, A Bibliography.* Santa Barbara, CA: ABC CLIO Press. Vol. 1, 1974; vol. 2, 1981.

Stevenson, Rosemary M. *Index to Afro-American Reference Sources.* New York; Greenwood, 1988.

Weinberg, Meyer, ed. *The Education of Poor and Minority Children. A World Bibliography.* Westport, CT: Greenwood, 1981.

Willis-Thomas, Deborah. *A Bio-Bibliography of Black Photographers, 1940–1980.* New York: Garland, 1989.

Individual Biography

Davis, Lenwood, G. *A Paul Robeson Research Guide: A Selected Annotated Bibliography.* Westport, CT: Greenwood, 1982.

____, and Janet L. Sims. *Marcus Garvey: An Annotated Bibliography.* Westport, CT: Greenwood, 1980.

Duffy, Susan. *Shirley Chisholm: A Bibliography by and about Her.* Metuchen, NJ: Scarecrow, 1988.

Johnson, Timothy V. *Malcolm X: A Comprehensive Annotated Bibliography.* New York: Garland, 1986.

Kinnamon, Kenneth. *A Richard Wright Bibliography: Fifty Years of Criticism and Commentary, 1933–1982.* New York: Greenwood, 1982.

Newman, Richard. *Lemuel Haynes: A Bio-Bibliography.* New York: Lambeth, 1984.

Pratt, Louis H., and Darnell D. Pratt. *Alice Malsenior Walker: An Annotated Bibliography 1968–1986.* Westport, CT: Meckler, 1988.

Pyatt, Sherman. *Martin Luther King Jr.: An Annotated Bibliography.* New York: Greenwood, 1981.

Robinson, William H. *Phillis Wheatley: A Bio-Bibliography.* Westport, CT: Greenwood, 1981.

Scally, Sister Anthony. *Carter G. Woodson: A Bio-Bibliography.* Westport, CT: Greenwood, 1985.

Settle, Elizabeth A. *Ishmael Reed: A Primary and Secondary Bibliography.* Boston: G. K. Hall, 1982

Collective Biography

Black Writers: A Selection of Sketches from Contemporary Authors. Detroit: Gale Research, 1989.

Dance, Daryl Cumber. *Fifty Caribbean Writers: A Bio-Bibliographical Critical Sourcebook.* Westport, CT: Greenwood, 1986.

David, Thadious M., and Trudier Harris, eds. *Afro-American Fiction Writers after 1855.* Detroit: Gale Research, 1984. (Dictionary of Literary Biography, vol. 33)

____, eds. *Afro-American Poets since 1955.* Detroit: Gale Research. (Dictionary of Literary Biography, vol. 41)

____, eds. *Afro-American Writers after 1955: Dramatists and Prose Writers.* Detroit: Gale Research, 1987. (Dictionary of Literary Biography, vol. 38)

____. eds. *Afro-American Writers before the Harlem Renaissance.* Detroit: Gale Research, 1987. (Dictionary of Literary Biography, vol. 54)

____, eds. *Afro-American Writers, 1940–1955.* Detroit: Gale Research, 1988. (Dictionary of Literary Biography, vol. 76)

Joint Center Political Studies. *Black Elected Officials: A National Roster.* New York: Unipub, 1986.

Logan, Rayford W., and Michael R. Winston. *Dictionary of American Negro Biography.* New York: Norton, 1982.

Southern, Eileen. *Biographical Dictionary of Afro-American and African Musicians.* Westport, CT: Greenwood, 1982.

Speadling, Mary Mace. *Black and White. A Guide to Magazine Articles, Newspaper Articles, and Books Concerning More than 6,000 Black Individuals and Groups.* Detroit: Gale Research, 1980. Supplement, 1985.

Van Sertima, Ivan, ed. *Great Black Leaders: Ancient and Modern.* New Brunswick, NJ: Journal of African Civilizations, Ltd., 1988.

Histories and Critical Analyses

Asante, Kariamu Welsh, ed. *African Dance.* Lawrenceville, KS: Africa World Press, 1996.

Brawley, Benjamin. *A Short History of the American Negro.* New York: Macmillan, 1924.

Diop, Cheikh. *The African Origin of Civilzation.* New York: Lawrence Hill, 1974.

Dunn, Ross. *The Adventures of Ibn Battula.* Berkeley: University of California Press, 1986.

Du Bois, W. E. B. *The Souls of Black.* New York: Fawcett, 1961.

Gibbs, H. A. R. *The Travels of Ibn Battula A.D. 1325–1354.* Cambridge: Cambridge University Press, 1971.

Harding, Vincent. *There Is a River.* New York: Harcourt Brace, 1981.

Hine, Darlene Clark. *Black Women in White: Racial Conflict and Cooperation in the Nursing Profession, 1890–1950.* Bloomington: Indiana University Press, 1989.

Nash, Gary B. *Forging Freedom: The Formation of Philadelphia's Black Community, 1720–1800.* Cambridge, MA: Harvard University Press, 1988.

Jacobs, Donald M., ed. *Courage and Conscience: Black and White Abolitionists in Boston.* Bloomington: Indiana University Press, 1993.

Mills, Glendola Yhema. *Dancing in My Mother's Body.* Lawrenceville, KS: Alice World Press, 1999.

Okur, Nilgun. *Contemporary African American Theatre.* New York: Garland, 1996.

Omari, Ibn al. *Masalik il Absar el Amsar. Trans. Gaudefroy.* Paris: 1927.

Randall, Dudley. *The Black Poets.* New York: Bantam, 1972.

Rose, Tricia. *Black Noise: Rap Music and Black Culture in Contemporary America.* Hanover, NH: Wesleyan University Press, 1994.

Van Sertima, Ivan. *They Came Before Columbus.* New York: Random House, 1976.

West, Cornel. *Race Matters.* Boston: Beacon, 1993.

White, Walter. *Rope and Faggot.* New York: Arno, 1969.

INDEX

Lynch, John, 125
lynching, 120–22, 132

M

Maafa, 11
Maghan, Nare, I, 7
Mali, 5, 17, 43
Malcolm X, 157, 158–60
Mande, 7
Mandingo, 17
Marshall, Thurgood, 165, 165
Mazrui, Ali, 14
McKay, Claude, 145
Mentuhotep, 15
Meroe, 22
middle passage, 39
Miller, Dorie, 152
Mitchell, Arthur, 144
Mogadishu, 2
Monges, Miriam Maat Ka Re, 15
Morgan, Garrett A., 179
Morocco, 2
Morrison, Toni, 147, 190
Mossi, 5, 43
Motley, Constance Baker, 166
Mott, Lucretia, 132
Mound Bayou, 83
Mountains of the Moon, 2, 3
Mozambique, 4
Muhammad, Askia, 9
Muhammad, Elijah, 163
Munhu Matapa, 15–16
Musa, Mansa, 9
Musi waTunya, 3

N

Nascimento, Abdias do, 149
Nation of Islam, 163
National Association for the
     Advancement of Colored People
     (NAACP), 141, 150
Naylor, Gloria, 147
Nefertari, 15
Negritude, 141
Newton, Huey, 161
Nkrumah, Kwame, 17
Nino, Pedro Alonso, 23

Niane, D. T., 7
Nok, 5
Nova Scotia, 53

O

Obatala, 58
Obeah, 58
Ogun, 58
Okpewho, Isidore, 14
Olduvai Gorge, 3
Omo River Valley, 3
Organization of African Unity, 14
Organization of Afro-American
     Unity, 158–60
Oshun, 58
Ouagadougou, 2
Oyo, 5

P

Parker, Charlie, 183
Parks, Rosa, 93
Piankhy, 15
Pinchback, P. B. S., 114
Pleasant, Mammy, 24
Plessy v. Ferguson, 123
Poitier, Sidney, 188–89
Poor, Salem, 112
population, 204
Primus, Pearl, 11, 147, 148
Punt, 15
pyramids, 5

Q

Quakers, 85, 86

R

Rameses, 15
Randolph, A. Phillip, 146
Reconstruction, 125
Remond, Charles, 84, 87
Revels, Hiram Rhodes, 124, 126
Riding, Henry, 83
Robeson, Paul, 146, 189
Robinson, Jackie, 166, 167
Rodney, Walter, 41

root medicine, 176
Rowan, Carl, 167
Royal Company of Senegal, 34

S

Sahara, 2
Salem, Peter, 112
Sangoan culture, 4
San Lorenzo, 22
santeria, 58
Schwerner, Michael, 197
Scott, Dred, 97
Seale, Bobby, 161
Sengbe, 70
Sherman's March to Atlanta, 125
Shabaka, 15
Shango, 58
Skinner, Elliot Percival, 168
Smalls, Robert, 106, 107
Society for Promoting the
     Manumission of Slaves, 54
Songhay, 7, 9, 43
South Africa, 2
Southern Christian Leadership
     Council, 197
Soyinka, Wole, 14
spirituals, 191–93
Stone, Lucy, 132
Stowe, Harriet Beecher, 88
Stuckey, Sterling, 14
Student Nonviolent Coordinating
     Committee, 197
Sundiata, 7, 9
Sumanguru, 7

T

Tanner, Henry Ossawa, 180
Tarharka, 15
Terrell, Mary Church, 92
Thornton, Isaiah, 83
Tiemassas, 4
Timbuktu, 2, 3
Tolson, Melvin, 145
Trotter, W. Monroe, 133
Truth Sojourner, 84, 90–91
Ture, Mamadu, 9
Turner, Bishop Henry McNeal, 68

Turner, Nat, 73–76
Twenty-fourth Infantry, 150

u

Uganda, 4
Ukpa, 5
Uncle Tom's Cabin, 88
Underground Railroad, 94–96
UNESCO, 14
Universal Negro Improvement
    Association and African
    Communities League, 143
University of Sankore, 9
Urban League

v

violence, 207
voting rights, 217

w

Walker, Alice, 147
Walker, David, 85
Walker, Madame C. J., 92
Walker, Margaret, 145, 189
wars, 232

Revolutionary, 232
    World War I, 232
    World War II, 232
    Vietnam, 232
Washington, Booker T., 87, 133,
    136, 140, 141
Wells Barnett, Ida B., 133–35, 136
Wesley, Charles, 111
Wheatley, Phillis, 50, 51
White, Walter, 164
Wiener, Leo, 22
Wilkins, Roy, 197
Williams Dyana, 186
Williams, John A., 189
Woodson, Carter, 111, 142, 16
Wright, Richard, 148, 189

y

Yoruba, 5, 17
Young, Charles, 149
Young, Hiram, 27
Young, Whitney, 166

z

Zimbabwe, Great, 15
Zulu, 32